Global Apartheid

Global Apartheid

Refugees, Racism, and the New World Order

Anthony H. Richmond

OXFORD UNIVERSITY PRESS
Toronto   New York   Oxford
1994

Dedicated to

M.W.T.

who inherits

Oxford University Press
70 Wynford Drive, Don Mills, Ontario M3C 1J9

Toronto   Oxford   New York
Delhi   Bombay   Calcutta   Madras   Karachi
Kuala Lumpur   Singapore   Hong Kong   Tokyo
Nairobi   Dar es Salaam   Cape Town
Melbourne   Auckland   Madrid

and associated companies in
Berlin   Ibadan

Oxford is a trade mark of Oxford University Press

Canadian Cataloguing in Publication Data
Richmond, Anthony H., 1925–
    Global apartheid

Includes bibliographical references and index.
ISBN 0–19–541013–0

1. Emigration and immigration—Social aspects.
2. Emigration and immigration—Government policy.
3. Refugees.   4. Refugees—Government policy.
5. Ethnic relations.   6. Nationalism.
I. Title

JV6032.R53   1994   304.8'2   C94-931097-2

Contents

List of figures and charts

List of statistical tables

Preface and acknowledgements

While this book was being researched and written, the Centre for Refugee Studies at York University, Toronto, provided an office, research facilities, and funding. I wish to thank the former director of the Centre, Howard Adelman, for his continuing support and encouragement. I am also indebted to all my colleagues at the Centre, and in the departments of sociology and anthropology, York University, who contributed their critical comments and helpful suggestions at various stages of the work. In alphabetical order, they include: James Hathaway, Frances Henry, Clifford Jansen, Evelyn Kallen, Lawrence Lam, Michael Lanphier, Véronique Lassailly-Jacob, Janet McLellan, Raymond Morris, John O'Neill, and Alan Simmons. Special thanks are also due to those students who have assisted with the preparation of tables and the compilation of bibliographies.

Some chapters are edited and updated versions of previously published articles. I thank the editors and publishers of the journals in question for permission to reprint, in part or in full. Specifically, they are *Current Sociology, International Journal of Canadian Studies, International Journal of Comparative Sociology, International Migration Review, Journal of Refugee Studies, Population Bulletin*, and *Refuge*.

Valerie Ahwee of Oxford University Press Canada provided editorial help as the book was prepared for the press. My wife, Freda Richmond, read and criticized early drafts, and tolerated my choice of retirement activity with good cheer.

The following previously published materials are reproduced with permission of the publishers:

Figure 8.5: Refugee Affairs Branch, 1990. Reprinted by permission of Citizenship and Immigration Canada.

Figure 10.2: Bureau of Immigration and Population Research. *Australian Immigration Consolidated Statistics*, no. 17 (June 1993) AGPS Canberra. Commonwealth of Australia copyright, reproduced by permission.

Tables 2, 3, 5, and 6 are reprinted from *World Refugee Survey 1994* by permission of the US Committee for Refugees.

Table 7: *NATO Review*, no. 1 (February 1993).

Tables 9, 10, 14, and 15: Adapted from 'Profile of Immigrants', Statistics Canada, Cat. 93-155, Table 1. Reproduced by authority of the Ministry of Industry.

Tables 12 and 13: Adapted from *Immigrants in the Canadian Labour Force: Their Role in Structural Change* (1989), a publication of the Institute for Research on Public Policy. Permission to reproduce was granted by the publisher.

Introduction

The theme of this collection of essays is the impact of postindustrialism, postmodernism, and globalization on international migration, racial conflict, and ethnic nationalism. Throughout the developing world there are mass movements of population from rural to urban areas, driven by over-population and poverty. Some cross international borders in their search for a better life. An estimated 70 million persons live and work in other countries, and more than a million emigrate permanently every year (Appleyard 1991; UNFPA 1993). Migration in and between advanced postindustrial societies tends to be a multiway movement with only small net gains and losses. However, migration from less developed regions leads to enormous pressure on cities without much relief to the rural areas where rates of natural increase are high. The world's population is growing at an annual rate of 1.7 per cent, or more than 95 million. The total will exceed 6 billion by the end of the century. If present trends continue, the proportion of the world's population living in what are now industrialized countries will fall from one-fifth to one-sixth of the total by the year 2025 (see Appendix 2, Table 1). The International Institute for Applied Systems Analysis used world population projections and computer simulations that took into account ecological feedback effects. Various scenarios were explored with different assumptions concerning fertility, mortality, and migration. They concluded that:

> The population in today's less developed countries will under all scenarios increase by at least 70 percent, or 1.3% annually by 2030, while the direction of change is uncertain in the more developed countries. Without immigration and under low fertility assumptions TFR = 1.1) the MDC's population size would start to decline soon after the turn of the century (Lutz, Prinz, and Langgassner 1993:5). [TFR is total fertility rate; MDC is more developed countries]

Refugees are a growing element in the complex population movements associated with the new world order (or disorder) that followed the collapse of the Soviet Union. Western European countries have taken severe measures to deter and exclude spontaneous arrivals of asylum seekers. As a result, the numbers arriving fell from 693,100 in 1992 to nearly 543,200 in 1993. Europe is not the only continent to be affected. Superpower confrontations in Africa, Central America, the Middle East, and Asia left a legacy of ethnic conflict and population displacement that spilled over into Europe, North America, and Australasia. Radical changes in southern Africa have also created new challenges.

There are an estimated 16.3 million refugees and asylum seekers around the world (see Figure Intro. 1). The largest source countries are Afghanistan, Palestine, Mozambique and the former Yugoslavia. In addition, the UN High Commissioner for Refugees (UNHCR) recognizes 6.6 million people in refugee-like situations.[1] The majority are still in their regions of origin, having sought shelter in their own or neighbouring countries. In December 1993, only 104,000 of those currently seeking asylum were in the United States, 30,500 in Canada, and 3,000 in Australia. Those who had other humanitarian claims but did not meet the UN Convention definition (see Appendix 1), included people fleeing conflicts in the Middle East, Central America, and Asia. To these must be added 25 million people who were internally displaced within their own countries as a result of civil wars, ethnic conflicts, or environmental disasters. The largest numbers were in the Sudan, South Africa, Mozambique, Somalia, and the Philippines (US Committee for Refugees 1993: see Appendix 2, tables 2 to 6).

Population pressures are not the only cause of ethnic conflict, although they contribute to its intensity. Racism, ethnocentrism, religious bigotry and prejudice, nationalism and ancient rivalries, intensified by economic competition, all play a part. The economically privileged seek to protect their advantage while the absolutely and relatively deprived fight for their piece of the pie. One response to these conflicts is to create barriers to stem the flow of migrants and protect the political power, economic benefits, and social status of the numerical minority.

Apartheid

In 1955, just six years after the nationalist government came to power in South Africa, I wrote a book, *The Colour Problem*, which examined racial relations in various countries (Richmond 1955). At that time, I suggested that two elementary processes of social organization are involved in the examination of migration, race, and ethnic relations. The first is the principle of *superordination/subordination*. The second is the principle of *separation/integration*. Each is a continuum involving varying levels of inequality in the distribution of status and power, together with degrees of segregation and dispersion of the populations concerned. When these two bases of social organization are combined, four main types of system are possible, although there are many variations when other factors, such as demographic ratios, levels of economic development, and degrees of similarity and difference in language and culture are taken into account. Extreme differences in power and status, combined with geographic and social separation, lead to apartheid. Similar differences in power and status in an integrated system lead to class differentiation. When power and status are more equally distributed and combined with separation, the result is self-determination. This may take a variety of forms ranging from separate statehood to a high degree of autonomy within an existing state. The

Figure Int. 1 Refugees and asylum seekers

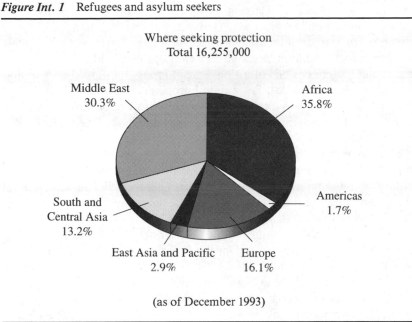

Where seeking protection
Total 16,255,000

Middle East
30.3%

Africa
35.8%

South and
Central Asia
13.2%

Americas
1.7%

East Asia and Pacific
2.9%

Europe
16.1%

(as of December 1993)

SOURCE: UN High Commissioner for Refugees and US Committee for Refugees

combination of relative equality on the dimension of superordination/
subordination and integration (in geographic as well as sociocultural
terms) leads to assimilation (Richmond 1955:27). In the latter case, there
may be convergence towards the characteristics of a numerical majority
group or various forms of *coaptation* in which different groups experience
change in response to endogenous and exogenous pressures (technological,
economic, political, and social). The first four chapters of this book are an
attempt to revise and elaborate the theoretical basis of my earlier work in
the light of contemporary developments in sociological thought.[2] Later
chapters apply this revised theoretical framework to various situations,
using a comparative perspective within the contemporary world system.

The Colour Problem (1955) contained a chapter entitled 'Apartheid and
White Supremacy in South Africa'. The book was banned in that country,
although a few copies were smuggled in by travellers who disguised it as a
novel. I wrote 'in South Africa a large majority of the European population
appears to be determined to hold on to, if not extend, its own privileged
position and to exclude non-Europeans from a full share in the government
of the country, now or in the future. For this reason racial relationships in
South Africa are bound to deteriorate until the pressure on non-Europeans
becomes so great that a major upheaval ensues. The only alternative would
appear to be a widespread change of attitude on the part of Europeans,
when and if the grim consequence of present policies is fully appreciated'

(Richmond 1955:81). Six years later when a revised edition of the book went to press, the treason trials started and Nelson Mandela began his long period of detention. I wrote then 'Afrikaner nationalism, as a sociological phenomenon is understandable enough. But it is obvious that the problems of a plural society cannot be solved by means of the unbridled assertiveness and unlimited pretensions of a single racial group, reinforced by fear and relying purely on violence. For a time Europeans in South Africa will be able to maintain their supremacy through political oppression backed by tanks and machine-guns such as those used at Sharpeville in 1960. But Nemesis is bound to follow' (Richmond 1961:134–5).

More than thirty years later, and after much more violence and bloodshed, the 'White' South African government finally recognized the impossibility of maintaining its exclusive power. Nelson Mandela was released and exiled leaders of the African National Congress were allowed to return. The first steps towards democracy and power-sharing were taken, although there is still resistance from 'White' extremists and factional fighting among the African population. For the first time, elections based on universal franchise were held in April 1994. It remains to be seen whether the transfer of power can be achieved peacefully. The attitudes, values, and social practices that constituted apartheid will not disappear overnight, although many were obsolete before being formally abolished (Adam and Moodley 1993). Already some 'White' Afrikaners are demanding a separate and independent state for themselves and are prepared to fight for it.

When the first Dutch settlers arrived in South Africa in 1660, they wanted to build a canal that would separate the Cape Peninsula from the rest of the continent, but that proved impractical. Instead, they planted a hedge of bitter wild almond in order to keep out the Hottentot and other 'Black' African peoples. The remnants of that hedge are still to be found in Cape Town's botanic garden. Symbolically, it persists in the numerous laws and customs that still keep 'Whites' and 'Blacks' apart (Hewson 1989; Sparks 1990:xvi).

The end of official apartheid in South Africa coincides with growing fears elsewhere in the world concerning the impact of mass migration and consequent conflicts in polyethnic and multiracial societies. New hedges are being built. Increasingly repressive and restrictive measures to restrain the flows of migrant labourers and refugees from Africa, Asia, the Caribbean, and Latin America are being imposed. Today we guard our airports, interdict undocumented travellers, build electronic fences, maintain coastguard patrols, and use computerized data banks to ensure that our borders are not infringed. Armed guards patrol frontiers and gunboats turn back ships loaded with asylum seekers and so-called 'illegal' immigrants. Advanced technologies, including infrared surveillance, fingerprinting, and computer data banks are being used to exclude unwanted persons. In some countries, voting rights and citizenship are denied, even to long-term residents, unless they are of the same ethnic origin as the majority group.

The term 'ethnic cleansing' has entered our vocabulary, although 'pogrom', 'genocide', and 'extermination' would be more apt descriptions of what is happening, not only in the former Yugoslavia but also in other parts of the world where indigenous populations and ethnic minorities are oppressed.

The predominantly 'White' and wealthy countries of North America, Europe, and Australasia endeavour to protect themselves from what they believe are imminent threats to their territorial integrity and privileged lifestyles. Wealthier enclaves in Asia and elsewhere follow suit. Global population pressures, economic crises, and shifts in political power generate profound insecurities in the old, new, third, and fourth worlds alike. Typically, dominant groups take defensive measures against external 'enemies' and threaten internal minorities. The result is further conflict and an even greater propensity to migrate. As economic interdependence encourages transnational movements of capital and tends towards a 'borderless world', political and social pressures pull in the opposite direction.

A central paradox emerges from an analysis of international migration in the last decade. The actual numbers crossing international borders, legally and illegally, rose substantially. One response was to offer amnesty, an adjustment of status, to *de facto* immigrants who had established themselves. At the same time, public opposition to immigration increased and, in some countries, precipitated violent protests and attacks on foreigners. Governments responded by tightening controls in an attempt to stem the flow. In so doing they labelled as 'illegal' or 'undesirable' people who earlier, would have been welcomed either as useful workers or as escapees from oppressive regimes. It now seems that a generous policy towards refugees was a cold war luxury, and even then one mainly reserved for Europeans. That is why new policies can be described as a form of *global apartheid*.

In order to understand the radical changes that are occurring in the world system, it is important to understand the demographic and sociological transformations that are occurring. This book is about those changes.

Notes

[1] Refugee movements are volatile and hard to quantify. Estimates vary according to the definition used and the time period under consideration. In late 1993, the UN High Commissioner for Refugees 'was responsible for the protection and assistance of an estimated 23 million persons in 143 countries, comprised of more than 16 million refugees, at least 2.9 million IDP's (internally displaced persons) and 3 million others, including victims of war and returnees' (UNHCR 1994:2).

[2] I have been influenced by the writings of Anthony Giddens, although the latter has no responsibility for my use or misuse of his ideas. For a critical discussion of Giddens's structuration theory, see Cohen (1989), Bryant and Jary (1991), and Craib (1992).

part one

Sociological theories

chapter one

Theoretical perspectives

There is no single theory of migration nor one sociological explanation of ethnic relations or racial conflict. Various writers have adopted different theoretical frameworks depending on their epistemological assumptions and value premises. Classical theorists, such as Marx and Weber, have been influential in Britain and Europe (Mason 1986). Robert Park, Louis Wirth, Herbert Blumer, and others in the 'Chicago School' laid the foundations for much of the writing about 'race' and 'ethnicity' in the United States (Lal 1986). In Canada, the Chicago influence was also present in the pioneer work of Carl Dawson, Lloyd Reynolds, and Everett Hughes at McGill (Clark 1975; Ostow 1984). Later John Porter brought ideas from the work of L.T. Hobhouse, Morris Ginsberg, and the Fabian-socialist traditions of the London School of Economics to an analysis of the Canadian 'vertical mosaic' (Helmes-Hayes 1990; Porter 1965). In the chapters that follow, I have adopted an eclectic approach endeavouring to achieve a synthesis of those theories that have explanatory value in particular context, especially those of Anthony Giddens. His work is grounded in classical sociology, but breaks away from it to provide in *structuration theory* 'a conceptual scheme that allows one to understand both how actors are at the same time the creators of social systems yet created by them' (Giddens 1991:204).

Among the key concepts necessary to understanding the sociological dimensions of international migration and related questions of 'race' and ethnic relations are power, conflict, agency, structuration, security, identity,

3

and communication. In turn these are related to questions of class, ethnicity, racism, domination, migration, and the coaptation of linguistic, religious, and cultural groups in quasi-sovereign states that are part of a world system. That system is currently experiencing radical change as it moves from modernity, through late modernity, to an uncertain postmodern phase that promises the possibility of chaos.

Power

Power is a key concept in social theory, although its precise definition and significance remain controversial. In its most abstract formulation, power is the capacity to achieve individual or collective goals through cooperation and, if necessary, by overcoming opposition. Sociologists writing in the 'political economy' tradition generally reduce questions of power to economic relations of production. In the classic version of Marxist theory, power derives from private property and capital accumulation and is expressed in class struggles. The state is an agent of the bourgeoisie. The military, the bureaucracy, and the legislative institutions of the modern state are not autonomous. They are the political arm or 'executive committee' of the ruling capitalist class. Only when revolution succeeds in overthrowing the capitalist system will the state wither away. Meanwhile, social conditioning induces subordination and can only be overcome by a demonstration of the false consciousness that diverts the proletariat from a recognition of their real interests. 'Race', ethnicity, and religion are among the forms of false consciousness in question. The ruling class exploits these divisions as a means of maintaining power and reducing the propensity to revolt. From this perspective, 'racism' is simply a manifestation of class struggle, particularly its colonial phase (Cox 1948). More sophisticated versions of neo-Marxist theory recognize the relative autonomy of the state and other institutions (Miles and Phitzakalea 1980; Poulantzas 1975). A good example of this approach is the work of Stuart Hall (1980). He identifies 'structures of dominance' in situations of racial conflict. While emphasizing the importance of class, he avoids the limitations of classical Marxism, including economic determinism, reductionism, and lack of historical specificity (Hall 1980:336). According to Hall, socially constructed definitions of 'race' are the 'modalities' and the 'medium' through which social and economic class relations are lived and experienced (Hall et al. 1978:394).

Others writing in a neo-Marxist tradition have followed Cox in recognizing the reality of a global economic system. For example, Miles (1987) emphasizes the importance of 'unfree labour' in capitalist societies. Beginning with slavery and proceeding through various forms of migrant labour ranging from convicts, indentured labour, and 'coolies' to contemporary *Gastarbeiter* and other temporary workers, there are pools of unfree labour. They are all subject to strict controls over their movements and have limited rights. Miles elaborated on the concept of a 'reserve army of labour' deemed necessary to profitability and capital formation. In the same theoretical framework, Satzewich (1991) examined the incorporation of foreign labour in Canada in the immediate postwar period when Canadian farmers relied heavily on European displaced persons to meet largely seasonal labour shortages. Later these were replaced by contract workers from the Caribbean.

An alternative view of power was put forward by Max Weber ([1925] 1947). His classic definition of power (*Macht*) is 'the probability that one actor within a social relationship will be in a position to carry out his own will despite resistance, regardless of the basis on which this probability rests.' He rejected the view that property was the sole source of power. He went on to define 'imperative control' (*Herrschaft*) as 'the probability that a command with given specific content will be obeyed by a given group of persons.' In turn this was related to the idea of discipline, or habitual and uncritical obedience. Weber elaborated the grounds on which power could be exercised legitimately, but said little about its illegitimate uses, including exploitation, domination, and coercion. Power was exercised as legitimate authority when it was based on tradition, bureaucratic rule of law, or through the charismatic influence of a leader who might challenge established systems by appealing to a higher moral authority.

Power in Max Weber's writings was related to questions of class, status, and political party. Status groups differed from classes in that the basis of their rank is related to their (often inherited) lifestyle and the honour and respect that they commanded. The latter was sustained through preserving social distance and a measure of exclusiveness. There were cross-cutting links between class and status groups to the extent that the latter could control the allocation of material and symbolic resources. For Weber, class relations are related to market situations, economic exchange, and competition. The distinction between status and class was connected with Weber's sociology of religion and his understanding of ethnicity. Status groups had their historic origins in feudal systems, but they are also linked to 'race', language, religion, nationality, and cultural differences. Social 'closure' arises as a result of defining membership in terms of ascriptive criteria. Competition creates interest groups that endeavour to control competition by monopolistic practices that in turn provoke retaliation by others (Weber 1968).

Neo-Weberian writers have related status groups to the cultural division of labour that occurs when ethnic or religious groups interact (Hechter 1978). When the occupational characteristics, income distribution, voting behaviour, and intermarriage patterns of ethnic groups in contemporary societies (such as Britain, the United States, or Australia) are examined, varying degrees of hierarchy and segmentation are observed. These reflect a cultural division of labour that has its roots in historical circumstances of conquest, migration, and ethnic stratification (Hechter 1975, 1978).

John Rex makes extensive use of Weber's theories of class and status in his discussion of 'race' and ethnicity in Britain (Rex 1986; Rex and Tomlinson 1979). He distinguishes between the situation of immigrant minorities in Britain and the United States. In the latter 'an individual is assimilated and accepted when he is capable of standing on his own feet as a property-owning individual' (Rex 1986:68). Although he sees the United States as an open society in which there are opportunities for immigrants to achieve social mobility, he recognizes that it is relatively closed to 'Black' Americans. The biggest divide in that country is racial (Rex 1986:62). In a welfare state such as Britain (at least before the Thatcher/Major era), immigrants were obliged to gain acceptance in a working class that had particular social rights relating to citizenship, collective bargaining, housing, and education. Noting that Weber defined class in terms of a market situation and a differential distribution of property, Rex argues:

> Taking this only a stage further we may say that wherever there is a system of allocation of scarce resources of any kind there will be classes. This Weberian revision of Marxism suggests that under the 'Welfare state deal' the position of the working class is defined in terms of certain social rights, and that whether or not any minority groups [sic] is part of the working class depends upon whether it shares fully these rights (Rex 1986:68)

Power and structuration theory

It is important to recognize that power is necessarily implicated in all forms of action whether cooperative or conflicting. It requires the mobilization of resources as a means towards the achievement of goals. These resources may be individual or collective. They are both material and symbolic. The principal components of power in any behavioural context are shown in Figure 1.1.

In Giddens's terminology, material resources are allocative and symbolic resources are authoritative (Giddens 1984:258–62). The latter are non-material resources that derive from social interaction and involve organization of social time-space. Material resources include energy, raw materials, and property as a means of production, together with the artefacts, goods, and services that are generated through action. Symbolic resources are derived initially from the acquisition of language and the capacity to communicate. Closely linked are intelligence, information, knowledge, art, science, and technology. In turn, these depend upon a capacity to organize, manage, and develop skills and perform efficiently. Individual action assumes will-power or a commitment to particular goals and a need for achievement. This is related to individual self-consciousness and a sense of identity. These propensities translate collectively into group consciousness through identification with leaders and the maintenance of group cohesion and solidarity in the pursuit of common objectives. Neither material nor symbolic resources are distributed equally between individuals and collec-

Figure 1.1   Power and mobilization

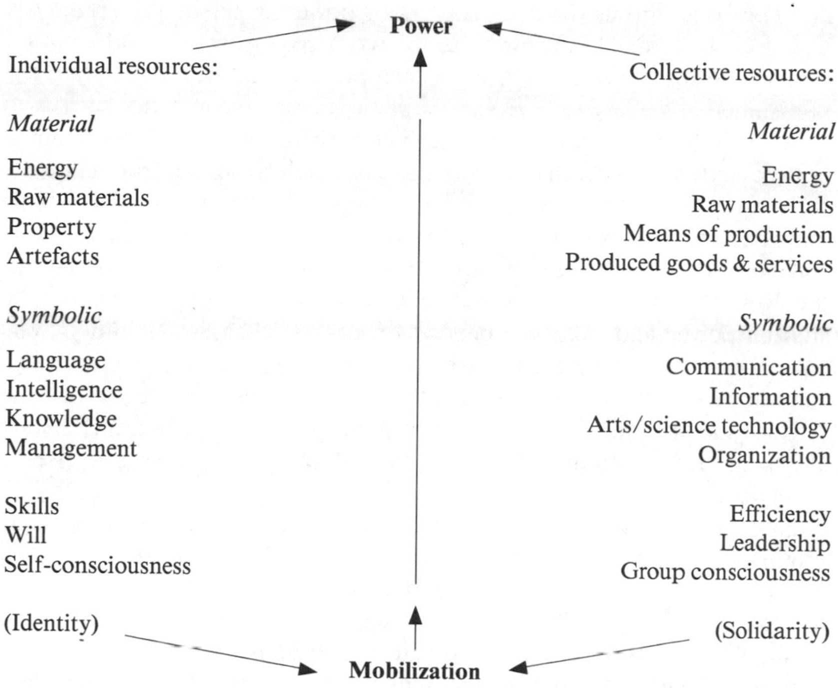

	Power	
Individual resources:		Collective resources:

Material

Energy
Raw materials
Property
Artefacts

Symbolic

Language
Intelligence
Knowledge
Management

Skills
Will
Self-consciousness

(Identity)

Material

Energy
Raw materials
Means of production
Produced goods & services

Symbolic

Communication
Information
Arts/science technology
Organization

Efficiency
Leadership
Group consciousness

(Solidarity)

Mobilization

tivities. This asymmetrical distribution gives rise to 'structures of domination' embedded in political, economic, and social institutions that can be oppressive. Giddens (1981:60) emphasizes that exploitation is more than purely economic in form. It can occur whenever power is used for sectional interests at the expense of other individuals or groups. Exploitation can be physical or psychological. It implies the manipulation of others through ideological indoctrination as well as material deprivation.

Power relations are not necessarily a zero-sum game, although they may be under some circumstances. As Parsons (1963) and others have shown, power (and the resources that create it) can be increased through the division of labour and cooperative activity. In this respect, power is like money. It facilitates the achievement of collective goals that can be expanded through the exercise of trust and confidence in others, including leaders. A process of legitimation generates authority and willing compliance by followers. Boulding (1989:25) distinguished three categories of power based upon threat, exchange, and 'love'. These are institutionalized in the political/military, economic and social systems, respectively, in different proportions. The political/military system relies primarily on threat (with an admixture of promises and rewards), the economic system depends primarily on exchange, and the social system on mutual support or integrative power. A somewhat similar view of power is expressed by Galbraith (1985) who identifies the main sources of power as personality, property, and organization. He distinguishes between compensatory and condign power in terms of the difference between positive and negative reward (or punishment).

Power relations are always two-way and involve varying degrees of autonomy and dependence. In this sense there is a dialectic of control, reflecting the capacity of the less powerful to manage resources (particularly symbolic ones) to their advantage, even when filling subordinate roles (Giddens 1984:16). Power implies the capacity to transform social relations and involves degrees of autonomy and dependence. Even those exercising substantial power and influence depend on others to carry out orders, but compliance cannot be assumed in all circumstances. The Parsonian or functionalist view of system integration assumes a greater degree of consensus than is characteristic of most organizations and societies (Parsons 1971). Norms are frequently contested and scarce resources give rise to struggle.

Force is an option not infrequently used by dominant individuals and groups to overcome opposition, and may be used by minorities in defence or retaliation. Violence is not to be equated with power. In fact, the resort to violence is itself an indication that legitimate power and authority are weak. Violence is instrumental, requiring weapons ranging from fists to bombs; 'like all means, it always stands in need of guidance and justification through the end it pursues'(Arendt 1970:51). Coercion may be physical or psychological. It involves the threat of violence or deprivation and the generation of fear. However, conformity and submission may be achieved by a variety of measures, beginning with the earliest childhood socialization and educational experiences. Behavioural conformity may be based on conditioning, physical rewards and punishments, expressions (or withdrawal) of love and approval, as well as material inducements. In adults psychological indoctrination, shock treatment, brainwashing, and torture may be used. Between these extremes are the contemporary instruments of persuasion available to economic and political powers in the form of advertising and propaganda through the mass media. This facilitates what Noam Chomsky (Herman and Chomsky 1988) calls the 'manufacturing of consent'. In a totalitarian society or a democratic one during wartime, the state plays a significant role in this process. However, in a (relatively) free society opposing political parties ensure that there is more than one set of policy options and the degree of hegemony is reduced. At other times, religious leaders may be openly critical of government policies and materialistic philosophies of a consumer society.

Corporate advertising is clearly designed to generate a consumer mentality and influence choice and market share for particular products and services. Similar techniques are used by politicians competing for power in

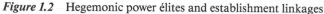

Figure 1.2   Hegemonic power élites and establishment linkages

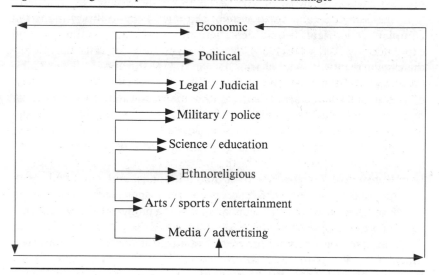

Economic

Political

Legal / Judicial

Military / police

Science / education

Ethnoreligious

Arts / sports / entertainment

Media / advertising

a (relatively) democratic society. The degree of competition may vary in both political and economic systems. There are marked tendencies towards oligopoly in contemporary capitalist societies, particularly since the collapse of the Soviet system, which used central state control of the economy, a more widespread adoption of free market ideologies has occurred. In other situations, religious denominations may apply their formidable resources of indoctrination (now reinforced by the use of television) to influencing attitudes, values, and behaviour. In some situations such as war, religious leaders appear to concur with the political and economic élites in the demands made upon people to make sacrifices and fight in defence of a given nation or cultural entity. However, in a plural society, the competing expectations and ideologies of different authorities may cancel each other out, leaving individuals in an anomic state of indecision or conflicting aspirations.

A key question concerns the degree of concentration and dispersion of power in a given system. A structure of domination may be totalitarian and highly centralized with close links between those exercising power in different spheres. Alternatively, more democratic systems exhibit greater equality in the distribution of resources and the capacity to fulfil individual and minority aspirations. The concept of a power élite implies a high degree of connectedness between the institutional spheres of power and the incumbents of powerful positions, who form a self-perpetuating establishment. The term 'hegemony' describes a situation in which a dominant class or group is able to influence the symbol systems of a society in such a way that their own position is accepted as legitimate with a minimum of doubt or opposition (Gramsci 1988). Such a closely knit system is represented in Figure 1.2 where the network linkages are mutually reinforcing.

In the contemporary world system, the role of the 'military-industrial complex' is critical. First identified by President Eisenhower and expounded by C.W. Mills (1956), the term has conspiratorial flavour. Nevertheless, the reality of a global arms bazaar and the threat of nuclear annihilation cannot be ignored. In the aftermath of the cold war and the collapse of the Soviet Union, armament manufacturers continue to compete for markets, new states and old have access to enormous stockpiles of nuclear and conventional weapons, while defence expenditures by superpowers and the governments of developed and developing countries have been only slightly reduced (see Table 7). Furthermore, terrorist groups purporting to represent minority interests or frustrated nationalist ambitions endeavour to force concessions from those they perceive as oppressors. There are not only more overt ethnic conflicts but an increasing propensity to use violence to promote or suppress them.

Power is not only centred in formal organizations and institutions. It is inherent in the day-to-day relations of people, beginning in parent-child relationships and continuing through life. In this sense, it is embedded in discourse and everyday practices. This aspect has been well documented in the writings of French philosopher Michel Foucault in his studies of power and knowledge, the history of prisons and mental hospitals, and in research dealing with sexuality (Foucault 1973, 1978; Rabinow 1984). In various disciplinary situations, human beings are made subjects and 'objectified'. That is, they are treated in categorical ways and divided from others. What Foucault calls 'dividing practices' separate people according to criteria such as age, gender, 'race', class, religion, or other ascriptive criteria. Such categories become 'discursive facts' that influence how people interact and perceive others. Behaviour may be termed 'deviant' if it is perceived as threatening to a dominant group; it may also be invoked to justify incarceration in prisons, hospitals, or asylums or to justify expulsion from a community. In some institutions, 'expert' knowledge is used to impose discipline and achieve behavioural modification. Dividing practices are techniques of domination that tend to be reinforced in the individual through the process of internalization. Others' perceptions of the person, his or her identity and 'place' in society, are actively incorporated into the subject's self-image. Classification of people as 'immigrants', 'refugees', 'visible minorities', etc., controls and facilitates techniques of administration (Wong 1989). Apartheid institutionalizes such dividing practices.

Foucault (1978) traced a direct link between the objectification of the subject and the growth of government controls and policing, the collection of demographic statistics and the emergence of what he calls 'bio-power'. He examined the history of the death penalty, the technology of war, and the techniques of power available to the state and its representatives.

Among the most important is the capacity for surveillance. Beginning with the simplest forms of observation and record keeping by bureaucrats, this process has become one of the most important *loci* of power in late modern society. Security systems, electronic record keeping, computerization, identity cards, passwords, and restricted access to databases are all ways in which information has become a powerful tool in the hands of those exercising power (Poster 1990). States wishing to exercise control over people entering and leaving their territory have been quick to grasp the importance of these surveillance techniques.

Foucault (1978) also demonstrated the relation between sexism and racism. He recognized blood relations as an important element in the mechanism of power. Kinship relations, alliances, the inheritance of property and sovereignty, and differentiation into estates and castes were all manifestations of this. A preoccupation with 'blood and the law' influenced the administration of rules concerned with sex and marriage. He suggested that in the second half of the nineteenth century, consanguinity became linked to a biological concept of 'race'. 'Racism took shape at this point (racism in its modern "biologizing" statist form): it was then that a whole politics of settlement (*peuplement*), family, marriage, education, social hierarchization, and property, accompanied by a long series of permanent interventions at the level of the body, conduct, health, and everyday life, received their color and their justification from the mythical concern with protecting the purity of the blood and ensuring the triumph of the race' (Rabinow 1984:270–1). He linked this tendency to the growth of the eugenics movement and eventually to the fanatical concerns of Hitler and the Nazis with questions of 'blood' and 'race'.

The process of 'racialization' of the world's population has also been traced by Banton (1977). The earliest European explorations of Africa, Asia, and the Americas led to a preoccupation with categorizing human beings into types on the basis of physical and cultural characteristics that were assumed to be biologically determined and hierarchically arranged. From Gobineau's *Essay on the Inequality of Human Races* ([1853] 1915) through the pseudo-scientific writings of the Social Darwinists to the eugenics movement, there was a direct intellectual link to the excesses of racism, anti-Semitism, and the Jewish Holocaust under the Nazis. Ironically, Banton (1977:155) noted that 'although racial identification was first employed by whites as a tool for putting blacks at a distance', some Afro-Americans and other politically organized minorities use the concept of 'racial solidarity' to promote ethnic pride and counter the dominance of 'Whites'. Militant anticolonialists adopted a similar position in an effort to mobilize opposition to imperialist domination (Fanon 1967). More recently, 'political correctness' has become a slogan and a means for minorities to pressure majorities into changing attitudes and behaviour, sometimes at the risk of reactionary intolerance.

Conflict

Although conflict is not a necessary outcome of the asymmetrical distribution of power and resources, it is a frequent concomitant. As Giddens (1984:283) states:

> It is a mistake to treat power as inherently divisive but there is no doubt that some of the most bitter conflicts in social life are accurately seen as 'power struggles'. Such struggles can be regarded as to do with efforts to subdivide resources which yield modalities of control in social systems.

Conflict arises when there is competition for scarce resources (material and symbolic) and/or when there is an opposition or lack of consensus concerning goals to be achieved. Conflict may also be the result of contradiction. This occurs when there is an opposition of structural principles or when the core value system of a society defines certain goals and ideals, but fails to provide the necessary institutional means for their achievement. Giddens suggests 'contradiction is likely to be linked directly to conflict where perverse consequences ensue' (1984:317). He gives, as an example, the urban rioting that occurred in Detroit in the late 1960s. This was seen at the time to be related to inadequate welfare services and employment opportunities for 'Blacks' in the city. When these were improved, it encouraged more poor people to migrate to the city to take advantage of the programs offered. This exacerbated rather than improved the situation.

Blalock (1989) examined the relation between power and conflict within the framework of a general systems theory. He treated power as a multiplicative function of resources combined with the degree and efficiency of their mobilization. When two or more individuals or groups interact, the outcome of a conflict will depend upon definition of goals, choice of means, and effective mobilization of resources. These in turn may be influenced by various environmental constraints. His models of power and conflict are predicated upon a 'modified subjective expected utility' perspective (Blalock 1989:33). This assumes 'rational actors', but the approach is modified by a recognition of the bounded nature of decision making and the influence of various situational determinants. The resulting models incorporate factors such as alliances, ideology, degrees of consensus, myths of invincibility, fatigue levels, willingness to negotiate, etc. Such multivariate complexity makes it extremely difficult to predict the actual outcome of conflicts. Blalock concludes his analysis by warning against the dangers of oversimplified explanations and subsequent naive policy recommendations (1989:251).

Agency

The study of social systems and behaviour raises difficult questions concerning the freedom of individuals and collectivities to determine their own futures. This is particularly evident in the sociological study of nationalism, migration, 'race', and ethnic relations. Deterministic theories, whether formulated in terms of 'manifest destinies', 'chosen peoples', evolutionary theories of change, or materialist views of history and class conflict leave little room for individual choice. Marx's famous dictum that people make history but not in circumstances of their own choosing has been generally interpreted in a deterministic way, but it can also be understood as a more dynamic relation between individual choices and the structural constraints and facilitators within which those choices are made. The role of leaders is critical. Power-holders in all spheres of life, but particularly in economic and political organizations, can have a substantial impact on history. So also can those in minority status when consciousness is raised and collective action occurs.

There is a long-standing dispute in the social sciences between 'structural' analyses and those that emphasize 'methodological individualism' (O'Neill 1973). Those who advocate the former eschew explanations of behaviour that depend upon the subjective state of mind of individuals or that attribute purpose and goals to collectivities. They believe that structures or networks of social relations can be studied independently of the actors. Social systems exhibit properties that are more than the sum of their parts. The proponents of methodological individualism insist that society can only be understood in terms of the individuals who participate in it. Only individuals are real, it is argued; everything else is abstraction or metaphor. Such a view insists that there can be no social scientific 'laws' unless they are expressed in terms of the psychological predispositions of individuals. Structural theorists, whether those of the functionalist and consensus school or those who adopt a more radical conflict approach, regard such assertions as reductionist.

The debate concerning agency is evident in the writings of various sociologists who have addressed issues of racism and ethnic relations. It is sometimes confused with alternative radical or conservative views, on the one hand, and with disputes concerning the extent to which competition gives rise to social exchange and rational choice on the other. For example, Hechter (1975) began his own research on colonialism and nationalism by emphasizing the importance of structural determinants embedded in historical circumstances. Subsequently, he recognized the limitations of this approach. 'Individuals typically have some choice-making discretion in all groups and societies. To the extent that they have such discretion, their behaviour will confound expectations derived from theories that only countenance aggregate-level causal factors' (Hechter 1986:267).

Both Hechter (1986) and Banton (1983) emphasize the importance of rational choice. The approach has its roots in economic theories of market behaviour. It has been adapted by anthropologists and sociologists who focus on questions of social exchange and the transactional nature of human interaction. Thus, Frederik Barth (1969) developed a theory of ethnic groups, social exchange, and boundaries of social relations that was heavily influenced by 'games theories' in micro-economics. As developed by Banton, the theory is predicated on the assumption that individuals endeavour to maximize net advantage, and that choices made in the past constrain those that can be made now and in the future (Banton 1983:104). Individual competition for resources (including such symbolic ones as status and prestige) tends to break down group boundaries, whereas group competition tends to reinforce them.

Transactional theories based on the premise of individuals making rational choices in order to maximize or achieve optimal satisfaction leave open the question of how value preferences arise in the first place or how they may be changed. There are elements of tautology and other weaknesses in the explanations provided (Dex 1985). Such theories have been severely criticized by writers in both the Marxian and Weberian traditions of sociology. For example, M.G. Smith (1985:495) points out the failure to incorporate power differentials into the models. The theory is biased towards the perspective of dominant groups.

> Anyone acquainted with the historical record of white and non-white relations in Africa, Australia, Melanesia, the Caribbean and the Americas will be surprised that one of the leading experts in this field has tried to analyze and 'explain' them as outcomes of rational choice and action to maximize net advantage by all their participants ... one wonders what a rational choice theory applied to contexts of this kind written by a scholar of the dispossessed, exploited or exterminated peoples would look like (Smith 1985:497)?

While adopting the perspective of methodological individualism, John Rex is also critical of rational choice theory. He emphasizes the importance of structural factors as well as the actions of individuals. He notes that 'the external social constraints upon our conduct can be analyzed in terms of the actions of other individuals, even though these themselves have been organized in long chains in which the constraints are themselves constrained' (Rex 1985:560). He suggests that a theory of 'race' and ethnic relations must explain what separates groups and what brings them together, what leads to increased or diminished salience of group boundaries as well as how 'race' and ethnicity are related to political and economic structures, including questions of class conflict (Rex 1986:18–37).

Questions of human agency and the dispute between structural theorists and methodological individualists have been helpfully reviewed in the work of Anthony Giddens (1984:207, 221). He argues that structural sociology and methodological individualism are not mutually exclusive alternatives.

> The methodological individualists are wrong in so far as they claim that social categories can be reduced to descriptions in terms of individual predicates. But they are right to suspect 'structural sociology' blots out, or at least radically underestimates, the knowledgeability of human agents, and they are right to insist that 'social forces' are always nothing more and nothing less than mixes

of intended or unintended consequences of action undertaken in specifiable contexts (Giddens 1984:220).

Giddens raises the further question of whether collectivities are actors. When we say 'the government' did this, or 'Blacks in Los Angeles' reacted in a certain way, we are using a shorthand description of a complex process that involves the reflexive monitoring of behaviour.[1] Formal organizations such as corporations and governments have elaborate decision-making rules that legitimate certain actions taken in the name of the organization, even when not all its members concur in the decision. The same is not true of looser associations of individuals and groups whose behaviour may appear to be more spontaneous and disorganized. However, even in the extreme case of crowd behaviour and rioting, there is still a feedback element. The actions of individuals have significant repercussions for others and for the system within which they play a variety of different roles.

The multivariate complexity of human behaviour and the social systems they create produces a high degree of indeterminacy in outcome. It must be understood that theories in the social sciences are necessarily probabilistic, not deterministic. The variables studied in social systems are interactive (in the sense that the consequence of event A may be different in the presence of variable B than in the presence of variable C); they are generally multiplicative rather than additive, meaning that a combination of circumstances will generate consequences that are more than the sum of the parts. Models of social behaviour are recursive in the sense that subsequent actions can feed back on previous ones, thereby having either positive (exaggerating) or negative (inhibiting) effects.

It is tempting to draw an analogy between the characteristics of social systems and mathematical 'chaos theory', although care must be taken not to stretch the comparisons too far. At best, they serve as a metaphor. Chaos theory is based on the proposition that random behaviour, irregularities, bifurcations, and apparently chaotic observations may, over a long period, display regularities that can be expressed mathematically. Crystallographers, ecologists, meteorologists, cosmologists, and other scientists have found unexpected order emerging out of systematic observation of events that cannot be experimentally controlled in a positivistic manner. One important contribution of chaos theory has been the realization that randomness (including noise and error) must be built into realistic theories. Very small differences in input can produce unexpected outcomes. One of the best examples has been labelled the 'butterfly effect'. It helps to explain why meteorological forecasting is so difficult. Hypothetically, the flight of a butterfly in a certain location could so affect wind currents in one place that it could whip up a storm in another. The theory suggests that in any system there is a sensitive dependence on initial conditions, but small interferences can have enormous and unpredictable consequences (Gleick 1987). By analogy, the assassination of a leader in one country may result in a world war, or a small fluctuation in the price of oil could lead to the fall of a government. There is a sense in which human societies are open and 'fractal' rather than closed and cybernetic. That is, they are the result of numerous coordinated, uncoordinated, and random events rather than directed and strictly determined, either by past history or central controls. Some patterns and some order may emerge out of the chaos, but it is doubtful if these can be reduced to mathematical formulae. Even though computer modelling of demographic and economic systems has become quite sophisticated, it is only possible to make limited projections based upon the parameters and assumptions built into the models. Most of these are 'linear'; they rarely incorporate the feedback effects that are critical in the modelling of mathematical chaos systems. This is partly because social scientists still have inadequate measures of the many behavioural variables that enter into the system.

Other mathematical theories that, again by analogy, throw some light on social behaviour are those associated with stress. Catastrophe theories have been developed in engineering and the study of the physical properties of metals, etc. The cumulative effects of small stresses can lead to the total collapse of a complex structure, a breakdown in the functioning of a machine, or the phenomenon of metal fatigue, leading to changes in the chemical or physical characteristics of the material, often with catastrophic results (Zeeman 1977). Again, it would be inappropriate to apply such mathematical theories directly to the study of social systems. Nevertheless, in a qualitative rather than quantitative sense, there is no doubt that cumulative stress and tension can have very harmful effects, both on the physiological and psychological well-bring of individuals, but also on the social systems of which they are a part. Rapid and unpredictable change is a major source of stress.

The concept of 'hyperchange' describes a combination of linear, exponential, discontinuous, and chaotic (or random, disorderly, and unpredictable) change. To this should be added the possibility of regressive or retroactive change and the consequences of positive and negative feedback that may lead to a slowing down or acceleration of change and influence the direction of movement. Learning from experience is rendered difficult under these conditions.

Under normal conditions, the reflexive nature of human behaviour enables learning to occur, which, in turn, makes forethought and planning possible. When situations are changing rapidly, this may not be possible. Furthermore, human behaviour is not governed by cognitive processes and rational choices alone. Even when all the necessary information is available to make decisions that will maximize net advantage, non-rational and irrational choices are often made. Instinctive drives, unconscious desires, and overriding passions frequently subordinate rational calculation. The situation is further complicated by the question of time-span. Choices that may seem rational in the pursuit of short-term goals, that are designed to benefit particular individuals and groups, may be counterproductive, and even seriously destructive when longer-term consequences and the effect on others (or on the biophysical environment) are taken into account.

It is no exaggeration to link persistent racial, ethnic, and national conflict to the collapse of stable political orders, economic crises, social upheavals, and violence, ranging from murder and suicide to civil war. Giddens's theories of structuration are helpful in understanding both the nature of social order and the spread of violence (Giddens 1985, 1987).

Structuration

By emphasizing the importance of agency, Giddens is able to transcend the split between structural theories and individualistic ones. He defines 'structuration' in terms of process, i.e., 'the structuring of social relations across time and space, in virtue of the duality of structure' (Giddens 1984:376). By 'duality' he means that structures are both the medium and the outcome of recursively organized conduct. Systems do not exist outside of action, but are being constantly produced and reproduced (with or without modification) over time and space. Structures are themselves derived from rules and resources, as systems are patterned with varying degrees of internal cohesion and conflict. Structures are virtual in the sense that they have no physical reality. Nevertheless, they exist as principles that govern conduct and social practices. Structural properties are expressed as forms of domination and power (Giddens 1984:18). Rules exhibit varying degrees of intensity, explicitness, formality, and sanctioning. Social structures constrain behaviour, limiting choices and narrowing options, but they also enable, thus facilitating action that could not occur otherwise. Giddens distinguishes structures of signification, domination, and legitimation. Each has a corresponding institutional order. *Signification* refers to symbolic orders and modes of discourse; *domination* to political and economic institutions (resource allocation) and *legitimation* to legal institutions (Giddens 1984:31).

In applying structuration theory to the study of migration, 'race', and ethnic relations, signification, domination, and legitimation are key concepts. Each interacts with the other. Terms such as 'race', 'ethnicity', 'migrant', 'refugee', and 'visible minority' are *symbolic signifiers*. They categorize people according to particular criteria that, in turn, convey complex sets of meaning according to the historical context and specific situations. They are closely linked to 'structures of domination' due to the unequal distribution of resources. Legitimation involves normative regulation and determines the rights and obligations pertaining to particular statuses.

Following Weber, Giddens distinguishes between class and status. Classes are economic interest groups arising from the allocation of property and other resources, including human capital. They reflect market positions and the degree to which mobility opportunities exist. Class-divided societies are those in which position is largely determined by birth, where the state plays a dominant role, and there is a marked division between urban and rural areas. Modern capitalist societies are class societies in which there is a competitive labour market involving all economically active populations. A distinction is made between class 'consciousness' and class 'awareness'. The latter implies shared attitudes, values, and lifestyles, but not necessarily awareness of collective class interests.

Giddens modifies Weber's view of status groups by separating distributive groupings, based on consumption patterns, from forms of social differentiation derived from non-economic criteria of honour and prestige. Giddens rejects the view that racial and religious divisions are necessarily incompatible with the formation of class consciousness. Rather than hindering such class formations, he suggests that where class coincides with the criteria of status group membership, class *consciousness* may be enhanced. He states that class structuration may be increased:

> ... where structuration deriving from economic organization 'overlaps' with, or. ... is 'superimposed' upon, that deriving from evaluative categorisations based upon ethnic or cultural differences. Where this is so, status group membership itself becomes a form of market capacity. Such a situation frequently offers the strongest possible source of class structuration (Giddens 1981:112).

I follow the terminology introduced by Milton Gordon, who uses the term *ethclass* to describe the intersection of class and ethnicity (Gordon 1978:134–6). In the United States and Canada, relative concentrations of particular immigrant and ethnic groups in certain industries and occupations have persisted since the turn of the century (Lieberson and Waters 1988:249). However, the relations of a postindustrial ethclass are not necessarily limited by the boundaries of a single state. Within a global system, an ethclass may be located in another region or continent and still experience a conflict of interest with classes located elsewhere in the world. Such transnational ethclasses do not interact on a local neighbourhood or community basis, nor are they formally organized in labour unions or professional associations. They are loosely connected by transnational communication networks. Examples range from Hong Kong entrepreneurs and Arab oil magnates at one end of the scale to Mexican farm workers and Filipino domestics on the other. In between are Amerindian steel rig workers and Japanese auto industry managers. The single common denominator is their motility. They follow the global demand for their services.

There is no logical reason why the relations between ethnic groups should not be based on equality, cooperation, and social exchange, but in practice this is rarely the case. Initial inequalities in the distribution of resources are exacerbated by uneven development and exploitation. War, racism, and colonialism have created a complex system of ethclass relations that extend throughout the global system. It is the basis of much overt conflict. Economic insecurity is a critical factor in structuration of ethclass relations.

Security and insecurity

Everyday life depends upon routine that, in turn, assumes a degree of predictability and trust in others. Feelings of anxiety are generated when routines are interrupted. Confidence and trust are essential elements in early socialization, creating feelings of ontological security. R.D. Laing (1960:39) defined primary ontological security in terms of an individual's self-confidence, derived from a sense of the permanency of things and the reliability of natural processes. He notes that in extreme cases, a person may experience engulfment, implosion, or petrification when faced with life-threatening crises or the collapse of the normal routines of daily life. Becoming a refugee, a prisoner-of-war, or the victim of torture, a pogrom, or systemic 'ethnic cleansing' generates extreme ontological insecurity. Reaction may take various forms ranging from fear, rage, and retaliation to hiding, flight, apathy, temporary derangement, psychosis, murder, or suicide.

Giddens (1990:7–10) draws attention to the themes of security versus danger, and trust versus risk in the development of modern social institutions. Modernity opens up numerous opportunities for material advantage and rewards. It increases life expectancy and enhances security in many ways. However, it also has negative consequences. Industrial work can be exploitive and degrading; political power may be abused through surveillance, bureaucratization, and oppressive treatment of minorities; economic systems may collapse and service delivery fail; ecological disasters are imminent as the environment is threatened by global warming and ultraviolet radiation; above all, military power generates enormous risks in an age of nuclear weapons and other means of mass destruction. These are the 'dark sides' of modernity (Giddens 1990:151–8).

Secondary ontological insecurity arises when particular spheres of social life are threatened. The death of a loved one, the experience of divorce, or the loss of a job are among the traumatic events that can generate extreme anxiety, the depth of which will depend upon the availability of practical and moral support systems. The duration of the feelings of insecurity will depend upon the individual's ability to restore normal routines, re-establish trust, and achieve confidence in himself or herself and others. Secondary security depends upon the predictability and reliability of key political, economic, and social institutions. When political systems degenerate into anarchy and civil war, or revolutions overthrow established forms of government, security is threatened. Giddens (1985:196) identifies the 'existential contradiction' between nature and society, life and death, which in the modern state is replaced by a structural contradiction reflected in the 'sequestration' of the experiences of sexuality, birth, death, and sickness.

When the routines of social life are seriously disrupted, 'large segments of modern life engender a basis for affiliation to symbols that can both promote solidarity and cause schism' (Giddens 1985:197). One of these is the phenomenon of nationalism.

Sovereignty, citizenship, and nationalism are related to the administrative unity of the state. All are affected by contemporary trends towards regionalization and globalization. There are contradictory pressures towards increased autonomy and local control on the one hand and loss of sovereignty through military and political alliances and economic union on the other. Giddens notes the 'Janus-faced' character of nationalism, vacillating between democratic and 'exclusivists' forms. When the ontological security of individuals is in jeopardy and there are high levels of anxiety, mass support may be generated for populist causes. Nationalism is rooted in the history of modern societies that form conceptual or 'imagined' communities with invented traditions (Giddens 1985:219; Hobsbawm and Ranger 1983). Postindustrial societies have experienced a resurgence of nationalism that is related to globalization on the one hand and competition for power by local, regional, and ethnic power élites on the other (Richmond 1988c:141–82). Political and economic insecurity are concomitant outcomes.

Economic insecurity is the consequence of various factors ranging from crop failure and famine, through recession and prolonged unemployment, to structural adjustment and the long-term consequences of industrial or postindustrial revolution. Economic insecurity is closely correlated with manifestations of ethnic prejudice and discrimination (Richmond 1950, 1988c). This does not mean that it is the only determinant. Prejudice and discrimination, including anti-Semitism, racism, and other forms of ethnocentrism and conflict, have complex roots in historical contexts, cultural traditions, religious beliefs, social institutions, and psychological predispositions (Sniderman et al. 1993). Prolonged unemployment or other threats to income security and livelihood generate feelings of insecurity that may result in the scapegoating of ethnic minorities. Periods of economic recession provide the underlying conditions that increase the probability of ethnic conflict. Sudden increases in the level of unemployment may precipitate outbreaks of violence. Given the multivariate and probabilistic nature of social causality, there is no determinate link between unemployment and ethnic tension. However, when full employment ceases to be a goal of economic policy and competition in the labour market is intense, racial conflict is likely to intensify. Questions of primary and secondary ontological security are closely related to those of individual and collective identity.

Identity

As mentioned earlier, gender, age, 'race', language, nationality, and religion are among the ascriptive bases on which people define their identities.

To these may be added achieved characteristics, such as occupation, which play an important part in the formation of personality and self-definitions. The plural noun is necessary because individual identities are multiple, situationally determined, and influenced by context. They are reflexively organized and redefined subjectively over time. Self-definitions of identity do not always correspond with the identities attributed by others, which may be based upon different criteria and perceptions.

An ontologically secure individual is able to integrate different facets of self-identity into a consistent whole. Anxiety-creating situations threaten that sense of wholeness and continuity through time and space. Modern social life tends to be pluralistic and segmented. It is also changing rapidly and involves risk. This can lead to the fragmentation of identity. A cosmopolitan person may thrive in a situation of ethnic diversity and rapid social change. A less secure person may experience a serious identity crisis. Anyone faced with a devastating loss will feel threatened. Examples include members of a dominant group experiencing decline in power and prestige, or others who are chronically unemployed, those who become refugees, together with the victims of war or racial oppression. They may react by becoming confused, or by seeking someone to blame. Others may compulsively and rigidly emphasize one aspect of their experience, asserting their identity through authoritarian conformity (Fromm 1941; Giddens 1991:189–91). In turn, authoritarianism is closely linked to expressions of ethnic prejudice, adherence to fascist-type ideologies and membership in neo-Nazi parties (Adorno 1950; Altemeyer 1988).

Even when there is biological basis for defining identity, as in the case of gender, the actual behavioural manifestations are socially constructed and culturally determined. Both the subjective and objective aspects of gender identity vary according to historical era and cultural milieu. From infancy, children are taught how to behave in accordance with gender roles, which begin with dress and proceed through toilet training, dolls, toys and games played, to rules governing appropriate behaviour in adolescence and adult life. Sexual orientation may or may not involve an element of choice after puberty, but in almost all other respects, gender roles are ascribed, as are those pertaining to age.

'Race' is similarly a social construct, the cultural meaning of which varies according to time and place. From a strictly biological point of view, there are no 'races', only gene pools that determine the statistical probability that certain physical traits, such as skin pigmentation or hair form, will appear in each generation. There has been so much miscegenation over the centuries that almost any large population will exhibit a mixture of such physical traits (Hulse 1969). Notwithstanding the claims of some pseudo-scientific studies, there is no reliable evidence that they are linked to any cultural, social, or psychological characteristics. It is the mark of a racist society that skin colour or other physical attributes are used as a basis of social (and sometimes legal) classification. A society 'structured in dominance' tends to use gender and 'race' as bases of superordination and subordination. Furthermore, persons of mixed Afro-European or Eurasian descent are often allocated to subordinate status, irrespective of their actual genetic inheritance or physical appearance. In extremely racist systems, such as those prevailing in South Africa or the southern United States until recently, light-skinned persons who might have been able to 'pass as White' were nevertheless compelled to remain within segregated communities and suffered the same discrimination as their darker complexioned relatives.

Terms such as 'White', 'Coloured', 'Negro', 'Black', 'person of colour', or 'visible minority' are all social constructs, the use of which reflects changing perceptions and shifting power relations. Political mobilization and consciousness-raising efforts have tried to unite disparate communities under a single banner. Slogans such as 'Black is beautiful' and 'Black power' have been used, with varying degrees of success, to bring together subordinated minorities of ultimately African, Asian or other non-European descent. However, antiracist movements have tended to split as some minorities become more socially mobile than others and cultural divisions assume greater salience. As Rattansi (1992:40) notes in the case of Britain, 'Partly influenced by the Black Power Movement in the US, the category "black" became, for the late 1960s, an important focus, especially among left anti-racists, for mobilizing the growing communities of Afro-Caribbean and Asian descent . . . But the cultural essentialism at its core has begun to disintegrate.' There has been an ethnic backlash and protest against cultural homogenization as well as neglect of the problems facing other immigrants groups, such as Turks and Greek Cypriots.

In Canada, there are similar difficulties with the term 'visible minority'. It was first introduced in the context of employment equity and affirmative action programs as a euphemism for 'race' (Abella 1984:46). Visible minorities were among several target groups that also included women, native peoples, and the disabled, all of whom were recognized as having suffered systemic and institutionalized discrimination in the past. Subsequently, Statistics Canada was asked to provide estimates of the numbers of people at risk in each of these categories (Boxhill 1984, 1990). This statistical exercise, using census data and immigration figures, aggregated people by various criteria, including birthplace, ethnic origin, and language. As a result, the Canadian-born descendants of 'Black' Empire Loyalists, who had been in Canada for generations, were lumped together with recently arrived refugees from Africa and Asia, immigrants from Latin America, and affluent business investors from Hong Kong!

There are cross-cutting links between sexism and racism to the extent that both gender and 'race' have been used to oppress. The status of women in particular ethnocultural groups varies considerably. In the United States and elsewhere, the feminist movement has sometimes brought together women of different 'races' and at other times they have been divided in their fight against discrimination (Davis 1983). In Canada, Aboriginal women have experienced discrimination within their own communities. Together with 'Black' feminists, they tend to regard the concerns of 'White' middle-class women as irrelevant to their fight against oppression. As stated by Stasiulis (1990:288), 'Black feminist analyses reveal how, for *both* white women and women of colour, the relationship to the family, state, production and reproduction has been mediated simultaneously by class interests, gender divisions, and white supremacist logics, in a way that has constructed barriers to sisterhood across racial lines.'

Attempts to categorize people by 'race' must be distinguished from ethnicity. The latter combines different dimensions of cultural identity into a relatively coherent whole. It is not synonymous with minority status or with the whole of culture. Only those aspects that are salient in group formation are selectively used as signifiers. It is a 'self-other' or 'us and them' definition using particular attributes that are socially constructed and then internalized in the process of personality development and identity formation. Language, religion, and nationality combine in different ways to form ethnocultural groupings and ethnonational political movements. Language plays a critical role, not only as an ethnic signifier in its own right, but also as the medium through which ethnic consciousness and ethnic groups are formed. Fishman (1989:7) emphasized this aspect when he stated:

> At every stage, ethnicity is linked to language, whether indexically, implementationally or symbolically. There is no escaping the primary symbol-system of our species, certainly not where the phenomenonology of aggregational definition and boundary maintenance is involved, when ethnic being, doing and knowing is involved. Initially however, language is but one of a myriad of minimally conscious discriminanda.

Fishman goes on to point out that language may become a rallying cry, and that it also plays a part in defining religious identity by raising 'language into the pale of sanctity even in a secular culture'. In the Canadian case, there are strong historical links between religion (Roman Catholicism) and the French language, particularly in Quebec. In turn, these have been moulded into a powerful sense of national identity. For generations, Quebecers have been taught that they have a unique heritage that differs profoundly from that of *les anglais*, who are seen as conquerors and oppressors. Even when English Canadians or immigrants living in Quebec speak French fluently, they are not regarded as *pur laine* or 'true' French Canadians.

Care must be taken to distinguish ways in which people may be categorized by 'ethnic origin' (for census-taking purposes or legal registration) and the way in which they define themselves. In censuses it is clear that multiple ethnic origins are characteristic of contemporary societies, such as the United States and Canada, that have experienced substantial waves of immigration over long periods. There has been extensive intermarriage between ethnoreligious groups with consequent diversification of the population even though complete assimilation to the characteristics of the majority of dominant group has not occurred. Lieberson and Waters (1988) described the many strands that have contributed to the American cultural fabric and the extent of intermarriage. They describe the resulting patterns as an 'ethnic flux' (Lieberson and Waters 1988:267). Many respondents in censuses and surveys decline to use an ethnic designation. In 1980, 12 per cent of the population preferred simply to define themselves as 'American'. Similarly in Canada in 1991, 29 per cent of the population reported more than one ethnic origin, and over a million people insisted on describing themselves as 'Canadian', although this was not an option on the census form.

Communication

Humans communicate through all five senses: touch, taste, smell, sight, and hearing. Each is important, particularly sight and hearing, which play a critical role in the development and learning of language. When either or both of these senses are impaired, touching assumes greater significance, making communication possible through braille and other means. There are cognitive and conative aspects to all communication. Understanding is more than the exercise of reason. It involves feelings and emotions. It is a social act. To be intelligible, communicative actions must take place within a given speech community. This involves a shared culture and symbolic interaction according to learned rules of behaviour. Language is at the core of self-identity. 'Unless the subject externalises himself by participating in interpersonal relations through language, he is unable to form that inner center that is his personal identity. This explains the almost constitutional insecurity and chronic fragility of personal identity—an insecurity that is antecedent to cruder threats to the integrity of life and limb' (Habermas 1990:199).

Habermas (1990) defines the *lifeworld* in terms of symbolic structures reproduced through cultural tradition, social integration, and socialization. Strategic behaviour oriented towards success in a power struggle or competitive situation may involve manipulating others' definition of the situation. Action oriented towards understanding must go further. It involves reaching agreement as a means of coordinating action and reaching consensus. The lifeworld is the context in which communicative action takes place. It is a circular process that feeds back on itself and is modified by the actors as they communicate. 'The shared lifeworld offers a storehouse of unquestioned cultural givens from which those participating in communication draw agreed-upon patterns of interpretation . . . '(Habermas 1990:135).

Habermas defines an 'ideal speech situation' as one that is free from systemic distortion. This means an absence of constraint or domination, unrestricted discussion, a complementarity of expectations, and unimpaired self-presentation. Needless to say, such conditions are not easily achieved and much communication in practice is impaired as a result. Although Habermas defines *ideology* as 'systematically distorted communication', it is more appropriate to recognize with Giddens (1987:270) that 'modes of signification are ideological when they are pressed into service of sectional interests via the use of power'. Racism is such an ideology and so also are sexism, chauvinism, and jingoistic forms of nationalism. Following Freire (1973), O'Neill points out that 'the oppressed are the instruments of a culture of silence, which is maintained by the political control of language and education' (O'Neill 1985:66). Human dialogue requires common understanding and a removal of barriers.

There are barriers to communication between people who speak a different language, which are not completely overcome by the use of interpreters and translators. Even when language itself is not the obstacle, there are other impediments to mutual understanding. Human beings depend upon those with whom they habitually interact for a conception of 'reality'. Hostility towards other individuals and groups is reinforced by shared frames of reference derived from the subject's own group membership. These have to do with perceived status relationships, power differentials, and expectations of the others' intentions based on stereotypes. Fixed perceptions and the frames of reference that sustain them are maintained by barriers to communication with the object of hostility. Hostility is likely to be reduced only when institutionalized barriers to communication with others are removed and when there is shared support from the subject's own group (Newcomb and Hartley 1947; Richmond 1954:4–7). Even then, it requires more than a cognitive effort. A degree of empathy and an appreciation of where the other is 'coming from' is also required. Violence is the negation of such empathy. 'Language is the soul of our lives together. Today we must work to restore language, to speak where violence puts an end to speech' (O'Neill 1972:67).

Communication may be sensual (as in music), verbal, written, symbolic, or transmitted electronically as encoded signals. Linguistic analysts have focused on *texts* as the medium of cultural discourse, but, in contemporary societies, electronic communications have assumed growing importance as means for the storage, retrieval, and transmission of information. This creates a new domain of language experience that is neither speech nor writing. Together with the images conveyed by television, it is a powerful new tool in the hands of those who aim to manipulate behaviour or influence consciousness. This has given rise to a 'mode of information' parallel to the 'mode of production' and the 'mode of distribution' in the ordering of social systems.

In the mode of information the subject is no longer located in a point in absolute time/space, enjoying a physical, fixed vantage point from which rationally to calculate its options. Instead it is multiplied by databases, dispensed by computer messaging and conferencing, decontextualized and reidentified by TV ads, dissolved and materialized continuously in the electronic transmission of symbols (Poster 1990:15).

Giddens uses the concept of 'time-space distanciation' to describe the effects that improved communications have on social system integration and the distribution of administrative power (Giddens 1985; Urry 1991:160–75). From the development of timetables to the use of various forms of segregation and sequestration of minorities and deviants, time, space, and information have been linked as agents of social control. That control now extends worldwide as states determine who may cross borders and what rights and privileges (if any) that citizens and non-citizens may enjoy. The importance of postmodern communication networks in the contemporary world system and their impact on international migration, 'race', and ethnic relations is the topic of the next chapter.

Note

[1] The term 'reflexive' in this context does not mean a knee-jerk reaction. It implies reflection and intention. 'Reflexive self-regulation' involves information feedback as a means of control and system reproduction (Giddens 1984:376). It does not follow that all behaviour is rational, or that there is anything automatic or cybernetic about the way systems perpetuate themselves. In some situations, the feedback process may be self-destructive.

chapter two

Postindustrialism, postmodernism, and ethnic conflict

The terms 'postindustrial' and 'postmodern' are sometimes used synonymously, but it is more appropriate to confine the former to the technological and economic developments that have occurred in the second half of the twentieth century, and the latter to the social and cultural changes that have taken place. It is debatable whether the postindustrial revolution (consequent upon the use of advanced technologies such as nuclear energy, jet propulsion, computers, automation, and telecommunication) is a radical departure from the changes initiated by the earlier Industrial Revolution or simply a logical continuation of trends that were already evident in the nineteenth century (Kumar 1978). In either case, it is clear that there has been a tremendous acceleration in the rate of change, consequent upon these technological advances. By the same token, it is arguable that contemporary societies that are part of the global capitalist system, as well as those in the less developed world, are in a transitional phase. Whether moving from traditional to modern or from modern to late modern, there is a potential for conflict arising from competing interests and values.

Edward Tiryakian, discussing the global crisis in the mid-1980s, showed that there has been a geographic shift in the centre of modernization from North America to East Asia. He noted that the deindustrialization of large zones within advanced Western societies was matched by the relocation of manufacturing investment in Third World countries and that the information processing revolution led to new modes of production: 'the global crisis is one not only of decline and destructuration but also one of underlying currents of restructuration' (Tiryakian 1984:125). The last decade (1981–90) has been one of those critical epochs that has profound implications for international migration, now and in the future.

Although interdependent, the global *ecological* system is analytically distinct from the global *state* system, the *military* order, the *information* system and world *capitalism* (Giddens 1985; Robertson 1990a). There has always been a global system of commerce extending from the Mediterranean to the far north and from Ireland to the far east. What is new is the emergence of a global system of *production*, as well as commerce and communications. This is now truly universal. In its present form, this world system originated with the Eurocentred mercantile adventurers of the sixteenth and seventeenth centuries. Their exploits linked the New World with the Old, and led to the agrarian and industrial revolutions in western Europe. This paved the way for imperialist expansion and the beginnings of modern capitalism (Wallerstein 1974). Today, however, the global economy is multicentred and dominated by what has been called the ILE (i.e., the interlinked economies of the United States, Europe, and Japan, together with rapidly expanding economies such as those of Taiwan, Hong Kong, and Singapore). The interdependence of these economies is such that, as in chaos theory, a small movement anywhere can trigger a recession, a stock-market crash, or a massive movement of capital and foreign exchange from one country to another. One of the major contradictions inherent in the current process of global change is that, notwithstanding residual protectionism (particularly in the agricultural sphere), money, goods, and information flow relatively freely across borders, but *people do not*. While economists examine the consequences of lowering barriers to trade, removing protectionism, and seeking ways of promoting prosperity through greater sensitivity to consumer preferences, sociologists and political scientists draw attention to the closing of doors to immigrants and refugees, and what Alan Dowty calls 'the contemporary assault on freedom of movement' between one country or continent and another (Dowty 1987).

Industrialism and postindustrialism

Pre-industrial societies were typically small, closely-knit, and territorially-bounded communities based upon kinship. Tonnies [1887] (1957) used the term *Gemeinschaft* to describe such a system of social relations. Relatively undifferentiated in terms of social position, such communities exhibited only an elementary division of labour based on age and gender. Status and political power were ascribed by birth and descent. There was little geographic or social mobility. Governed by orally transmitted traditions, such societies were slow to change. Beginning gradually with the iron and bronze ages and accelerating with the application of steam-generated power to transportation and manufacturing, the impact of industrialization transformed such communities into more complex social systems based upon association or *Gesellschaft*.

These new forms of social organization were superimposed on the old, transforming them without always eliminating them altogether. Family, kinship, neighbourhood, and a sense of community based on shared language, religion, and loyalty to traditional customs persisted, even when the effects of urbanization and industrialization introduced different ways and created new demands. Formal organizations, bureaucratic systems of government, and economic associations with complex systems of production and distribution created new classes with both cooperative and antagonistic interests. Simple barter and economic exchange gave way to complex markets facilitated by the development of money as a currency and a measure of the price, not only of goods and services but of labour itself. Through saving and investment, money became a source of power. When contracts were enforceable by law, the state became the agency through which property was protected. Inherited title to land and property survived the feudal system in which it originated, but a new bourgeois class of business persons, merchants, and entrepreneurs grew in size and importance. In the nineteenth century, the creation of the limited liability company with multiple investors brought industrial capitalism as we know it today. It became the dominant form of economic organization. Again, earlier forms persisted, particularly in the less developed regions of the world still dependent on subsistence agriculture. Meanwhile, the political and economic expansion of industrial capitalist societies seeking abundant supplies of energy, raw materials, and cheap labour led to the imperial domination and colonization of whole continents.

Although the concept was used by earlier writers, the term 'postindustrial' entered the sociological lexicon in the 1960s and was popularized in the writings of David Riesman (1958), Daniel Bell (1973), Amitai Etzioni (1968), Alan Touraine ([1969], 1971) and Alvin Toffler (1970). As well as recognizing the impact of advanced technologies, these writers anticipated significant social changes, not all of which have been realized in the form that they expected. For example, Riesman expected that the increased industrial productivity resulting from new inventions would give rise to a leisure-oriented society, liberating people from the more arduous tasks associated with earlier phases of industrialism. Similar utopian visions were projected by others who were inclined to attribute benign consequences to technological innovation (Frankel 1987). In reality, the second half of the twentieth century has been characterized by higher labour force participation rates (particularly by women), cyclical economic fluctuations, and chronically high unemployment rates in most late capitalist societies. In other words, the 'leisure' anticipated by Riesman has been unevenly distributed and largely involuntary.

Daniel Bell (1973) forecast a shift from employment in primary and secondary industries into the tertiary and quaternary sectors of the economy.[1] In this respect, a distinction between service occupations and service industries is important. As Kumar (1978) pointed out, service occupations were widely held in the nineteenth century, particularly by women in domestic service. Many of the occupations currently filled by women are simply the same jobs transferred to a new site, as in mass food processing and distribution, office cleaning, and hotel services. However, there has also been a growth in industries that are more closely linked to the techno-logical innovations of postindustrialism. They include financial and man-agement services, information processing, telecommunications and media, together with the education and health industries. All of these industries have a range of occupations requiring different levels of skill. As well as a professional and technocratic élite, there are also more routinized jobs (such as data entry and keypunching), although these may still require a level of education that traditional service occupations did not. Altogether service sector jobs in advanced industrial societies have doubled in the period 1960–90, while the share of manufacturing jobs has fallen to only one in five of all occupations. Agricultural employment is now only 4 per cent of all jobs (Akyeampong and Winters 1993). Contemporary labour markets have become global in extent. They are also highly stratified and seg-mented. Not only is there a hierarchy in terms of status and rewards, but skills have become less transferable. Prolonged periods of education and training are a prerequisite for employment in specialized fields. Further-more, labour unions and professional organizations are protective of their privileged access to employment. Credentialism governs hiring and there are barriers to the employment of those who lack the appropriate qualifica-tion or local experience.

A theme common to a number of writers concerning postindustrialism is the importance of applied science and technology and the emergence of a knowledge-based system. This, in turn, creates a class of information man-agers, technocrats, and decision makers with exceptional power to influ-ence opinion and determine policies, leading to a 'technology of knowledge' and a 'programmed society' (Etzioni 1968; Touraine [1969] 1971). Peter Drucker (1993:19–47) described 'post-capitalist' society as one that has become a 'knowledge society'. While it is probably premature to speak of the end of capitalism, it is true that applied science and the 'application of knowledge to knowledge' has generated profound eco-nomic, political, and social changes. Among them are transformations in the characteristic forms of social organization.

The impact of structural change is most evident in transportation, com-munication, and the transmission of information and images. Beginning with the invention of printing and the spread of mass literacy, on the one hand, and the building of railways, steamships, and, in due course, the airplane, on the other, transportation and communications have been revo-lutionized. Marshall McLuhan was one of the first to recognize the impor-tance of these developments, pointing out that 'when information moves at the speed of signals in the central nervous system, man is confronted with the obsolescence of all earlier forms of acceleration, such as road and rail. What emerges is a total field of inclusive awareness. The patterns of psychic and social adjustment become irrelevant' (McLuhan 1964:103).

I have argued elsewhere (Richmond 1969, 1988c) that these postindustrial developments have important consequences for education, migration, and ethnic relations. Automation makes paid learning, experimentation, and programming the principal sources of increased productivity. All aspects of production, consumption, and recreation are rendered incidental to communication and the electronic feedback of information. Higher education and technical training, once the privilege of a minority, became prerequisites for all but the most menial forms of employment. International (and internal) migration becomes a multiway process of exchange based upon ease of access to information and transportation, in which net gains and losses of population in particular localities are a small proportion of the gross movements involved in labour migration, business, and tourism. The concept of transilient migration, originally limited to the highly qualified professional and managerial strata, is now applicable to a much wider range of movers whose permanence in any one locality is neither necessary nor expected, given the ease with which return and remigration can occur. The predominant mode of coaptation of migrants in postindustrial societies is active mobilization, i.e., a 'dynamic interaction between motile individuals and collectivities giving rise to information flow and feed-back effecting greater control over material and human resources' (Richmond 1969:281).

The instantaneous communication made possible through telephones, fax machines, satellite links, videotapes, etc., means that the maintenance of ethnic identity is no longer dependent on a territorial community (*Gemeinschaft*) or on formal organizations (*Gesellschaft*) but on networks (*Verbindungsnetzschaft*). Ethnic links are maintained with others of similar language and cultural background throughout the world (Richmond 1988c:167–82). The political, economic, and social consequences of globalization are central features of both the postindustrial and postmodern revolution.

Globalization

The geography of labour migration is related to globalization and structural changes that are changing the international division of labour:

> The globalization of international labor migration is manifest in two ways. Firstly, all countries now engage in migration systems growing in size and complexity and producing an increasing diversity of flows. Second, many of the processes that create and drive these systems operate on a worldwide basis, the consequence of economic globalization, capital mobility, the activities of international business corporations, and the widespread realization by govern-

ments that human resources can be traded for profit like any other resource (Salt 1992:1080).

Remittance from overseas workers are an important source of foreign currency for many developing countries. These transfers contribute to material development of the countries concerned, contributing to education, welfare, improving the status of women, and contributing to infrastructure building. They also facilitate debt repayment (Stahl 1988).

In terms of trade and commerce, transnational exchanges of goods have always occurred. Beginning in the Mediterranean and Asia Minor, the world system gradually spread to the rest of the globe with the incorporation of the New World into a system of exploitation and colonization (Wallerstein 1974). Money as a medium of exchange was universalized, first through the adoption of a gold standard, later through international banking and money markets, and, by 1986, through the electronic linkage of capital, stock exchanges, and commodity markets into a single system operating twenty-four hours a day. The so-called 'big bang' symbolized the economic integration of a world system (Dezalay 1990). There remained internal conflicts and contradictions between the proponents of free trade and those who continue to seek protection for agricultural and manufacturing industries in particular countries and regions. An international division of labour, with substantial inequalities in the distribution of wealth and in the level of technological and economic development, persists despite the relative integration of the world economic system. In turn, this gives rise to mass migrations of labour from the less to the more developed regions (Appleyard 1988).

The movement of people is also as old as history itself. From nomadic hunters and pastoralists to the inhabitants of space stations, human migration is a universal experience. Early traders, military invaders, explorers, religious evangelists (of many different faiths), pilgrims, travelling entertainers, pirates, and highway robbers have carried languages and cultures around the globe. In more recent times, immigrants, refugees, guest workers, tourists, drug peddlers, journalists, students, and scientists have been added to the growing body of motile individuals and groups. The revolution in transportation and communication that began with the railway and the steamship, accelerated with the automobile, the airplane, and the telegraph, became a dominant factor in the contemporary world system with the spread of radio, TV, telecommunications, satellites, and spacecraft. These new technologies not only convey people and information, they are also the vehicles through which political ideologies, alternative lifestyles, oppositional values, and social movements are spread. Appadurai (1990:295–310) calls these various dimensions of the globalization process ethnoscapes, technoscapes, finanscapes, mediascapes, and ideoscapes. He emphasizes that these are social constructs 'inflected very much by the historical, linguistic and political situatedness of different sorts of actors:

Figure 2.1 Global networks

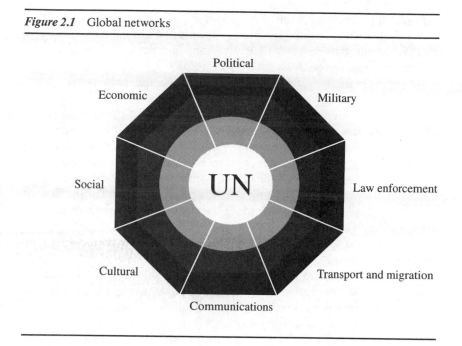

nation-states, multinationals, diasporic communities, as well as sub-national groupings and movements . . . ' (1990:296). One could add to this list mediscapes as the universal consequences of the AIDS epidemic unfold. 'Thus the global health system is only the promissory side of a world disease system. Each generates the other. Here, once again, there is a potential for a rebarbarization of the global order through quarantine orders, immunization control and racism—witness the construction of Afro-AIDS' (O'Neill 1990:338).

Metaphorically, the global system can be understood as an immense spider's web of interlinked networks, without a spider in the middle! It would be tempting to consider the position of secretary-general of the United Nations as the spider at the centre of the web, but this is clearly not the case. In the absence of a system of world government, there is no central direction. States operate with a significant degree of autonomy, even though there is clearly a structure of dominance resulting from unequal economic, political, and military power. Nevertheless, there are many cross-cutting ties and the influence of the UN has increased considerably in recent years. The web of interlinked networks has many sectors (see Figure 2.1). They include the interlinked economies of various countries, their political systems and diplomatic corps, as well as a variety of other networks, together with those of non-governmental and non-economic organizations representing various interests, ranging from religious faiths and humanitarian agencies to subversive political groups and terrorist organizations.[2] Superimposed on all of these are the interpersonal networks based on kinship, friendship, ethnoreligious affiliation, and shared interests. The ability to maintain these links across long distances has been greatly assisted by modern communications technology.

Beginning with the postal system, telegraph, and ham radio, global interpersonal and interorganizational networks have been facilitated by telephone, fax, satellite links, camcorders and VCRs. The cross-cutting flows of goods, services, money, people, diseases, symbols, and information leads to deterritorialization. Whether in terms of economic interests, corporate organization, political affiliation, preventive medicine, or cultural activity, the state is no longer the only or primary frame of reference. Borders have become permeable as never before. This is particularly true of the flow of capital for investment. As a leading Japanese management consultant explains, 'the global economy follows its own logic and develops its own webs of interest, which rarely duplicate the historical borders between nations' (Ohmae 1990:183).

The borderless world is not yet a complete reality and there is clearly resistance to its implications. Lip-service is paid to free trade while economic protectionism persists, despite regional integration. Passports may not be needed by people moving within the European community, or across the US–Canada border, but stringent controls are being imposed on foreign entry to these regions. The flow of cultural products—from films and television programs to newspapers, magazines, and popular music—is resisted by those who are concerned about American cultural imperialism. Cross-border movements of Islamic fundamentalism, Chinese communism, pornographic literature, hard drugs, contagious diseases, terrorism, organized crime, and illegal immigrants are similarly restricted. To this end, borders are patrolled by customs agents, health officials, immigration officers, coastguards, and quasi-military agencies using the latest surveillance and deterrence devices. Immigrants and refugees are caught in this countervailing effort to combat the onslaught of a global system on the sovereignty of states.

Notwithstanding the trend towards globalization, states remain the units upon which the world system is based. The principle of self-determination is at the core of the United Nations and its organizations. However, a common error among social scientists is to conflate 'nation' and 'state', combining them in the single designation 'nation-state'. This is an ideological formulation, reflecting the interests of dominant groups in the era of industrialism and imperialism, imposing a single language and identity on subordinate peoples. In reality, states are frequently multinational and nations are often polyethnic (Richmond 1988c:143). In Britain, the Celtic minorities (themselves heterogeneous in terms of religion and language) have been suppressed under the hegemonic influence of anglophone élites. Basques in Spain and the Languedoc and Bretons in France experienced a similar fate, as did other linguistic and religious minorities in various parts of Europe and the former Soviet Union. Asian and African states recognized by the United Nations almost all exhibit substantial heterogeneity in ethnocultural characteristics. Many also face internal conflicts arising from the nationalist aspirations of these minorities. The North and South American states are no exception, particularly where indigenous peoples resisting the consequences of colonization claim never to have relinquished their sovereignty and/or seek to reassert their claims to independence and self-government.

It is often suggested that states have a monopoly in the legitimate use of violence. The accuracy of this assertion depends on the interpretation given to the term 'legitimate'. Clearly, states do not have a monopoly on violence, or even the use of weapons of mass destruction. Violence begins at the interpersonal level in the relations between parents and children, spouses and peers. Weapons ranging from knives and handguns to highly sophisticated automatic weapons are readily available. Attempts to control their manufacture and distribution have been thwarted by the gun lobby, particularly in the United States. Terrorist organizations are able to obtain high explosives, and civil wars are conducted with the most up-to-date weaponry available in a global arms bazaar, in which states themselves are active promoters of the arms trade. Before the demise of the Soviet empire, as Giddens (1985:293) notes:

> The industrialization of war conjoined science to technological research in such a way to concentrate weapons development in the more economically advanced states. This initially reinforced the position of these states in the world at large, and today places the USA and the Soviet Union at the centre of the weapons development globally, as well as in chronic competition with one another militarily. But while virtually all military research and development takes place in the advanced industrialized countries, the world-wide distribution of armed forces and weaponry does not correspond directly to the conventional global divisions.

Giddens (1985:255, 293) identifies four major subdivisions of the current world system: 1) a global information system reflecting symbolic orders and modes of discourse; 2) a system of relations between states involving political institutions and a growing number of international agencies; 3) the world capitalist economy and related economic institutions, and 4) a world military order enforcing law and imposing sanctions. He rejects the view that globalization necessarily leads to a complete loss of sovereignty. 'Since states exist in an environment of other states, "power politics" have inevitably been a fundamental element of the geo-political make-up of the state system' (1985:292).

Numerous commentators have drawn attention to the dangers of the military-industrial complex endemic in twentieth-century states, capitalist and socialist, imperial and ex-colonial, developed and developing. President Eisenhower warned against its propensity to dominate the American economy; C. Wright Mills observed the integration of political, economic, and military power élites and, more recently, Soviet analyst Georgy Arbotov drew attention to the role of the military in the USSR in opposing *glasnost*, *perestroika*, and independence movements in the Baltic states and elsewhere (Kondrashov 1991; Mills 1956). The international ramifications and dangers of arms manufacture and distribution were noted by the inventor of dynamite (Alfred Nobel) in 1876, by the Peace Congress in Berne in 1899, by Bernard Shaw in *Major Barbara* (1905), by the British Admiralty in 1919, a British Royal Commission on the Private Manufacture of and Trading in Arms (1935–6), and by the UN on many occasions since (Gleditsch and Njolstadt 1990; Krause 1992; Myrdal 1976; Samson 1977). Firms such as Krupp in Germany and Vickers-Armstrong in Britain supplied arms to both sides in the 1914–18 war and since then, a worldwide armaments industry has developed in which Third World countries are heavily involved. The role that Western countries and the Soviet Union played in arming Iraq has been highlighted. An estimated $50 billion worth of weapons and advanced technology (plus the components for biochemical warfare) were sold to Iraq. This is only one segment of the international arms trade (Smolowe 1991).

The worldwide arms bazaar may not have been the beginning of the global economic system as we know it today, but it remains a significant component of it. Since the end of the cold war, there has been some reduction in the stockpiles of nuclear weapons, but vast quantities of these and so-called 'conventional' weapons remain in the hands of countries whose internal stability and relations with their neighbours raise serious doubts about the legitimacy of any ensuing violence. The situation is further complicated by the role the United States and the UN have assumed as self-designated peacekeepers and peacemakers in various parts of the world. It is questionable whether armed intervention will ever achieve the objective of reconciling hostile communities or pacifying warlords as long as the latter have access to the means for prolonging the armed conflicts. Precise estimates of world military spending are hard to obtain because much defence expenditure is covert and secret or subsumed under other budget categories. In the 1990s, annual expenditures in the region of US $975 billion, or more than 5 per cent of world average GNP, were officially confirmed. NATO countries spent an estimated US $516 billion in 1992. The United States spent approximately $300 billion annually and Canada over $13 billion (see Table 7). Sales to other countries, including those in the Third World, were approximately US $41 billion globally, the United States and Russia being the largest suppliers. Canada's arms exports were over $1 billion, of which an estimated $253.4 million went to Third World countries in 1992 and 1993. This was largely due to a huge increase in exports to Saudi Arabia, notwithstanding the latter's poor human rights record (Regehr 1993:9). (See Table 8.) Ironically, maintaining and boosting arms sales abroad have been defended on the ground that such activity creates employment and combats economic recession.

In 'mapping the global condition', Robertson (1990a:27) suggests that the period since 1960 has been a 'phase of uncertainty'. This phase of globalization has brought inherent contradictions arising from the inclusion of Third World countries in the global system, the increase in global institutions and media influence, problems of multiculturalism and polyethnicity, concern with humankind as a 'species community', and interest in world civil society and world citizenship. The resolution of these contradictions and their consequent conflicts will determine whether an integrated global economy, polity, and society can become a reality. Postindustrialism, globalization, the communications revolution, and a resurgence of nationalism are related phenomena. In turn, they are connected to the political, social, and cultural movement that has been labelled 'postmodern'.

Postmodernism

The terms 'industrial' and 'postindustrial' refer to technological and economic developments. 'Traditional', 'modern', 'late modern', and 'postmodern' describe the social and cultural changes that are concomitant with the economic and technological ones, although they are not necessarily predetermined by them in any absolute way. There is scope for considerable selectivity and variation in the ways in which particular individuals and groups respond to the challenges presented by globalization. Postmodernism is a philosophical and cultural movement. It is a reaction against previous forms of expression in art, architecture, literature, music, and theatre. It emphasizes the uniqueness of particular cultures and the relativity of aesthetic and value judgements. Its ideas have also been influential in the social sciences, giving rise to considerable controversy concerning the validity of theories and methods that claim 'scientific' or universal applicability. Some writers continue to defend the positivist view that there can be a 'natural science of society', but even they agree that contemporary sociology does not claim such a status (Turner 1992:156–76).

In reviewing the literature on postmodernism, Margaret Rose (1991) distinguishes deconstructionist theories from double-coded and alternative theories. The former focus on textual analysis and emphasize the break with modernism. They highlight latent meanings and reject the metanarratives supposedly inherent in earlier writings, notably those that claim universality for the ideas originating in Europe since the eighteenth century. Double-coded theories reflect the cultural diversity of postmodern societies and, particularly in art and architecture, reject functionalism, rationalism, and holism in favour of pluralism, activism, participation, and hybridism (Rose 1991:40–149). A leading exponent of postmodernism suggests that 'in the last ten years post-modernism has become more than a social condition and cultural movement. It has become a world view. But its exact nature is strongly contested . . . ' (Jencks 1992:10).

Giddens (1990:149–73) identifies some of the differences between post-modernity and what he prefers to call 'late modernity' or, in its projected futuristic form, 'radicalized modernity'. He rejects the view that contemporary trends must necessarily lead to fragmentation, dislocation, relativity, and powerlessness. Instead, he emphasizes the reflexive nature of human behaviour, the trend towards global integration, and the potential for empowerment—particularly for women and minorities who, in pre-modern and modern societies, were largely excluded from the decision-making process. He emphasizes the role of radical social movements and 'utopian realism' in achieving positive change in spheres such as political representation, the status of women and minorities, labour conditions, peace, and the protection of the environment.

One characteristic of the postmodern perspective is the recognition of the role of irony in the vocabulary of philosophy and sociology. This involves the conjunction of opposites, the recognition of unintended consequences, and a questioning of once taken-for-granted assumptions. Specifically, it casts doubt upon the view that modernity is the necessary and inevitable outcome of forces that must carry other countries and continents in the same direction as Europe and America. The legitimating discourses of rationality, secularization, and the values of the 'Enlightenment' are seen as having devastating consequences that other societies (as well as our own) may wish to avoid by rejecting their underlying premises. For example, J.R. Saul (1992) decries the 'dictatorship of reason in the west' and attributes such phenomena as the Jewish Holocaust in Nazi Germany, the development of the atomic bomb and the proliferation of the arms race, the degradation of the environment, and other disasters to the application of science and technology in the service of the state. He regards the most common characteristic of power élites as 'cynicism, rhetoric, and the worship of both ambition and power' (1992:580). However, care must be taken not to confuse postmodernism with antimodernism. The former looks forward, whereas the latter is a romantic nostalgia for an often mythical past and is a reaction against trends characteristic of postindustrial and late modern societies (Turner 1990).

Postmodernism rejects the view that postindustrialism and globalization must lead to cultural homogenization through the spread of capitalism and mass markets. Although the instrumental forms of advanced technology may become universal, their expressive and symbolic meanings are used selectively, transformed, and adapted to the needs and interests of local communities. 'Indigenous cultural values shape the transformations that external forces engender and the ironies and resistances they generate' (Coombe 1991:198). If this is true of non-Western societies, it may also apply to the cultural minorities within Western societies whose voices are being heard and responded to as never before. Frederic Jameson (1991:17) makes this point when he states that 'if the ideas of a ruling class were once the dominant (or hegemonic) ideology of bourgeois society, the advanced capitalist countries today are now a field of stylistic and discursive heterogeneity without a norm.' The micropolitics of gender, ethnicity, race and religion—that is, the politics of difference—ensure that new social and linguistic codes are more freely expressed. In turn, this raises the question whether 'anything goes'.

Taken to extremes, postmodernism leans towards nihilism and the rejection of all claims to knowledge as 'truth'. Objective truths are replaced by hermeneutic truths, which are entirely subjective and relative to the point of view of the interpreter. This argument fails to distinguish between instrumental and expressive knowledge. As Gellner suggests, scientific knowledge 'has proved so overwhelmingly powerful, economically, militarily, administratively, that all societies have to make their peace with it and adopt it' (Gellner 1992:61). However, this still leaves fundamental questions concerning human rights and political organization in dispute. Issues such as private property ownership, territorial claims, torture and the death penalty, the status of women, the rights of minorities, the preservation of lifestyles, the survival of languages, the practice of religion, and freedom of expression are caught in the paradox of universalism versus particularism. Whose values are to prevail? What if the values in question are themselves contradictory? How does one respond to the claims of fundamentalists (of whatever religious or political persuasion) who insist upon imposing their particular ideas and practices on others, by force if necessary, or of eliminating, through expulsion or genocide, those who are different? Such ideological fanaticism is one of the contributory factors in the spread of ethnic conflict today.

Ethnic conflict

Ethnolinguistic and ethnoreligious heterogeneity by themselves are not a sufficient cause of conflict. In fact, I have argued that 'the complex communication networks of postindustrial societies will create the possibility of a new type of society, free of both religious and ethnic intolerance, by permitting great diversity within the structure of a supra-national state' (Richmond 1988c:181–2). However, I went on to say that such a transition would not come about without conflict, and that there would be reactionary movements reasserting national sovereignty and seeking to impose ethnic and cultural uniformity. Fishman (1989:18) makes the same point when he states that 'a characteristic of postmodern ethnicity is the stance of simultaneously transcending ethnicity as a complete, self-contained system, but of retaining it as a selectively preferred, evolving, participatory system.' Fishman then identifies some of the factors that hinder the emergence of such benign forms of ethnic identification. They include the communication barriers induced by language and the persistence of nationalism and its manipulation by power élites. Also important are the contributions that economic deprivation, political authoritarianism, and the rapid changes induced by modernization make towards the generation of civil strife. He concludes that 'linguistic homogeneity/heterogeneity cannot be considered an important independent predictor of civil strife when an extensive panoply of deprivational, modernizational and non-ideological authoritarianism predictors are also considered' (Fishman 1989:623). In other words, a multivariate model of ethnic conflict is required in which the role of underlying conditions, intervening variables, precipitating events, and interacting feedback effects of policy responses by local and international agencies are taken into account (Richmond 1988c:3–10).

Ethnic conflict takes several different forms and sometimes combines different elements. Firstly, there are the state-supported systems of domination and exploitation of minorities that may lead eventually to the extermination of a people or their relegation to the geographic and social margins of the society. This was the typical fate of indigenous populations in the colonial era and continues in varying degrees today. Neocolonialism is often more economic than political in form, but does not preclude the state's connivance in the activities of national and transnational corporations exploiting natural and human resources. Secondly, there are the conflicts that result from the emancipatory efforts of such minorities endeavouring to reclaim territory and reassert human rights, with or without the support of outside agencies such as the UN, churches, and other minorities joining in the common cause. Thirdly, there are interstate conflicts in which questions of language, religion, and irredentist aspirations are involved. Fourthly, intrastate conflict (sometimes leading to civil war) may occur when interethnic antagonisms, competition for scarce resources, political power struggles, and ideological disputes fail to be resolved by other means, such as negotiation, conciliation, and the peace-keeping efforts of outside bodies. Fifthly, various manifestations of ethnic nationalism give rise to overt conflict when other constraining factors are removed. The lifting of imperialist rule or the end of a totalitarian system of government may precipitate latent conflicts that have been held in check by the superior military power and ruthlessly suppressive measures used by the previously governing parties. Sectarian violence, communal conflict, civil wars, and independence movements may assert themselves under these conditions. Finally, there are the conflicts that arise as a consequence of past and present migrations, particularly the movements from less developed to more economically developed countries. Beginning with the movements of slaves and indentured labourers, and continuing to the present day with migrant workers and asylum applicants, such migrations have left substantial ethnocultural minorities in Europe, North America, and elsewhere. Originally sought after for their contribution to the labour force or welcomed as political refugees, such minorities may face severe opposition and demands for their repatriation during times of economic recession.

In 1992–3, there were more than sixty-five ethnic conflicts raging, with varying degrees of severity in different parts of the world (see Chapter Eleven). Two-thirds of these were ongoing armed conflicts, responsible for a thousand or more combat-related deaths. Others were of a lesser degree of severity, but were potentially as dangerous. They included interstate wars, civil wars, and terrorist activities. Many involved ethnic or national identity issues and more than a third had secessionist goals (Regehr 1992). In examining the role of ethnicity in contemporary international politics, Daniel Moynihan (1993:24) chose to describe it as promoting pandaemonium. He cited the IRA bombings in Britain and the riots in Los Angeles, as well as the ethnic conflicts in Africa, Asia, and Europe as evidence that we have so far failed 'to make the world safe for and from ethnicity' (1993:173). He chided social scientists for having paid insufficient attention to its significance. It is a mistake to equate the revival of ethnicity in the late twentieth century with 'tribalism'. The latter term refers to relationships within a territorially bounded community or *Gemeinschaft*. Contemporary manifestations of ethnicity transcend geographic limits. They involve global networks and connections that facilitate the mobilization of resources and the exercise of power beyond the limits of states and societies as previously understood by anthropologists and sociologists.

Anthony Smith (1991, 1992) examined some of the factors associated with the survival of ethnic groups and the resurgence of ethnic nationalism in the context of global movements of ethnic mobilization. He noted the importance of political élites, the emergence of a literary high culture, and the creation of invented traditions, which turn a passive *ethnie* into an active political community determined to relive past glories. Old myths of ethnic election as a 'chosen people' are revived, and fuel neonationalist movements. He agreed that this renewal fits my previously argued thesis that the communication networks of postindustrial societies facilitate the proliferation of linguistic and ethnic nationalisms, and provoke the revival of majority nationalism as well. Examples include the revival of ethnic nationalism among Serbs, Czechs, Germans, Poles, and Russians. Pan-nationalist movements and attempts at regional integration may also revive specific ethnic nationalisms among majorities and minorities alike. The effect of immigration, guest workers, and waves of refugees on hitherto relatively homogeneous societies can induce reactionary forms of nationalism that threaten democratic values. It may also induce a revival of interethnic tension and fascist movements in countries of immigration (Richmond 1988c:167–82; Smith 1991:143–77). This leads to the question of multiculturalism and its implications for postmodern societies.

Multiculturalism

It is necessary to distinguish the descriptive and the prescriptive aspects of multiculturalism. Contemporary societies, whether in a premodern, modern, or late modern stage of development (and most countries have sectors in all three stages simultaneously), are generally pluralistic in terms of their ethnic composition. Some have indigenous minorities that have retained their distinctive languages and cultures despite the pressures towards assimilation that accompanied industrialization and colonization. Others have experienced substantial migrations (inward and outward), leading to a spread of languages, religions, and cultures throughout the world. In demographic and statistical terms, the degree of heterogeneity of a population may vary, but nowhere can the reality of ethnic pluralism be denied altogether. The degree to which majority groups accept and encourage this diversity also varies. Multiculturalism as a policy has been adopted in a number of countries, although the intent and purposes of these policies vary, and their degree of success in containing the potential for conflict is a matter of debate.

There are certain key areas in which multicultural policies have been applied. They include the treatment of indigenous minorities, the integration of immigrants, the development of educational curricula and (in some cases) separate school systems, support for linguistic and cultural diversity in the arts, employment equity or affirmative action in the labour force, and representation in political institutions. Such policies range from legislative measures and direct government funding to voluntary grass roots movements that have the tacit approval of mainstream political parties and economic élites. Included are measures designed to combat racism and diminish ethnoreligious discrimination and more actively promote minority interests and power. In some cases, multicultural programs have been linked with those endeavouring to advance the status of women. In others, there have been ideological disputes and a conflict of interest between the two. Black women (sometimes referring to themselves as 'women of colour') do not necessarily share the same feminist agenda as 'White', liberal, middle-class women (Stasiulis 1990).

Racism and antiracism

Although it is generally recognized that 'race' is a social construct, there remain deeply felt prejudices and systemic discrimination based on categories defined in terms of physical appearance. Often these are rationalized and justified in terms of perceived cultural differences that are linked to ethnicity and nationality. Majority 'White' interests and the survival of traditional national characteristics in Britain, France, and Germany (as well as traditional immigration countries such as Australia, Canada, and the United States) are thought to be threatened by the claims of immigrants and their children. Neoconservative philosophers and politicians rally to defend immigration controls, the expulsion of foreigners, and the preservation of traditional Christian and family values, simultaneously denying that they are racist. In education, multiculturalism tends to be identified with such phenomena as Black studies and other liberal attempts to broaden the curriculum. At the same time, antiracism assumes a more radical stance, opposing the patronizing attitude of teachers and the discrimination embedded in institutions, ranging from the police and the judicial system to municipal and national politics. Antiracist discourse becomes more vehement and intolerant itself, sometimes resulting in violent clashes with neo-Nazi and other right-wing groups. Furthermore, racism and ethnocentrism are not confined to 'White' groups. 'Visible minorities' can be intolerant of other minorities, stereotyping them, while denying that 'Blacks' can be racist. Some activists are hostile towards anyone considered insufficiently militant. Ali Rattansi (1992:37) asked how various forms of racism, ethnocentrism, and nationalism interact with discourses and practises in official policy programs and popular culture around 'Asian women' or 'Black youth'. He criticized what he calls 'cultural essentialism' and the tendency to subsume the experience of all minorities under a single rubric such as 'the Black struggle'. He noted the emergence of new syncretic cultures, particularly among second-generation youth in Britain, and argued that multiculturalists must abandon their 'additive models' of cultural diversity and confront issues of cultural difference (1992:39). One of the consequences of multicultural policies, which deliberately highlight and celebrate cultural differences, is a renewed trend towards separation. This manifests itself in education, the arts, and recreation. Ethnocultural and religious minorities sometimes insist that they must have their own schools and that there should be government funding to assist them. A proprietary attitude may enter into art, music, and literary expression, where there is resentment of the expropriation of such modes of expression by persons of different ethnic or 'racial' origin.

This raises a question of the politics of recognition in a multicultural society. Charles Taylor (1992) proposes that the key criterion for recognizing minority claims should be their 'authenticity'. The latter is understood as being 'true to oneself', but, at the same time, recognizing that the self is not a monologic outcome of introspection but a dialogic result of interaction with others. From a sociological perspective, Giddens (1987:47) also emphasizes the importance of dialogue in the formulation of social research, applied sociology, and social policy. He recognizes the importance of close communication between researchers, policy makers, and those whose behaviour is the subject of study and action.

There remain some inherent contradictions and dilemmas in the pursuit of the multicultural ideal and the politics of difference. Ethnic identity is not the only basis on which individuals may claim recognition. Gender, age, nationality, citizenship, property ownership, and tax-paying status may impose conflicting claims on the body politic and confuse issues concerning human rights. In responding to Taylor's argument concerning the politics of recognition, Steven Rockefeller (1992:88) notes that 'our universal identity as human beings is our primary identity and is more fundamental than any particular identity, whether it be a matter of citizenship, gender, race, or ethnic origin.' Policies that promote particular identities and the interests associated with them may lead to intolerance, separatism, and rivalry. This is particularly true when the resources available are in short supply, whether they are government grants, jobs during a recession, or places in institutions of higher education.

There is an inevitable tension between the pursuit of multicultural policies and the promotion of a sense of a national unity and commitment, particularly in those countries that have experienced substantial immigration. Australia is a good example of a country that has tried to balance a recognition of its growing ethnic diversity and the need for special services for immigrants without abandoning the concept of a 'dinkum Aussie' or loyal Australian. The government's own *Agenda for Multicultural Australia* (Commonwealth of Australia, Office of Multicultural Affairs 1989) stated that everyone must accept the basic structures and principles of Australian society, including the principles of the Constitution and English as the national language. The emphasis was on multiculturalism for all Australians, irrespective of birthplace or ethnic origin. 'For the essence of this vision is priority of the wholeness and welfare of the entire society engaged in developing a new nationhood, a new Australian identity' (Zubrzycki 1991:136). It is the absence of such a sense of national identity (or the possible threat to it) that worries many North American critics of multicultural ideologies. Schlesinger (1992) examined the growing influence of multiculturalism in the United States, particularly as reflected in what he called the 'battle of the schools' over curriculum and the teaching of history. He deplored the 'disuniting of America' and affirmed that the ideas that defined American nationality were 'individual freedom, political democracy and human rights'. 'The question America confronts as a pluralistic society is how to vindicate cherished cultures and traditions without breaking the bonds of cohesion' (Schlesinger 1992:138). Similar concerns have been expressed in Canada, where the secessionist pressures of francophone Quebecois and some Aboriginal communities combine with the multicultural claims of immigrant minorities and their descendants to generate what Reginald Bibby (1990) called 'mosaic madness'. He is critical of excessive individualism and the pursuit of sectional interests at the expense of society as a whole.

The idea of society as a whole is precisely what postmodernist critics are sceptical of. Who determines what constitutes the whole society and whose voices will be heard in a system that is structured in dominance and that is hierarchical, patriarchal, competitive, and motivated by profit? Drawing on Derrida, Foucault, and poststructuralist writers, Radhakrishnan (1990) relates questions of ethnic identity to questions of difference and the politics of heterogeneity. He uses the example of Jesse Jackson's candidacy for the leadership of the Democratic party in the United States, the so-called 'rainbow coalition' that tried to bring together a wide spectrum of minority groups. Jackson was seen as representing special interests whereas, Radhakrishnan claimed, 'Corporate, military, business, male, "White," "non-ethnic interests" were regarded as "natural," "general," "representative," ideologically neutral and value-free' (1990:66).

In Canada there are similar tensions and conflicts between particular minorities competing for power, status, and recognition, as well as between these minorities and the dominant or founding anglophone and francophone majorities. The failure of several decades of effort to achieve constitutional reform in Canada (as in Australia) is evidence of the difficulty of reconciling competing interests. It is also evidence of globalization as both countries restrict immigration, adopt concepts such as 'multiculturalism', endeavour to accommodate Aboriginal concerns, and come to terms with the realities of a global economy (Russell 1993:41–61). There are inherent contradictions between the emphasis on individual rights, including those relating to property, which stem from the Western liberal philosophy and the recognition of collective rights. Quebec Premier Robert Bourassa defended his use of the 'Notwithstanding' clause in the Canadian Charter of Rights on the grounds that he had a special responsibility to defend French language and culture in North America. Similar arguments have been used by Aboriginal representatives, who consider that the cultural traditions of some Aboriginal communities place more emphasis upon the communal sharing of land than upon individualistic ideas about property rights (Hiebert 1993; Turpel 1990).

The combined effects of postindustrialism, postmodernism, and globalization have generated a crisis of integration in contemporary societies (McLellan and Richmond 1994). There are systemic contradictions between homogeneity and universalism, on the one hand, and heterogeneity and particularism, on the other. In extreme circumstances, other countries could follow the example of Yugoslavia and disintegrate into warring factions, acting out historic animosities and seeking revenge for past and present atrocities. All forms of collectivism (ethnicism, nationalism, statism, regionalism, and globalism) are in dialectical contradiction to the thesis of individualism. It remains to be seen whether a new synthesis will take the form of humanism. Ernest Gellner rejects both postmodern and fundamentalist positions when he makes a case for 'enlightened rationalism' (Gellner 1992). He rightly points out that societies are systems of real constraints and not just systems of 'meanings', as hermeneutics would suggest. Unfortunately, however enlightened it may be, rationalism does not carry with it the emotional appeal—the gut reaction—that ethnic nationalism provides.

As mentioned earlier, Anthony Giddens (1990:151–73) prefers the idea of 'utopian realism' as expressed in emancipatory social movements, such as those concerned with economic equality, participatory democracy, human rights, demilitarization, and the protection of the environment. In the face of high-consequence risks, we (i.e., humanity as a whole) must 'harness the juggernaut' in order to minimize the dangers of a 'runaway world'. Among those dangers are the growth of racism, the revival of Nazi movements in Europe and elsewhere, the perceived threat of mass migration and refugee flows, and the consequent imposition of forms of global apartheid.

Notes

[1] Industrial classifications are not the same as occupations that may range from low to high status and income in any industry. Primary industries include agriculture, horticulture, animal farming, forestry, fishing, mining, and all forms of natural resource exploitation.

Secondary industries include all craft, manufacturing, and construction activities. Tertiary industries include wholesale and retail distribution, domestic and professional services, including health, banking, and insurance.

Quaternary industries are those that have grown fastest as a result of the postindustrial revolution. They are mostly information-based and include education, telecommunications, mass media, and computer-based technologies.

[2] Special examples of international networks include the International Postal Union, Interpol, World Health Organization, International Civil Aviation Authority, World Council of Churches, YMCA/YWCA, and numerous other governmental and non-governmental agencies that have proliferated in the late twentieth century as communication networks were extended and facilitated by new information technologies.

chapter three

Proactive and reactive migration[1]

Sociological theories of international migration should be capable of explaining the scale, direction, and composition of population movements that cross state boundaries; the factors that determine the decision to move and the choice of destination; the characteristic modes of social integration in the receiving country; and the eventual outcome, including remigration and return movements. Studies of international migration have not attempted such an ambitious agenda. Research has generally focused on specific aspects, such as the demographic characteristics of immigrants, migration decision making, economic and social adaptation in receiving countries, the policies of sending and receiving countries, or global trends in population movement. Empirical studies have been conducted on an *ad hoc* basis, largely uninformed by developments in general sociological theory.

Typologies

Early writers utilized simple typologies to classify migratory movements. Fairchild (1913) distinguished invasion, conquest, and colonization from immigration as such. He classified societies as 'peaceful or warlike' and 'low or high culture'. He endeavoured to show that the types of migration and their consequences were influenced by this distinction. Later writers emphasized the difference between voluntary and involuntary movements. Included in the former were seasonal, nomadic, and other temporary moves as well as more permanent migrations that were largely economic in nature. Involuntary movements included those of slaves and others who were impelled by war and other political pressures (Price 1969).

Petersen (1958) developed a more elaborate typology using several dimensions. The first involved the relation of 'man' to nature, the state, norms, and other men. The second concerned the migratory force linked to each of the former, i.e., ecological push (nature), migration policy (state), aspirations (norms), and what he called 'social momentum'. These elements generated different classes of migration that he labelled (i) primitive, (ii) forced/impelled, (iii) free, and (iv) mass. Petersen introduced further classifications of 'conservative' and 'innovating' types based on the consequences of the movement. For example, group settlements were essentially conservative, enabling the migrants to preserve a traditional lifestyle in varying degrees. In contrast, individuals who migrated on their own led to 'pioneer' situations and large-scale voluntary movements led to urbanization and social change.

Typologies of this kind fail to go beyond the descriptive level and have little explanatory or predictive value. Advances in the sociological analysis of developmental processes throw doubt upon the validity of distinguishing evolutionary stages or postulating essential correlations between technology, economic growth, political systems, social institutions, and demographic behaviour. To the extent that there are causal relations between these variables, they are more complex than such simple typologies would suggest. Furthermore, as will be shown below, the distinction between movements of population that are voluntary and involuntary, or forced and free, is of doubtful validity. There is a convergence of these two forms, and differences depend on relationships to the state (Hein 1993).

Theories of migration

Theories of international migration can be broadly classified as macro and micro in their level of analysis. In the former category are those that focus on migration streams, identifying those conditions under which large-scale movements occur and describing the demographic, economic, and social characteristics of the migrants in aggregate terms. The macro level also includes most theories concerning the immigrant adaptation process, economic and social integration, assimilation, etc., when regarded from a structural or cultural perspective. The micro level includes studies of sociopsychological factors that differentiate migrants from non-migrants, together with theories concerning motivation, decision making, satisfaction, and identification. It may also include some aspects of immigrant adaptation when regarded from a strictly individualistic perspective as distinct from the broader societal consequences.

It should be noted that almost all the theories address voluntary migration. In most cases economic factors are assumed to be predominant in determining the outflow and interpreting the experience after migration. Often the writers explicitly state that they are not concerned with refugees or politically motivated migrants. Whereas it is taken for granted that some regularity can be detected in the flows of economic migrants, it is generally assumed that refugee movements are spontaneous and unpredictable, although there is growing evidence that this is not the case. When questions of absorption in receiving countries are considered, the experiences of refugees are rarely distinguished from those of economic migrants.

Macro theories

Ravenstein (1885) put forward so-called 'laws of migration' based on empirical observation of internal migration in the nineteenth century. Some of his generalizations have stood the test of time, such as the fact that most migrations are over short distances, that they generate counter-streams, and that they are related to technological development. Others have been contradicted, including the suggestion that urban populations are less migratory than rural, that females predominate among short-distance movers, or that migration proceeds by stages from rural areas to small towns, and then to larger cities and metropolitan areas.

Stouffer (1940, 1960) also considered internal migration, related mobility, and distance while introducing the concept of 'intervening opportunities'. Lee (1966), building on Ravenstein's observations, offered a model of migration that linked positive and negative factors at the areas of origin and destination with the decision to migrate, taking into account intervening obstacles and personal factors. He related the volume of migration to the diversity of the territory and the composition of its population, to fluctuations in the economy, and to difficulties in surmounting any intervening obstacles.

Mabogunje (1970) developed a systems model, recognizing an interdependence between sending and receiving areas. He identified four components in migration movements: economic, social, technological, and environmental. He described migration as a 'circular, interdependent, progressively complex and self-modifying system.' A systems approach was also used by Tos and Klinar (1976) in examining the experience of Yugoslavian temporary workers, including the question of return migration. A theory of societal systems was applied by Hoffman-Nowotny (1981) to generate a general theory of migration based on the relation between power and prestige in a society. It emphasized the importance of structural tensions derived from inequalities and status inconsistencies in the sending country, which generated anomic tendencies. The tensions may be resolved by emigration to a country where status aspirations can be attained. He uses the term 'under-casting' to describe a process where structural tensions in the sending country are relieved by emigration but may be transferred instead to the receiving country, which must find ways of integrating the newcomers.

Although the model was developed with economic migration largely in mind, Ferris (1985:17) suggests that it may also be applicable to the movement of refugees.

The question of immigrant adaptation has generated a variety of theoretical perspectives at the macro level. Richmond and Zubrzycki (1984) identified six different models of migration and occupational status, each derived from alternative theoretical premises. The classical approach focused on assimilation and was functionalist in orientation. It contrasted with a Marxian or conflict model that emphasized class differences between immigrants and indigenous populations. Colonial situations gave rise to a form of élite migration, while the more common experience in the twentieth century has been cross-sectional in terms of occupational status, and pluralistic from a cultural point of view. Recent theories have focused upon stratification and segmentation of labour markets, which lead to ethnic enclaves. Finally, the importance of structural changes generated by technological innovation and postindustrial developments have also influenced the flow of migrants and their modes of integration in advanced societies. Comparative studies of Canada and Australia suggested that not one of these models by itself was sufficient to account for the experience of post-Second World War immigrants in these countries, although each throws some light on particular aspects of adaptation (Burnley and Kalbach 1985; Rao et al. 1984; Richmond and Zubrzycki 1984) Studies of the labour market and other experiences of Cuban and Haitian refugees in the United States also demonstrated the heterogeneity of the experience. They pointed to the need for alternative theoretical models to account for different modes of incorporation, which were not always disadvantageous to the newcomers, despite an initially unfavourable economic and social climate (Pedraza-Bailey 1985; Portes and Mozo 1986; Portes and Stepick 1985).

Global systems

It is generally recognized that in the study of international migration, the reality of a global economy, polity, and social system must be recognized, however much conflict and contradiction there may be in the interface between quasi-sovereign states (Richmond 1988c:1–27). Wallerstein (1974) traced the origins of the present world system to the mercantilist period in the seventeenth century. Contemporary economists and sociologists have shown that there is a global labour market in the modern world economy (Amin 1974; Petras 1981; Portes 1983). They distinguish core, semi-peripheral, and peripheral areas and relate the flow of labour to capital investment and resource development. Drawing on Marxist theory, they identify a reserve army of labour in developing countries that may be exploited by wealthier imperialist powers. Richmond and Verma (1978) suggested a 'global system of international migration' with four subsystems, each of which may also be internally differentiated according to level of development. The most advanced postindustrial societies have high rates of exchange migration, particularly of highly qualified people, but they note that tremendous pressures to emigrate have built up in less developed areas of the world. They predicted that 'this process will only be contained by increasingly restrictive immigration policies in the more advanced countries who will be compelled to adopt punitive measures to combat illegal immigration' (Richmond and Verma 1978:32).

Political economy

A central issue in the study of refugee movements is the relation between economic and political determinants of population movement. The theories considered so far have been generally applicable to movements of people from poorer to richer areas, from regions of economic underdevelopment to those experiencing growth, or to the exchanges of skilled and highly qualified migrants between advanced societies to which the term 'transilience' has been applied (Richmond 1969). Although the de jure definition of refugee status (a 'Convention refugee'), used by the United Nations[2] and adopted by various countries in determining eligibility for admission, emphasizes 'a well founded fear of persecution', it is no longer possible to treat 'refugee' movements as completely independent of the state of the global economy.[3] Complex questions of sovereignty, perceived interests, international relations, and ideological considerations are also involved (Weiner 1985).

The situations that most commonly give rise to large refugee movements and requests for asylum include external and civil wars, political unrest and revolution, terrorism, the expulsion of ethnic minorities, ethnoreligious and communal conflict, displacement of populations through technological developments such as mechanization of agriculture and hydroelectric schemes, land reforms and resettlement programs, famines and other 'natural' disasters, as well as a wide variety of human rights violations and oppressive state regimes.[4] In all these cases economic, social, and political factors are interdependent. It is not necessary to invoke Marxist assumptions concerning the ultimate determining influence of modes of production on state formations or to attribute all forms of political oppression to the interests of 'bourgeois capitalism' to recognize that crises in the Middle East, Central America, and Asia are not unrelated to the ideological and military confrontation of the superpowers, the competing interests of multinational companies, and the problems of development facing Third World countries (Sivard 1985; World Bank 1984).

Zolberg et al. (1986) have pointed out that refugee movements 'do not constitute a collection of random events' but form distinct patterns that are related to political transformations, such as the breakup of former colonial empires. The formation of new states and nation building are rendered more difficult by economic underdevelopment. Even the economic aid and refugee policies of the wealthier and more powerful countries are dictated by their narrowly defined interests (Harrell-Bond 1986). Dowty (1987:183) notes that 'So-called economic migrants are often responding as much to political repression as to material deprivation.' He gives examples of refugees from Ethiopia where political pressures and war combine with famine to cause massive flight, Haiti where political repression and economic underdevelopment go together, and El Salvador where would-be refugees have been returned because they are regarded as 'victims of generalized violence' rather than individual persecution. Dowty states that 'In such circumstances, the distinction between "economic" and "political" refugees becomes meaningless' (1987:236). From a sociological point of view, this is true. However, it does not prevent governments from making a *de jure* distinction between Convention refugees and others, refusing asylum to those who do not meet the strict criteria of the UN Protocol.

Micro theories

Social psychologists have addressed questions of motivation and the decision to move. As a last resort, migration is an individual choice, although such decisions may be made in consultation with family members or others in a close-knit community or religious group. Most micro-level studies of migration decision making have been conducted among those whose main motivation has been economic or family related. An assumption of rational choice, following a considered evaluation of options available, is implicit in most theories of motivation. A distinction is generally made between push and pull factors, which must be taken into account.[5] Human needs and aspirations are generally represented in terms of economic benefits, social mobility, or family reunion. Costs and benefits of migration are then calculated according to the individual's own hierarchy of values and presumed net advantage. So-called place-utility theories endeavour to explain why individuals decide to move or choose particular locations in terms of perceived advantages and anticipated satisfaction. Empiricial studies using this concept have lent only partial support to it and suggest that a more sophisticated formulation of human aspirations and needs is required (Simmons 1985–6). Place-utility is one version of a more generalized value-expectancy model that relates goals to expectations in terms of subjective probabilities of achievement. It is a cognitive model that assumes the availability of adequate information on which to base decisions. More complex psychological explanations take into account the influence of 'significant others' in the decision-making process, the role of cognitive dissonance, and the tendency to adhere to a decision once made, despite negative feedback (de Jong and Gardner 1981). Although theoretically elegant, such explanations are only weakly supported by empirical evidence and tend to overlook the multiple cognitive and conative influences that prevail in a media-saturated information environment.

Although refugee movements are usually represented as 'forced', they are only an extreme case of the constraints that are placed upon the choices available to an individual in particular circumstances. The choices facing a landless peasant displaced by a multinational company producing for export may be unemployment, begging, stealing, sickness, starvation, and death for him and his family. Choices facing an ethnic or political minority may be to join a dissident army, face political imprisonment, torture, or death. In either case, the limited options available involve excruciating choices. Flight is one of these options. Kunz (1973, 1981) put forward an explanation of refugee behaviour in terms of what he called 'kinetic models'. He differentiated 'anticipatory' from 'acute' movements and further distinguished 'majority identified', 'alienated' refugees, and 'reactive-fate groups' from those with a clearer purpose. The common denominator is a sense of loss of control over one's own fate. Kunz noted, 'The borderline between political refugees and those dissatisfied economically can indeed be blurred when displacement occurs in reaction to events. Yet, the magnitude of the decision should be kept in mind as well as the pressures of the social forces which finally result in the seeking of exile'(1981:50–1).

Keller (1975) described the trauma of becoming a refugee, using examples from the experience of the 15 million people displaced by the partition of India and Pakistan in 1947 when a million people died. The author suggested stages in the refugee generating process, starting with a rejection of the idea that disaster is imminent and a determination to carry on as normal a life as possible, followed by the trauma of flight, which in turn leads to long-term effects, including feelings of guilt, invulnerability, and aggressiveness. A study of Vietnamese-Chinese refugees in Canada showed that the resettlement process often involved downward occupational mobility, fatalistic attitudes, a preoccupation with family reunification, and a profound desire to escape dependency (Lam 1983).

Various studies have examined the psychological aspects of immigrant adaptation, emphasizing the more serious trauma faced by refugees and the mental health problems they experienced (Cohon 1981). A social displacement syndrome can be identified. An incubation period may be followed by paranoid symptoms, hypochondria, anxiety, and depression (Tyhurst 1977). However unrealistic, some may cling to the idea of returning home or working politically for the 'liberation' of the home country (Anwar 1979; Luciuk 1986; Stein 1981; Zwingmann and Pfister-Ammende 1973).

Structuration and voluntaristic action

The relation between structural constraints and individual choice is a central problem in sociological theory. It involves fundamental questions of free will and agency versus theories that imply behavioural determination by forces over which we have little or no control. The nature of the problem was expressed in oversimplified form by Marx when he wrote, 'Men make history, but not in circumstances of their own choosing.' Almost all social theorists have recognized the paradox that this reflects. Is the recognition of structural constraint compatible with a voluntaristic theory of action?

Talcott Parsons addressed this issue throughout his work, commencing with his synthesis of the writings of classical theorists in *The Structure of Social Action* ([1937] 1961). Sciulli (1986) noted that the term 'voluntaristic action', as used by Parsons and others, has several different meanings. Firstly, it can refer to the actor's free will or capacity to make choices despite constraints. Secondly, it can mean a capacity for self-initiated action, whether or not this capacity is realized. Thirdly, it can refer to the concept of individual autonomy despite the limitations of ideal or material conditions. Fourthly, it may represent individual autonomy as an unstable element in the social order. Fifthly, voluntaristic action may be understood as the residual normative elements not subsumed under behavioural, conditional, or material categories. Sciulli himself prefers a reformulated distinction that Parsons implicitly developed when he distinguished 'purposeful rational action toward quantifiable ends' from 'non-rational action, directed toward transcendental ends', as in the case of religious rituals. This left a third type of social action that involved 'normative practices'. Although within the sphere of non-rational action, the latter cannot be regarded as ultimate or transcendental. 'Voluntaristic action is comprised, therefore, of qualitative worldly ends as well as the shared symbols and norms which allow actors to simply maintain a shared recognition of these ends'(Sciulli 1986:748). It is the recognition of these shared values that provides a bulwark against an arbitrary exercise of power. Without voluntaristic action and the institution-alized values that support it, direct coercion or the manipulation of belief by the dominant minority is likely to occur.

In somewhat different terms the same point is made by Giddens (1984:174) when he distinguishes various forms of constraint, which may be material, associated with sanctions, or are structural in form. The latter are derived from the given nature of structural properties that the individual is unable to change and that limit the range of options. Giddens's concept of structuration, however, replaces a static view of social structures as completely external to the individual with one that emphasizes the process by which social structures are created and changed through the exercise of freedom of action. It is necessary to explore this idea further if we are to develop a satisfactory sociological theory of motivation that will account for the behaviour of migrants and refugees.

Turner (1987) reviewed various sociological theories of motivation, including that of Giddens, which he sees as having a psychoanalytic basis in that it identifies both conscious and unconscious determinants of social action. Key elements are unconscious needs for security and trust in relations with others. Practical consciousness and reflective monitoring lead to routinization and social integration. Unconscious needs increase in salience when these established institutions break down (Giddens 1984:4–7,

281–4; Turner 1987:20–1). Turner incorporates several other social psychological traditions into his synthetic model, including those of social exchange, interactionist theories, and ethnomethodology. He postulates a hierarchy of needs. These go beyond the primordial requirements of biological survival. They are socially determined and include needs for group inclusion, trust, security, symbolic and material gratification, self-conception, and 'facticity', i.e, the shared understanding of intersubjective and external worlds, which in turn is linked to power and the ability to achieve goals through negotiation and exchange with others. Turner's model involves complex feedback loops and assumes that failure to achieve these goals leads to diffuse anxiety and strategies to avoid such feelings. One of these strategies may be exit from a situation that persistently fails to satisfy needs (Turner 1987:24).

The implications of this sociological theory of motivation for studies of migration and refugee movements are complex. A few key points will be highlighted. Firstly, migratory decisions, even those made under conditions of extreme stress, do not differ from other kinds of decision-governing social behaviour. The same sociological model of motivation is applicable. Secondly, the distinction between free and forced or voluntary and involuntary is a misleading one. All human behaviour is constrained. Choices are not unlimited but are determined by the structuration process. However, degrees of freedom may vary. Individual and group autonomy and potency are situationally determined. It would be more appropriate to recognize a continuum at one end of which individuals and collectivities are proactive and at the other reactive. Under certain conditions, the decision to move may be made after due consideration of all relevant information, rationally calculated to maximize net advantage, including both material and symbolic rewards. At the other extreme, the decision to move may be made in a state of panic during a crisis that leaves few alternatives but escape from intolerable threats. Between these two extremes, many of the decisions made by both economic and political migrants are a response to diffuse anxiety generated by a failure of the social system to provide for the fundamental biological, economic, and social needs of the individual. Thirdly, a reasonable hypothesis would be that when societal institutions disintegrate or are weakened to the point that they are unable to provide a substantial section of the population with an adequate sense of group inclusion, trust, and ontological security, a refugee situation is created.[6]

Structural constraints and facilitators

I have argued elsewhere (Richmond 1988c:38) that an adequate sociological theory of migration must incorporate an understanding of social action and human agency, the question of conflict, contradiction and opposition in social systems, the meaning of structure and change, and the importance of power. A key element in structuration theory is the recogni-

Figure 3.1   Structuration of migration

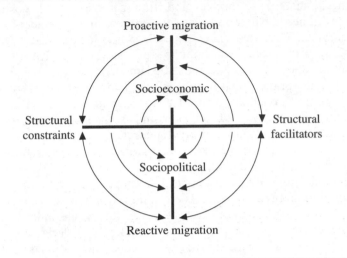

tion that social structures not only constrain but enable. Constraint involves an asymmetrical distribution of power, which may involve naked force and physical coercion, material rewards, threats of deprivation, or various forms of persuasion and inducement. However, Giddens (1984:173) points out that sources of constraint are also means of enablement: 'They open up certain possibilities of action at the same time as they restrict or deny others.' Parson's use of the concepts of power and influence are relevant here. Power is not necessarily a zero-sum concept (Giddens 1968; Parsons 1960, 1963). Its unequal distribution may lead to conflict, but it must also be understood as a resource that facilitates the achievement of collective goals. It is notable that in his review of the studies of place-utility and intention to migrate, Simmons (1985–6) concluded that background variables (constraints and facilitators) had a stronger association with actual migration than expressed intentions. A simplified representation of the structuration of migration is shown in Figure 3.1.

Based on her experiences in an African refugee camp, Harrell-Bond (1986:283–329) discussed the 'oversocialized concept of Man', which fails to recognize the extent to which, in critical situations, individual survival undermines social values, including those that normally induce humane responses. Following Bettelheim's account of life in a concentration camp, Giddens (1984:63) makes the same point when he notes that any sustained attack on the routines of social life produces a high level of anxiety and a stripping away of socialized responses. It takes time to rebuild social structures and attempts to impose order often fail for lack of grass roots cooperation. Psychological stress and accompanying levels of depression and anxiety may reach pathological levels. Bereavement exacerbates the problem, but a crisis can be perceived as a threat, a loss, or a challenge. Adaptive and coping mechanisms can be generated, although outside help may be needed to do so.

Harrell-Bond goes on to point out that, in order to answer the question of how refugees survive, their relationship with the host society must be considered. Refugees are generally perceived as a 'problem' or a 'threat' to those countries whose borders they cross. However, they may also generate opportunities and become a source of positive social change. As in the case of other immigrants, they may bring human capital, skills, or experience that benefit the receiving society. International agencies may become involved, attracting investment in transportation or new industries. Markets may be created, marginal land cultivated, schools started, or health services established. Short-sighted interference by outside agencies pursuing policies dictated by the interests of foreign powers or private corporations, whether represented as well meaning or not, may have the opposite of the desired effect. Harrell-Bond (1986:366) argues that humanitarians and researchers alike should become facilitators, using their resources to enable refugees to help themselves. Either way, the outsiders are necessarily agents of social change, as are the refugees themselves.

Conflicts and contradictions

No society is without conflicts arising from the unequal distribution of resources, competing interests, opposing values, and internal contradictions. Giddens (1984:193–4) distinguishes between existential contradiction and structural contradiction. The former concerns human existence in relation to the natural world. It comes to the forefront when people are faced with the question of absolute survival and must make choices that could mean sacrificing their own lives for the sake of others, a not unreal conflict in disasters and under oppressive regimes. More familiar are the structural contradictions that arise out of changing social systems. Giddens notes that 'the emergence of state-based societies also alters the scope and pace of "history" by stimulating secondary contradictions. States bring into being, or at least greatly accentuate, social relations across considerable reaches of time and space' (1984:196).

One example of structural contradiction in this context is the provision of international law and the UN Convention on Human Rights (not observed in practice by all states), which provides the right to leave a country without any complementary right of admission elsewnere. The result is the creation of stateless persons and refugees in orbit, i.e., reactive migrants who have escaped intolerable conditions in one place but who can find no state willing to offer asylum or resettlement opportunities. Dowty (1987) has chronicled the 'contemporary assault on freedom of movement' that has led to the closing of borders and increasingly restrictive immigration and refugee policies in many countries. A further contradiction, following from this, is that it is mainly the poorest countries in Africa and Asia that presently shoulder the burden of providing shelter and aid for the millions of people displaced by wars that are fuelled by superpower confrontation and the arms bazaar (Ferris 1985; Myrdal 1976; Samson 1977; Sivard 1985).

The above review of sociological and social psychological theories pertaining to international migration leads to two key conclusions. Firstly, an absolutely clear distinction between the economic and the sociopolitical determinants of population movement is not appropriate. A multivariate approach is necessary. There may be exceptional cases where both the underlying and precipitating causes can be identified as 'purely' economic or political. However, in the modern world where states, religious leaders, multinational corporations, and suprastate agencies (such as the International Monetary Fund and the World Bank) are involved in decisions that affect the lives of millions of people, the majority of population movements are a complex response to the reality of a global society in which ethnoreligious, social, economic, and political determinants are inextricably bound together.

Secondly, a distinction between voluntary and involuntary movements is also untenable. All human behaviour is constrained and enabled by the structuration process, within which degrees of freedom of choice are limited. Individual autonomy is relative to opportunity structures, which are themselves determined by social forces. The distribution of economic and political power is central to the decision-making process at the individual and collective level. 'Rational choice' within a means-end schema, in which individuals maximize net advantage, is a special case rarely found in isolation from decisions that are influenced by direct coercion, manipulated opinion and value systems, the non-rational pursuit of transcendental goals, and normatively oriented voluntaristic action. In this context, decisions regarding migration are more appropriately designated proactive or reactive, according to the degree of autonomy exhibited by the actors involved.

The resulting paradigm of international migration is diagrammatically represented in Figure 3.2 as a matrix.[7] The vertical axis represents decision making on a continuum from maximum to minimum autonomy. The horizontal axis represents the interaction of economic and sociopolitical forces, reflecting that they come full circle as internal and external state powers converge. Proactive migrants include retirees, transilients, returnees, reunited families, and ordinary emigrants.

Multivariate model of proactive migration

Recognizing that there is a continuum between the extremes on the axis of proactive and reactive migration, it is possible to describe some of the key factors likely to affect a decision to migrate by those who have relatively unconstrained choice, unlike refugees and others reacting to circumstances

Figure 3.2 Paradigm of international population movements

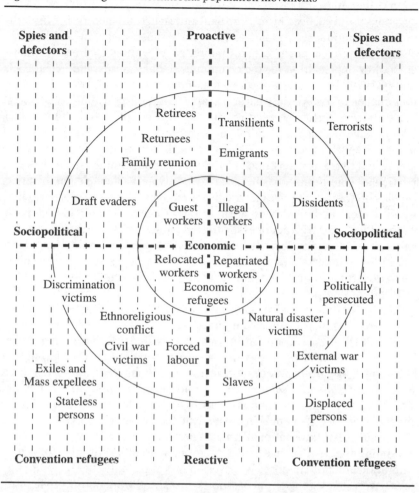

almost entirely beyond their control. The choices facing proactive migrants include whether to move at all, when to move, whether to go a long or a short distance, and whether to cross an international border in the process. Questions of place-utility enter into these deliberations. As well as choosing between alternative destinations, the migrants may take into account intervening opportunities. More decisions must be made concerning whether to travel alone or with family members or friends, and whether to follow a route already established by others with whom there may be prior connections. Such networks may also be able to assist in the initial reception and settlement process. Further questions arise concerning how long to stay in the new location. The duration may be short term, long term, or permanent. If not permanent, choices must be made regarding remigration to another location or return to the original place of residence, when to do so, and in what circumstances. Although relatively unconstrained, such decisions are influenced by institutional and structural factors that limit the proactive migrant's freedom. Such factors must weigh in any rational choice, although in practice, many people move without a complete knowledge of or appreciation for the economic, social, and psychological costs and benefits. Subjective aspects such as a desire for travel, adventure, risk, and challenge, or even a wish to escape family responsibilities or social pressures may affect the decision-making process (de Jong and Gardner 1981). Some people may exhibit 'hypermobility' when they make several moves in quick succession. This is generally more characteristic of the young and those not constrained by family responsibilities, strong ties to a particular community, or the need to cultivate a clientele for business purposes. Transilient migrants are those who, by virtue of their particular qualifications and experience, are able to find employment in various parts of the world, and who adapt easily to the requirements of the new location in terms of language, local customs, standards, and technologies. Adaptability is not necessarily correlated to higher education. It is also exhibited by many people in unskilled labouring and service occupations.

In examining propensities to migrate, it is important to consider local political, economic, social, and cultural conditions. Some communities have a long history of choosing migration as an option in the fulfilment of personal, family, and community goals. The precedents thus set may influence others at a later date, whereas other populations without such a tradition of migration may be more inclined to remain sedentary, even when a rational weighing of economic costs and benefits might favour moving. For this reason, it may be inappropriate to apply to developing countries the predictive models that apply in more advanced urban societies (Tuck 1981). The influence of transnational ethclass networks is also important.

Among the institutional and structural factors constraining proactive migration are those imposed by governments at the national, regional, and local levels. These range from passports, visas, and work permits to requirements involving health checks, assessment of qualifications, or other eligibility criteria. There may be limits on eligibility for health and social service benefits, non-recognition of occupational qualifications, or the imposition of special taxes. Non-governmental factors may include questions relating to language and cultural similarity or dissimilarity, climate, cost of living, educational, and employment opportunities, etc.

Structural facilitators for proactive migration include financial incentives that may be provided by governments in the sending and/or receiving areas, such as free passages or subsidized transport, assistance with housing, and special incentives for investors and entrepreneurs. Similar incentives may be provided by the private sector when transnational or other corporations wish to recruit abroad or encourage the mobility of their own workforce. Career mobility (sometimes called spiralism) is often dependent upon the acquisition of experience in other localities or through working abroad. Other facilitating factors include agreements for the transfer of pension funds, reciprocity with regard to health and other social services, and special settlement adjustment programs, including language and cultural orientation, retraining, and the recognition of credentials.

The majority of proactive migrants are likely to be motivated by socioeconomic considerations, but there are exceptions. Retirees may be influenced by climatic concerns or the proximity to family as well as the portability of pension benefits and the cost of living. Politically motivated proactive migrants include those who, while not forced to move by conditions in their own country, are prompted by the desire to advance an ideological cause or to induce changes in the country to which they move. Government employees in external affairs, diplomatic personnel, trade representatives, consuls, and immigration officials may all experience considerable international migration in the course of their careers. Spies, terrorists, and dissidents are also closer to the proactive than the reactive end of the scale. As indicated in Figure 3.2, guest workers, 'illegal' workers, relocated workers, and repatriates cluster somewhere in the middle of the proactive-reactive axis.

Multivariate model of reactive migration

UN Convention refugees, stateless persons, slaves, and forced labourers are clear examples of reactive migrants. Between the two extremes of proactive and reactive migrants are a large proportion of people crossing state boundaries who combine characteristics, responding to economic, social, and political pressures over which they have little control, but exercising a limited degree of choice in the selection of destinations and the timing of their movements. The nearer the category falls to the vertical axis, the more important are the economic determinants, while those closer to the horizontal periphery are more in the political domain, although no clear-cut boundary between these factors can be drawn. Some elaboration of the concept of reactive migration and the factors giving rise to such movements is required, keeping in mind that there is no hard and fast line dividing reactive and proactive, although migrants in the latter category have more options open to them. They have greater freedom in deciding whether to move as well as in their choice of destination and the opportunity of returning. International laws and conventions generally define as 'refugees' only those who have crossed an international border, although, from a sociological perspective, they may be indistinguishable from internally displaced persons reacting to similar circumstances. Feelings of group exclusion, loss of trust, and a sense of threat and insecurity can occur independently of each other, although one frequently leads to the others. Some combination of political, economic, environmental, social, and psychological variables is generally involved. They range from external and internal war, state-initiated genocidal policies towards minorities (which involve mass extermination), to the aftermath of volcanic eruptions or earthquakes where the civil authorities are unable to provide the victims with adequate protection or rehabilitation. The inclusion of environmental determinants in this schema reflects a growing recognition that climatic changes, drought, and famine are not independent of the sociopolitical and economic causes of migration, including revolution and civil war. The situation in the sub-Saharan regions, Ethiopia, the Sudan, and Somalia is evidence of this link, as is the effect of drought and crop failure in Bolivia and Peru (Hampson in Mungall and McLaren 1990). The effects of global warming and other ecological disasters in the future could also give rise to a growing problem of environmental refugees (Suhrke and Visentin 1991). The environmental hazards of war, including chemical weapons and oil pollution, about which scientists had previously warned (Westing 1990), were highlighted by recent events in the Persian Gulf.

A multivariate systems model of the relations between these elements in the aetiology of refugee movements is shown in Figure 3.3. The figure illustrates the interaction between economic, political, social, environmental, and biopsychological determinants, on the one hand, and, on the other, the importance of distinguishing predisposing factors, structural constraints, precipitating events, enabling circumstances, and feedback effects of reactive migration on the states concerned as well as the global system.

Predisposing factors

The above account indicates that political factors are important but not exclusive determinants of reactive migration. Extreme inequalities of wealth and resources between different countries and regions of the world are among the predisposing factors increasing the probability of reactive migration. Such inequalities, when combined with political instability, create the conditions under which refugee movements are likely to occur unless severely constrained by other factors. New state formation and decolonization, including the rise of nationalist and separatist movements, also provide fertile ground for refugee movements to occur (Smith 1991; Zolberg 1989). States are generally defined as sovereign organizations having supreme coercive power and a monopoly of the legitimate use of violence for external defence and the maintenance of internal law and order. At the same time, it is recognized that states may abuse their powers and that other agencies may also use violence in the pursuit of their goals, with or without the connivance of state authorities, thereby creating the potential for flight from danger.

The boundaries of states have their origin in war, imperial conquest, and treaties designed to stabilize a balance of power in a given region. However artificial and lacking in correspondence to geographic factors or the ethno-linguistic composition of the population, such boundaries assume a

Figure 3.3 Reactive migration—multivariate factor analysis

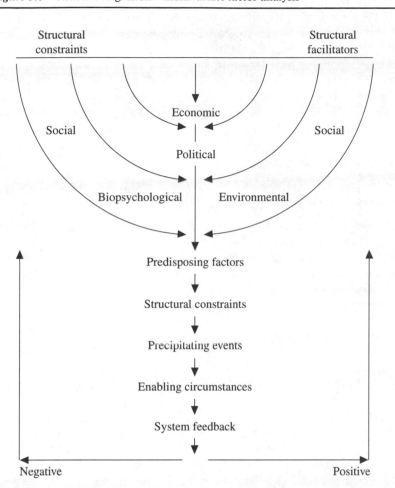

'sacred' status. The right to defend them is entrenched in international law and attempts to extend them are met with opposition. The ideology of a relatively homogeneous nation-state has been used to mobilize support for the defence of existing state boundaries and for their extension to incorporate neighbouring (and even distant) territories where close allies and friends, fellow nationals, or co-religionists reside, supposedly under the domination of alien rulers. In reality, the populations of modern states are generally polyethnic and multinational in composition (Richmond 1988c:141–66). Ethnic nationalism and aspirations for independence lead to wars of national liberation and revolutions, which, in turn, give rise to reactive population movements across borders. Prolonged incarceration in camps can lead to militant 'refugee warriors' and to 'exiles' in their own birthplace (Abu-Lughod 1988; Zolberg et al. 1989).

The process of globalization has increased the propensity for both proactive and reactive migration. Improved transportation and communication links increase awareness of mobility opportunities in sending and receiving areas. The global market for arms, superpower intervention in local conflicts, the spread of nationalism and the breakdown of the former 'balance of terror' between the West and the former Soviet Union have created instabilities in the world system. Aspirations to improve economic prospects by migration to the West increased with the destruction of the Berlin Wall and all that it symbolized. Reactive migration increased as a result of civil war and 'ethnic cleansing'.

Structural constraints

The persistence of quasi-sovereign states intent on protecting their borders against illegal migrants and other unwanted persons (such as drug dealers, smugglers, and other criminals) is among the factors constraining the movement of reactive migrants. Although economic and other influences (including mass communications) may transcend state boundaries, there are powerful political forces reinforcing borders and controlling population movements across them. There is a contradiction between the long-term trend of the global economy towards a borderless world, which Ohmae (1990:xii–xiii) describes as 'ensuring the free flow of information, money, goods and services as well as the free migration of people and corporations', and the reality of a world of closed borders and reluctant hosts, shutting the doors to refugees and all but a select few economic migrants (Dowty 1987; Joly and Cohen 1989; Matas 1989; Richmond 1991a).

States continue to pursue policies that are in their own collective self-interest, including the protection of their economic system, education, housing, health and welfare services, and their political borders. Draconian enforcement measures are used by most governments against those perceived as illegal immigrants or overstayers. In the case of the more industrially developed countries, these standards include the provision of health and welfare services, unemployment insurance and pension plans, income maintenance programs, educational services, and minimum housing standards. Uncontrolled immigration, including the admission of large numbers of refugees, is seen as a potential threat to these standards. In this respect, the immigration control measures instituted resemble the actions of the South African government when apartheid was enforced. Pass laws, work permits, segregated housing locations, restricted travel, deprivation of voting and other citizenship rights, removal to 'homelands', and draconian enforcement measures have all been used by governments against illegal immigrants and asylum seekers.

The situation has been aggravated by recent developments in eastern

Europe. As long as the Berlin Wall separated Warsaw Pact countries from those in the NATO Alliance and the countries of eastern Europe and the Soviet Union, and placed severe restrictions on emigration, western European countries (together with the United States, Canada, and Australia) were prepared to recognize as 'refugees' almost anyone who wished to leave a communist country, whether their motivation was economic or political. The reverse is now the case. Given the severe economic crisis in eastern Europe and the lifting of the ban on exit, there is potential for an enormous exodus. Ethnic conflicts in the former Soviet Union, nationalist movements in the Baltic states, Yugoslavia, and elsewhere, together with evidence of growing anti-Semitism, racism, and xenophobia throughout Europe, all create the conditions for substantial reactive migration. In the face of these potential pressures towards mass migration from eastern to western Europe, a variety of control measures are being put in place to deter and limit both proactive and reactive migrants. Not only are western European countries restricting entry but countries such as Poland have been obliged to control the movement of Romanians and are afraid that there could be a large exodus from the Soviet Union if conditions deteriorate further there. Some Albanians, seeking to escape repressive political and deteriorating economic conditions recently fled to Italy. Western European countries, together with the United States, Canada, and Australia, have tried to formulate a common response to these emerging crises.[8]

Other structural constraints on the incidence and scale of reactive migration are the emigration laws of potential sending countries and the use of coercive measures on either or both sides of state borders to deter such movements. Armed border guards prepared to shoot, strict deportation measures for illegal migrants, and coastguards who intercept boats carrying potential refugees are among the most obvious examples. While all forms of authoritarian repression may add to the predisposition to migrate, those same repressive laws and totalitarian measures make actual flight more difficult. At the same time, critical turning points in the history of such societies may precipitate long-suppressed aspirations to escape.

Precipitating events

Sudden changes in the economic, political, social, or environmental situation may precipitate reactive migration. Critical events include the outbreak of war, internal revolution, or the institution of racist or religious programs and genocidal policies. Outbreaks of terrorist activity by dissident or separatist groups or other sources of violent conflict may be involved. Reactive migration may also be precipitated by natural and technological disasters that destroy food supplies or housing, threatening the lives, health, and livelihood of local residents. Generally, the precipitating event is one that disrupts the normal functioning of the system and thus destroys the capacity of a population to survive under the prevailing conditions. The social systems that provide people with an ongoing sense of ontological security may collapse in the face of what Giddens (1990:171) calls the 'high consequence risks of modernity', such as ecological disaster, economic collapse, war, nuclear threats, the coming to power of a military dictatorship, or the end of a totalitarian regime.

Enabling circumstances

Not all predisposing factors and precipitating events actually generate large-scale reactive migration, although some proactive movements may occur under these conditions. Some additional enabling circumstances are needed. These are generally the obverse of the structural constraints already discussed. Thus, the end of a dictatorial regime and the relaxing of border controls may make reactive migration feasible. Extreme poverty remains a deterrent because the migrants must have access to some resources to provide for their journey and interim support. Often bribes must be paid, documents acquired, tickets bought, and provisions obtained. Reactive migration may be demographically and economically selective, favouring the young, the healthy, the able-bodied and those with some material resources that can be traded or converted into foreign currency. It may also be gender selective as adult males may be more proactive than women and children, who are often left behind with few options, except to react to circumstances beyond their control.

Other enabling circumstances depend on the actions of governmental and non-governmental agencies that may institute rescue missions, establish refugee camps, issue travel documents, relax entry requirements, and set up asylum application procedures. Generous immigration programs and steps to promote human rights by international agencies may also facilitate reactive migration and eventual resettlement.

System feedback

The processes of structuration as consequences of reactive migration, and the response of individuals and collectivities to such movements, has positive and negative feedback effects on the societies in question and on the global system of which they are a part. Under some conditions reactive migration may grow at an exponential rate until it reaches a level that is perceived as threatening to the stability of receiving countries, which then institute measures to deter and restrict further arrivals. Such countries may experience a backlash by their own population against further immigration. There may be efforts to deport those not meeting strict standards of eligibility for refugee status. Voluntary and involuntary repatriation schemes may be instituted.

As the number of reactive migrants (whether legally defined as Convention refugees or not) reaches the levels currently estimated as 17,556,900

Figure 3.4 Reactive migration

	TYPOLOGY				
	POLITICAL	ECONOMIC	ENVIRONMENTAL	SOCIAL	BIOPSYCHO-LOGICAL
Political	1	2	3	4	5
Economic	6	10	14	18	22
Environmental	7	11	15	19	23
Social	8	12	16	20	24
Biopsychological	9	13	17	21	25

refugees and asylum seekers and a further 24 million internally displaced civilians (US Committee for Refugees 1993), attention turns to questions of root causes and preventative action. Clearly, as the above analysis shows, there are no simple solutions. However, measures that reduce economic inequality and dependency, promote political stability and democratization, achieve arms control and demilitarization, and facilitate the peaceful settlement of disputes all contribute in the long run to a reduction in scale of the problem. Failure to do so results in whole generations who are born, live, and die in transit camps. The insecurity created under these condition may lead to the formation of militant protest groups and refugee warriors ready to fight for their individual and collective human rights.

Typology of reactive migration

Using the multivariate approach outlined above, it is possible to delineate a typology of reactive migration as shown in Figure 3.4.

The horizontal dimension of the figure lists the major determinants of particular kinds of reactive migration and the vertical column indicates the principal secondary factors reinforcing the breakdown in institutions previously providing political protection, economic support, and a sense of group inclusion, trust, and security. Major determinants include the precipitating events discussed earlier, together with enabling circumstances, while principal secondary factors include the predisposing factors, although in particular cases, there may be interaction between all of these. The categories thus created do not preclude the possible added effects of any tertiary factors that may be present, or of overlapping categories and concomitant or sequential calamities, thus increasing the propensity to migrate. In categories one to nine, political determinants are involved either as primary or secondary determinants of movement. These types of reactive migration are generally more readily recognized as refugee movements than others.

1. *Political/Political*: People fleeing from wartorn countries, whether the war is a result of external invasion or internal civil conflict. Political exiles,

the potential victims of state-induced genocidal policies, nationalist movements, ethnic conflicts, and death threats to minorities are also included. The largest single example today is the number of Afghan refugees in Pakistan and Iran, as well as those internally displaced in Afghanistan. Recent events in the former Yugoslav republic have also generated large reactive migrations as a result of political conflicts.

2. *Political/Economic*: Those compelled to move as a result of slave trading and other forms of forced labour, backed by coercive laws and quasi-military threats, including the forcible recruitment of children into military service. The UN Working Group on Contemporary Forms of Slavery monitors this type of reactive migration.

3. *Political/Environmental*: Victims of nuclear and biochemical weapons or accidental nuclear and biochemical disasters that are the direct or indirect result of governmental policies and programs, including failure to enforce appropriate safety standards. The Chernobyl nuclear disaster is one example that resulted in the evacuation of the exposed population. Kurdish refugees escaping chemical weapons use by Iraq is another.

4. *Political/Social*: Those escaping from political regimes perpetrating major human rights violations of the kind identified by agencies such as Amnesty International, e.g., mass executions, 'disappearances', systematic terrorism, etc. The activities of the *Sendero Luminoso* in Peru is an example. Individual migrants may not always meet the UN Convention definition of a 'refugee' if they cannot show that they are personally at risk.

5. *Political/Biopsychological*: Those threatened with execution, torture, brainwashing, or 'cruel and unusual' punishment for political protest, crimes against the state, etc. Those escaping imprisonment under the Stalinist regime or Communist China are examples.

6. *Economic/Political*: Persons forced to move by government-backed policies of forced relocation, transmigration, clearances, etc., are in this category. Thailand's program of reforestation by forced eviction is an example (Hubbel and Rajesh 1992), as is migration necessitated by compliance with externally imposed 'structural adjustment' programs designed to satisfy requirements for international loans and aid.

7. *Environmental/Political*: Includes migration induced by politically motivated actions that result in environmental disasters, e.g., deliberate oil spills, fires, water or air pollution, and/or famine conditions resulting from civil conflict. Refugees and internally displaced persons in the Sudan and Somalia are examples (Otunnu 1992).

8. *Social/Political*: Escape from general deprivation of human rights, civic, social, and economic, as in totalitarian regimes, or from South Africa under apartheid are examples.

9. *Biopsychological/Political*: Includes migration induced by psychological warfare, terrorism, or widespread hate-mongering towards particular ethnic or religious minorities. Examples include Tibetan monks in Nepal fleeing Chinese persecution of those suspected of pro-independence sympathies.

10. *Economic/Economic*: Persons forced to migrate as a result of bankruptcies, total economic collapse, chronic unemployment, and loss of livelihood without safety-net social security measures are in this category. Recent developments in eastern Europe and periodic economic crises in developing countries have induced such economically motivated reactive migration.

11. *Economic/Environmental*: Comprises migration induced by the effects of deforestation, deliberate flooding, opencast mining, hydroelectric dams, or other economic actions causing environmental damage. The internal displacement of Aboriginal populations in Canada following the James Bay hydroelectric project is an example.

12. *Economic/Social*: Migration induced by structural changes in the economy leading to rural depopulation, urbanization, regional disparities, etc., fall into this category. Loss of livelihood due to international free trade agreements and industrial relocations are examples.

13. *Economic/Biopsychological*: Closure of mines or other economic enterprises following major accidents, together with occupational health hazards and injuries, may result in reactive migration.

14. *Environmental/Economic*: Includes population movements consequent upon drought, soil depletion, etc., with consequent famine conditions. In 1992, Zimbabwe and other areas in southern Africa were facing a desperate water shortage and mass starvation that resulted in reactive migration.

15. *Environmental/Environmental*: Migration compelled by earthquakes, volcanic eruptions, or other 'natural' disasters are included here, although a neglect to take precautionary measures may be a tertiary factor.

16. *Environmental/Social*: Migration following loss of livelihood induced by animal rights, antifur trapping, and general conservationist policies. Ironically, some populations may be forced to move as a consequence of policies adopted by the recent Earth Summit conference designed to combat overfishing, destruction of rain forests, etc.

17. *Environmental/Biopsychological*: This includes migration induced by soil, water, and air contamination by pollutants, total allergy syndrome, etc. People may be forced to move as a result of anticipated radiation hazards, lead poisoning, etc., particularly if children are affected.

18. *Social/Economic*: This includes migration induced by strikes, lock-outs, curfews, boycotts, social unrest, etc. Escape from riot-prone inner-city areas to safer suburban neighbourhoods is an example.

19. *Social/Environmental*: Migration may be induced by a threat to life-style, loss of roots, desire for preservation of community etc., in the face of industrialization, urban sprawl, or encroachment on rural areas, leading to a re-establishment of traditional ways. Although often individually proactive, such movements may be reactive when whole communities are affected.

20. *Social/Social*: Migration may be impelled by laws and customs that enforce racial or ethnoreligious discrimination and segregation, forbid intermarriage, etc., or is motivated by racially reserved occupations, deprivation of access to education or qualifications, and limit social mobility for minorities.

21. *Social/Biopsychological*: Includes migration induced by age or gender discrimination, language loss, 'cultural genocide', forced assimilation, etc.

22. *Biopsychological/Economic*: This category covers migration necessitated by industrial injuries, physical and mental health disabilities, occupational stress and burnout, etc., which render the person incapable of economic self-support in the previous location.

23. *Biopsychological/Environmental*: Migration caused by plagues, epidemics such as cholera, or other major health hazards is included here.

24. *Biopsychological/Social*: Escape from race prejudice, anti-Semitism, and other forms of ethnoreligious intolerance or abuse (not institutionalized in the political or economic system) belongs in this category.

25. *Biopsychological/Biopsychological*: Includes flight from eugenic or psychiatric experimentation, brainwashing, indoctrination, etc., as well as escape from spousal abuse and violence, sexual assault, child abuse or domestic or institutional violence.

As noted above, there is a continuum between proactive and reactive migration in all of the above cases, but the structural constraints are greater in the latter, and the scope for rational choice by reactive migrants is limited.

Policy conclusions

The above is more than just a list of the traditionally understood push factors contributing to migration because it recognizes the interaction between motivational factors, on the one hand, and the social structural determinants, on the other. It also emphasizes the complex interaction between political, economic, environmental, social, and biopsychological factors in determining the propensity to migrate. Thus it demonstrates the inadequacy of any definition of 'refugee' that singles out one element in the causal chain, such as having a 'genuine fear of persecution', because such fear is often only one factor in a much more complicated relation between predisposing factors, structural constraints, precipitating events, and enabling circumstances.

In the context of an emerging new world order, the policies that should be adopted towards refugees and other reactive migrants are those that ensure the viability of a global social system. States can no longer isolate themselves geographically, economically, politically, or socially from the actions of other collectivities. Whether it is the effect of destroying the rain forests or building dams; inducing large-scale unemployment through externally imposed monetary policies; accumulating agricultural surpluses in one region while famine reigns in another; invading another state; creating a violent revolution or nationalist insurrection; persecuting ethnic, religious, or political minorities; or causing a fallout from a nuclear disaster—all of us are implicated in the causes and directly affected by the outcomes.

Worldwide mass migration will be a major force for change and a potential source of disastrous conflict in the future unless our dominant values and the policies based on them are radically changed. We must recognize that our postmodern society is a global one, the survival of which requires the institutionalization of universal values respecting human rights, including the right to asylum. It is imperative that the definition of a 'refugee' be widened to include all those in peril from natural and unnatural disasters. It is also essential that the political will and the means be created to end the global arms bazaar, together with the violent conflicts that it sustains. Innovative responses from the international community, through the UN and its various agencies, will be needed to ensure reflexive self-regulation. It will be necessary to determine priorities, develop rules, allocate resources, and take appropriate preventive and rehabilitative action to create new global structures.

The central core of international migration consists of those responding to the uneven development of the global economy, the demands for labour in oil-rich and economically advanced societies, and the displacement consequent upon urbanization in the Third World. These economic determinants are not independent of the sociopolitical context in which they occur. Such migrants are vulnerable to cyclical fluctuations of the global economy as well as political instability and changing policies in sending and receiving countries alike. At times they find opportunities available as contract or guest workers, but they are subject to repatriation or exclusion when the perceived interests of traditional receiving countries change. Many are treated as 'illegals' and are subject to deportation when discovered.

Convention refugees are the prototypical political migrants, although the historical circumstances in which the precise legal definition of a 'refugee' in the UN Protocol was formulated limits its applicability to the contemporary world system. At the opposite extreme to those who qualify as Convention refugees on the basis of their demonstrated fear of persecution, are those politically motivated proactive migrants who fall into the category of spies, terrorists, or defectors. In some cases, they may deliberately infiltrate genuine refugee movements. Furthermore, there is growing evidence of collusion between the intelligence agencies in various countries that have allowed actual or former agents, political activists, and war criminals to enter other countries under the guise of refugees (Deschenes 1986; Rodal 1987; Wright 1987). Intermediate cases, also combining sociopolitical and economic determinants, include American draft evaders (Kasinsky 1976), other political dissidents, victims of ethnic discrimination, and those who may be persecuted because of their religious or political beliefs, together with a growing class of so-called 'economic refugees'. The extent to which they are regarded as admissible in other countries often depends upon ideological considerations and cross-cultural understanding (Kalin 1986:230–40).

Sociologists are still a long way from being able to explain all aspects of international migration within a single theoretical framework. The paradigm outlined above brings together certain key elements in structuration and social psychological theory to explain certain broad features of contemporary international migration, particularly that of refugees. At the risk of gross oversimplification, it may be stated that: $M = P + R$, where M is the total number of international migrants, P is the number of proactive migrants, and R is the number of reactive migrants. In turn, $P_{a \cdot b \cdot t}$ is the number of proactive migrants from place $_a$ seeking entry to place $_b$ in time period $_t$. It is likely to be a function of distance, intervening opportunities and obstacles, rationally calculated net advantages (not exclusively economic in nature), qualified by a variety of non-rational considerations derived from the voluntaristic nature of social action. The number actually admitted to country $_b$ will depend upon a variety of policy considerations, themselves combining rational and non-rational elements.

Similarly, $R_{a \cdot b \cdot t}$ is the number of reactive migrants from place $_a$ seeking entry to place $_b$ in time period $_t$. This is likely to be a function of the degree to which societal institutions in place $_a$ have disintegrated to the point that they are unable to provide a substantial section of the population with an adequate sense of group inclusion, trust, and ontological security, qualified by the perception of place $_b$ as capable of reducing the anxiety thus created. The receptivity of those in place $_a$ to R will depend upon the same considerations applied to P, with additional non-rational elements, likely to be invoked as a consequence of a conflict between humanitarian values and strictly self-interested motives.

Certain policy conclusions can be drawn from the above analysis. Firstly, the present UN definition of a 'Convention refugee' is inadequate in the face of the contemporary demographic realities. Even the adoption of a 'B' category, or designated class of persons who do not meet the *de jure* requirements but are admissible on other grounds, does not do justice to the scale or complexity of the global situation facing reactive migrants. Attention needs to be given to a reformulation of the concept of 'refugee' to take into account a variety of crises and disasters that warrant international collaborative relief effort. It raises issues of sovereignty and international law that only jurists are qualified to address. Sociological theory can only point to the inadequacy of existing international codes.

Secondly, the right to leave must be matched by the right of asylum. Wealthy countries should not close their borders or adopt more restrictive immigration policies merely because the scale of reactive migration has increased or the racial and cultural characteristics of those seeking refuge has changed. Finally, it is evident that the 'refugee problem' is only a symptom of much more profound conflicts and contradictions within our global system. Ultimately, the flow of international migrants, both proactive and reactive, will be responsive to a more egalitarian economic order and to the creation of a more peaceful, demilitarized society.

Notes

[1] This chapter is an extensively revised and extended version of two previously published papers, which appeared in *Current Sociology* 36, no. 2 (1988) and *Journal of Refugee Studies* 6, no. 1 (1993).

[2] The 1951 United Nations Convention relating to the Status of Refugees and the 1967 Protocol define a refugee as one who 'by reason of a well-founded fear of persecution for reasons of race, religion, nationality, membership in a particular social group or political opinion, a) is outside the country of his nationality and is unable or, by reason of such fear, is unwilling to avail himself of the protection of that country, or b) not having a country of nationality, is outside the country of his former habitual residence and is unable, or by reason of such fear, is unwilling to return to that country.'

[3] Although quite evident in the contemporary world, the connection between economic conditions and political persecution is not new. Marrus (1985:31) notes that in the case of the Jewish exodus from eastern Europe in the nineteenth century, 'Neither in the persecution policy nor in the motivation for emigration do we find forcible uprooting in the usual sense. Jews from the tsarist empire seem to represent an intermediate case . . . neither entirely refugees nor entirely voluntary emigrants, they included elements of both, sometimes to the confusion of outside observers.' He goes on to give other more recent examples of economic and political factors combining to induce migration.

[4] Even 'natural' disasters involve a large element of human responsibility, to the extent that such events as earthquakes and volcanic eruptions can be predicted with some degree of probability and their effects can be minimized with appropriate building and other codes. Floods, famines, and fires are all preventable and in many cases are actually caused by humans. It goes without saying that chemical spills, mining disasters, and nuclear 'accidents' are all man-made. Once the disaster has occurred, the speed and efficiency of remedial action is closely related to the

economic and political context of the relief operations and the degree of cooperation between government and non-governmental agencies. Ideological considerations frequently intervene to inhibit early warning or effective relief of disastrous population movements (Gordenker 1986:170–89). (For further discussion, see Chapter Four.)

[5] Push factors are generally understood to mean economic and political insecurity in the sending country, while pull factors refer to perceived opportunities for economic benefits, family reunion, or political asylum. However, push and pull factors are not necessarily independent and there is an interaction between them that is better understood in a system framework.

[6] 'Ontological security' in this context means confidence in the social world and one's ability to survive in it and in terms of social identity (see Chapter One).

[7] The figure is drawn in the form of a Mercator projection of a sphere, although no geographic connotation is intended. The distribution of types of migrants within the quadrants indicates relative degrees of autonomy in decision making, together with the relative importance of economic and sociopolitical determinants. Empirical research is needed, using reliable measures of these variables, in order to place a particular movement of population into its appropriate location within the matrix.

[8] An intergovernmental agency called Informal Consultations on Asylum, Refugee and Migration Policies in Europe, North America, and Australia is based in Geneva. The participating states are Australia, Austria, Belgium, Canada, Denmark, Finland, France, Germany, Italy, Netherlands, Norway, Spain, Sweden, Switzerland, the United Kingdom, and the United States. Several of these countries have recently introduced new immigration legislation and some are parties to the Schengen Agreement, Dublin Convention, and the Maastricht Treaty when ratified. The aim is to harmonize policies regulating population movement.

chapter four

Environmental refugees[1]

The term 'environmental refugee' has gained currency in recent years, following reports by the UN Environmental Program and the Worldwatch Institute (El-Hinnawi 1985; Jacobson 1988). The former defined the term very broadly to include anyone forced to leave his or her traditional habitat because of marked environmental disruption. Other more or less synonymous terms have been used to describe the plight of those fleeing long-term environmental degradation or short-term disaster. They include 'ecological refugees' and 'resource refugees'. None of these concepts has any standing in international law. According to the 1951 UN Convention and 1967 Protocol (see Appendix 1), people in need of humanitarian assistance are not refugees if they are still in their own state, even when they have been displaced by violent upheavals. When they flee their country, it is not enough to be a victim of war, disaster, or generalized violence; there must be evidence of persecution directed against the individual claimant.[2] Canada, among other countries, has incorporated this definition into its own legislation and refugee determination system. Asylum applicants who do not meet these criteria are subject to removal unless there are other compelling reasons of a humanitarian or compassionate nature to justify a review of the case before deportation is enforced. Economic or environmental conditions in the country of origin are not deemed adequate grounds to permit postdetermination judicial review (MacMillan 1993).

The scale of environmentally induced migration (whether defined as a refugee movement or not) is difficult to estimate.[3] Much depends upon whether past, present, or possible future movements are considered; whether worldwide migration or only that occurring in developing countries is considered; whether internal as well as external migrations are taken into account; and whether environmental degradation is considered in isolation or in conjunction with other political, economic, and social determinants of population movement.

Demographic aspects

The distinction between internal and external migration has long been recognized in demographic studies, despite the artificiality of state boundaries. As previously noted, although they do not meet the Convention definition of a 'refugee', there is a growing recognition of the humanitarian needs of populations internally displaced as a result of civil war, political persecution, etc. Recent developments in eastern Europe and the legacy of colonialism in Africa and Asia are evidence of the lack of correspondence between state boundaries and the ethnic ties that cut across them. Nationalist and irredentist movements have led to the definition of new boundaries and claims to self-determination. India, the Soviet Union, Yugoslavia, and Mozambique are examples of states that have disintegrated in the aftermath of colonialism or as a result of the collapse of a totalitarian regime. Population movements that would once have been regarded as internal become external. The reverse can occur when neighbouring territories are annexed. Although states are reluctant to interfere in the internal affairs of other sovereign countries, there is a growing recognition that civil wars and environmental catastrophes have consequences for the global system. In the future, UN intervention is likely to occur more often for peacekeeping purposes or for the prevention of (and rehabilitation after) ecological disasters of various kinds. In these circumstances, the distinction between external and internal population displacement is a political one without demographic or sociological foundation.

Sociologists and demographers also recognize a distinction between movers and migrants. The difference depends on the duration of the move. As well as involving some consideration of distance and boundaries (whether those of a state or an administrative subdivision within a country), the difference depends on the duration of the move. Temporary movements are not regarded as migration. Somewhat arbitrarily, demographic convention regards movements across state boundaries for one year or more as 'migration', and those of a lesser duration as temporary movements. The same criterion is not normally applied to internal movements, although people commuting daily or periodically and others who travel for business or pleasure, later returning to a fixed place of abode, are not defined as 'migrants'. Seasonal and other short-term movers may still qualify as external or internal migrants if they have their own place of abode and establish economic and social ties in the locations concerned. In considering the question of environmental disasters, the distinction between temporary and permanent movers is important. Life-threatening situations may call for the temporary evacuation of a population from an area that is overcome by a natural disaster or by some technological catastrophe such as a chemical spill, gas leak or nuclear fallout. However, if the population in question is allowed to return in a period of days, weeks, or even months, they do not qualify as environmental migrants or 'refugees'. Nevertheless, they may be in need of humanitarian assistance if they have lost their livelihood or if their homes have been destroyed.

Given the limitations of the UN Convention, it has been suggested that alternative concepts such as environmental migration or, in the case of those who have not crossed an international boundary, environmentally induced internal displacement might be more appropriate. If a new category of environmental refugees were to be recognized in international law, it would be designed to supplement present usage and not compromise the existing definition under the Convention. Those favouring an additional category emphasize that environmental refugees would have to be those *forced* to leave their homes and who had crossed an international border as a result (Suhrke and Visentin 1991; Trolldalen et al. 1992).

Following the distinctions made in the last chapter, proactive migrations induced by purely environmental considerations include movements of population in response to climatic conditions when these are not directly linked to economic needs and livelihood. Examples would include the summer homes of wealthier families retreating from the heat, or the winter movements of retirees and others in northern climates, who seek greater warmth and sun in the south. Reactive migrations, exclusively in response to environmental factors, include the flight from earthquakes, volcanoes, floods, and other 'natural' disasters where these could not have been predicted. As scientific knowledge of the factors likely to cause these geophysical catastrophes increases, it is impossible to separate purely environmental causes from economic and political questions. By anticipating possible disasters and taking appropriate precautions, it is possible to save lives and avoid the necessity for reactive migration. The building of dikes and dams, the application of strict building standards and the introduction of emergency procedures (including temporary evacuation) may reduce the necessity for permanent environmental refugee movements.

Many of the environmental influences associated with both proactive and reactive movements are inseparable from political determinants. What Kunz (1973) calls 'anticipatory refugee' movements may result from a recognition of the potential environmental disasters induced by war or terrorist activity, such as bombing dams or setting fire to oil wells. It is hard to separate such proactive movements from the acute reactive migration that occurs after such events. The use of defoliants and scorched earth tactics by armed forces may have devastating and long-lasting consequences for the environment. Political and economic considerations may also determine whether adequate precautionary measures are taken in anticipation of earthquakes or other natural disasters. Failure to do so may generate an environmental refugee movement. Although the direct cause of a migration may be famine or drought, civil wars or other political upheavals may contribute to the crisis by preventing the planting of crops, the transport of water, or the supply of emergency aid. As Suhrke (1992:28) notes, when environmental degradation leads to migration, it is generally a proximate cause linked to questions of economic growth, poverty, population pressure, and political conflict.

When environmental factors are combined with economic considerations and earning a livelihood, proactive migration includes the hunting and trapping lifestyles of Aboriginal populations in various parts of the world, including the Arctic and some tropical regions in Africa and South America. Migration is also typical of pastoral and 'slash and burn' subsistence economies. Seasonal factors play an important part as well as the necessity of following the trail of migrating animals and fish. Reactive migration under these circumstances occurs when diminishing natural resources threaten the livelihood of the populations concerned. Such resource depletion may occur under natural conditions, but it is now often induced by environmental pollution or commercial and industrial practices that destroy the resources Aboriginal populations have traditionally relied upon, thus giving rise to environmental refugee movements.

Another example of proactive migration related to environment and economic determinants is that of gypsies, peddlers, and trading communities carrying supplies of raw materials or artefacts to remote destinations where these products are not available. Classical examples were the caravans that carried silk, spices, and other Oriental goods from Asia to Europe in return for gold or manufactured goods. Modern methods of transportation have made such migrations anachronistic. The jet-flying traders and executives of the twentieth century are proactive movers who may spend more time in airports and hotels than at home, but they do not qualify as migrants. The reactive equivalent would be gypsies who are refused permission to stay in a particular location or country and are subject to coercive expulsion. Other examples include asylum applicants escaping natural disasters who are refused admission to other countries on the grounds that they do not meet the Convention definition of a refugee.

Social and environmental factors interact to facilitate proactive as well as reactive migration. Examples of the former include migration to reunite families or maintain communities with strong linguistic or religious ties. The desire to preserve a particular lifestyle or begin a new life in communes, cooperative ventures, and the like may result in proactive migration. The environmental influence may be present as either a push or a pull factor or some combination of both. Gradual environmental deterioration, soil erosion etc., may initially lead to proactive migration, but eventually result in reactive movements as the process of degradation accelerates. Reactive migration that combines environmental and social determinants occurs when whole communities are forced to move as a consequence of environmental degradation or disaster and re-establish in a new location.

Environmental factors may combine with biopsychological factors to induce migration. Proactive examples include migration to health spas or movements of people deliberately seeking rural communities or isolation from noisy or stressful situations likely to affect their physical or mental health. Reactive migration under these conditions would include escape from plagues, epidemics, pollution, and other health hazards. Environmental disasters such as hazardous radiation or chemical contamination of the air or soil result in environmental refugee movements of this kind.

Systems model

It is necessary to go beyond a descriptive typology of environmental reactive migration (whether or not defined as a 'refugee' movement) and to understand the dynamic interaction of multivariate causal factors that are likely to generate such population movements. This involves a definition of predisposing conditions, structural constraints, facilitating factors, and precipitating events. It also requires some examination of the feedback effects of environmental reactive migration on the national and the global system. Positive effects (i.e., those that exacerbate and accelerate reactive migration) include conflicts related to the environment and access to resources. Negative, or mitigating feedback, reducing the damaging effects of acute reactive migration, include measures such as emergency aid and humanitarian intervention by governmental and non-governmental agencies. Immediate and long-term policy responses, including preventive measures, must be considered.

Predisposing factors include geophysical conditions over which there is no control, although advancing scientific knowledge may make some contingency planning possible. Examples are research on geological fault lines, volcanic conditions, atmospheric, oceanic, and meteorological studies. The possibility of predicting catastrophic events and measuring their probable strength provides a basis for early warning and the prevention of disaster. However, scientific knowledge in these fields is far from reaching a point where a total elimination of all potential hazards is possible. Unfortunately, technological developments may themselves create predisposing conditions that have potentially disastrous consequences. Obvious examples are the long-term consequences of global warming and/or damage to the ozone layer. There are other human interventions in the environment such as industrial pollution, waste disposal, and deforestation, which contribute to ecological damage, place this planet under stress, and predispose reactive migration (Mungall and McLaren 1990).

Figure 4.1 Typology of environmentally related disasters

Naturally induced disasters

Hurricanes	Tornadoes	Whirlwinds
Earthquakes	Volcanic eruptions	Avalanches
Floods (freshwater)	Floods (salt water)	Hail and snowstorms
Fires	Electric storms	Lightning
Droughts	Famines	Plagues

Technologically induced disasters

Chemical	Nuclear	Oil spills
Pollution (air)	Pollution (water)	Pollution (soil)
Explosions	Building collapse	Railway or airplane crash
Dams (floods, etc.)	Mining accidents	Power cuts
Factory accidents	Soil exhaustion	Urban dereliction

Economically induced disasters

Deforestation	Crop failure	Fishery exhaustion
Mineral exhaustion	Species extinction	Human redundancy
Population clearances	Relocation	Structural adjustment

Politically induced disasters

War (external)	War (internal)	Terrorism
Apartheid	Ethnic cleansing	Holocaust
Exile	Persecution	Rights violations
Totalitarianism	Anarchy	Extremism/intolerance

Socially induced disasters

Ecological extremism	Animal rights activism	Green crusaders
Fanaticism	Excommunication	Jihad
Class war	Shunning	Boycott

Notwithstanding the predisposing factors increasing the probability of reactive migration, the environment may also limit the possibility of flight in some circumstances while facilitating it in others. Populations living in an earthquake zone, in the vicinity of a volcano or in a flood path, may have little opportunity to escape if they are surrounded by mountains or the sea. The very suddenness of the disaster may preclude effective escape or rescue measures. Under other circumstances, environmental conditions may render escape more feasible and survival more likely. The availability of natural shelter (as in caves), or the use of trees or other natural objects to cling to or shelter under, may facilitate flight and rescue. More gradual forms of environmental degradation may be recognized ahead of time and contribute to proactive rather than reactive migration.

Environmentally induced reactive migration generally occurs as a result of a precipitating event that may or may not have been preceded by some warning of the impending disaster. Figure 4.1 identifies some of the principal factors likely to precipitate reactive migration and that have direct or indirect environmental implications. They may be categorized as natural, technological, economic, social, and political. It is important to emphasize that they are not independent of each other but may be interactive and mutually aggravating. The political precipitants are closer to the legally defined Convention definition of a 'refugee', although they may also combine with other factors of an environmental type to produce reactive migration. For example, war almost invariably has deleterious environmental effects, destroying food supplies, contributing to crop failure, resource depletion, pollution, and damage to dikes, dams, bridges, and other technological controls used to restrain environmental hazards. Ironically, overzealous action by those who wish to protect the environment, save species, or proclaim animal rights may induce reactive migration when the livelihoods of those who have depended on resource exploitation are threatened by such campaigns. Examples are seal hunting, whaling, fishing, fur trapping, and forestry. Those working in these occupations may be compelled to move when the markets for their products collapse or when laws are passed forbidding or limiting their activity.

Other social and religious movements may induce migration that falls somewhere halfway on the scale between proactive and reactive. For example, fundamentalist or fanatical religious beliefs may lead to schisms or sectarian conflict, or to the routine division of communities (such as the Hutterites) with resulting migration of whole populations to new land. Other social and religiously related migrations may occur as a result of persecution and such practices as shunning, excommunication, religious wars (jihad), class conflicts, labour union disputes, etc. The environmental connection with the latter may be remote, although there may be indirect links through political movements, technological change, and economic pressures. Examples include conflict arising over oil in the Middle East, or the closing of coal mines in Britain. These cannot be completely separated from Islamic fundamentalism in the former case and socialist versus neoconservative ideologies in the latter. Both are connected to natural resource consumption and depletion.

Figure 4.1 also identifies some of the more obvious natural disasters likely to precipitate reactive migration over which human intervention can have little influence except to provide contingency planning and emergency response capability. More direct human responsibility is involved in technologically and economically induced disasters. These may sometimes appear to be 'natural' when, in reality, they are the result of previous actions such as the building of dams, the diverting of rivers, or the cutting of forests. Calculated risks are taken and cost-benefit analyses made when major projects, such as nuclear power, hydroelectricity, irrigation schemes, and the development of mines are involved. There is growing recognition of the need for environmental assessment before major projects are undertaken, with or without public funding. Population displacement, relocation, and compensation may be among the economic and social costs that must be

Figure 4.2 Environmentally related population movements—multivariate model

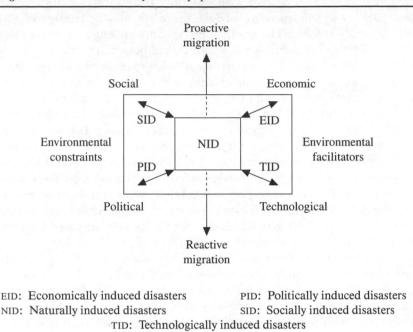

EID: Economically induced disasters   PID: Politically induced disasters
NID: Naturally induced disasters   SID: Socially induced disasters
              TID: Technologically induced disasters

considered. Past experience suggests that the consequent human trauma is often underestimated.

The interaction of economic determinants and environmental factors is evident in resource depletion and species extinction, as well as in unemployment, which comes with changing market conditions and technological change. At the Earth Summit conference in 1992 it was recognized that rapid population growth, poverty, and environmental degradation are closely related and may be exacerbated by the structural adjustment programs imposed on developing countries by banks and international agencies concerned with inflation control or loan repayments (George 1992). The export of raw materials and the exploitation of mineral or forestry resources may be the only way to deal with balance of payment crises and meet interest payments. The resulting environmental devastation may make reactive migration inevitable and add to urbanization trends that in turn cause pollution and problems of inadequate waste disposal (Homer-Dixon et al. 1993; UN Association of Canada 1991).

The complex interactive and multivariate nature of proactive and reactive migration related to environmental factors is illustrated in Figure 4.2. Social and economic determinants tend to be more closely linked to proactive movements, while political and technological factors are more likely to result in reactive migration. However, it must be emphasized that the proactive-reactive axis is a continuum, and that many large-scale population movements may fall between these extremes. Environmental conditions may predispose, enable, and precipitate migration, but also impose restrictions and constraints on population movements, thus determining their scale and direction.

System feedback

Proactive and reactive migration may be induced by the preventive measures designed to reduce the effects of environmental degradation or catastrophe, as well as the measures needed to clean up after disasters. As noted earlier, policies that aim to reduce environmental damage may affect the livelihoods of those who have depended on resource exploitation for employment. They are unlikely to induce sympathy or humanitarian aid for the movers, although some compensation may be demanded by corporations if their economic interests and contractual obligations have been adversely affected. Clean-up operations after environmental disasters may induce temporary in-migrations of personnel with equipment and expertise in such matters. There may be long delays before the original inhabitants or others can return to the area of the disaster.

Among the more serious feedback effects of environmental change is the possibility of violent conflict that occurs when population growth and movement result in competition for scarce resources. Further conflicts are generated when hitherto separate and potentially antagonistic ethnic groups are brought into close proximity as a result of environmentally induced migration. When resource scarcity and competition combine with nationalistic, racial, linguistic, or religious differences, the probability of overt conflict is increased.

Environmental issues as a source of violence

Researchers studying environmental change and acute conflict have identified various ways in which ecosystem vulnerability may combine with scarcity of renewable resources and political factors to generate acute conflict (Homer-Dixon et al. 1993). Internal and external migration may give rise to ethnic conflict, urban unrest, and weaken governments and promote insurgency. These factors, in turn, may exacerbate pressure on the environment by interrupting planting, causing crop failure, and destroying food or fuel supplies. Political, economic, and environmental forms of reactive migration may all increase as a result. China provides numerous examples of the interaction between population growth, industrialization, political conflict, and reactive migration linked to environmental change (Smil and Gladstone 1992). Other Asian and African countries experiencing growing pressure of population on the environment are facing rapid transformation of their political and economic systems. These countries could be a serious threat to global security if not given constructive aid. Recent examples of such menacing situations include Somalia and Cambodia where civil war and famine are combined threats. Despite the lip-service paid to environmental issues at the Earth Summit in 1992 (and in other forums such as the UN Conference on Environmental Development) Canada, the United States, and other countries are diverting external aid from developing countries to eastern Europe for economic, political, and strategic reasons. One of these is the perceived need to stem the flow of reactive migrants from eastern to western Europe. The result is likely to be greater pressure for migration from south to north, i.e., from Africa, Asia, and Latin America to North America and Europe.

The most critical conflicts arising from environmental factors are likely to be those related to land, water, and energy, including fossil fuels. Disputes over land rights have traditionally given rise to war and colonial conquest. As Fourth World (Aboriginal) populations and previously subjugated peoples seek their independence, issues of self-determination and sovereignty are major underlying, intervening, and precipitating causes of reactive migration. Attempts to gain control over territory lead to 'ethnic cleansing' and civil war, as well as attacks on neighbouring countries. Aboriginal populations seek redress for past deprivation and the right to control their own land and its resources, which could lead to the expulsion of those deemed not to belong to the ancestral community. Although violence is always a possible consequence of acute conflicts, comparative studies of environmental degradation in Africa, India, Thailand, and elsewhere led to the conclusion that 'environmental degradation, in so far as it causes displacement of people, is more likely to generate exploitation than acute conflict' (Suhrke 1992:31). This is because the populations concerned are likely to be weak and small in numbers relative to the surrounding communities. However, in the case of Bangladesh, the combined effects of population growth, movements of political refugees, pressure on land resources, and the trauma of flooding have exacerbated existing ethnic conflicts and contributed to violence (Hazarika 1993:45–63).

In many parts of the world, water has become a major source of conflict when combined with hydroelectric power, or projects that divert water supplies from one area to flood another. Once abundant sources of potable water are rendered scarce by pollution, dam building, and the diversion of rivers. Examples range from northern Quebec (James Bay) to the Hungary/ Slovakian region of the Danube, the Jordan river basin and megaprojects in Africa, Asia, and Latin America. Nearly all have resulted in significant population displacement and subsequent disputes (Gleick and Lowi 1992; Zmolek 1992).

Fossil fuels continue to be a source of acute conflict. Advanced industrial countries' dependence on cheap oil has created an arena in which superpower interests are directly affected by any threat to supply. Oil exploration, extraction, and transportation pose serious environmental hazards. Supply management and control over markets for oil is a potent source of economic and political conflict and has led to war in the Middle East and elsewhere. Developing countries rely heavily on the exploitation of forest products for export, while advanced industrial countries are faced with the necessity of finding alternatives to coal. All of these situations increase the probability of environmentally induced reactive migration.

Policy implications

The above analysis suggests a number of policy initiatives and programs that are needed at the international and state level. From an ecological perspective, better planning, irrigation, soil conservation, and reforestation are clearly essential. Collaborative efforts are also needed to deal with air and water pollution, ozone depletion, and global warming. A 1992 conference on migration and development identified a number of areas for policy development (IOM 1992). The emphasis was on organizational roles, relationships, and responsibilities, including the need for coordinating the many UN, other international, national, and non-governmental agencies involved that may have competing or contradictory interests (IOM:25–8). Other issues included defining state responsibility, developing a legal regime, identifying resources and mechanisms to respond to the needs of people forced to move, and long-range planning for sustainable environmental change. The human rights aspects of international migration and environmental refugee situation were emphasized and the need for new strategies of prevention and rehabilitation were urged (*International Migration* 1992:225–8).

Some additional questions arise. Firstly, it is clear that the present UN Convention relating to the Status of Refugees is not an appropriate instrument to deal with the needs of reactive migrants, particularly those whose external or internal displacement is directly or indirectly induced by environmental factors. There may be financial and politically expedient reasons for not attempting to amend the existing Convention and Protocol at this time. However, a new instrument may be necessary. This should address the humanitarian needs of all those displaced from their homes (whether or not they cross an international border) by circumstances beyond their control. Environmental factors should be one concern, although these may be linked to other economic, political, and social influences promoting reactive migration. Secondly, given that development aid and humanitarian effort are inevitably scarce resources, it may be necessary to develop a system of priorities in which weight is given to certain critical factors in order to measure the severity of a given threat. Early warning systems need to combine indicators of impending environmental disaster with concomitant political, economic, social, and biopsychological variables to determine the degree of urgency and scale of preventive and ameliorative measures required. Thirdly, there is a need for more effective coordination of effort by various UN and other agencies as well as an efficient targeting of assistance to the most acute areas of conflict and deprivation. Fourthly, the governments of developed and developing countries alike need to take a long-term view of resource utilization. The concept of sustainable development requires greater elaboration and specification. It must take into account the needs of sedentary and motile populations in the context of a postindustrial global society in which proactive migration will probably increase. Reactive migration should be rendered anachronistic as people are able to exercise greater freedom of choice and are not constrained by environmental or other conditions beyond their control.

Canada can take a leadership role in the development of international strategies to deal with environmental and migration issues. It could also serve as a role model for other countries, although this would require the reversal of some present tendencies. The private sector, including large companies and transnational corporations, must be prepared to assume a more responsible role in environmental conservation. Areas of particular geographic concern include:

1. The Arctic: The effects of pollution are already evident in the ecosystems of polar regions where PCBs and other industrial pollutants originating elsewhere are already at dangerous levels. Aboriginal communities dependent on the caribou, seals, whales, and fishing are already obliged to modify their traditional lifestyles. Military activity, oil spills, and mineral exploration are exacerbating a situation that could also be affected by global warming and damage to the ozone layer. Greater sensitivity to the environmental and human consequences of development in these regions is needed.

2. Northern Quebec: The James Bay hydroelectric scheme has already displaced Aboriginal populations and there is controversy over the compensation paid. The proposed Great Whale project (temporarily on hold) would have even more serious consequences, both to the environment and to the human and wildlife populations inhabiting the region. Although a feasibility study by Hydro-Quebec claimed that the impact on the atmosphere, fish, migratory birds, mammals, and vegetation would be minimal, it admitted that there will be negative consequences for the Cree who have traditionally hunted and fished in the area.

3. Western Canada (particularly the coastal region of British Columbia) is vulnerable to earthquakes. Greater efforts are needed to develop early warning systems, emergency measures, and preventive action to ensure building safety and shelter. The clear-cutting of forests is also causing serious environmental damage, and there are dangers of further oil spills from tankers.

4. The Great Lakes: The major issue here is pollution, although global

warming could also generate flooding. Improved emergency measures are needed.

5. Nuclear energy: The risks associated with the use of atomic generators in Canada may not be as great as at Three Mile Island or Chernobyl, but they cannot be ignored. There remain serious risks associated with the military and peaceful uses of nuclear energy. The disposal of nuclear waste is still an unsolved problem.

As the Norwegian delegate to the Helsinki Conference on Security and Cooperation proposed, we should transplant the concept of confidence and security-building measures, usually understood in strictly political and military terms, to the environment (Brett 1992:38). This would mean not only arms reduction and an end to the dumping of nuclear and chemical wastes but an active promotion of peace, security, and mutual cooperation. We worry about the toxic wastes we dump in our rivers and garbage landfills. We should also recognize the threatening consequences of arms proliferation. Trickle-down economics may not have worked well, but trickle-down munitions sales have turned the world into a huge bazaar for weapons deemed by the manufacturing countries to be surplus or technologically redundant. Arms production and sales are seen as the politicians' answer to economic recession. We have created a global garbage dump full of explosives ready to ignite at the slightest increase in political heat or ethnic conflict anywhere in the world. The weapons range from the handguns frightened citizens place under the counter or beside the bed at night, through high-velocity rifles and AK 47s, to weapons of mass destruction immensely more powerful than those used in the bombing of Hiroshima and Nagasaki. Delivery is possible by sea, land, or air, including short- and long-range missiles. Such weapons are now controlled by relatively small and politically unstable states. They could eventually get into the hands of unscrupulous politicians or terrorists determined to hold the world at ransom. The global refugee problem will never be solved as long as the militarization of the global economy continues. Any attempt to deal with root causes must address the issue of multilateral disarmament, as well as all the other factors contributing to reactive migration, including those related to the environment.

Notes

[1] This is a revised version of a paper presented at the meetings of the International Union for the Scientific Study of Population (IUSSP), held in Montreal, 24–31 August 1993. A slightly different version was published in *Population Bulletin* (1994).

[2] The Organization of African States and some Central American governments have adopted a broader definition of a refugee. This includes people who are compelled to move as a result of 'events seriously disturbing public order'. In principle, such a

definition might be interpreted to include those escaping environmental crises, although in practice it is unlikely that the governments concerned would recognize them as genuine refugees (IOM 1992:23).

[3] Using a very broad definition of an environmental refugee to include all those forced to move temporarily or permanently as a result of environmental disruption or degradation, the Worldwatch estimated the number as 10 million in 1988 (Jacobson 1988). Extrapolating from that figure, an IOM/Refugee Policy Group report suggested that as many as 1 billion may be displaced by the end of the century (IOM 1992:9). These estimates fail to recognize the complexity of reactive migration, its relation to other than environmental determinants, and the non-recognition of environmental refugees in international law.

chapter five

'Race' and urban violence

In an open democratic society, conflict is positively valued and rewarded as long as it is acted out within socially approved limits. Competition (academic, political, economic, sports, etc.) is encouraged and institutionalized. Only when resources are scarce and inequitably or unjustly distributed does such competition lead to disintegrative forms of conflict. Political dissent and opposition is encouraged as long as it is expressed through proper channels and protest is peaceful. Constructive conflict includes recognition of different needs and interests (individual and collective) and provides means for participation, negotiation, mediation, conciliation, arbitration, and settlement. Such mechanisms avoid the necessity for confrontation and violence. They are particularly important in a polyethnic, multiracial society.

Violence takes many forms, not all of which are necessarily unacceptable in contemporary Western societies. Some forms of violence are positively approved and encouraged, as in military ventures rationalized as 'just wars', or efforts that are meant to overthrow oppressive regimes. Violence is also acceptable in self-defence and in sports events (such as boxing, wrestling, hockey, football, hunting, and big-game fishing). The widespread possession and use of rifles, handguns, and automatic weapons in North America (and the persistent failure to legislate effective gun control) is evidence of the extent to which violence is condoned or positively promoted. There is also general approval of the use of violence by police or the army to deal with riots, vandalism, urban disorder, or unruly protests and to respond to terrorist threats. The violent imposition of law and order is not confined to totalitarian societies. The police are authorized to use all necessary means to apprehend a fleeing suspect, to subdue someone resisting arrest or apparently threatening others. However, the use of excessive violence by the police in the course of arrests has become contentious, particularly where allegations of racism are involved.

In considering questions of ethnic or racial violence, care must be taken to distinguish interpersonal violence from collective violence (Richmond 1976). Although not generally approved, interpersonal violence against women, gays, and visible minorities is endemic in Canada, as in other Western countries. This kind of victimization tends to be more frequent at times of economic recession, or when there are other factors undermining ontological security. A further distinction is necessary between violence perpetrated by a majority or its representatives (such as the police) towards a minority person, and the actions of minorities in retaliation or self-protection. In turn, these may differ from interethnic violence, in which one minority group is in violent confrontation with another. Sometimes this involves displacing hostility towards the majority or using another group as a scapegoat. Riots, disorders, or disturbances may involve one ethnic group attacking another, racist or antiracists attacking each other in a protest, or several groups uniting in opposition to the police.

Classical sociological theories do not throw much light on the origins of racial violence. A functionalist approach, which emphasizes the importance of consensus on shared values as the basis for social integration, leads to an examination of contradictory values or anomie and the failure of tension management techniques to improve community relations. Such an analysis defines violence as 'deviant behaviour' that must be corrected. There is a tendency to blame the victim, to represent the violence as hooliganism, and to emphasize the breakdown in family and community values. It leads to a diagnosis of a societal dilemma. Conservative politicians call for an enforcement of law and order, while the liberal response is to urge a restoration of confidence and a commitment to justice and equality (Myrdal 1944; Richmond 1988b; Rose et al. 1969).

Social exchange theories stress the role of individual and group competition, the exercise of rational choice, and cost-benefit assessments (Banton 1985). Some theorists have argued that violence as a strategy may actually pay by drawing public attention to problems and leading politicians to redirect resources to the areas affected. This institutional-structural perspective regards violence as rational, purposeful, and politically effective (Patel 1980). Such a view suggests that racial harmony is a public good that must be weighed against other priorities, and that violence is a legitimate strategy for minorities in a struggle for power and influence (Banton 1985).

Urban sociologists have approached the question in terms of city neighbourhoods and ecology, highlighting the effects of ethnic and racial segregation, poor housing, and squalid environments on the inhabitants, particularly young people facing high unemployment and poor prospects (Gurr and Graham 1989; Peach et al. 1986; Rex and Moore 1967). Absolute and relative deprivation, unrealized hopes and expectations, and frustration and disillusionment may lead to violence towards other groups, the police, property, and the symbols of authority.

Conflict models, based on Marxian or Weberian premises have also been used to account for racial tensions and violence, defining immigrants and minorities as a reserve army of labour. Such theories underline the importance of competition for scarce resources such as jobs, housing, educational opportunities, and social status (Cashmore and Troyna 1982; Clarke and Obler 1976; Gilroy 1982; Rex and Tomlinson 1979). Immigrants and other minorities are allocated to a perpetual underclass, experiencing high unemployment, low pay, and providing society with a pool of labour that can be called upon when needed and subsequently discarded. Violence in such a situation is seen as part of a class struggle, arising from the position of visible minorities in relations of production that are inherent in the capitalist system. As this system assumes global dimensions, the reserve army becomes worldwide. Advanced capitalist societies depend upon a supply of men and women from less developed countries to fill the unskilled labouring and service jobs. Although perceived as 'racial' because they involve 'Black' and Asian workers, such conflict and the violence associated with it is regarded as an inevitable outcome of class struggles (Miles 1987).

In a pioneer study of violence in American cities, Lieberson and Silverman (1965) distinguished 'underlying conditions' and 'precipitating events', but this distinction fails to take into account a variety of intervening variables that may determine whether certain events actually lead to violence or may be contained or channelled in other directions. Waddington et al. (1989, 1992) emphasize the significance of flashpoints in precipitating public disorder, recognizing that these occur in a context that includes structural, political, cultural, and situational determinants. It is also important to recognize the effects of social policies (or the lack of them), which serve as feedback mechanisms that either exacerbate the conflict or reduce the potential for violence. In a simplified form the model is represented in Figure 5.1.

Underlying conditions

Global conditions and external conflicts (wars and civil conflicts in other countries) can influence the incidence of domestic conflict, particularly in a polyethnic/multiracial society where international conflicts may have repercussions upon immigrant minorities or particular ethnic groups whose countries of origin are parties to the conflict. Latent animosities

Figure 5.1 Systems models of ethnic violence

Underlying conditions (global and national)
    External conflicts
    Demographic change
    Economic conditions
    Political relations
    Institutional forms
    Cultural characteristics
    Sociopsychological factors

Intervening variables (provincial and local)
    Demographic
    Economic
    Political
    Institutional
    Cultural
    Sociopsychological

Precipitating events (flashpoints)
    Individual
    Collective
    Symbolic

Policy responses
    Short term
    Long term

Feedback
    Positive (exacerbating conflict)
    Negative (containing and reducing conflict)

whose historical roots go back more than one generation may flare up under these conditions.

Demographic factors may contribute to heightened racial conflict and tension under certain conditions, although their importance can be exaggerated. Often a perception of demographic pressure is more important than actual population change. Rapid population growth as a result of natural increase or net migration can put pressure on scarce resources such as food, housing, jobs, and social services. If one ethnic/racial group is believed to be growing more rapidly than others (through higher fertility or immigration rates) this may generate hostility towards that minority. However, selective immigration controls based on race or ethnicity may simply exacerbate any existing tendency to regard the minority in question as 'different' or 'inferior'.

Other demographic factors that may be influential include the geographic distribution of ethnic/racial groups in the society concerned. Where there is a historic link between a particular territory and a certain group that lays claim to it (whether or not the group in question still occupies that territory exclusively), ethnic nationalism and political activism may at times become violent. This is most likely to occur when the legitimate claims of minorities conflict with those of a conquering or occupying power (governmental or corporate) that wishes to exploit the resources of that territory. If claims are ignored or their settlement delayed by prolonged judicial proceedings, patience may be exhausted and violence can ensue. Such a territorial claim is unlikely to arise in the case of immigrant minorities. Immigrants or indigenous ethnic-racial minorities without territorial claims are faced with contradictory forces. When given a choice, many minorities prefer some degree of geographic and residential concentration to create ethnic community facilities, generate a voting base, promote family reunion, and provide support services. However, such relative concentration must be voluntary. If it results from perceived prejudices or explicit discrimination in the housing market or the community at large, it is more conducive to resentment and likely to give rise to conflict.

Economic factors are those most often cited as predisposing ones in conflicts. Extreme poverty may induce apathy, but a sense of relative deprivation or raised expectations that are not fulfilled is often an underlying condition (Gurr 1970; Richmond 1976). Entrenched inequalities between one ethnic-racial group and another are usually associated with lack of educational opportunities and a cycle of poverty persisting from one generation to another. This, in turn, generates a self-fulfilling expectation on the part of dominant groups that the minority lacks the skills, motivation, or ability to perform anything other than menial tasks. At times of economic growth and labour shortages these prejudices may be overcome and special efforts made to hire minorities, but the reverse may occur at times of economic recession or 'stagflation'. Chronic unemployment among minorities, especially youth, provides fertile ground for violent conflict.

Economic insecurity may be accompanied by political conditions that are threatening to the majority or the minorities concerned. Reference has been made to external conflicts and their possible domestic implications, but internal political disputes between 'charter groups' (founding peoples) or between such groups and indigenous populations may degenerate to the point where violent rather than peaceful means of resolution are adopted. When violent means are adopted by one group, there is a 'demonstration' effect that may lead others to conclude that such tactics are appropriate for them too.

Sociocultural conditions are among the underlying factors in any society that may contribute directly or indirectly to conflict. The role of violence depicted in the media, films, TV, and video games is controversial, although there is evidence that a minority may become conditioned to violence and prone to copycat crimes (Paik 1991; Sparks 1992.) Dominant value systems are often created or reinforced by the media. When such values emphasize masculinity, assertiveness, or competition (macho values) and condone violence, they contribute to a potentially violent climate if explosives and guns or other weapons are readily accessible. In such a situation, minor disputes may escalate into major confrontations. Terrorist activities remain clearly outlawed, but a philosophy in which ends justify the means (as in the resolution of international disputes) may encourage minorities to believe that such activities can be justified in their case. Violence may be the means of drawing attention to minority grievances or used as a bargaining factor in negotiations.

Psychological factors are closely related to sociocultural conditions and are mediated through the socialization and learning experiences of children and adults. An authoritarian upbringing by itself may not breed prejudice, but numerous studies have shown that there is a relationship between authoritarianism, conservatism, status insecurity, intolerance of ambiguity, alienation, and the propensity to express racial prejudice and practise discrimination. (A number of situational determinants must also be present before these personality factors are outwardly expressed.) It follows that some societies (and some individuals and groups within a society) may have a greater propensity to resolve their frustrations through scapegoating or be more inclined to join extremist organizations.

Intervening variables

The boundary between underlying conditions and intervening variables is not hard and fast. For purposes of this analysis, the underlying conditions are assumed to be those prevailing at the global and national level (although not necessarily uniformly or at all times). Intervening factors are generally those found at the regional or local level, more often understood as situational. The term 'situational' has both geographic and temporal significance. From a policy perspective such factors may be more immediately capable of direct intervention, control, or change than the 'underlying conditions'.

Local and immediate demographic changes may or may not reflect national or longer-term trends. If a particular 'visible minority' is believed to be rapidly increasing in numbers, and if this also appears to cause increasing competition for housing, jobs, schooling, and welfare services, the result may be an increase in ethnic tension (although not necessarily in its violent expression). Intervening factors that have been associated in the past with outbreaks of violence include a sudden upsurge in youth unemployment (among majority, minority, or both), perceived competition for places in public housing, the allocation of places in schools or colleges, the desegregation of public transportation, bars, restaurants, and the busing of children to schools in a different ethnic neighbourhood.

The extent of institutional discrimination against minorities varies by region, locality, and institutional sphere. The extent to which ethnic/racial groups have access to resources and representation in the political decision-making process is critical. Feelings of exclusion and powerlessness are highly conducive to pent-up frustration, which in turn can lead to aggressive behaviour directed towards others. In this connection the presence or absence of credible and trusted leaders capable of representing minorities and articulating their claims is important.

Among other situational determinants are those relating to particular institutional contexts and subcultures, such as those found in neighbourhoods, schools, colleges, and workplaces. A hegemonic culture and dominant value system that ignores the ethnic diversity of the population concerned may alienate minorities and add to frustration. When the media fail to reflect local ethnic community diversity in newscasts, advertisements, or entertainment, or when they actually denigrate the group in question, there is a greater potential for violence. More specific factors may include the availability of hate literature, hostile tape recordings, telephone messages, T-shirts, and video games targeting particular groups as victims. The role of neofascist groups in deliberately spreading hate messages and provoking violence is critical.

Other intervening variables related to prevailing subcultural conditions are those in which it is possible for organized crime, prostitution, drug rings, smugglers (of cigarettes, alcohol, drugs, guns, and people) to perpetrate violence.

Precipitating events

The analytic model proposed is a probabilistic one. None of the underlying conditions or intervening variables by themselves constitute a necessary or sufficient cause of violence. However, the probability of a violent incident occurring, or of a single incident leading to a sequence of violent events, is greatly increased when one or more of the underlying conditions is combined with particular situational determinants. The cumulative and multiplicative effects create the flashpoint conditions that only require a sometimes apparently trivial precipitating event to ignite (Waddington et al. 1989).

Precipitating events can be individual actions, various types of collective behaviour, or symbolic phenomena. In some cases a combination of these is involved as, for example, when a crowd incites an individual to burn a flag, which then starts a riot. Individual acts of violence often spark a collective response. Thus a homicide involving a minority group member could be the result of a bar brawl, a traffic accident, police overreaction to a threatening situation, or a deliberately racial attack. Rape and other assaults, whether intended to be racial or not, may also lead to further violence. The way in which such an incident is perceived by others, particularly members of the victim's own group, may be critical in determining the outcome.

Crowd behaviour may also be a precipitating event, particularly when levels of excitement are enhanced by alcohol consumption. Football (soccer) matches in Europe and other sports in North America have been associated with a high degree of violence during and after the game. Street violence is often accompanied by looting and a general relaxation of inhibitions against theft, arson, and other forms of destructive behaviour induced by the anonymity afforded by the crowd. The homes and stores of particular ethnic minorities may be targeted for arson attacks or trashed by hostile crowds or organized groups.

Certain symbols are highly evocative of group pride and self-esteem. They assume a 'sacred' status in the eyes of the group. Attacks on these symbols are not only a form of violence in themselves but are likely to precipitate retaliatory action. Examples include desecration of burial grounds, cross and effigy burning, graffiti on churches and temples, together with flag trampling, burning, etc.

In a democratic society, peaceful protest against injustice and demonstrations for or against specific political parties or programs are legal and appropriate. However, when ideological opposition is strong and extremists become involved, such events may be disrupted or otherwise become the precipitating cause of violence. The listing in Figure 5.2 summarizes the forms of minority protest and majority response that have been experienced in Canada and elsewhere. In the section on policy responses and their feedback effects, the question of their effectiveness in preventing or containing violence will be considered. An elaborated version of the systems model is shown in Figure 5.3. It incorporates what Habermas (1976:68–75) calls a 'legitimation crisis' into the sequence of events. When constitutional and democratic means fail to redress grievances, minority alienation leads to more violent forms of protest. In turn, this contributes to more repressive action by governments faced with an obligation to maintain public order (Richmond 1988c:5–8).

Policy responses

Precipitating events or flashpoints that in some circumstances might easily lead to widespread urban disorders may under other conditions produce fairly peaceful demonstrations. Protest may be channelled through institutions and agencies that provide an opportunity for minorities to be heard. Although authorities may often be slow to respond and the recommendations of advisory bodies not always acted upon, such measures may successfully defuse the situations in question. However, in the long run, such tension management strategies may be self-defeating. Expectations are created that lead to greater frustration if they are not fulfilled. The minorities concerned may decide they cannot wait indefinitely for society to ensure that justice is done, discrimination ended, and equality achieved. New leaders may emerge with a more militant agenda, demanding immediate action, using violent means if necessary. Dominant groups, in turn, may demand firmer action by authorities and the imposition of tougher law and order measures.

The role of the police as representatives of the dominant group is critical.

Figure 5.2 Forms of minority protest and majority response

	MINORITY PROTEST	MAJORITY RESPONSES
Constitutional	Voting	Delayed action
	Party lobbying	Promises
	Education	Policy statements
	Conferences	Commissions
	Negotiation	Investigative committees
	Judicial appeals	Legislation
		Judicial determinations
Non-violent	Civil disobedience	Inquiries
	Passive resistance	Police protection
	Strikes/boycotts	Community policing
	Conciliation	Mediation
	Pickets	Arbitration
	Marches	Surveillance
	Rallies	Limited arrests
	Demonstrations	Detentions
	Propaganda	Fines
	Media events	Censorship
	Blockades	Curfews
	Fasting	Bureaucracies
	Nude parades	Grants-in-aid
	SUICIDE	CO-OPTATION
Violent	Terrorism	Infiltration
	Hijacking	Provocation
	Arson/sabotage	SWAT teams
	Bombing	Military actions
	Murder	Mass arrests
	Assassination	Life imprisonments
	Mass killing	Corporal punishment
	Civil war	Torture
		'Disappearances'
		Suspend civil liberties

Depending upon the definition of their role as keepers of the peace or as enforcers of law and order, they may inhibit a propensity towards violence or, in an atmosphere of suspicion and mistrust, they become the catalyst, their actions serving as a principal precipitating event. There is a tendency for the police to stereotype particular ethnic minorities, associating illegal gambling with Aboriginals and Chinese, drug dealing with 'Blacks' or Latin Americans, extortion with Vietnamese, etc. When an organized sweep, or special surveillance of particular neighbourhoods is undertaken,

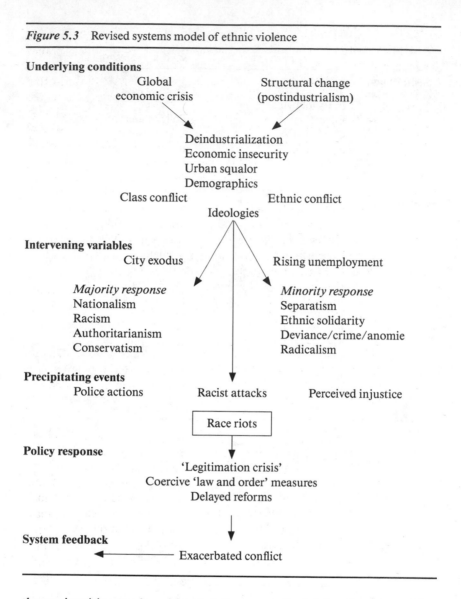

Figure 5.3 Revised systems model of ethnic violence

Underlying conditions

Global economic crisis

Structural change (postindustrialism)

Deindustrialization
Economic insecurity
Urban squalor
Demographics

Class conflict   Ethnic conflict
Ideologies

Intervening variables

City exodus   Rising unemployment

Majority response   *Minority response*
Nationalism   Separatism
Racism   Ethnic solidarity
Authoritarianism   Deviance/crime/anomie
Conservatism   Radicalism

Precipitating events

Police actions   Racist attacks   Perceived injustice

Race riots

Policy response

'Legitimation crisis'
Coercive 'law and order' measures
Delayed reforms

System feedback

Exacerbated conflict

these minorities may be subject to harassment. Social class factors combine with age, resulting in young (often male) members of 'visible minorities' appearing in court more often than their 'White' counterparts. When a reputation for frequent harassment of or brutality towards minorities occurs, even routine investigations and arrests may become occasions for onlookers to react violently. The same may be said of court hearings and sentences if these are perceived to be unjust.

The experience in various countries suggests that coercive responses to individual or collective violence are generally counterproductive. The use of a massive show of force involving police SWAT teams, or calling in the army and using confrontational tactics, including tanks and heavy armour, may quell a disturbance, but at great cost. There are costs in the allocation of resources to deal with the disturbance, loss of human life, and the trust that must eventually be re-established between the people involved and the wider community. A failure to respond to violent incidents at all, resulting in prolonged disorder, and an inability to protect the public from dissident elements, criminals, and extremists is also unproductive. Police and other authorities require specialized training and experience in order to respond to violence with a minimum of bloodshed. At the same time, the steps taken must leave opportunities for face-saving on both sides and open the way to negotiation, conciliation, mediation, arbitration, and cooperation. Community relations personnel may have something to learn from labour relations experts and conciliators in this regard. However, industrial disputes may be more confrontational when economic conditions are deteriorating and 'racial' minorities are blamed for taking the jobs of others.

Other responses by the police and judicial authorities that exacerbate conflict and perpetuate violence include framing arrested persons, beating prisoners, using excessive force in restraints, planting evidence against alleged perpetrators, taking punitive action against selected ringleaders who are treated as scapegoats, and blaming victims (e.g., dismissing riots as hooliganism and blaming lack of parental control). Official cover-up, bureaucratic buck-passing, token measures, media hype, and pious promises designed to disguise official inaction also serve to heighten dissatisfaction and increase tension.

The cost of dealing with ethnic/racial conflict and combatting violence competes with other policy priorities in the allocation of scarce community resources and tax dollars. At a time of fiscal restraint, budget cut-backs, deficit reduction, and anti-inflation measures, there is always a temptation to postpone action on all but those measures that are deemed to be most likely to win votes or please investors. Short-term palliative measures may be preferred to more expensive long-term programs. Education, social services, low-cost housing, employment equity, and community relations programs may be subject to severe financial constraints. There are practical limits to effective intervention strategies in a climate of 'stagflation', and one where there is little or no political will to act. Politicians, bureaucrats, and community leaders may be afraid of a backlash if they appear to be giving too high a priority to the needs and interests of minorities.

It is in just such a climate that minority leaders sometimes conclude that violence is their only effective weapon. Such action may be a last resort, or it may become a deliberate tactic designed to draw attention to their community's complaints when these have otherwise been neglected or given very low priority. The propensity of the media to cover violent events and to neglect more mundane activities such as peaceful negotiations means that the temptation to stage confrontations is very great. While sometimes achieving short-term attention, such a use of violence tends to exacerbate long-term conflict.

Effective policies and programs

Given the complex interactive nature of any social system, no single policy or program, no one type of intervention or preventive measure will guarantee that violent conflict will not occur. By the same token, a single response to a violent event or ongoing conflict will not resolve the issues once and for all. There have been numerous *ad hoc* measures in policy areas, such as immigration, multiculturalism, education, housing, urban renewal, employment, community relations, the judiciary, human rights, affirmative action, sensitivity training for managers, police recruitment and training, riot control, etc. Some of these have had a measure of success in the short term, but none has succeeded in eradicating the problem altogether (Glazer and Young 1983). The consensus is that most the programs have, in practice, been too little, too late. They have been underfunded, short-term, palliative measures that lack coordination and do not address the root causes. Another major criticism is that they are often paternalistic, imposed by outsiders without adequate consultation with the communities concerned.

Successful conflict resolution requires cross-cutting ties between communities, shared interests in common goals that transcend sectional interests, the development of security and trust, and a consensus on appropriate measures. It also requires active cooperation to increase jobs, housing, economic and social benefits, rather than a zero-sum competition for scarce resources. Government agencies need to work with voluntary agencies and corporations to achieve coordinated long-term programs in order to be more effective.

Minority political representation and participation in the decisions that affect them is a necessary precondition for non-violent conflict resolution. This is true for Aboriginal land claims, educational services, employment equity, and community relations. The question of police relations with ethnic minorities raises issues that go to the heart of democratic accountability and government by consent. Minorities must be represented in the police force at all ranks and on the boards that manage them. The use of police or the army to deal with protest reflects a legitimation crisis in which inequalities of power and status, class, and ethnic conflicts combine to undermine loyalty, creating contradictions that threaten social integration. When such conflicts result in violent protest by minorities and a coercive response by authorities, the moral basis of society and the integrity of the state are undermined. Only a comprehensive approach that addresses underlying conditions, intervening factors, and facilitates constructive responses to precipitating events will avoid a repetition of urban violence.

As a leading American sociologist, writing about the nature of power and conflict, stated, 'if social processes are indeed complex, so must be our models of these processes if we are to achieve our policy objectives . . . [and] . . . any policy recommendations we wish to make concerning how these processes may be modified or controlled. Otherwise we run the risk of making recommendations that, although they may seem on the face of it to make considerable sense, may do far more harm than good' (Blalock 1989:250–1).

part two

Comparative aspects

chapter six

Comparative perspectives on immigration and ethnicity[1]

It is a paradox that in the world today, some people remain exiles in the country of their birth, while others are at home on continents far away from their place of origin. Whole generations are born, live, and die in refugee camps. Aboriginal Fourth World populations do the same on reserves, occupying a minuscule part of the territory that their ancestors once roamed freely. At the same time, migrants settle in large cities, work temporarily in seasonal industries (while remitting their earnings to families they rarely see) or, as privileged entrepreneurs and managers, commute between the financial capitals of the world, whose skyscrapers and airports are hardly distinguishable from each other. Some of the people who live all their lives in one place feel alienated by the transformation of their once familiar, homogeneous neighbourhood into a vibrant polyethnic, multi-cultural, cosmopolitan metropolis. As sociologists we must ask who is adjusting to whom and to what. Once familiar concepts, such as accultura-tion, assimilation, and integration no longer make sense in a rapidly chang-ing world of satellite communications and global culture. Instead, the predominant mode of coaptation of migrants in postindustrial societies is one of active mobilization, defined as a 'dynamic interaction between motile individuals and collectivities giving rise to information flow and feed-back effecting greater control over material and human resources' (Richmond 1969:281). The dimensions of immigrant coaptation are also the dimensions of social survival for sedentary populations with whom the migrants interact. Movers and non-movers alike must respond to the endogenous and exogenous forces that are transforming local as well as global systems.

Dimensions of social survival

The term 'survival' is used deliberately to highlight the fact that the human race has at its disposal the capacity for individual and collective self-destruction. Drug addiction and epidemic diseases threaten rich and poor alike. A nuclear holocaust might not immediately kill everyone in the world, but it would create such environmental and genetic damage that human civilization would likely disappear. Other unnatural disasters could also have devastating effects. Global warming, the effects of pollution, changes in the atmosphere, inadequate waste management, destruction of the rain forests (or other non-renewable resources), all place our planet under stress and constitute 'the challenge of global change' (Mungall and McLaren 1990). 'Environmental refugees' and 'Green crusaders' must be added to the categories of international migrants (Homer-Dixon 1991). Sociologists who once treated so-called nation-states as closed systems must now address the reality of an interconnected global society, i.e., the world as a total system (Boulding 1989; Giddens 1985). As Robertson (1990a:22) argues, 'the systematic comprehension of the macrostructuration of world order is essential to any form of contemporary theory.'

Already we recognize the existence of an interdependent global economy in which information, goods, services, and money move relatively freely in what has been described as a 'borderless world' (Ohmae 1990). The goal of the so-called interlinked economy (in which multinational enterprises based in the United States, Japan, and Germany are the major players) may be a free movement of labour across borders, but this is far from having been achieved. On the contrary, immigration doors are closing and freedom of movement is limited for refugees and others. Regional economic communities, such as the European Union and the proposed US–Canada–Mexico free trade area, are facilitating movement within the region while more severely restricting access to it (Bean, Edmonston, and Passell 1990; Dowty 1987; Joly and Cohen 1989; Matas 1989). Nevertheless, international migration is an integral part of the world capitalist economy and the flow of refugees reflects the lack of political integration and instability of that system (Petras 1981; Zolberg 1989).

In such a global system, the dimensions of social survival are biological, economic, political, social, cultural, and psychological. Migration may be literally a matter of life and death for those escaping repressive regimes and violent situations. For the least fortunate, survival may mean exile, homelessness, scraping a livelihood by begging, or relying on food banks or international humanitarian aid. Others become members of an underclass of temporary migrant workers or a middle class of transilient professionals, while the economically successful business-class immigrants transfer millions of dollars for investment from one country to another. In other words, immigrants are part of a global system of social stratification and ethclass conflict.[2] Consequent upon the effects of postindustrialism, that system is undergoing major structural changes that have important consequences for external migration. There is a new international division of labour and a balance of economic power that no longer necessarily favours the formerly dominant Euro-American axis.

Postindustrialism and structural change

The postindustrial revolution associated with advanced technologies in communication, transportation, automation, and 'fourth-generation' computerization is an acceleration of trends that go back to the beginning of the Industrial Revolution itself (Kumar 1978). What is new is the redistribution of power and the restructuring of the global economy that this entails. Western Europe and North America are experiencing a process of deindustrialization with the relocation of many manufacturing operations to low-wage regions of Asia and Central America. New modes of production are being created through satellite communications, information processing, and computer-linked financial networks. The number of people employed in tertiary and quaternary sectors of industry has increased steadily in the last quarter of the twentieth century. Agricultural employment has declined steadily in absolute and relative terms, while the service sector has expanded everywhere.

In ten advanced industrial countries, employment in services doubled and the share of total employment rose to two-thirds by 1990 (Akyeampong and Winters 1993). However, these sectors are themselves segmented and stratified. Immigrants and temporary workers (including undocumented and illegal migrants) are an important part of this restructuring process. This is determined by controls exercised over immigration by the receiving country, and by a combination of demographic and economic conditions that create a demand for particular types of labour and human capital (Stahl 1988). A process of segmented structural change occurs in which immigrants are differentially incorporated into both the rapidly growing and declining sectors of industry. Canada provides an interesting case-study in this respect.[3] Similar trends are evident in other traditional immigrant-receiving countries as well as those (such as Germany) that have admitted large numbers of guest workers and asylum applicants, but who do not regard themselves as countries of immigration in the same way as those in the 'New World' (Freeman 1992). The main regions of birth of the 4.5 million immigrants in Canada in 1991 are shown in Table 21 and Figure 6.1.

Figure 6.1 Canada, 1991, birthplace of immigrants

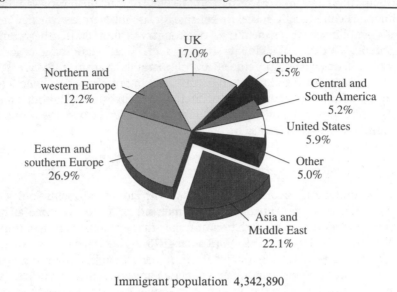

Immigrant population 4,342,890

SOURCE: Census of Canada, 1991

Immigrants in global cities

An almost universal characteristic of immigrants in the contemporary world system is that they live and work in the major metropolitan areas and 'global cities' that are part of the interlinked economy and the world system.[4] The concept of a 'world city' was first suggested as early as 1915 by Patrick Geddes, a Scottish pioneer of urban planning. Such cities function as hubs of economic activity, centres of communication, transportation meeting points, and cultural nodes. The idea was further developed by Lewis Mumford (1938:295–6), who recognized that, in order to function effectively, a 'world city' required a world order. However, both these idealists were appalled by the squalor and congestion that already characterized the megalopolis.

The conditions have been exacerbated in Third World countries by the urbanization that has occurred since that time. Today, Mexico City has a population of over 25 million, São Paulo 22 million, and Calcutta nearly 16 million. There is now a world city hierarchy that reflects the multicentred core and peripheral regions of the global economy (King 1990). The major metropolitan areas of the more advanced postindustrial societies are the control centres of the global economic system (Sassen 1988; Sassen-Koob 1986). As such, they serve as a magnet for immigrants ranging from itinerant capitalist investors and managers of multinational corporations, through transilient professionals, educators, and technicians, to temporary and permanent migrants who provide the less well-paid services necessary to sustain the system. Cities, such as New York, London (England), and Toronto, reflect in microcosm the stratification of the global capitalist system and the class relations within it (Ross and Trachte 1990:148–71).

In major metropolitan areas, the rich and poor of all nationalities, races, and religions are brought together, although not necessarily into close primary-group relations. Global inequalities tend to be reflected in the spatial relations within world cities, which are often more closely integrated into the global system than with the region or state in which they are located (King 1990:145; Sassen 1988, 1991). The social ecology of metropolitan areas has been profoundly influenced by international migration. Varying degrees of ethnic residential segregation are typical. The relative concentration of immigrants and their descendants in particular neighbourhoods need not necessarily be equated with ghettoization. The latter implies involuntary isolation, together with economic exploitation and social exclusion. This may occur in the case of some immigrant minorities, particularly where racial or religious characteristics contribute to a high degree of visibility, and when the latter is associated with low education and a cycle of unemployment and poverty.

However, even when immigrant socio-economic status is high, there may be preference for neighbourhoods that, while exhibiting heterogeneity and ethnic diversity, provide an opportunity to maintain social networks based on family, kinship, and ethnic ties. As the absolute numbers of immigrants from particular countries and world regions increase, so does the possibility of creating institutions to serve these populations. Cities in Australia, Britain, Canada, and elsewhere that were once dominated architecturally by church spires now have synagogues, mosques, and Buddhist temples alongside office towers and suburban shopping malls. The goods and services provided in the malls reflect the ethnic heterogeneity of the populations they serve (Richmond 1988c:57). Ethnic schools, newspapers, credit unions, theatres, social clubs, travel agents, doctors, lawyers, accountants, architects, real estate agents, and social workers contribute to the institutional completeness of the city populations.

The metropolitan areas of Canada are typical of the heterogeneity and institutional completeness characteristic of global cities in many parts of the world. Inner and outer suburbs have grown rapidly as a result of immigration and internal migration, while the populations of the city centres have declined in the face of massive office development. Ethnic diversity indexes for fourteen metropolitan areas in 1981 ranged from 0.41 to 0.83 and mean segregation indexes from 0.253 to 0.574. When the socio-economic status of census tracts was controlled (for Montreal and Toronto), mean segregation indexes ranged from a high of 0.825 for Scandinavians in poorer areas of Montreal to 0.299 for British in the high-status areas of Toronto. However, even in the higher socio-economic status areas, the mean segregation index was 0.458 in Montreal and 0.376 in Toronto (Balakrishnan and Selvanathan 1990).

Survey data concerning participation in ethnic-related activities in Toronto support the conclusions based upon measures of ethnic residential segregation. Kalbach (1990:132-3) determined that the classical assimilation model only applied to the British and northwest European groups. Other ethnic minorities retain a high degree of residential concentration and ethnic involvement into the second and third generations. This raises some critical questions concerning the nature of ethnic identity and the potential for social conflict in metropolitan areas with a high proportion of immigrants.

Ethnic identity and social conflict

The cities in which most immigrants live are cosmopolitan, multiracial, polyethnic, culturally plural, religiously diverse, and polyglot. The experiences of Australia, Britain, and Canada are similar to that of the United States in that 'the most important division is between whites and non-European groups such as Blacks and Hispanics, as well as peoples from Asia, Latin America and the Caribbean' (Lieberson and Waters 1988:247). As in the United States, there has been considerable intermarriage between European-origin groups in Canada, giving rise to multiple ethnic ancestry (Krotki and Odinak 1990). However, this has not created a melting-pot so much as a process of ethnic flux in which ethnicity assumes varying forms and different subjective meanings over time and according to generation and various situational determinants (Krotki and Odinak 251-3).

Based on European-origin groups in Toronto, Isajiw (1990:87-8) identified five different forms or dimensions of identity retention that may persist singly or in combination. They are ritual and symbolic, marriage and friendship, social participation, language, and group support. To these should be added racialization and religious restructuration. The latter are important bases of ethnic identity formation and change for many 'Black' and Asian immigrants and their descendants (McLellan 1987; Nagata 1985).

The most serious manifestations of ethnic conflict in contemporary post-industrial societies do not arise from immigration. They are the result of long-standing grievances and feelings of deprivation or oppression experienced by indigenous populations. Aboriginal peoples, linguistic minorities, religious groups, and marginalized populations who have historic claims to particular territories seek power for themselves. Such ethnic minorities may have harboured nationalistic aspirations for political autonomy and self-determination over several generations. Examples include the Irish, Basques, Croatians, Serbs, Armenians, Kurds, Palestinians, Quebecois, Sikhs, Tamils, 'Blacks' in South Africa, and Aboriginal peoples in Canada and Australia. However, these long-standing ethnic conflicts may spill over into immigrant- and refugee-receiving societies through the networks connecting them with the countries of origin, which are facilitated by modern mass communications and transportation. In immigrant-receiving countries (such as the United States, Australia, and Canada), Arabs and Jews, Armenians and Turks, Kurds and Iraqis, Sikhs and Hindus, Vietnamese and Chinese, Irish Protestants and Catholics, Serbs and Croats, all must live together while agonizing over the fate of their friends and close relatives in their former countries. Furthermore, these ethnic tensions are played out symbolically and sometimes realistically in the immigrant communities. Terrorism has become a global phenomenon through which local conflicts have become internationalized. The worldwide arms trade and the involvement of superpowers in regional struggles and civil wars further exacerbate conflict and directly affect expatriate communities everywhere (Intriligator and Brito 1990:380).

Other types of ethnic conflict arise more directly from immigration, particularly when the immigrants and their immediate descendants face systemic barriers to full incorporation, economic opportunity, and social acceptance. Racism persists in most contemporary societies, even those that have adopted human rights codes and official policies of multiculturalism. It may take a covert form as privately expressed prejudice and subtle avoidance, or more public manifestations of harassment, abuse, racial hatred, and violence. The incidence of all of these has increased recently. The experiences of Britain, Canada, the United States, and Germany suggest some common denominators and significant differences in terms of the incidence of violence and community responses to it.

Race and urban violence

In Canada, as in other countries, racism ranges from stereotyping and prejudice, through explicit discrimination in the labour force, to violent confrontations between the police and 'Black' youth. It finds its way symbolically into litigation over the right of Sikhs to wear a turban or a *kirpan*, or the use of the classroom and the telephone to spread neo-Nazi propaganda. Institutionalized discrimination in hiring and promotion may not be effectively removed, despite employment equity and affirmative action programs. Precipitating events, such as police brutality, painting of swastikas on a synagogue, or the threatened desecration of an Aboriginal burial ground, lead to collective violence and/or organized protest. Such situations are frequently dealt with by a reflexive insistence upon maintaining law and order, using coercive measures that further inflame the situation (Reitz 1988; Richmond 1988b, 1991). Alternatively, commissions are set up to investigate and report, although recommendations may be subsequently ignored or only selectively implemented. In Ontario, *The Report of the Race Relations and Policing Task Force* (Lewis 1989) cited studies conducted since 1974 whose recommendations had not been implemented. It made a further fifty-eight recommendations. Only a few of these had been adopted before more disturbances occurred in Toronto. These followed close on the heels of those in Los Angeles, which received considerable media attention in 1992. Another report on *Race Relations in Ontario* (Lewis 1992) noted that there was 'a strong perception that the implementation of its [the earlier report's] recommendations has slowed.' A reconstitution of the task force was recommended together with a series of further proposals ranging from a race relations audit for the police forces of Ontario, the setting up of a special investigation unit, improved training and limits on the use of force by the police, expediting employment equity programs, more effective antiracist programs for schools, improved access to trades and professions for immigrants and their children, and increased resources for community development, particularly in those areas with high concentrations of immigrants and visible minorities. Ironically, the report was submitted shortly before the provincial government entered into a major budget reduction exercise!

However, the overall incidence of violence in Canada, including cases that have a clear racial component, is much lower than in the United States. The rate of serious violent offences known to the police is five times higher in the United States than in Canada. The rates for Britain and Germany are also lower than those of the United States. One thing all four countries have in common is a trend in the past decade towards more crimes of violence and more individual acts of violence specifically directed at immigrants or other ethnic minorities. Racial and ethnic harassment is not a new phenomenon, but the number of reported cases in Britain and Germany has been rising. In the latter country, Turkish immigrants who were long-term residents were singled out. Attacks on homes and hostels resulted in some fatalities. Governments in several countries, including Britain, Germany, France, and Sweden, reacted to heightened racism by tightening immigration controls and threatening to deport illegal immigrants.

Postmodernism and global culture

The ethnic diversity of almost all postindustrial societies today raises the question whether equality of opportunity and the coaptation of immigrants with each other and with indigenous populations can be reconciled with the maintenance of separate identities and cultural pluralism. Is a harmonious coexistence of people with different linguistic, religious, and cultural characteristics possible? Will the process of globalization eventually lead to homogeneity or to the 'deterritorialization of cultures' and the persistence of heterogeneity? If the latter occurs, what will it mean in terms of societal integration? This is a debate that is currently being conducted among sociologists who are concerned with questions of modernity and postmodernity.[5]

The material and instrumental artefacts of postindustrial society are universal. In consumer markets, technology is clearly imposing homogeneity under the guise of choice within a market system, differentiated only by price. The same is true of defence spending and military procurement. Automobiles, tanks, airplanes, Scud missiles and Patriot interceptors, hamburgers and soft drinks, telecommunication systems, fax machines, remote control and heat-seeking devices, rockets and radar, televisions, computers, robots, and spy satellites recognize no frontiers. As O'Neill puts it:

> Nothing can be more curious than the annual flocking of American immigrants to their former homelands to discover the omnipresent toilet roll, toothpaste, central heating, hamburger, and Coca Cola signs for which their ancestors displaced themselves and with which they identify America as the ultimate trip. What is sad in all this is that the real history of immigrant labour and political refugees recedes into the background of canned cultures created for the international tourist who travels as nearly as possible with the same technosphere as he or she enjoys at home (O'Neill 1988a:20).

However, this is not the whole story. Two hundred years of industrialism and state formation (democratic and authoritarian) have failed to suppress the languages, religions, and aspirations for self-determination of ethnic minorities throughout the world. The non-material, expressive dimensions of ethnicity are not exclusively primordial, but they are profoundly related to identity and, as such, they are powerful motivators. They continue to dominate human consciousness, usurping the role that *class* was expected to play in the late stages of capitalism, according to classical Marxist theory. When socio-economic status and ethnicity come together in relations of economic and political domination, the resulting ethclass conflicts explode in violent confrontations on a global scale.

As Robertson (1990a:57) points out, 'National societies are increasingly exposed, internally, to problems of heterogeneity and diversity and, at the same time, are experiencing both external and internal pressures to reconstruct their collective identities along pluralistic lines.' There are competing reference points for individuals in terms of ethnicity, culture, and religion and the system of international relations is becoming more and more fluid and 'multipolar'. The United States, like many other countries, is ethnically stratified and culturally pluralistic and, as a conseqence, there is no single 'American way of life' into which immigrants must eventually be assimilated. The same is true for European and other receiving countries. Australia, Britain, and Canada are among those that have adopted educational and social policies that are specifically defined as 'multicultural'. However, there is much debate and uncertainty concerning what such policies and programs mean in practice (Bullivant 1981; Burnet 1987; Foster and Stockley 1988a and 1988b; Zubrzycki 1986). One critic has gone so far as to describe Canada as a case of 'mosaic madness' because, in his view, official bilingualism and multiculturalism have contributed to divisiveness, a lack of national unity, and no sense of common purpose (Bibby 1990). The possible secession of Quebec from the Canadian federation and the separatist tendencies evident in the western provinces lend some support to this view.

Citizenship and human rights

The ethnic diversity of contemporary cities/states and the existence of a global system of international migration raises fundamental questions concerning the meaning of citizenship. The UN Charter of Human Rights bestows the right to leave a country, but other states are not obligated to allow entry. In Roman times, citizenship was a privileged status accorded only to the imperial élites who could travel freely within that far-reaching domain. Everyone else was either captive, slave, or freeman with little say in the political arena and without the rights accorded to a citizen. Today, the franchise has been extended in many countries to women and those without property, but not to immigrants, refugees, or temporary workers. In some countries, citizenship is not even a birthright. It is denied to the adult children born to immigrants long resident in the receiving country. Germany is a case in point (Brubaker 1989; Hammar 1990a). More than civic rights are involved. Marshall (1965) pointed out that economic and social rights, such as education and income security, are implicit in the twentieth-century idea of democratic citizenship. Wexler (1990:164–75) argues that citizenship is an archaic term because society has changed since Marshall examined its relation to social class. Citizenship is built on rationality and solidarity, but these have disappeared in a postmodern society where 'the autonomous individual has been decomposed into a network of non-synchronous signs.' He concludes that 'semiotic citizenship' is possible through the collective reconstruction of shared individual life histories and the realization of new collective identities (Wexler 1990:173). One such collective identity must be a citizen of the world, the very survival of which depends upon our willingness to recognize our common humanity.[6]

The 1951 UN Convention on the Status of Refugees, as amended in 1967, is the only instrument available in international law to implement the right of movement. It is generally recognized as inadequate for present global realities. As noted by the president of the Commission on the Protection of Refugees in 1989, the circumstances under which the 1951 Convention was adopted no longer prevail, but efforts to adopt a convention on territorial asylum have failed. He stated that 'in a growing number of instances, refugees were not granted any status, be it refugee or any other status, by the Government concerned, and were merely tolerated as non-persons. This major problem called for international co-operation and not unilateral solutions—if refugees were not granted any status, they were frequently subject to exploitation or racial antagonism' (United Nations 1989:27).

It is not only those who can establish a well-founded fear of persecution who need the support of an international system for the protection and promotion of human rights. Other immigrants and temporary workers need protection too (Goodwin-Gill 1989). Not all countries have committed themselves to the UN Charter of Human Rights (1945); the Convention on the Elimination of all Forms of Racial Discrimination (1965); the International Covenant on Civil and Political Rights (1966); the Covenant on Economic, Social, and Cultural Rights (1966); the Convention on the Elimination of all Forms of Discrimination Against Women (1979). These instruments and other treaties commit their signatories to a broad range of policies designed to promote greater equality and justice within and between states. Among other things, they are designed to outlaw genocide, apartheid, racial discrimination, forced labour, and slavery. However, their full implementation remains to be achieved (Banton 1990).

The economically advanced countries of the world have welcomed temporary and permanent migrants (including refugees) when their own economies were in need of labour and skills, and imposed restrictions when economic and political conditions changed. Furthermore, the involvement of the superpowers in Third World conflicts (together with the actions of multinational companies, banks, and international agencies such as the International Monetary Fund in dealing with international debt) have contributed to the economic hardship and civil unrest that have precipitated refugee crises in various parts of the world. The fact that a large majority of the estimated 23 million refugees and displaced persons in the world today are of non-European ethnic origin raises the question of racism because of the inhospitable responses of developed countries.

It has been shown that there is an assault on freedom of movement and a closing of borders by the more advanced industrial countries of the world. In the name of state sovereignty, border control, and humane deterrence, we are placing more and more barriers in the way of the fundamental human right to leave a country where there is a well-founded fear of persecution or other serious threat to personal security and well-being. The global system is failing to provide temporary asylum or permanent refuge for the multitude of displaced persons who happen not to be regarded as culturally compatible or eligible for full citizenship and its associated civil rights. There is a danger of repeating the shameful record of the pre-war period when so many Jews were left to their fate in Nazi Germany. The economically developed countries are practising global apartheid through their restrictive immigration and refugee policies. The select few who are deemed admissible because their skills are needed are exposed to the prospect of further systemic discrimination, personal prejudice, and structured inequality when they attempt to settle in their new country. There has been a resurgence of domestic nationalism, racism, anti-Semitism, and ethnic conflict in Europe and North America. This does not augur well for the survival of immigrant populations or their neighbours in our global cities

(De Vos and Suarez-Orozco 1990; Richmond 1991a). However, it is not an adequate reason for closing borders or expelling long-term residents.

The global economic recession that began in the 1980s and continues through the 1990s generated profound insecurities. They were exacerbated by the collapse of communism in the Soviet Union and eastern Europe and the political turmoil that followed. When the huge differences in material standards between east and west, south and north are taken into consideration, it is obvious that the rich feel threatened and the poor envy the real or imagined wealth to be gained by escaping from their present state. Migratory pressure is the result of political, economic, and social factors that create a potential that is then impeded by lack of receptiveness in other countries. 'It is the dam against free flow of migration that creates migration pressure' (Straubhaar 1993). As the pressure builds, so does the possibility of violence, civil war, and a variety of clandestine movements to evade the obstacles placed in the way of moving. 'Illegal' migration, asylum applications that do not meet the Convention criteria for refugee status, the use of forged travel documents, stowing away or smuggling people across borders are all symptoms of disequilibrium. They are also a safety-valve without which many would be without hope. Such a despairing population is also a threat to peace and order, ready to respond to a call to arms by fervent nationalists and petty dictators. A vicious circle of reactive migration is thus created.

Notes

[1] This is a revised version of a working paper published by the Urban Institute, Washington, August 1991.

[2] For a fuller discussion of global ethclass conflict, see Chapter One.

[3] See Chapter Seven.

[4] Major metropolitan areas and 'megacities', such as Mexico City or Calcutta, are defined in terms of population size alone. A 'global city' is one that is also a centre of wealth and power connected through banking and stock exchange networks to the key financial institutions of the global economy.

[5] See Chapter Two.

[6] As Francis Bacon (1561-1626) expressed it (albeit in sexist language!), 'If a man be gracious and courteous to strangers, it shows he is a citizen of the world.'

chapter seven

Immigration and structural change:
The Canadian experience[1]

The economic and social systems of advanced industrial societies have undergone major structural changes in the last twenty years. These changes have a significant impact on the process of immigrant absorption. Among the most important effects are the growth of metropolitan areas, the improved level of education of the populations of sending and receiving societies, together with the transition from industrialism to post-industrialism. The latter is evident in the declining importance of the primary and secondary sectors of industry and the growth of the tertiary sectors, which include technologically advanced fields such as banking, finance, and information processing associated with computerization, as well as traditional service industries such as domestic employment, catering, etc. These economic and social changes have occurred simultaneously with demographic shifts from baby boom to baby bust, a consequent aging population, and a substantial increase in female labour force participation. In the case of Canada, the structural changes have also been accompanied by deliberate attempts to recruit well-qualified immigrants and a business class of entrepreneurs with capital to invest. At the same time, there has been an emphasis on family reunion and some refugee migration. There has been a substantial shift from traditional to non-traditional source countries.[2]

In the postwar period up to 1961, immigrants from Britain were the largest single source; those surviving constituted almost 22 per cent of that cohort in 1986. However, those of British origin were only 7.5 per cent of those who arrived in the mid-1980s. In 1988, they were less than 5 per cent of the total intake. Other traditional source countries in Europe now supply only 20 per cent of the total arrivals. Since 1962, the Asian populations have been the fastest growing. Almost three-quarters of Canada's annual immigration presently comes from Third World countries, with Asia, the Caribbean, and Latin America predominating. The composition of the Canadian population in 1986, by ethnic origin and period of immigration, is shown in Table 9.

Immigrants are not evenly distributed throughout the country. Postwar immigrants, as well as more recent arrivals, have gravitated to Canada's metropolitan centres, which are growing economically, while Canada's older established populations (the Canadian-born of Canadian parentage of largely British and French origin) are disproportionately represented in the rural and maritime hinterlands, where economic opportunities are limited.[3] In 1986, 15.6 per cent of the total population was foreign-born, but the average for twenty-five metropolitan census areas was 21.2 per cent. The proportion for Toronto was 36.3 per cent, about a quarter of whom arrived in the decade 1976–86. The 'Black' and Asian populations were even more highly concentrated in Montreal, Toronto, and Vancouver.

Among the changes in the last two decades in the characteristics of the immigrant population, the level of education is particularly important. Overall, 10 per cent of the Canadian population in 1986 had a university degree, 44.5 per cent a high school diploma or better, and 18.2 per cent had less than a grade nine education. Table 10 shows that there was considerable variation by age, sex, birthplace, and period of immigration. Among the foreign-born, males who arrived in the decade 1967–77 were the best educated—almost one in five had a degree. With a growing emphasis on family reunion and the admission of refugees, there has been a decline in the number and proportion of highly selected independent immigrants in the last decade. As a result, there is evidence of a less-well educated stream, especially among recently arrived women. However, even among the 1983–6 cohort, the level of education of males is generally above the Canadian average. In this category of immigrant women, there is some clustering at the highest and lowest ends of the scale.

Economic dimensions

In the first fifteen years after the Second World War (1946–61) the total labour force of Canada increased by 1.9 million and postwar immigration accounted for 42 per cent of that growth. In the following decade (1961–71) another 2.15 million workers were added, and net immigration accounted for 16.4 per cent of that growth. Between 1971 and 1981, net immigration accounted for 20 per cent of the growth of over 3.5 million, but in the next five years (1981–6) there was a slight decline in the number of immigrants in the labour force, despite the addition of approximately 175,000 workers who had immigrated in that period. This was a consequence of the remigration, retirement, and mortality of the earlier cohorts. By far the largest single source of growth in the labour force in recent years has been the participation rates of Canadian-born women, which on an age-standardized basis rose from 39 per cent in 1971 to 55.4 per cent in 1986—still slightly below that of immigrant women (57.8 per cent).

Structural change

Detailed analyses of 1971 census data led to the conclusion that no single theoretical model of immigrant adaptation and incorporation of the foreign-born into the economy could explain the complex distribution of immigrants in the industrial and occupational system of Canada (Richmond and Kalbach 1980; Richmond and Zubrzycki 1984). Functionalist theories, ethnic pluralism, class conflict, colonial and labour market segmentation models all received some support when partial and limited aspects of the phenomenon were considered. However, one aspect of the experience of immigrants between 1951 and 1971 was highlighted, that is, the influence of postindustrial development and structural changes taking place in the distribution of workers by industry. It was found that, generally speaking, immigrants avoided the declining primary sector and that an increasing proportion of those arriving before 1971 had entered the expanding secondary and tertiary sectors, lending support to a 'structural change' model of immigrant absorption. The various theoretical models of immigrant adaptation and occupational status are illustrated in Figure 7.1.[4]

In the fifteen years following 1971, the Canadian experience continued to support the importance of structural change, while at the same time reinforcing the conclusion that in order to arrive at even a 'rough approximation to the complex realities of immigration', no single theoretical perspective is adequate and that 'the institutional structures of receiving societies, already experiencing exogenous pressure to change and to respond to world-wide economic forces and technological innovations, react also to endogenous pressures which emanate from demographic sources'(Richmond and Zubrzycki 1984:133). Analyses of 1981 census data for Canada confirmed that no one model was adequate for explaining the occupational distribution of immigrants and their income levels. It was necessary to distinguish between the experience of those who came from traditional source countries and those who came from others, to differentiate between men and women, and to take into account the effect of length of residence and the auspices of immigration. Beaujot et al. (1988:88) noted that immigrants might include an American engineer recruited to work in a Canadian subsidiary, an Indo-Chinese refugee rescued from the boats leaving Vietnam and a teacher who arrived from the Netherlands as a very young child some thirty years ago.' No one theory could explain the experiences of all.

Figure 7.1 Models of migration and occupational status

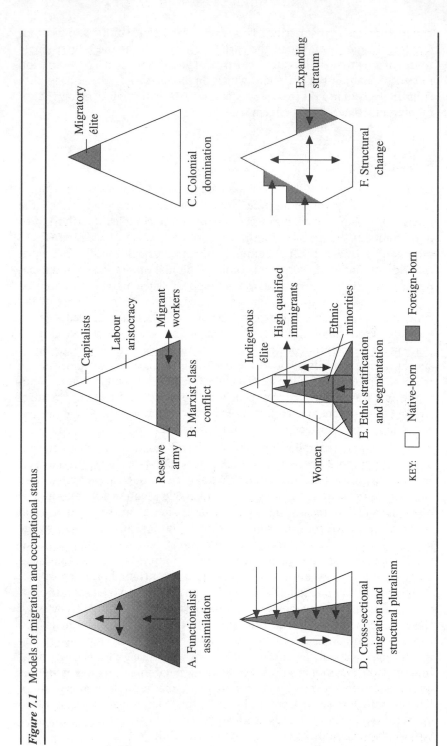

Figure 7.2a   Index of relative concentration, industrial sectors

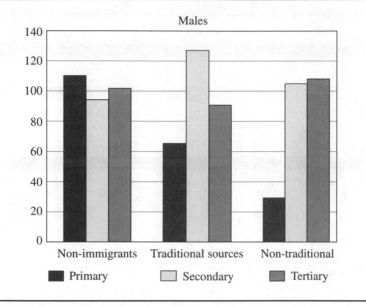

SOURCE: Census of Canada, 1986

Although processes of structural change alone may not be able to explain all the trends in immigrant adaptation, shifts in the distribution of a much-expanded labour force in 1971–86 have an important bearing on the process of absorption. Table 11 shows the pattern of structural change that occurred in the Canadian labour force by industry in this period. Overall, the labour force grew by nearly 4 million people. The primary sector (agriculture, mining, etc.) only added 6 per cent compared with a growth of 17 per cent in the secondary (mainly manufacturing) industries. By far the most rapid expansion was in the tertiary sector (69 per cent). Some industries that were expanding up to 1971 have since begun to decline, but only tobacco, leather, and textiles experienced an absolute decline in the fifteen-year period. Clothing and textiles survived largely through tariff protection. Some, such as agriculture, fishing, oil exploration, and rail transportation benefited from direct government subsidies, supply management, and tax incentives.

Table 12 shows the percentage distribution and relative concentration of immigrants by industrial sector, comparing males and females, and those from traditional and non-traditional source countries by period of immigration (see also figures 7.2a and 7.2b).[5] The data confirm the continued underrepresentation of immigrants in the primary sector (although this is more true of men than women). It also confirms the relative concentration of immigrants (from both traditional and non-traditional sources) in the

Figure 7.2b   Index of relative concentration, industrial sectors

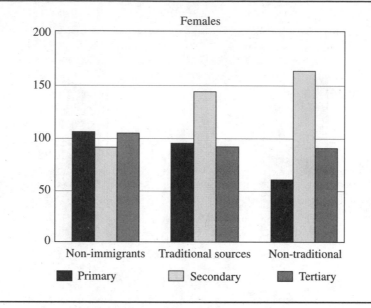

SOURCE: Census of Canada, 1986

secondary (mainly manufacturing and construction) industries. Males from non-traditional source countries are also overrepresented in the tertiary sector. However, immigrant women are the most overrepresented in the secondary manufacturing sector. This is particularly true of the most recent arrivals from non-traditional source countries. With the exception of the longer-term immigrants from non-traditional sources, foreign-born women are underrepresented in tertiary industries.

Further light is thrown on the question of immigration and structural change when the distribution of immigrants in the fastest-growing industries is compared with that in declining sectors (Table 13). The seven fastest-growing industrial subsectors between 1971 and 1986 were business services, finance insurance and real estate, accommodations and food services, health and welfare (social services), leisure and recreation, and other personal and miscellaneous services. Altogether, they accounted for 43 per cent of the total labour force in 1986 and almost half of the immigrants from non-traditional source countries. The relative concentration of immigrants was greatest in the accommodation and food services sector, business services, finance, insurance, and real estate. Only in accommodation and food services, together with business services, were the most recently arrived immigrants from non-traditional source countries overrepresented. However, as shown in Table 13, there was also some overrepresentation of immigrants in declining industries such as leather and textiles, but these accounted for only 0.5 per cent of the total labour force and only 1.1 per cent of the most recent immigrants. It must be noted that accommodations and food services, while growth industries in terms of employment, are also subject to seasonal fluctuations, high unemployment, and traditionally low wages. They are at the unskilled end of the expanding service sector, employing many immigrant women. This industry contrasts with business services, where immigrants are also over-represented, but which are part of the high-tech expansion in computers and communications technology characteristic of postindustrial societies.

Structural changes in the industrial distribution of the labour force accelerated in the mid-1970s and by 1981, some industries began to decline in terms of the absolute numbers employed. The decline continued between 1981 and 1986 and was evident in a number of secondary industries, notwithstanding some overall growth (albeit slow) over the longer period 1971–86, which occurred mainly in the early part of the decade. In fact, almost all secondary industries experienced some loss of employment in 1981–6 when the overall decline in that sector was –5.0 per cent. The largest losses were in metals, machinery, wood, paper, and primary textiles. A recent monograph, based on the 1986 census, examined the relevance of the aforementioned theoretical models and tested the hypothesis that structural change is important in explaining the occupational and industrial distribution of immigrants in Canada (Seward and Tremblay 1989). More support was found for the structural change model with respect to male immigrants than for females. Men from non-traditional source countries had higher levels of education and were responding to the needs of rapidly expanding industries, whereas recently arrived immigrant women from similar countries were not responding as effectively to changing labour markets as non-immigrant women, although both were overrepresented in lower paid jobs in the expanding service sector (Seward and Tremblay 1989:36). A further analysis found that rapidly growing industries had a more highly educated labour force with better official language skills, but no clear association between growth and employment income (Seward and Tremblay 1990:19).

Occupations and incomes

The economic aspects of immigrant absorption and the effect of structural change can be further analysed by an examination of occupational distributions. Marr (1986:770–1) showed that in 1981, foreign-born males were proportionally overrepresented in nine out of the twelve fastest-growing occupations for men, and immigrant females in seven out of sixteen fastest-growing occupations for women. However, the most recently arrived were somewhat less likely to follow this trend than those who had arrived before 1971. When the total foreign-born population is considered, there are few significant differences between them and the Canadian-born except those that would be expected, given the small number of immigrants in rural areas and primary industries. However, when specific birthplaces were taken into account, male immigrants (in 1981) from the United States, Great Britain, western Europe, and Asia were overrepresented in professional and managerial occupations, while those from southern Europe were relatively concentrated in manufacturing and construction. Immigrant women, particularly those from southern Europe, tended to be in services and product fabricating (Beaujot et al. 1988:40–4). The effect of length of residence on occupational distributions (in 1986) is shown in Table 14. It is evident that the most recently arrived immigrants are overrepresented in product fabricating and service occupations, confirming the evidence of numerous previous studies that, notwithstanding high educational qualifications and occupational selection, immigrants frequently do not pursue their intended occupations during their first few years in Canada (Beaujot et al. 1988; Manpower and Immigration 1974; Richmond 1967). Language difficulties and non-recognition of qualifications are contributory factors in this initial adjustment period.

Evidence from the 1971 census suggested that, notwithstanding early adjustment difficulties and setbacks, immigrants eventually recovered and generally surpassed the Canadian-born in terms of income (Richmond and Kalbach 1980). This continues to be the case. In 1980, unadjusted immigrant male incomes were $18,553 compared with $16,577 for Canadian-born men; the equivalent figures for women were $8,872 and $8,322, respectively (Beaujot et al. 1988:49). In 1985, median total incomes were $19,797 for males and $9,540 for females (Statistics Canada 1989, Table 1). The distribution by sex, birthplace, and period of immigration is shown in Table 15. Although median incomes of postwar immigrants who had been in the country ten years or more exceeded those of the Canadian-born, more recent immigrants fell below the average. Males who arrived in 1983–6 received only $9,323 and females $8,219, respectively. Male immigrants in 1970 had arithmetic average total incomes that were 7.7 per cent above those of the Canadian-born, 12.8 per cent higher in 1980, and 11.8 per cent above in 1985. The averages for female immigrants were about the same in 1970, but 6.7 per cent above in 1980 and 5.6 per cent higher in 1985.

Employment incomes for those working full-time and part-time in 1985 are also shown in Table 15. Immigrants arriving in the period 1978–86 were clearly falling below the average, whereas earlier arrivals were earning more than non-immigrants. When overall comparisons are confined to earned incomes for those working full-time for forty weeks or more in the year, *and then standardized for age and education*, a different picture emerges. In 1970, the relative advantage of male immigrants persisted, with standardized earned income that was 2 per cent above the Canadian-born average. However, in 1980 the standardized comparison fell 1.1 per cent below and, by 1985, immigrant men were 2.6 per cent below their Canadian-born equivalents. Comparable figures for immigrant women were 2.2 per cent above in 1970, 1.7 per cent below in 1980, and no difference in 1985 (Beaujot and Rappak 1989:59).

It seems that immigrants in Canada have lost some of their earlier advantage. A combination of cohort differences in origin and level of education, combined with increased adaptation for those having longer residence, accounts for some of the difference between earlier and later immigrants. Further differences are due to the clustering of immigrants in metropolitan areas. Generally, they have retained a closely comparable level of earning capacity to that of the Canadian-born as a whole, qualified only by the high cost of living (and particularly housing) in the metropolitan centres in which the majority live. Verma and Basavarajappa (1989:448) examined income levels for immigrants in metropolitan areas in 1980 and found that overall, men earned 1.9 and women 5.9 per cent less than the Canadian-born living in those areas, but the differences were greater when age and education were controlled. There was considerable variation by birthplace and period of immigration. Recently arrived immigrants from non-traditional source countries earned the lowest incomes. They found evidence of ethnic labour market segmentation as well as a relative concentration of immigrants in service industries. However, they concluded that 'the differential labour market entry of immigrant groups is better explained by the structural pluralism model or the ethnic stratification and segmentation model' (Verma and Basavarajappa 1989:449).

The overall picture, based on averages for all immigrants, disguises some of the variations within the immigrant population, particularly when comparisons are made between those from traditional source countries and those from Third World countries. In 1985, among those who arrived during 1975–9, standardized employment incomes for non-traditional source countries were 21.2 per cent below those of traditional immigrant groups in the case of men and 10.7 per cent below for women (Beaujot and Rappak 1989).[6] More recent arrivals were further disadvantaged. The situation of Caribbean immigrants in 1980 is a specific case in point. A detailed analysis of the economic experience of Caribbean men and women in Canada (based on 1981 census data) revealed a pattern of absolute and relative deprivation, compared with other immigrants and the Canadian-born (Richmond 1989). When standardized for age and education, the employment incomes of francophone Caribbean males was only 67 per cent of that of comparable Canadian-born men; the proportion for anglophone Caribbean males was 83 per cent. Comparable figures for Caribbean women were 79 per cent and 90 per cent, respectively (Richmond 1989:61). It was notable that the degree of disadvantage was greater in Montreal than in Toronto, lending support to the conclusion that Haitian immigrants in Quebec faced even greater prejudice and discrimination than their West Indian counterparts in Ontario. The study also demonstrated that Caribbean women faced the same substantial gender gap in incomes as other women, but that they recovered from the initial adjustment difficulties more quickly than Caribbean men. Furthermore, the data also show that the gap between actual and expected employment incomes (after standardizing for sex, age, and education) grew wider as educational levels rose. In other words, well-educated Caribbean immigrants had greater difficulty achieving an occupational status and income comparable with their qualifications than those with less education. Those with university degrees had greater difficulty than similarly qualified immigrants from other countries (Richmond 1989:44).

The problem of credentialism has been a persistent source of difficulty for wave after wave of immigrants in Canada who find their university degrees discounted, their professional qualifications unrecognized, and their trade diplomas useless. The problem has been particularly acute in recent years as the number of Canadian-trained students entering the labour market increased and competition for jobs has intensified. Refugee doctors have been especially hard hit. While being allowed to sit written examinations to prove their competence, often they have been refused the necessary period of hospital internship, which is mandatory before they can be licensed to practice. A recent study of the barriers to the recognition of immigrant credentials concluded that these varied according to occupation, country of origin, and province of settlement. Doctors, teachers, social workers, nurses, and tradesmen all faced barriers. Ethnic prejudice and discrimination in hiring and promotion added to these difficulties (Cumming et al. 1989; McDade 1988).

Is it possible to formulate a revised, composite model of immigrant adaptation in a postindustrial society, such as Canada, that accounts for the complex empirical findings of recent research? It is evident that a number of factors are involved, some of which are countervailing or even contradictory.

The government encourages well-educated and qualified immigrants, but there are obstacles in recognizing their credentials. Canadian experience is valued and preference given to established immigrants over recent arrivals. Immigrants from non-traditional source countries are encouraged through a non-discriminatory admission policy, but 'Black' and Asian immigrants face race prejudice and barriers to hiring and promotion. Female labour force participation has increased dramatically and women are increasingly employed in professional, technical, and managerial positions. But married women with children need assistance with housework and child care if they are to work full-time, creating a demand for immigrant women in low-paid domestic employment. While well-qualified immigrants eventually move into better paid professional employment in expanding sectors, many of those not so qualified or whose language skills are inadequate appear to be a replacement population in manufacturing industries that are losing older workers (immigrant and non-immigrant). Pay and working conditions in such industries are no longer attractive to a younger generation of well-educated Canadians who have entered the labour force in the last decade or so.

The resulting economic picture is a complicated one, but it may be

Figure 7.3 Economic adaptation of immigrants—revised model G—segmented structural change

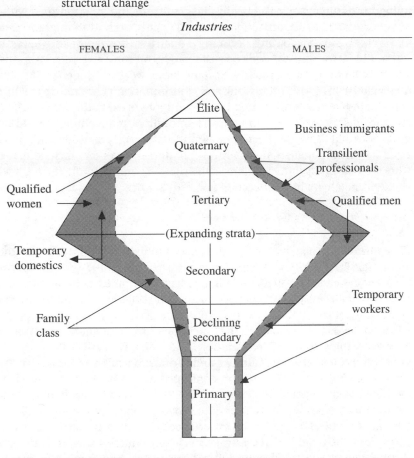

represented in a somewhat simplified form by superimposing the characteristics of the ethnic stratification and segmentation model E on the structural change model F (Figure 7.1). The result is diagrammatically represented in Figure 7.3 (model G) and titled the segmented structural change model. It recognizes the existence of a corporate élite consisting mainly of indigenous managers and entrepreneurs, but including a few business-class immigrants who bring with them capital for investment. There is also a multiway movement of highly qualified immigrants and transilient professionals who do not necessarily settle permanently but whose skills are in demand in a technologically advanced society. Expanding industries draw their labour from immigrant and non-immigrant sources alike. Women are found at all levels of the system, but immigrant females are overrepresented in many of the poorly paid service industries and in those manufacturing industries where semi-skilled manual labour is employed, but a knowledge of English (or French) is not necessary. Many immigrant women are in the family class category and are sponsored without regard to their qualifications. Some recently arrived immigrant men and women gravitate towards declining industries whose competitiveness in international markets can only be sustained by offering wages and working conditions that are unattractive to indigenous workers. Older workers in these industries (both immigrant and non-immigrant) are retiring, while younger indigenous workers take better-paid jobs in expanding sectors. The effect of discrimination is to block the mobility opportunities for ethnic minorities and delay the effective integration of recently arrived immigrants from non-traditional source countries. Temporary workers include males who are employed in agriculture, construction, and manufacturing, and women who are mainly engaged in domestic service.

Postscript

A segmented structural change model of immigrant adaptation to the labour market describes the experience of Canada from 1971–86. Since that time, the processes of structural change have continued at an accelerated pace. Global recession contributed to a further reduction in the agricultural and manufacturing labour force. Resource depletion has had a devastating effect on the fishing industry in the Maritime provinces, where the majority of those employed were Canadian-born and whose roots went back several generations. The absolute number and proportion of the experienced labour force in the service sector continued to grow. Business services increased by an average of 15 per cent in 1986–91, including a 70 per cent increase for computer-related services (Akyeampong and Winters 1993). Similar structural change was experienced by all advanced industrial countries. The largest increases were in those countries such as Italy and France, which had relatively small service sector employment in earlier decades (Akyeampong and Winters 1993). In the Canadian case, immigrants continued to be allocated across all industrial and occupational divisions, but with a marked tendency for the unselected categories to experience greater unemployment and lower incomes than earlier cohorts.

The experience of the United States appears to be similar to that of Canada, modified by the impact of illegal immigration, the effects of employer sanctions, and a different 'mix' of immigrants admitted for settlement. The US Department of Labor noted that immigrant workers can revive (or at least prevent further decline) of certain failing local industries that face strong import competition. Business immigrants create employment opportunities and foreign-born professionals meet special needs. At the same time, specialities and job locations least desirable to US workers have been available to immigrants. This may have led to some exploitation. Structural changes benefit some and penalize others in the context of a global capitalist system. Manufacturing jobs may be lost more rapidly than service employment increases (Ross and Trachte 1990:148–71). However, American studies have shown how immigrant workers permitted new industries and the entire service sector to expand. Electronics, restaurants, and the construction sector are cases in point. 'In all but isolated instances, domestic workers and American consumers benefit from the continued viability of these industries' (US Department of Labor, 1991:194–5). Studies comparing the experience of immigrants in Canada and the United States suggest that 'the Canadian skills-based immigration policy is apparently successful in selecting immigrants who are younger and more language proficient. Canadian policy does not appear to have a consistent effect on the educational levels of immigrants' (Duleep and Regrets 1992:431). However, Asian immigrants in Canada did not earn more than their American counterparts.

It remains for further comparative research to be undertaken to determine whether the experience of other countries can be explained in terms of the segmented structural change model.

Notes

[1] This is a revised version of a paper published in *International Migration Review* 26, Winter 1992.

[2] Traditional source countries are Britain, Europe, and the United States; non-traditional sources are all other countries, including Asia, Africa, the Caribbean, and Latin America.

[3] For example, throughout the 1970s and 1980s, unemployment rates in Newfoundland were two to four-and-a-half times the rate in metropolitan Toronto. In rural areas of Newfoundland, they were even higher. In 1985, they were 24 per cent compared with 6.7 per cent in metropolitan Toronto.

[4] Prepared by the present author in 1979 and used for teaching purposes, the models were first published in Richmond and Zubrzycki (1984). They have since been reproduced and/or discussed in Beaujot et al. (1988), Verma and Basavarajappa (1989), and Seward and Tremblay (1989, 1990).

[5] The tables and Figure 7.2 show indexes of relative concentration compared with the average for the same sex. Women are more likely to be in tertiary industries than men, but immigrant women are relatively more concentrated in the secondary manufacturing sector than other women.

[6] Borjas (1988:64) also noted that the 1960–4 cohort in Canada started out at a 14.3 per cent wage disadvantage, but for 1975–9 immigrants, the wage disadvantage increased to 44.8 per cent. The greatest disadvantage was for those from Africa and Asia.

chapter eight

Immigrants and refugees in Canada and the United States: Policy dilemmas[1]

Policies concerning immigrants in Canada and the United States focus on three concerns: 1) those who are admissible to the country for temporary or permanent residence, 2) initial settlement, and 3) long-term absorption into Canada's officially bilingual, multicultural society, and the (officially) monolingual but increasingly diverse population of the United States.

Canadians and Americans both make rhetorical claims that their country is 'a land of immigrants', although the perception of who is an immigrant is probably quite different. The nearly 300,000 Americans and 728,000 people born in Britain who live in Canada are rarely perceived as 'immigrants', although they may be so designated in official records. The same may be true of the almost 1 million Canadians living in the United States, unless they happen to be francophone Quebecers, in which case their 'stranger' status is defined by language.[2] When discussing immigration, most people have in mind recent arrivals from non-traditional sources. In Canada, this means Chinese, Vietnamese, Laotians, Filipinos, South Asians (India, Pakistan, and Sri Lanka), Afro-Caribbeans, and Lebanese, among many other nationalities. In the United States, the term 'immigrant', in popular usage, applies to those recently arrived from Hispanic and Asian countries. The adjective 'illegal' often accompanies this perception.

The reality is that 16 per cent of the population of Canada and 7 per cent of that the United States were born outside the country. Canada admitted

1.7 million persons for permanent residence between 1984 and 1993. In the same period, the US admitted approximately 7 million immigrants, including those already resident whose status was legalized by various amnesty programs. However, allowance must be made for emigration so that the net effect on population growth was less than these figures suggest.[3]

There are substantial movements of population between the two countries consisting of visitors, tourists, students, cross-border shoppers, commuters, temporary workers, and more permanent emigrants. Since 1979, net migration favoured the United States from Canada, which lost an estimated 163,500 people to the US from 1981–5 (Buttrick 1992:1454; Pryor et al. 1990). There is an enormous ebb and flow of travellers every year, making border control extremely difficult. In 1990, a record 17.6 million visa non-immigrants entered the US. Statistics on air travel and border crossings to and from the United States and from overseas indicate that in 1989, there was a record number of 106 million Canadian border crossings. Transborder aircraft movements in Canada rose from 259,647 in 1980 to 356,218 in 1990. Although non-resident visits to Canada from abroad (including road and rail movements) remained between 35 and 40 million throughout the decade, the number from countries other than the United States rose from 2.1 million in 1980 to 3.3. million in 1989 (Aircraft Movement Statistics 1990; Statistics Canada 1990). Amid this throng, immigrants, temporary workers, and asylum seekers constitute a relatively small proportion of the total movement.

More than 10 million non-immigrants legally enter the US every year, the majority of whom leave again after a short visit, although more than 1 per cent is likely to stay more than a year (Kraly and Warren 1991). (These figures do not include the Canada–US border crossings by citizens and permanent residents, which are not subject to control.) Illegal (i.e., undocumented) migration into the US is mainly from Mexico and Central America. In 1986, there were 1.3 million apprehensions of illegal migrants; the number has since fallen to more than half a million annually. Many illegal entrants return to their countries of origin after a short period of employment. Others who entered the country legally may overstay their visa stipulation. In 1989, an estimated 1.7 to 2.9 million persons were illegally resident in the US (Bean, Edmonston, and Passel 1990:27). This was a significant decline from earlier in the decade as a consequence of legalization under the 1986 Immigration Reform and Control Act, discussed below.

Immigrants in Canada

In Canada, there are no defined quotas by country or world region, although the location of Canadian immigration offices abroad may influence accessibility to the country. Recent trends in the country of last permanent residence of immigrants to Canada are shown in Table 16. For several years Hong Kong has been the largest single source country of immigration. Canada distinguishes between landed immigrants—roughly equivalent to those in the US who have permanent residence status—and others who enter the country as temporary workers, asylum applicants, visitors, students, or on minister's permits.[4] If any of these remain for one year or more, they are technically 'immigrants', according to United Nations demographic usage, but they are not so classified in the annual immigration statistics.[5] The 1991 census of Canada enumerated 223,410 persons legally in the country on a temporary basis, although this may be an underestimate. In 1990, an estimated 240,000 long-term, non-permanent residents were admitted, of whom 71 per cent were workers on temporary employment visas (Michalowski 1993:67). Undocumented or illegal immigrants are mostly those who entered the country legally and overstay the temporary short-term status accorded to them. Precise numbers are hard to estimate, but are thought to be relatively small. More critical from a policy perspective are the increasing numbers arriving at the borders (by land or sea, but mainly air) and immediately applying for refugee status. The Supreme Court of Canada held that anyone making such a claim has a right to an oral hearing and a right of appeal.[6]

Legally, admission to Canada is governed by the 1976 Immigration Act, as amended by subsequent legislation, including bills C55, C84, and C86. The act of 1976 (which came into force in 1978) set out the main objectives and principles guiding legislators at that time. These included the pursuit of demographic goals; strengthening the cultural and social fabric; family reunion; facilitating immigrant adaptation; promoting trade, tourism, culture, science, and international understanding; and fostering a strong and viable economy. It also upheld Canada's humanitarian tradition with respect to the displaced and persecuted and its international obligations to refugees. For the first time, the act incorporated the Convention definition of a refugee into the law. The act also noted the need to protect the health, safety, security, and good order of Canadian society, all without discrimination on grounds of race, national or ethnic origin, colour, religion, or sex (Hawkins 1988, 1989).

The three broad categories admissible for permanent residence were independents, selected primarily for their potential economic contribution (i.e., selected workers, business immigrants, or investors); family class,[7] who were nominated by close relatives; and refugees who were required to meet the UN Convention definition of a refugee, or to fall into one of several designated classes deemed to warrant humanitarian consideration. Canada's postwar record of accepting refugees, displaced persons, expellees, and other humanitarian movements is shown in Table 17. Notable were the Hungarian refugees (1956), Czechs (1968), Ugandan Asians (1972), Vietnamese/Cambodians (1975), and Lebanese (1976). Refugees may be privately sponsored by churches and other bodies or government sponsored. The government's plan for 1991–5 envisages an annual intake of

---

Figure 8.1 Immigration to Canada by class

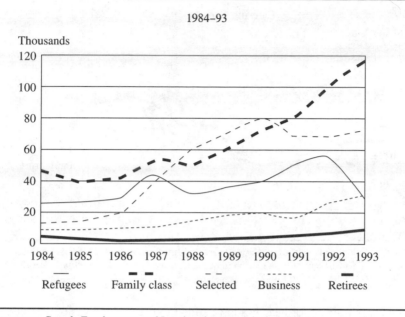

SOURCE: Canada Employment and Immigration (special tabulations)

13,000 government-assisted, 20,000 privately sponsored refugees and designated classes (from abroad), and 25,000 asylum applicants landed in Canada.

Recent trends by classes of immigration are shown in Figure 8.1 and Table 18. The family class continued to be the largest single category but declined proportionately after 1984.[8] The table excludes the temporary migrant category. Not counting those who live or work in Canada for less than one year, the numbers entering the country annually exceeded the number recorded as landed immigrants (Michalowski 1991, 1993). For example, in 1990, 209,630 immigrants (excluding the backlog of asylum applicants processed in Canada) were landed, 224,500 long-term temporary residents were admitted and 144,600 short-term (see Figure 8.2). The long-term category includes documented visitors, those on minister's permits, students, and those receiving temporary employment authorizations valid for more than a year. In recent years, these have included asylum applicants. When measured in person-years of employment, temporary employment authorizations (short- and long-term) are generally larger than the number of landed immigrants intending to enter the labour force annually.

Ministers of immigration are required to consult with provincial authorities concerning annual immigration levels. The question of temporary movements is not normally considered, despite the fact that asylum

Figure 8.2 Permanent and non-permanent admissions to Canada

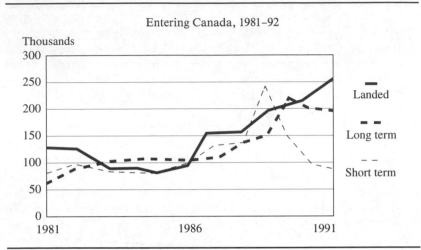

Entering Canada, 1981–92

SOURCE: Compiled from Canada Employment and Immigration, and M. Michelowski, 'Redefining the Concept of Immigration to Canada', *Canadian Studies in Population* 20, no. 1 (1993): 59–84. 1991 and 1992 are estimated

applicants waiting for hearings have added to the social costs of immigration, which are largely borne by provincial and municipal authorities. Longer-term immigration policies have been reviewed by a federal government demographic review and by the Economic Council of Canada (Beattie 1989; Swan 1991). The demographic review concluded that declining birth rates (particularly in Quebec), combined with the aging of the population and the level of emigration, justified continuing a moderate immigration program (Beaujot 1991). Subsequently, the department announced an increased annual immigration level, but this was before the recession became obvious and a temporary freeze was placed on further selected worker admissions, although projected levels remained at 250,000 p.a.

The Canada Employment and Immigration Advisory Council recommended increasing the number of children and young persons, including foreign adoptions, as a means of compensating for low birth rates in Quebec and the rest of Canada (CEIAC 1991b:7). However, this would place an added burden on education authorities, which are under provincial and municipal jurisdiction and consequently have little input into immigration decision making.

The Economic Council of Canada examined the economic and social consequences of immigration. It concluded that the impact of immigration on standard economic indicators such as GNP per capita, unemployment, productivity, tax and dependency burdens, etc., was very small but nevertheless positive over the long run. Therefore, it favoured gradually increasing gross immigration over the next twenty-five years until it reached an annual level of 1 per cent of the population by the year 2015 (Swan 1991:133).[9]

In practice, Canadian policy with regard to permanent admission has vacillated. With economic recession at the beginning and the end of the eighties, fewer independent immigrants were selected according to a points system based on language, education, skills, and qualifications (see Figure 8.3), but the proportion of business immigrants admitted on the basis of entrepreneurial experience and investment plans increased. Numerically more significant was the growth in family class admissions, partly as a result of extending the definition of eligible relatives. This initiative, much favoured by ethnic lobby groups, was reversed in 1991 when it was discovered that many of those arriving were not well qualified to compete in a declining labour market.[10] Refugees and designated classes selected abroad, combined with those applying for asylum after arrival, were less than 20 per cent of the total.[11] The numbers and sources of Convention refugees and designated classes admitted as permanent residents from 1990–2 is shown in Table 19. The figures include those coming from abroad and those approved for asylum status in Canada. The two largest categories of designated classes were from Poland and El Salvador. The top ten countries of admission are shown in Figure 8.4.

The bureaucratic and quasi-judicial system of refugee determination used before and after 1993 is shown in Figure 8.5. At either the initial or full hearing stage, only one member has to decide in favour of the applicant. In 1993, the initial hearing stage was abolished and now immigration officials at the border have more discretion in referral. The board's procedures have been criticized on a number of occasions. Individual adjudicators were allegedly prejudiced or suffering from compassion fatigue, with the result that acceptances and rejections were not consistent. In 1993, it was revealed that tribunals sometimes met privately with immigration officials to be briefed on individual cases without the knowledge of the asylum seekers or their lawyers. One newspaper editorial described this as a 'star chamber' type of justice that was clearly unconstitutional.[12] The record of asylum application hearings and acceptance rates for 1993 is shown in Table 20. The Convention Refugee Determination Division heard 29,838 claims to completion in 1992. The overall rate was of acceptance was 57 per cent, down from 64 per cent in 1991 and 70 per cent in 1990. There was a further drop to 54 per cent in 1993. Major source countries were Sri Lanka, the former USSR, and Somalia, followed by Soviet Jews (coming from Israel), Pakistan, and Yugoslavia.

A major revision of Canadian immigration law occurred with the passing of Bill C-86, which came into force in January 1993. It aims to expedite administrative procedures by creating three streams. The first, which includes spouses and dependent children together with business immigrants, will have priority. The second stream will be dealt with on a first-come, first-served basis, and the third will be subject to numerical limits

Figure 8.3 Selection criteria (the points system)*

FACTOR	UNITS OF ASSESSMENT	NOTES
Education	12 maximum	
Specific vocational preparation	15 maximum	
Experience	8 maximum	0 units is an automatic processing bar unless (i) applicant has arranged employment and (ii) employer accepts lack of experience
Occupation	10 maximum	0 units is an automatic processing bar unless applicant has arranged employment
Arranged employment	10	
Age	10 maximum	10 units if 21 to 44; 2 units deducted for each year under 21 or over 44
Knowledge of official language(s)	15 maximum	
Personal suitability	10 maximum	
Levels control	10 maximum	
TOTAL	100	
PASS MARK	70	
Bonus for all assisted relatives	10 (60 pass mark)	If application is accompanied by an undertaking of assistance
Additional bonus for these assisted relatives: married sons and daughters, brothers, and sisters	5 (55 pass mark)	

*The Quebec selection system has some differences in factors and units of assessment, but the intent and results are similar.

SOURCE: Canada Employment and Immigration

Figure 8.4 Ten largest refugee source countries

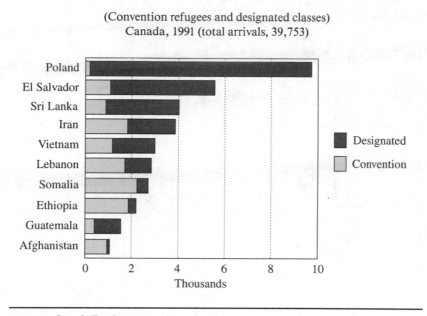

(Convention refugees and designated classes)
Canada, 1991 (total arrivals, 39,753)

SOURCE: Canada Employment and Immigration

and *relative* excellence. This means that earning enough points will not be sufficient if there are others in line who are better qualified.

A key feature of the new legislation is that it gives greater power to the minister in Council to make regulations governing the admissibility of immigrants and refugees. In practice, what this means is that the bureaucracy has greater influence and can control immigration with a greater degree of flexibility. Temporary employment and resident permits may be issued for up to three years. Specifically, it can harmonize Canada's immigration and refugee policies with those of other countries, such as the United States, the EEC, and Australia. The minister is empowered to enter into agreements with other countries for sharing information and responsibility for examining refugee claims. This can be done without explicit parliamentary approval. Refugee claimants may be refused a hearing if they have travelled to Canada through a safe country, or one where they could have made a refugee claim.

The minister may also enter into agreements with provincial governments concerning immigration selection and provision for settlement services. Quebec has had such an agreement with the federal government since 1978, but other provinces, including British Columbia, have expressed an interest in exercising more control over the numbers and types of immigrants that arrive. The new legislation also permits the fingerprint-

Figure 8.5 Refugee status determination system (new)

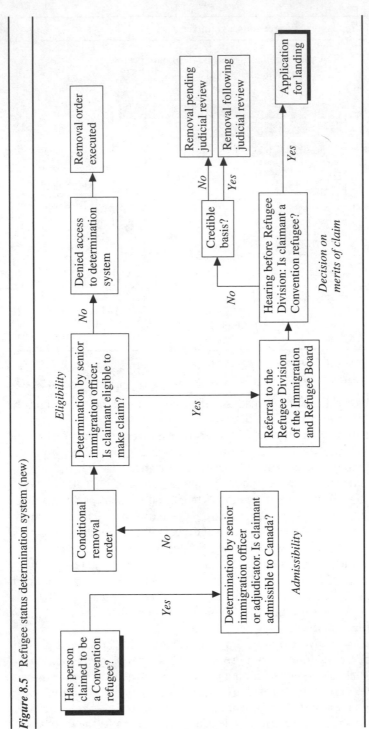

SOURCE: Refugee Affairs Branch

Figure 8.5 (continued) Refugee status determination system (old)

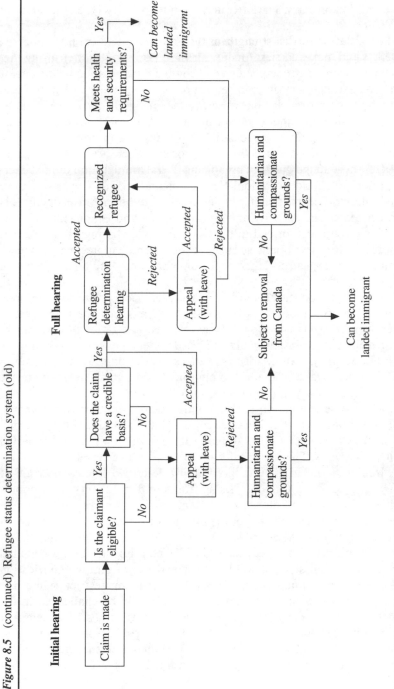

SOURCE: Based on Auditor General of Canada (1990)

ing of asylum applicants, tightens requirements regarding medical examinations, and makes it possible for immigration authorities to impose terms
and condition on entry. The latter may include specified type or location of
employment.

The legislation further strengthens the power to interdict undocumented
travellers and makes carriers (mainly airlines) responsible for ensuring that
travellers are properly documented and eligible for admission before departure. It also strengthens the enforcement powers and ability to deport illegal
immigrants or those who have been found ineligible for refugee status.
Grounds for inadmissibility include a range of criminal and security questions, including guilt by association with any group considered to be
involved in espionage, subversion, or terrorism. There are substantial penalties for those found guilty of organizing illegal immigration or of shelter-
ing persons due for deportation. New search and seizure powers will allow
immigration officers to search people suspected of hiding travel documents
or other materials. As early as 1988, a Control and Enforcement Policy
Working Group was formed in the Department of Immigration and was
responsible for developing strategic control and enforcement policies,
including training airport personnel on visas and fraudulent detection
techniques.

The immigration authorities' increasing preoccupation with enforcement and control is reflected in the announcement by the Conservative
government in 1993 that (as part of a general reorganization of government
departments) immigration would be placed under a newly created Ministry
of Public Security.[13] Many critics saw this as a criminalization of immigration and a betrayal of Canada's commitment to a humane response to the
needs of refugees, asylum applicants, and others with legitimate aspirations
to migrate. The number of removals under the old immigration system in
1988 was 2,057. By 1991, it had risen to 4,408, excluding 4,016 interdictions. In 1992, there were 7,138 removals, of which 4,672 were rejected
asylum claimants. The rest were illegal entrants or overstayers.[14]

A leading authority on immigration law described 'the conundrum of
refugee protection in Canada' arising from conflicting aims and responsibilities. If Canada administers its inland refugee determination system
generously and independently of the policies of other industrialized countries that are closing the doors, it will be flooded by protection requests. If it
raises the number of refugees accepted while retaining the ceiling on annual
immigration admissions, it will be at the expense of family reunification
and independent immigrants. If Canada adopts a more restrictive interpretation of the Convention refugee definition, it will be challenged in the
courts. The preferred course is the use of visa controls and stricter deterrent
and interdiction measures 'to prevent the flow of truly desperate humanity'
(Hathaway 1992:85). Canada's dilemma is shared with the United States.
Both countries continue to receive immigrants in increasing numbers, but

are seeking ways and means of stemming the flow and exercising greater powers of selection and rejection.

Immigrants in the United States

Three main bodies of legislation govern the admission of immigrants and refugees to the United States. They are the Refugee Act of 1980, the Immigration Reform and Control Act of 1986, and the Immigration Act of 1990. Prior to 1980, refugees were admitted to the US using presidential parole authority. For example, 130,000 Vietnamese were paroled into the country by President Ford. The 1980 legislation was intended to abolish the parole authority. It established a quota of 50,000 refugees annually. The law incorporated the UN definition of a Convention refugee. It allowed an alien to file an application for asylum at an Immigration and Naturalization Service office and/or appeal a deportation order to an immigration judge. Almost immediately, the new system was thrown into crisis by the arrival of large numbers of Cubans in the Mariel Boatlift. President Carter was forced to use parole power and the annual cap of 50,000 has been exceeded ever since (Yarnold 1990:16). The Immigration Act of 1990 made further changes to make it easier for those who were granted asylum to obtain permanent residence status. It also revised grounds for deportation and modified provisions for naturalization (US Department of Justice 1991:25).

Inflows of permanent settlers to the US from 1980–90 (by birthplace) are shown in Table 22. Until 1988, the annual admissions ranged between 530,000 and 643,000, after which the inclusion of internal legalizations increased the number to a million in 1989 and 1.5 million in 1990. Asia and Latin America, including Mexico, were the main sources. Table 23 shows the inflow of permanent settlers by entry class, indicating that refugees ranged from 156,600 in 1982 to 84,300 in 1989. The ten largest refugee source countries for the United States in 1991 are shown in Figure 8.6. As in the case of Canada, inflows of authorized temporary workers increased over the decade from 44,800 in 1981 to 144,900 in 1990.

US immigration policy and practice have been severely criticized for favouring applicants from 'hostile' (mainly communist countries) and routinely rejecting those from elsewhere. For example, between 1983 and 1986, the rates of approval of asylum applicants ranged from 73 per cent (306/321) from the USSR to 2.5 per cent (1,004/38,670) from El Salvador (Zucker and Zucker 1991:240). Haitian applicants have a similar low rate of acceptance and many of those endeavouring to reach the US by boat were intercepted by the coastguard and detained in a naval base in Cuba or returned to Haiti. Central American asylum applicants who do manage to reach the US are detained in camps, pending a hearing. The majority are eventually deported.

The 1986 Immigration Reform and Control Act was designed to reform

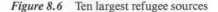

Figure 8.6   Ten largest refugee sources

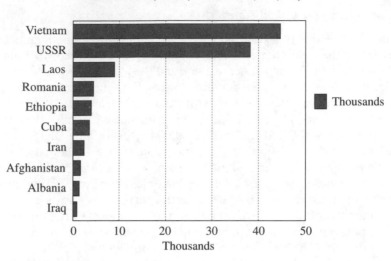

United States, 1991 (total arrivals, 113,799)

SOURCE: Report to Congress, 1992

earlier legislation and deal with the problem of illegal immigrants. It gave temporary residence status to aliens who had lived illegally in the US from 1981 or earlier. A legalization program was instituted to adjust the status of such migrants together with those illegal aliens who had worked at least ninety days in seasonal agriculture during the year ending 1 May 1986 (US Department of Justice 1991:25). The aim was to reduce the stock and flow of undocumented immigrants. It has been only partially successful (Bean, Edmonston, and Passel 1990). The Immigration and Naturalization Service has increased its 'line watch' and border patrols with Mexico, even building a fence near Tijuana to deter would-be migrants to California. This was countered by an attempt to tunnel under the border! The use of electronic surveillance equipment has increased.

The Immigration Act of 1990 extensively revised earlier provisions concerning visa categories and preferences regarding regular immigration into the US. Up to that time, 85 per cent of all immigrants were coming from Central America or Asia, 95 per cent were admitted because of family ties (although there were very long waiting periods for brothers and sisters of US citizens), and little priority was given to persons with skills. Exclusion categories (such as those relating to health, sexual orientation, or political affiliation) had not changed since 1924 (Tinker 1992:10). The act created new immigration categories, distinguishing family-sponsored, employment-based, and other immigrant categories. Within the family category, first preference was given to unmarried sons and daughters of US citizens; within the employment category, first preference was given to aliens 'with extraordinary ability, outstanding professors and researchers, multinational executives', and the spouses and children of these persons. A new visa category ('diversity' immigrants) enables those from previously under-represented countries to be admitted. There is a special class of business immigrants from Hong Kong, and an investor class for those with a million dollars or more to put into a commercial enterprise in the US. Further provisions were made for a growing category of non-immigrant profession-als, entertainers, athletes, etc. (Miller 1992:14–28). Although the new pro-cedures were designed to facilitate employment-based immigration for those with appropriate education and skills, an emphasis on family-based migration was reinforced. Although intended to be non-discriminatory in its effects, penalties imposed on employers who hire illegal immigrants may have repercussions on established workers who appear to be of foreign origin.

The Canada–US free trade agreement makes provision for certain cat-egories of professionals and managers to move between the two countries with a minimum bureaucratic interference. It is likely that the net flow will be outward from Canada. The proposed North American Free Trade Agreement, which would include Mexico, is intended in part to stimulate the economy of Mexico so that it will reduce the incentive to move illegally to the US. Canada and the US have approved the agreement after demand-ing certain side agreements concerning working conditions and pollution controls on the Mexican border. There is no guarantee that even with these additional conditions, it will inhibit the movement north.

Settlement policies in Canada and the United States

The United States makes no pretence of being a 'welfare state'. It lacks the universal health care services available in Canada. Other educational and social services, even where some government funding is available, rely much more on the voluntary principle. The idea of universality, which, until recently, governed Canada's income maintenance programs, is not an American value. The cult of competitive individualism and self-sufficiency precludes such policies. Indeed, the alleged entrepreneurial capacities of immigrants are sometimes held up as an example to other Americans (Skerry 1993:174–88)!

The Migrant Health program, administered by the US Public Health Service, provides primary health care services to migrant farm workers. There is some question as to how effective it is in reaching those whose need is greatest. Language barriers, transportation problems, and ignorance of the facilities available render farm workers particularly vulnerable to ser-ious health problems (Egan 1992:155–8). Refugee resettlement is another area in which much has been achieved, but more needs to be done, particularly with respect to mental health. In 1991, $410 million was provided by US federal departments for the refugee domestic assistance program, which was channelled through state-administered resettlement programs. Although immigration to the US has increased, funding for special programs, such as ESL (English as a second language) has not grown proportionally.

Canada

Under the Canadian Constitution, immigration is a shared responsibility of the federal and provincial governments, although the federal authorities make the final determination of admissibility. Only Quebec has its own immigration department and special criteria for admission. It endeavours to encourage francophone immigration to that province and undertakes intensive 'francization' programs for those who do not speak French on arrival, although funding is limited and the results disappointing (CEIAC 1991b:35–44; McAll 1991). Other provinces have similar ESL programs, but they are also limited in their effectiveness. A third of all immigrants arriving speak neither of the official languages, but 60 per cent of the women and 10 per cent of the men are not eligible for government-funded language training programs, either because they have been privately sponsored or they are not expected initially to enter the labour force. (In practice, many spouses and young people do seek employment soon after arrival.) The actual training provided is largely confined to achieving a modest level of oral fluency. It is of little help to those seeking clerical or professional employment, where a high level of literacy is needed. The government's own advisory council has been critical of the uncoordinated nature of existing programs, their short duration (maximum thirty weeks), restricted entry conditions, and lack of national standards for instructors and graduation (CEIAC 1991b:55–6). The Economic Council has recommended giving equal access to men and women and the introduction of a partial fee-charging system, together with loans and subsidies (Swan 1991:138).

A major problem that immigrants have faced since the end of the Second World War concerns the recognition of skills and professional qualifications. This is largely a provincial responsibility; even qualifications obtained in one province are not necessarily recognized in another. Consequently, there has been resistance to making special arrangements, either by licensing people with foreign trade or professional qualifications on the basis of previously determined equivalence, or providing special arrangements for immigrants to upgrade or requalify in Canada. Labour unions and professional associations are also resistant to any suggestion that immigrants should be given direct assistance. There is a vicious circle in which some employers hire immigrants only when they can show they have 'Canadian experience', but they cannot obtain that experience without the proper credentials, which may require several years of further study, apprenticeships, internships, and Canadian certification. The situation makes a mockery of efforts by the immigration department to recruit well-educated immigrants whose skills are in short supply, or who have a potential for contributing to the economy in other than unskilled jobs. Several federal and provincial government agencies have recommended the establishment of a national body to assess and establish the equivalence of education, training, and experience obtained abroad, but there has been no action in this regard (CEIAC 1991c:19; Cumming et al. 1989).

The federal government regards the first three years as critical to the settlement process. It funds various non-governmental agencies to provide a variety of community-based information, advisory, and counselling services to immigrants. Some of these are ethnic-specific, based on particular linguistic or religious service agencies, while others are more comprehensive and non-sectarian. All complain of the inadequacy of the funding and the arbitrariness of the three-year term. Often adjustment problems do not surface until families are reunited, children enter school or reach adolescence, or recession brings unemployment and financial stress (Sharma 1981b).

The most frequent settlement problems experienced by recent immigrants, in addition to those concerning language and employment, are those related to affordable housing, law enforcement, and racial discrimination (Sharma 1981a). The majority of immigrants and refugees settle in the major metropolitan areas where job opportunities are greater and where relatives and others of the same ethnic background can provide some support. Various authorities have argued that immigrants should be encouraged to settle in the smaller towns and in provinces (such as the Atlantic region) that received few immigrants in the past. It is believed that this would relieve congestion in larger cities, provide cheaper housing, and reduce strain on educational and other services. However, when the Economic Council addressed this issue, it concluded that immigrant adaptation was facilitated by the presence of others of the same ethnic origin and that no recommendation concerning overall regional distribution was required. However, it did suggest that local community sponsorship of refugees to remoter places might be worth considering (Swan 1991:41).

Municipalities bear the burden of education, housing, and welfare costs consequent upon immigration. At a time of fiscal constraint when all levels of government are cutting expenditure and are politically hesitant to raise taxes, new or enhanced services for immigrants are not likely to be provided. Nevertheless, the federal advisory council recommended that municipal governments expand services to newcomers and adopt special measures to deal with racism and other sources of conflict. It suggested that 'the efforts of inter-faith, anti-racist and human rights groups be strengthened and coordinated' (CEIAC 1991c:10). A similar recommendation was made by a task force on mental health issues affecting immigrants and refugees. This study also recommended premigration orientation programs, more ethnic minorities and interpreters to be employed in health and welfare services, and funding for ethno-specific rehabilitation and reintegration facilities, particularly for refugees who were the victims of torture (Beiser 1988). Unfortunately, little action has followed the publication of this report.

In the context of contemporary global migration patterns the use of terms such as 'adjustment', 'adaptation', and 'settlement' is anachronistic. Canada and the United States are part of a world system of international migration; there are multiway flows of people in all directions. The number of people entering and leaving the North American continent as visitors, short- and long-term temporary workers, asylum applicants, and illegally, far exceeds those arriving as immigrants. Furthermore, those who are entering as immigrants are not necessarily permanent. There is a significant flow of return and remigration as well as the emigration and return of those born in Canada and the US. Key characteristics of contemporary international population movements are motility and transilience.

In the context of this global system, the appropriate focus should be upon the coaptation of polyethnic populations in a multicultural society, irrespective of birthplace. As suggested in Chapter Two, the essence of postmodernism is rapid change, diversity, differentiation, relativism, hybridization, fragmentation, loss of identity, and rejection of traditional mores. It is accompanied by power shifts, assertion of minority rights, and subversion of established authorities. The insecurities generated by these rapid changes create deep-seated fear and anxiety among movers and non-movers alike. These fears are exacerbated by economic uncertainty. The result is reaction, resistance, racism, and 'reform' (meaning a nostalgic yearning for a more familiar and stable society). In extreme cases, it results in neofascism, scapegoating, discrimination, violence towards 'visible' minorities, religious fundamentalism, exclusionary attitudes towards strangers, and a 'fortress' mentality designed to protect the family, neighbourhood, and country against perceived threats.

The goal of government policy should be to alleviate fears, generate economic and social security, promote conflict resolution, tension management, and cope with change among the population as a whole. Special programs focusing on the settlement and adaptation of recently arrived immigrants (with restricted eligibility criteria) for one, two, or three years do little to help. This does not mean that governmental and non-governmental agencies should not be providing initial adjustment services, including language training and skill retraining. It does mean that such services alone are not enough to ensure a smooth transition.

It must be recognized that some of the most severe strains generated by contemporary postindustrial/postmodern changes are experienced by older people, non-movers, and by a younger generation growing up in North America who are torn between the traditional attitudes and values of their parents and those to which they are exposed through the consumer-oriented media. When economic opportunities are frustrated, rage and rebellion result. As well as rioting, drugs, alcohol addiction, prostitution, smuggling, and other forms of deviant behaviour, repressive measures by police, anti-immigrant demonstrations, hate-mongering, and all forms of intolerance are symptomatic of a failure to achieve satisfactory coaptation.

Successful coaptation may be defined as a process whereby migrants and non-migrants achieve an optimal level of participation in the economic, political, and social institutions of society. An optimal level is one that maximizes an individual or group's contribution while minimizing strain, maintaining satisfaction, and promoting identification with (rather than alienation from) society. This means that short-term adjustment cannot be separated from questions of the longer-term absorption into North American society.

Long-term trends

In 1971, former Prime Minister Pierre Trudeau announced a policy of multiculturalism within a bilingual framework designed to recognize the ethnically plural nature of Canadian society, and to encourage pride in linguistic and cultural heritage while facilitating the full integration of immigrants and their descendants in the country. Subsequently, official bilingualism at the federal level (and in New Brunswick) was entrenched in the Constitution in 1982. However, Quebec did not sign the constitutional document, preferring to emphasize its own distinctness and to promote a monolingual French environment for all Quebecois, internal migrants, and immigrants alike.[15] The constitutional issue of Quebec as a distinct society is still unresolved and could lead to the eventual secession of that province or some form of sovereignty association (Bercuson and Cooper 1991; McAll 1991).

Clause 27 of the constitutional Charter of Rights declares that 'This Charter shall be interpreted in a manner consistent with the preservation and enhancement of the multicultural heritage of Canadians.' To this end, an act (Bill C-93, 1988) spells out Canada's commitment to human rights and to the International Convention on the Elimination of all Forms of Racial Discrimination. It established an enlarged department of multiculturalism to promote antiracist programs and maintain heritage languages and cultures. It also encourages understanding and creativity between individuals and communities of different origins. Substantially increased funding towards these goals was promised, but, like many other programs, this one has subsequently suffered fiscal constraints that limit its effectiveness.

The Charter of Rights also provides for equality rights and specifically authorizes affirmative action programs to combat discrimination, particularly on grounds of 'race, national origin, colour, religion, sex, age or mental or physical disability' (section 15).[16] The federal government has passed an Employment Equity Act (1988) to enforce the equality rights clause in those areas under federal jurisdiction, but it is widely regarded as a weak measure that will be reinforced with parallel provincial legislation and stronger enforcement powers and sanctions (Employment Equity Commissioner 1991).

In the course of the national unity debate and constitutional wrangles over Quebec's place in confederation, policies of official bilingualism and multiculturalism were subject to much populist criticism and some reactionary protest from the extreme right. Both programs are widely misunderstood. They are often seen to be divisive when the aim has been to promote greater cohesion. The Citizens Forum on Canada's Future, which held public hearings throughout the country in 1991, concluded that it was wrong to encourage 'hyphenated-Canadians', and that there should be more emphasis on 'Canadians first' (Spicer 1991). While welcoming cultural diversity, there was a widespread feeling that this should not be government-sponsored or tax-funded but a result of voluntary action. Multicultural policies were seen as divisive by many of those who participated in the forum, although it is doubtful whether they were a representative cross-section of the population. Interestingly, there was more sympathy for the needs of Canada's native (Aboriginal) population than for immigrants and their descendants, or for the separatist aspirations of some Quebecers. A study of the costs and benefits of multiculturalism concluded that present policies were the only viable and realistic ones, but urged the need for more public education concerning the aims and objectives of the policies. It noted the danger of a backlash against immigrants and visible minorities and recommended more research, as well as a closer monitoring of ethnic tolerance levels and multicultural programs to measure their effectiveness (Berry 1991:33–7). Multiculturalism in Canada, as in other countries, is facing a crisis that is closely connected with a postmodern emphasis on the persistence of 'difference' and with the effects of globalization (McLellan and Richmond 1994).

Prior to the Canadian Citizenship Act (1947), as amended in 1976, Canadians were either British subjects or 'aliens'. Canadian citizenship is now obtained through birth or naturalization. A landed immigrant with three years or more of continuous residence may apply for Canadian citizenship. They must demonstrate a knowledge of one or both of the official languages, some knowledge of Canadian history, geography, and its political system. They must also swear or affirm allegiance to the Queen. Citizenship court judges vary considerably in their interpretation of these requirements, but, in most cases, the level of fluency and knowledge required is rudimentary. In due course, most immigrants who remain and settle take out citizenship. The 1986 census (Statistics Canada 1989) showed that 87.5 per cent of those who arrived before 1946 and 86.4 per cent of the

1946–66 cohort were Canadian citizens. The proportion of non-citizens among those who arrived between 1967–77 was 27.9 per cent. Among those most recently eligible to apply (1978–82 arrivals), 43.1 per cent were not yet Canadian citizens. The average number of years elapsed before applying for naturalization varied from nineteen for Italians, fifteen for Germans, and fourteen for those from the United States, to four years for those from Hong Kong, Iran, and Haiti. One factor promoting prompt application is political instability of the former country, so that refugees are more likely to apply early.

Citizenship is a prerequisite for voting in federal and provincial elections, as well as for joining the armed services, becoming a ship's master, obtaining permanent employment in the public service, and for certain professional licences.[17] It is also a requirement for public office. It is sometimes assumed that immigrants constitute part of an 'ethnic vote' that will support one particular political party or candidates of the same nationality. There is little evidence to support this view. Immigrants are influenced by the same considerations as other voters, including their own education, socio-economic status, and perception of the issues. However, in recent years better-educated immigrants arriving in Canada have been more politically sophisticated and keen to participate in political parties and to stand for office.

The United States

The myth of America as a melting-pot was first questioned after the Second World War. Persisting religious distinctions between Protestant, Catholics, and Jews led to the idea of a triple melting-pot in which the English language and a political allegiance to the US indicated a degree of assimilation. This stopped short of overcoming religious differences (Herberg 1960). Later studies in New York and elsewhere indicated that other ethnic minorities were retaining their language and identity, as well as organizing themselves as a political force (Glazer and Moynihan 1963). Above all, 'Blacks' in the US remained geographically segregated and increasingly militant in their demand for representation in municipal, state, and federal politics. Hispanic and Asian immigrants and their descendants followed this example in their endeavour to gain recognition for their language and traditions. Lieberson and Waters (1988) recognized that an ethnic flux was taking place among those of European origin with the emergence of 'non-hyphenated Whites', but the melting-pot was not occurring as expected. Above all, the greatest divisions in terms of residence, occupation, income, and intermarriage were between 'Whites' and non-European groups, such as 'Blacks' and Hispanics, as well as peoples from Asia, Latin America, and the Caribbean (Lieberson and Waters 1988:247).

The United States is no less a multicultural society than Canada, although the former is reluctant to recognize this officially. Attempts to make Spanish an official language in several states have been strongly resisted. Education authorities have experimented with 'Black studies' and introduced other cultural subjects into the curriculum of schools where there is a high proportion of 'Black' or immigrant children. Affirmative action for admission to colleges and universities and in determining eligibility for various employment and training programs has favoured selected minorities. The results have been disappointing and have incurred severe criticism by mainstream 'liberal' commentators (Glazer 1975). 'America increasingly sees itself as composed of groups more or less eradicable in their ethnic character. The multiethnic dogma abandons historic purposes, replacing assimilation by fragmentation, integration by separatism' Schlesinger 1992:16–17). In this respect, the United States is not only similar to Canada but reflects a global trend.

Canada's immigration, settlement, and long-term absorption policies cannot be considered in isolation from those of other countries. US policies undoubtedly influence those of Canada, although in connection with refugee determination, asylum, repatriation, and deportation, they are sometimes in conflict.[18] Other countries, such as Britain and Australia, are endeavouring to accommodate themselves to increasing ethnic and racial diversity by promoting multicultural policies (Richmond 1990, 1991a). European countries are facing critical issues arising from the end of the cold war and a flood of migrants and refugees arriving from eastern and central Europe, as well as many Arab, African, and Asian countries (Joly and Cohen 1989).

Politicians and bureaucrats would like to impose order on the present chaos, selecting only those they believe will contribute to their own country's economic and social well-being. They would like to exclude those who might become a public charge, or who are perceived as potentially disruptive of the social order, even when the disruption is a result of prejudice and discrimination exhibited by their own citizens. The frequency with which Canada and the United States have been compelled to grant amnesty to those who are in the country illegally or who have overstayed their temporary visas is evidence of the futility of exclusionary measures. We live in a world system in which mass movements of population have become endemic. Most countries today place strict control over who is admissible. Nevertheless, vast numbers of people (particularly those from developing countries or states experiencing political upheaval) are clamouring for admission to the more economically developed and politically stable countries. Short of declaring outright war on those who seek to cross state borders in search of political asylum and economic security, it is difficult for these countries to resist the pressure. It would be virtually impossible to exclude everyone except by building the equivalent of the Berlin Wall around each and every country. Policy makers must come to terms with this reality.

Throughout the nineteenth and twentieth centuries, the answer to the largely rhetorical question of whether Canada needs more people has been in the affirmative. With a geographic area larger than that of the US and a population only one-tenth its size, growth through positive net immigration makes prima facie sense. However, this view has been questioned by environmentalists and advocates of zero-population growth, who point to the ecological fragility of much of the territory north of the forty-ninth parallel. Forests are in danger of depletion, arctic permafrost and wildlife breeding grounds could be permanently damaged by oil exploration, hydroelectric dams, or other development. The Aboriginal populations that claim these vast land masses as their own and seek self-government are not likely to encourage immigration or increased population density. Against the views of some environmentalists, it can be argued that the population's rate of natural increase has slowed substantially in recent years. Increased emigration from Canada (particularly to the United States) is a highly plausible outcome of current economic and postindustrial developments, including the North American Free Trade Agreement. Just to sustain a slow rate of growth (to approximately 32 million in the year 2015) will require levels of immigration at least equal to the average of the last decade. This raises the question of selection and control.

The evidence suggests that the enormously expensive bureaucratic system that Canada has created to select immigrants abroad and to process asylum applicants after arrival has failed to achieve the goals set out in the Immigration Act of 1976.[19] There is no longer any need for an agency whose mandate is to actively seek out and promote immigration because the numbers finding their own way to Canada's borders far exceed the demographic or economic requirements. On the basis of economic criteria, selection abroad has also proved ineffective as the majority of those coming to live and work in the country are not in the selected worker category. (Not counting accompanying dependants, this component is currently 10 per cent to 15 per cent of all landed immigrants.) With the exception of those who have prearranged employment, many workers selected according to the points system are unable to find employment in their area of experience and expertise. The global economic recession has made immigrants everywhere the scapegoats for high unemployment, and subsequently there is increased hostility to them. The dilemma as seen by immigration officials in Canada and the United States is how to reduce the potential flow of legal and illegal immigrants while preserving the option of utilizing their labour when seasonal and cyclical economic fluctuations make that the profitable course. Those who emphasize humanitarian considerations argue that short-term economic self-interest should not be the foundation of immigration policies. Worldwide demographic pressures in the future may preempt such a choice. With birth rates declining in the north and populations burgeoning in the south, the dam will likely burst.

Notes

[1] This is an extensively revised version of a paper presented at a seminar at the School of International and Public Affairs, Columbia University, New York, 21 April 1992.

[2] The population of Canada was approximately 27.3 million in 1991, of whom less than 7 million were French-speaking. The majority of the latter reside in Quebec.

[3] Emigration from Canada is estimated at approximately 500,000 in the same decade, including the return migration of former immigrants. There were approximately 1 million US-born persons resident abroad in 1980; emigration from the United States is estimated as 100,000 annually for the decade 1981–90.

[4] A minister's permit is issued when a person is precluded by statute or regulation from admission for permanent residence because of health, disability, or other reason, but is granted an annually renewable permission to enter the country. Permits are usually issued to a family member accompanying a landed immigrant who has accepted full responsibility for the individual concerned.

[5] The political and public discourse immigration rarely takes into account the effect of emigration of the Canadian-born and the return or remigration of landed immigrants. Most people are also unaware of the scale of temporary migration and its use to meet specific economic needs. It is estimated that between 80,000 and 90,000 person-years of employment are provided annually by temporary workers on visas (Boyd et al. 1986; Richmond 1991a).

[6] The *Singh* case (SCR 177 [1985]) was decided under the Charter of Rights and the Bill of Rights. It focused on the unwarranted infringement of the right to an oral hearing imposed by the examination-under-oath process that was previously in force.

[7] The family class includes relatives of citizens or landed immigrants who were not assessed under the points system. They included spouses, fiancés, fiancées, unmarried children, parents, grandparents over sixty, orphaned brothers, sisters, nephews, nieces, or grandchildren (not yet married) under eighteen years, or any other relative if the sponsor had no close relative in Canada.

There is growing uncertainty concerning how a 'family' should be defined. Some ethnic groups have a concept of the family as an extended one. Also, there are now common-law relationships, same-sex couples, polygamous spouses (and their children), spouses and children from a former marriage, as well as parents, grandchildren and lateral relatives such as brothers and sisters (and their children) who are potentially eligible. There is clearly a snowball effect from sponsorship.

[8] In February 1992, the immigration department announced a revised order of priority for processing immigrant applications abroad. Spouses, fiancés and fiancées, and children of immigrants already in Canada would receive the highest priority in order to reduce delays in family reunion. Other close relatives such as parents, brothers, sisters, and grandparents would receive the lowest priority. Refugees selected abroad would also be in the top priority category, followed by independent immigrants with prearranged employment, business immigrants,

immigrants nominated by provinces, and skilled workers in occupations deemed in short supply, in that order of preference.

[9] The council did not take into account emigration levels or the flow of temporary workers, which makes any recommendation concerning gross immigration somewhat dubious.

[10] In 1992, regulations were changed so that non-dependent children over nineteen were ineligible to immigrate under the family class. Some social workers and others complained that this discriminated against those in the refugee backlog who had been waiting several years to become landed immigrants, and whose children had grown up in the meantime.

[11] Designated classes were immigrants who did not meet the Convention definition of a refugee, but who were admitted on other humanitarian grounds.

[12] In late 1993, the Immigration and Refugee Board commissioned the *Review of Fundamental Justice* by a leading academic lawyer and expert on refugee determination procedure. The report advocated a non-adversarial approach by refugee hearing officers and made forty recommendations to improve the quality and fairness of the proceedings (Hathaway and MacMillan 1993).

[13] However, this decision was reversed by the incoming Liberal administration, which reunited citizenship and immigration under one minister, an arrangement not known since 1966.

[14] In 1994, the shooting death of a policeman by an immigrant, who had been ordered deported for previous criminal offences, brought to light the fact that the department had been under political pressure to increase the number of deportations by concentrating on the easy-to-locate cases. A misplaced file and a reluctance to expose immigration officers to dangerous arrest situations meant that criminal cases had low priority. An estimated 1,500 people with criminal records facing deportation had not been removed as of June 1994. Subsequently, an RCMP task force was set up to enforce the deportation of foreign-born criminals; at the same time, failed refugee claimants from China and elsewhere were required to depart unless they met certain conditions. Those from Afghanistan, Burundi, Haiti, and Rwanda were exempt due to human rights violations in those countries.

[15] Only persons born in Quebec of English-speaking parents have a right to English-language schooling. Sign laws restrict the use of non-French languages.

[16] The Charter does not specifically refer to sexual orientation, but it is believed that the courts will interpret the 'in particular' wording to include other possible sources of discrimination. In January 1992, a homosexual male from the Argentine successfully established a claim to refugee status in Canada on the ground that his sexual orientation would result in his persecution if he was returned to the Argentine. The issue of gender-related persecution has also been controversial. The Immigration and Refugee Board released *Guidelines for Women Refugees Fearing Gender-Related Persecution* in March 1993. While recognizing this as a humanitarian step forward, some refugee lawyers would have preferred to see wife assault and similar fears explicitly recognized in regulations as constituting grounds for recognizing a legitimate refugee claim (MacMillan 1993).

[17] In 1989, the Supreme Court held that Canadian citizenship was not a necessary requirement to practise law in British Columbia. It remains to be seen whether this ruling will affect the requirements for other professions or employment in the public service.

[18] A case in point is that of Ms Bembenick, a fugitive from US justice, whose extradition from Canada was delayed by her claim for refugee status in Canada on the ground that she had been framed and persecuted by the Wisconsin police.

She was eventually extradited to the US and pleaded 'no contest' in a retrial.

[19] In 1991, bureaucratic costs of processing asylum applicants were estimated at over $250 million (Swan 1991:102). This figure does not include the cost of removing the refugee backlog created before 1989. These costs may be compared with approximately $105 million annually spent by the federal government on language training and settlement, or the $35 million spent on long-term multicultural programming. These figures exclude expenditures by provincial or municipal authorities.

chapter nine

Racism and immigration: Britain and Canada[1]

The most prolonged and intense manifestations of racism and ethnic conflict are usually those directed against indigenous minorities. In Britain, the 'Celtic fringes' have been victimized by the dominant Anglo-Saxon population so that their languages have almost died out. Protestant-Catholic conflict in Northern Ireland has persisted for centuries, and terrorism has spread to the mainland. In Canada, the Aboriginal populations have experienced loss of land, language, and culture, as well as systemic discrimination following colonial settlement. However, in recent years immigration policies and the foreign-born populations of the two countries have been the locus of much racist discourse and practice.

Immigration policies need not completely exclude certain nationalities in order to warrant description as 'racist'. If the intended or unintended consequence of particular regulations is to put certain ethnic groups at a disadvantage while making it easier for others to gain admission, then such policies may be designated 'quasi-racist' or systemic forms of discrimination, even though the admissions criteria make no reference to 'race' as such. Thus visa requirements, literacy tests, health regulations and medical examinations, quotas, preference for close relatives, patrial clauses, the location of immigration offices abroad, and even exclusions based on environmental considerations can have a differential impact on particular ethnic groups (Richmond 1988c:95–106).

In examining British and Canadian immigration policies and related questions of ethnic conflict and racial violence, it is important to distinguish underlying conditions, intervening variables, and precipitating factors (see Chapter Five). It is also necessary to understand certain similarities and differences between the two countries in terms of demographic variables, education, and economic conditions. Variations in any of these may influence the probability of immigrants being accepted or rejected. Depending on these circumstances, specific events such as a racial assault or a homicide may lead to a violent confrontation or result in constructive responses designed to relieve tension and prevent a further escalation of conflict.

Underlying conditions

The underlying conditions influencing immigration policies in both countries are those that prevail at the global level. They include the economic disparities between developed and developing countries, the legacy of colonialism, the political confrontation of superpowers, recent changes in eastern Europe (including the disintegration of the Soviet empire), together with the continued instability of regions such as the Middle East, Southeast Asia, and Central America. The combined effect of all these has created a refugee crisis of immense proportions and overwhelming push factors promoting aspirations to emigrate from the Third World. The response of Britain, Canada, and most other Western countries has been to impose legal restrictions on immigration, adopting highly selective criteria for admission.

The immigration policies of countries such as Britain and other EEC countries, Australia, the United States, and Canada are contributing to a system of selective exclusion and repatriation. (The Maastrict Treaty, when fully ratified, will create the European Union, which will replace the European Economic Community.) Extensive use is being made of passports, travel documents, work permits, administrative tribunals, judicial hearings, police powers, 'requirement to depart' orders, voluntary repatriation, and deportation as a means of controlling who may and may not be allowed to live in the more affluent regions. Britain now permits free movement of EEC nationals, while Europe itself is becoming more restrictive. New regulations governing admission to EEC countries have warranted the description of its borders as 'fortress Europe' (Joly 1989).

In Britain, as in Canada, the emphasis is on the admission for permanent residence of close relatives, wealthy entrepreneurs, and persons with skills deemed to be in short supply in the labour force, thereby contributing to an international brain drain. At the same time, others (such as au pair girls and domestic servants) are admitted only on a temporary basis. The fact that a certain proportion of those allowed to settle are from Hong Kong or other 'New Commonwealth' countries is reminiscent of the 'honorary White' status formerly accorded to Japanese businesspersons and diplomats in

South Africa. Meanwhile, population pressures in Third World countries escalate and the gap between rich and poor nations widens. Aspirations to emigrate for economic reasons persist, and the number of refugees fleeing from violence continues to mount. While borders may not be completely closed, it is becoming more difficult for all but a select minority to obtain permanent residence in developed countries. Many who have been given temporary asylum or contract employment are subject to deportation or repatriation (Dowty 1987; Suyama 1989; Zolberg et al. 1989).

These underlying conditions influence government policies and the attitudes of the general public. Protecting borders from undocumented migrants is seen as necessary and desirable in order to maintain existing economic standards. Restrictions are intended to reduce competition for scarce resources such as jobs and housing, to limit overcrowding in schools, and avoid excessive demands on health services or the welfare (income security) system. None of these considerations are 'racist' in themselves, but they assume that immigration controls are a necessary precondition for social harmony. As British labour politician Roy Hattersley put it, 'integration without control is impossible, but control without integration is indefensible' (Hansard 1965). Restrictions on non-'White' immigration are seen as in the interest of existing ethnic minorities because it is feared that uncontrolled immigration will precipitate a backlash, exacerbating existing levels of prejudice and discrimination. In Canada, migrant farm labour and domestic workers from the Caribbean are among those who have been allowed only temporary visas, at least in part to avoid the creation of a permanent 'Black' working class (Bakan 1987; Satzewich 1988). However, restrictive immigration policies implicitly label non-'White' immigrants as less desirable and provide a spurious legitimation for racist attitudes. Immigrants themselves are seen as a 'problem' and policies are then directed towards exclusion instead of addressing the root causes and manifestations of racial prejudice and discrimination in the receiving society.

Intervening variables

Intervening variables influencing immigration and majority-minority relations include the institutional structure of the receiving countries, the ethnic composition of their respective populations, together with demographic, educational, and socio-economic characteristics of immigrants. Comparing Britain and Canada, Reitz (1988:118) noted that the institutions had a direct effect on the way immigrants were perceived, which, in turn, influenced interracial competition and conflict. Among the institutional differences were those relating to the legislative and administrative control of immigration itself. In this respect, the year 1961–2 was critical because it marked a turning point for both countries. Canada effectively lifted almost all legislative restrictions on non-European immigration in 1962 while at the same time introducing selection on the basis of education and occupation. The UK passed the first of a series of acts designed to limit immigration from the so-called 'new commonwealth' and Pakistan, but some immigration from the West Indies and the Indian subcontinent to Britain still continues, although under strictly controlled conditions and regulations. In recent years, it has been mainly spouses and other close relatives of former settlers who have been admitted (Home Office 1989). Nevertheless, Britain has generally experienced a net loss of population through migration when all countries of origin and destination are taken into account.[2]

In the 1970s, both countries accepted expellees from Uganda and other East African countries (mainly of Asian ethnic origin) and admitted a number of Vietnamese refugees. Currently, Canada has increasing immigration from Hong Kong, which is also a new source of immigration to Britain. Overall, Canada has more diverse immigration from both European and non-European sources, including the Philippines, the Middle East, Africa, and Latin America. Recently, Canada has moved towards a more restrictive control over immigration with the implementation of several new measures between 1989 and 1993 (see Chapter Eight). However, selective immigration motivated by a mixture of demographic, economic, and humanitarian policy considerations continues to be promoted. In contrast, Britain still sees immigration as a potential threat to national integration (Birch 1989:77–137). Altogether, only 6.7 per cent out of a total UK population of 54.2 million were born overseas, of whom 1.4 million (approximately 40 per cent) came from New Commonwealth countries and Pakistan (CRE 1985). Overall, out of a total of 27 million in 1991, 16 per cent of the population were born outside of Canada, of whom 30.7 per cent (or almost 1.2 million) came from Third World countries.

Recent immigration trends in Canada and Britain

Table 16 shows the overall trends in Canadian immigration from 1984–93. In this period, the number of annual arrivals ranged from a low of 84,493 in 1985 to a high of 252,574 in 1992.[3] The increase followed political lobbying to remove a growing backlog of relatives in the family reunion category, the need to deal with spontaneous arrivals claiming asylum, the promotion of business immigration for investment purposes, and Quebec's desire for a larger share of such immigration. The proportion of immigrants from Asia and the Pacific rose from 41 per cent in 1983 to more than half by 1992. The percentage of Caribbean and Central American immigrants fell after 1986. Hong Kong accounts for approximately 14 per cent of all immigrants. Throughout this period, family class immigration and assisted relatives have been an important component, accounting for about half of all immigrants.

High unemployment in the early 1980s led to a deliberate limitation in the number of selected workers (independent immigrants) admitted, although Canada continued to make use of temporary employment visas to fill short-term vacancies for certain classes of workers, particularly female domestics, some factory jobs, and seasonal employment in agriculture. As temporary employment authorizations are usually for less than one year, they must be converted for statistical purposes into equivalent person-years. In 1987 and 1988 (as in some earlier years) the equivalent person-years of employment provided through temporary authorizations exceeded that provided by annual immigration of a more permanent nature. By 1992, the number of temporary employment authorizations had risen to 228,000, including those issued to asylum applicants. (Trends in the admission of refugees, designated classes, and asylum applicants were examined in Chapter Eight.)

The government of Canada has encouraged business immigration in recent years. The numbers admitted under special entrepreneur and investor classes rose from less than 2,000 in 1985 to nearly 7,000 in 1992. When their dependents are included, the numbers rise to 5,000 and 15,684 respectively. In 1987, business immigrants brought an estimated $1.9 billion to Canada and in 1988 the figure was $3.1 billion. Hong Kong was the largest single source, accounting for 28 per cent of all business immigrants, followed by South Korea, Taiwan, and the United States. There has been much controversy over these programs, which have been subject to abuse by those merely endeavouring to obtain entry to Canada without necessarily fulfilling their obligations (Nash 1987). This led the minister of Employment and Immigration in 1989 to put in place a monitoring program to track entrepreneurs until they have complied with the terms and conditions of their landing. There are still problems with the program as some business immigrants settle their families in Canada and then return to their former country. Others complain that their investments have been misappropriated by syndicates soliciting funds.

As noted in Chapter Eight, enforcement and control measures have been strengthened by new legislation and the number of interdictions, removals, and requirements to depart from Canada have been rising annually since the mid-1980s.

Britain

Immigration to Britain is governed by earlier Aliens Acts, as well as by the Immigration Act of 1971, the British Nationality Act of 1981, the Immigration Act of 1988, and the Asylum and Immigration Appeals Act of 1993. Prior to 1962, British commonwealth and colonial subjects were free to enter the UK without restriction. Subsequently, limitations were placed on the right of abode, which differentiated between those whose parent or grandparent came from Britain and those without such patrial status. Further restrictions were imposed on spouses and children. The latter may be required to undertake DNA tests to prove a biological relationship. One-to four-year qualifying periods of residence were required before some categories of applicants could acquire permanent settlement and re-entry status (Home Office 1989). The 1993 legislation authorizes the fingerprinting of asylum applicants, restricts access by such applicants to public (council) housing in British municipalities, and curtails leave to enter or remain in the UK. It also provides limited rights of appeal against deportation when this would be against Britain's obligations under the UN Convention relating to the Status of Refugees. The act also extends carriers' liability in transporting passengers who are refused entry. A High Court judgement in 1993 confirmed that 'asylum buck passing' was legal in Britain, i.e., it was permissible to deport someone fleeing persecution in the home country if they arrived in Britain via a safe third country. Similar regulations now apply in other European countries and in Canada.

Population movement between Eire and the United Kingdom remained unrestricted and after Britain joined the EEC, nationals of western European countries were no longer subject to control. Excluding nationals of EEC countries, a total of 8.1 million passengers were admitted to the United Kingdom in 1991, less than the peak in 1990. The majority of passengers were short-term visitors, but 46,920 (including dependants) were allowed to remain for short-term employment, or education and training (see Table 25). The majority obtaining temporary work permits were from the United States, Europe, and the 'old commonwealth'. EEC nationals did not require permits.

Including those who were permitted to stay after removal of a time limit, 53,900 people were accepted for settlement in 1991. Table 24 shows the trends in immigration to Britain from 1984 to 1991 by geographic region and nationality. These figures are based on the number of those subject to control and accepted for settlement on arrival or after removal of a time limit. Excluded from control are people from Ireland and those from commonwealth countries who were entitled to patrial status, together with most entering from EEC countries.[4] The total of those subject to control and admitted for settlement was approximately 50,000 annually between 1982 and 1991. The majority of these were in Britain already on visas subject to a time limit. The number admitted immediately on arrival declined over the decade and was only 6,020 in 1991. There was an increase in acceptances following a time limit after 1987 due to efforts to remove a backlog of applicants from the Indian subcontinent for admission of a spouse. Of those admitted in 1991, 47 per cent were from Asia. However, when those not subject to control (from Ireland, the EEC, and commonwealth countries) are taken into account, gross immigration into Britain is about 130,000 annually and net migration slightly negative.

Between 1979 and 1988, Britain awarded refugee status to 9,585 persons and gave a right of residence because of exceptional humanitarian circumstances to an additional 1,960. During this period, 6,420 persons were refused refugee status and required to depart. In 1988, the number of refugees granted the right to settle in the UK after four or more years residence declined from 700 to 350. However, there was an increase in the number of refugees accepted on arrival from Vietnam and the government indicated that it would accept a further 2,000 Vietnamese from Hong Kong before June 1992. In 1991, 1,000 refugees were accepted for settlement, but there were nearly 24,000 asylum applications (see Table 26). In anticipation of the return of Hong Kong to mainland China in 1997, legislation allows a limited number of Hong Kong Chinese into Britain in the next few years. Enforcement of immigration controls became stricter. In 1991, 18,182 persons were refused entry to the UK and 5,600 were deported or required to depart. This was more than double the number in 1987. In 1993, the death of a West Indian woman deportee while in custody led to concern about the methods used by police to restrain those forcibly removed. Controversy arose over abuse of student visa regulations by language schools that permitted students to work full-time. At the same time, there was some support among politicians (not all on the extreme right) for the voluntary repatriation of any Caribbean immigrants as long as they were prepared to relinquish their right to return to Britain.

Ethnic and 'visible' minorities in Britain and Canada

In Canada, the concept of a 'visible minority' has entered the official vocabulary to the extent that Statistics Canada has been asked to estimate the numbers and distribution of such persons. Attempts to quantify the concept of a 'visible minority' rely upon cross-classifying such diverse criteria as birthplace, ancestry, language, and religion, or upon self-definition. The estimates, based on the 1986 census, are shown in Figure 9.1. This shows that 6.4 per cent of the population (or approximately 1.6 million persons) are so categorized. In addition, there were approximately 845,000 native or Aboriginal peoples.[5] Major groups included 390,000 Chinese and 355,600 'Blacks'.[6] Federal government agencies and federally funded organizations, together with corporations doing business with the government, are required to keep appropriate records in connection with the federal Employment Equity Act. Similar legislation requiring employers to reflect the ethnic composition of the local community in their labour force is proposed for Ontario. However, the legal and bureaucratic adoption of the term 'visible minority' fails to address the complex ethnocultural reality of the Canadian population. It implies an equation of genetically determined physical attributes (such as skin colour) with environmentally influenced cultural and socio-economic characteristics. Such a link has long been rejected by scientists.

The use of the term 'visible minority' gives a spurious legitimacy to a 'racial' categorization that has no biological or social reality. Furthermore, its use obscures the very different circumstances and needs of such widely different groups as the Canadian-born descendants of Afro-American

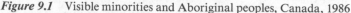

Figure 9.1 Visible minorities and Aboriginal peoples, Canada, 1986

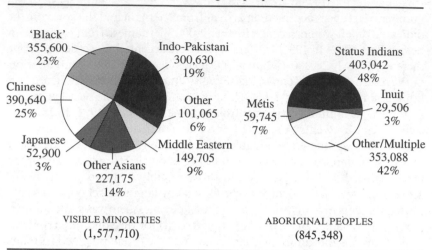

'Black'
355,600
23%

Chinese
390,640
25%

Japanese
52,900
3%

Other Asians
227,175
14%

Indo-Pakistani
300,630
19%

Other
101,065
6%

Middle Eastern
149,705
9%

Métis
59,745
7%

Status Indians
403,042
48%

Inuit
29,506
3%

Other/Multiple
353,088
42%

VISIBLE MINORITIES
(1,577,710)

ABORIGINAL PEOPLES
(845,348)

Indian and Northern Affairs (1989); Statistics Canada (1989, adapted)

slaves, wealthy Asian immigrants recently arrived from Hong Kong, Vietnamese refugees, Afro-Caribbean immigrants, and many others, including Arabs and Latin Americans. It also includes the Canadian-born children of these groups. No single policy or program designed to deal with discrimination, employment equity, or other dimensions of economic and social justice can respond to these very different situations by combining them all into one category of 'visible minority'. This is not to deny the reality of the discrimination and disadvantage experienced by many people perceived as 'racially' distinct.

In Britain, the term 'ethnic minority' has come to mean much the same as the term 'visible minority' in Canada. In both countries, these terms exclude other immigrant groups and indigenous minorities defined only in terms of birthplace, language, religion, or culture. The latest estimates of ethnic minority populations in Britain are based on labour force surveys conducted from 1984–6 (Shaw 1988). They are shown in Figure 9.2. In 1986, 2.43 million persons (or 4.5 per cent of the population) were designated 'ethnic minorities', and 43 per cent of these were born in the United Kingdom. The largest groups were those of Indian origin (760,000), followed by West Indian (534,000) and Pakistani (397,000).[7]

Education and socio-economic characteristics

Of all ethnic minorities in Canada, the Aboriginal population (whose preferred designation is 'First Nations') have experienced the worst deprivation, as measured by indexes of education, health, housing, occupational

Figure 9.2 Ethnic minorities in Britain

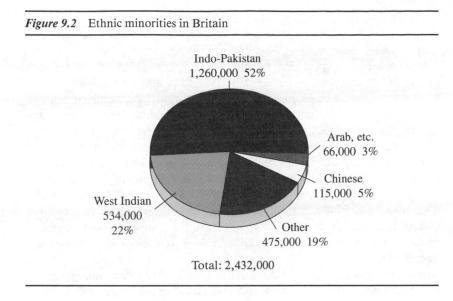

Indo-Pakistan
1,260,000 52%

Arab, etc.
66,000 3%

Chinese
115,000 5%

West Indian
534,000
22%

Other
475,000 19%

Total: 2,432,000

status, and income (Indian and Northern Affairs Canada 1989). Although there have been improvements in the last decade, life expectancy is considerably below the national average. Suicides and violent deaths are high, the latter rate being three times the national average. Functional illiteracy (defined as less than a grade nine education) among status Indians is more than double the rest of the population and the rate for Inuit is even higher. Average Aboriginal incomes are slightly more than half those of other Canadians and the gap appears to be widening (Indian and Northern Affairs Canada 1989, Part III).

Caribbean and Asian immigrants and their children in Canada were better educated than their counterparts in Britain, due largely to the policy of greater occupational selectivity exercised by the Canadian immigration authorities. However, more emphasis on family reunion in recent years resulted in some increase in immigrants with elementary education only, but the overall educational level remained higher than the national average. In 1986, 22 per cent of the Canadian population fifteen years of age and over had some university education compared with 36 per cent of immigrants from non-traditional source countries. Generally, Asian immigrants had higher qualifications than those from the Caribbean (Beaujot et al. 1988; Richmond and Mendoza 1990; Seward and Tremblay 1989). A study in Toronto showed that there was a decline in the educational level of Caribbean immigrants arriving after 1976, but that those who received most of their education in Canada were achieving qualifications at a level commensurate with that of the general population (Richmond 1993b).

Brown (1984:133) showed that in Britain, Asian men were as well qualified academically as 'White' men, but were less qualified vocationally, while West Indian men were less qualified than 'White' men in both respects. Asian and West Indian women had lower academic qualifications than 'White' women, but West Indian women were closer to 'White' women in terms of vocational training. In the period 1988–90, 48 per cent of 'White' males and 27 per cent of 'White' women had A-level (high school) or higher. The proportion for ethnic minority men and women was 38 per cent and 25 per cent, respectively. However, among the younger age groups, the differences were much reduced, and there was a marked tendency for ethnic minority youth to remain in school longer than their 'White' counterparts (Jones 1993:31–60). Nevertheless, there remains a perception that British-born youth of Caribbean origin underachieve in the educational system (Drew and Gray 1991; Rampton 1981; Swann 1985). This may be partially attributable to the school and the neighbourhood (Smith and Tomlinson 1989). Racial discrimination and abuse remain a serious issue in British and Canadian schools (Gillborn and Drew 1992; James 1990).

Notwithstanding their formal qualifications, many new immigrants to Canada have difficulty finding commensurate employment due to non-recognition of their credentials, lack of Canadian experience, and racial discrimination (Cumming et al. 1989; McDade 1988). As a consequence, occupations and incomes do not necessarily match those that would be expected when sex, age, and education are controlled. Based on the 1981 census, Caribbean-born males earned 82 per cent of the expected level of income, compared with 108 per cent for British-born, 91 per cent for south Asia, and 78 per cent for southeast Asia. Relative to other women, female immigrants were slightly less disadvantaged, although the gender gap in incomes remained high. The most recent arrivals earned proportionally even less than the average (Beaujot et al. 1988:68). Comparable income data are not available for minorities in Britain, but Brown (1984:212) showed that median weekly earnings for West Indian males in full-time employment were 85 per cent and Asian men 86 per cent of those of 'White' men. West Indian women actually earned more than 'White' or Asian women.

Unemployment has been a serious problem for ethnic minorities in both countries. In the UK, the unemployment rate for ethnic minority groups was nearly twice that of the 'White' population from 1984–6, and in 1987–8 it was 60 per cent higher. Unemployment was highest in the Pakistani/ Bangladesh communities and among West Indian men. In the age group of sixteen to twenty-four, unemployment from 1986–8 averaged 16 per cent for 'White' males and 31 per cent for West Indian males; they were slightly lower for young women, but still above average for the ethnic minorities (*Employment Gazette* 1990). Although unemployment rates had fallen by 1990, there was still a similar differential between the 'White' and ethnic minority populations (Jones 1993:112–33). In Canada, there were substantial regional differences in unemployment levels. In the metropolitan areas where most immigrants and their descendants have settled, unemployment rates were below the national average. However, in 1981, age-standardized unemployment rates for Caribbean-born males were twice those of Canadian-born males in Montreal and 50 per cent higher in Toronto. Unemployment was particularly high among West Indian youth. In 1981, one in four Caribbean-born males aged fifteen to twenty-four years in Montreal and one in eight in Toronto were unemployed. In both cases, these rates were roughly 50 per cent higher than those for the Canadian-born of the same age. Caribbean women also had high unemployment rates, particularly in Montreal (Richmond 1989:30–3). Recently arrived immigrants from non-traditional source countries had the highest unemployment rates. However, overall measures of socio-economic status show that Canada's Aboriginal population scores the lowest of all groups on measures of education, occupational status, and income (Indian and Northern Affairs Canada 1989).

Racism and violence in Britain and Canada

The term 'visible minority' has been adopted precisely because racism is a reality in Canada as in other countries. The reality of ethnic prejudice, discrimination, and disadvantage has been documented in a number of studies (Henry 1978; Ramcharan 1982; Richmond 1988b). Racist attitudes are widespread and expressed overtly or covertly, by up to a third of the population. A report by a parliamentary committee stated that 'one need only look at the employment practices of police departments, fire departments, government services, universities, the media and private companies to see that visible minorities are consciously or unconsciously denied full participation in almost all Canadian institutions' (Daudlin 1984:1).

The most dramatic example of violence in the relations between ethnic minorities in Canada and the 'White' population occurred in the summer of 1990 in a suburb of Montreal where a dispute over an Indian land claim led to a prolonged stand-off between police and armed Mohawk 'warriors'. The precipitating event was an attempt by the local municipality to acquire a sacred burial ground to expand a golf course. One policeman lost his life in the initial shooting. Eventually, the army used tanks to remove barricades and fortifications. The situation was complicated by sympathetic action taken by other Indian bands, leading to the blocking of traffic over a bridge and a main artery into the city of Montreal for several weeks.[8]

The media have focused on allegations of growing violence among teenage and young adult gangs in Canada's cities. The *Globe and Mail* in June 1990 had several articles on Asian crime and *Maclean's* weekly news magazine (22 May 1989) devoted its front cover and leading articles to 'Gang Terror: How Young Thugs Are Creating Fear in Canadian Cities'. Such sensational journalism ignores the fact that violent crime remains a fraction of that in most American cities. Some youth gangs in Toronto and elsewhere recruit members from a particular racial group, while others are mixed. One journalist quoted an interesting comment from the leader of a punk rock group whose members wear Mohawk-style haircuts and outlandish gear. 'We could have been good white folk but we made the choice to be a visible minority. We fit right into Toronto's multicultural society because we created our own ethnic group' (*Maclean's* 22 May 1989:41). In 1993, it was alleged that Filipino youths were being singled out by security guards at shopping malls and required to leave the malls on suspicion of criminal intent.

When demographic and socio-economic factors are taken into account, there is no statistically reliable evidence that any one ethnic minority is more likely to be engaged in crime than any other. Unfortunately, their visibility makes 'Black' and Asian youths targets for police surveillance, and so allegations of racial harassment are common. These have been reinforced by several incidents in Montreal and Toronto, where police have shot and wounded or killed 'Blacks' suspected of involvement in traffic offences, car theft, drug peddling, or gang violence. The *Report of the Race Relations and Policing Task Force*, established by the Ontario Solicitor General in 1988 following accusations of racism against the police, concluded that 'Relations between the police and visible minority communities in some parts of this province are strained at the best of times. Following a confrontation, they deteriorate dramatically, leaving a gulf of mutual misunderstanding and sometimes outright hostility' (Lewis 1989:152). The task force made some fifty-seven recommendations for the improvement of relations between the police and racial minorities, many of which have still to be implemented by the authorities concerned. When a further outbreak of violence occurred in Toronto in 1992, Stephen Lewis (former UN ambassador) was asked to investigate. He noted that racism was widespread. Visible minority communities throughout southern Ontario experienced indignities and systemic discrimination. He singled out the 'Black' (Afro-Canadian) population as the principal victims.

> It is Blacks who are being shot, it is Black youth that is unemployed in excessive numbers, it is Black students who are being inappropriately streamed in schools, it is Black kids who are disproportionately dropping out, it is housing communities with large concentrations of Black residents where a sense of vulnerability and disadvantage is most acute, it is Black employees, professional and non-professional, on whom the doors of upward equity slam shut (Lewis 1992:2).

Quebec also experienced several incidents of violence involving the police. Ethnocentrism among francophone Canadians is generally greater than among anglophones. One study attributed this to a 'siege culture' in Quebec, which feels threatened by English in the rest of the country and by American influences (Berry, Kalin, and Taylor 1977:247). Royal commissions in Nova Scotia and Manitoba have drawn attention to the failure of the justice system to deal fairly with native peoples. In other regions, hostilities towards Sikhs and other ethnic minorities take the form of harassment, vandalism, swastika painting, graffiti, and the spreading of racial hatred through telephone messages, buttons, and T-shirts with racist slogans. There have been attempts to mobilize support for neofascist organizations and to promote racism among young skinheads. However, with the exception of the confrontation between 'Whites' and Mohawks in Montreal and the post-Los Angeles disturbances in 1992, Canada has avoided the outbreaks of collective violence and rioting in the streets that have occurred frequently in Britain.

Violence in Britain

Britain has a long history of race prejudice, discrimination, and violence (Banton 1985; Rex and Tomlinson 1979; Richmond 1954, 1955). There were disturbances in various British port towns after the First World War and rioting erupted again in Liverpool in 1948. The Notting Hill area of London and Nottingham in the East Midlands experienced racial incidents in 1958, and again in Notting Hill in 1976. In 1979, clashes occurred in Southall, London, between Asians and supporters of the neofascist National Front, which resulted in fatalities. Earlier riots involved direct attacks by 'Whites' on 'Blacks', whereas in the 1980s in Brixton, Liverpool, Bristol, Birmingham, and elsewhere, 'Black' anger appears to have been directed against property and the police. Throughout the period, there were less publicized clashes in various neighbourhoods in which there was a high proportion of immigrant or British-born youths of Afro-Caribbean origin. Also, there have been violent incidents involving 'White' youths described as 'skinheads' or 'mods'. Harassment of 'Black' and Asian tenants in local authority housing estates is a major problem. A Home Office report noted the increase in racial attacks and the inadequate response of housing authorities and other agencies to the problem (Home Office 1989b). In addition, there has been increased violence at football matches, which sometimes appears to have racial undertones, suggested by the use of fascist slogans and antiracial slurs.

In September 1985, violence broke out in several British towns. The same inner-city localities that had erupted in 1981 were once more in the headlines. In others that had been relatively peaceful, fighting, window breaking, looting, burning, and direct clashes between the police and youths (both 'Black' and 'White') occurred. In Brixton, it was reported that, out of 212 arrests, 132 were 'Black', seventy-four were 'White', four were 'dark-skinned Europeans', one was Asian (meaning Indo-Pakistani), and one was Chinese. As in 1981, when a similar pattern was discernible, initial disturbances in Brixton were followed by outbreaks in Liverpool, Manchester, Bristol, and various parts of the West Midlands, including Birmingham (Benyon 1984; Richmond 1988b). In September 1993, there were violent clashes in the east end of London, coinciding with the election of a British

National Party candidate to the local town council. Subsequently, there were violent clashes between antiracist marchers and the the police, who tried to prevent the marchers from approaching the head office and bookstore run by the British National Party. In the course of the march, a 'Black' policeman was injured by antiracists, who called him a 'traitor'.

Ethnic conflicts in mainland cities of the British Isles are not yet as serious as those between Protestants and Catholics in Northern Ireland, where the level of violence has reached critical proportions. The IRA has been active in England as well causing casualties and much property damage. However, if economic and social policies do not respond to the real needs of areas with a high proportion of immigrants and their descendants, there will be further trouble. If residents are not involved in the decision-making processes affecting them by having full democratic participation at the local and central level, these cities may follow the Belfast example. So far, the British government's policy response to racial violence in the cities has been to treat the symptoms through a coercive law and order approach, rather than treating the underlying conditions or intervening factors. The result has been a feedback that reenforces conflict and exacerbates already tense race relations. Prevention is always better than belated attempts to cure a situation that has already seriously deteriorated.

So far in Canada, the confrontation with Aboriginal peoples has exhibited the same reflexive emphasis upon 'law and order, even to the point of relying on military force and intimidation. So far, the incidents of violence involving the police and 'Blacks' in Toronto and Montreal have been contained. They have resulted in orderly protest marches and representations to municipal and provincial authorities, leading to the establishment of investigative task forces and similar measures. However, promises of amendments to the Criminal Code and the Police Act, which are designed to limit the use of firearms by the police, and other recommended reforms, have yet to be implemented. The 'Black' and Asian populations, including the middle classes, are beginning to feel insecure and threatened. Further delays could aggravate an already tense situation.

The future economic and social conditions facing ethnic minorities born and raised in Canada will be critical. This includes the native peoples whose experience of racism has persisted since the earliest colonial contacts. The events in Montreal and elsewhere in the summer of 1990 heightened tension in native communities right across the country.[9] The rejection of constitutional amendments that would have recognized the inherent right to self-government for First Nations has left a legacy of frustration and disappointment.

The children of Caribbean and Asian immigrants must be able to look forward to a better future. Like their counterparts in Britain, they will not accept perpetual exclusion from the mainstream. Full employment policies designed to ensure economic security are vital. If persisting high rates of unemployment are the price to be paid for combatting inflation, promoting free trade with the US or Europe, and globalizing the economies of Britain and Canada, serious social consequences could result. There must be equality of opportunity for all, and this must be accompanied by a sense of dignity, social acceptance, and full participation by minorities in economic, political, and social life if further violence is to be avoided.

Notes

[1] This is an extensively revised and edited version of a paper first published in *International Journal of Comparative Sociology* 31 (1990):3–4.

[2] Britain experienced an overall net migration loss of population (including British subjects) from 1971, except in 1979 and 1983–7 when there were small gains due mainly to increased immigration from the European community. Canada does not keep records of people leaving the country, but emigration is generally estimated at 0.28 per cent of the population, or approximately 70,000 annually.

[3] The figures in Table 16 are for landed immigrants only. They exclude people legally in Canada with temporary employment visas, minister's permits, and those seeking asylum.

[4] Under the British Nationality Act (1981), persons born in the UK, together with their children and grandchildren, are not subject to immigration control. Persons holding European Economic Community passports are also no longer subject to control. Table 24 includes those accepted for settlement on arrival, and those accepted on removal of a time limit initially imposed (Home Office 1989). The numbers differ from the estimates of immigration and emigration based on the International Passenger Survey, which records arrivals and departures and includes those exempted from control, except those from Ireland.

[5] In 1991, 470,615 persons reported single Aboriginal origins, an increase of 26 per cent from 1986. A further 532,060 reported mixed Aboriginal and other origins, including Métis.

[6] Of those reporting Asian ethnic origin, 26 per cent were Canadian-born. Of the 'Black' population, which included Caribbean, approximately 20 per cent were born in Canada. The *Definition of Visible Minorities and Aboriginal People for Employment Equity* was prepared by the Census Custom Products Service, Census Operations Division, April 1989.

[7] An 'ethnic' question was asked in the 1991 census of England and Wales, the results of which are not yet available; the total ethnic minority population was estimated to be 2,577,000 in 1990 (Jones 1993:22).

[8] At the time of writing, the dispute remains unresolved. A major obstacle to a peaceful settlement has been the claim made by Mohawk negotiators to complete Iroquois sovereignty over extensive territory consisting of traditional lands on both sides of the US–Canada border.

[9] Further problems arose in 1993–94 due to smuggling of cigarettes and liquor across Mohawk territory bordering the US, Quebec, and Ontario.

chapter ten

Immigration and multiculturalism
in Canada and Australia[1]

Canadian and Australian immigration and multiculturalism policies in the last decade appear to be vacillating and inconsistent. They reflect the contradictions and crises inherent in the global system. The number of admissions fluctuated from year to year, the ethnic and skill composition changed, announced levels were exceeded or fell short. The large number of undocumented migrants threatened the integrity of selection procedures overseas and, in the case of Canada, almost overwhelmed border controls. Multicultural policies and funding experienced similar vicissitudes and generated much controversy and debate. Opposition grew in both countries to increased immigration and ethnic diversification, yet the numbers admitted from non-traditional sources continued their upward trend. The lack of a consistent policy resulted from *ad hoc* responses to global change. Exogenous and endogenous sources of demographic, economic, social, and political change generated conflicting pressures. Canada and Australia faced similar crises and their responses reflected the contradictions inherent in the situation.[2]

While the Third World population continued to grow rapidly throughout the decade, traditional immigrant-receiving countries experienced slow population growth as a consequence of low fertility. Long-term demographic projections suggested that increased immigration would delay an eventual population decline, but short-term economic and political conditions made it difficult for either Canada or Australia to adopt an open-door policy. Prevailing democratic and humanitarian values led to an emphasis on family reunification and refugee admissions amid fears that numbers could be overwhelming. Public opinion in both countries showed a marked ambivalence towards issues relating to immigration, refugees, and multicultural questions (Office of Multicultural Affairs 1989; Reid 1989). Legal, bureaucratic, and security considerations emphasized the need to maintain border control, and tough legislative measures were taken to deport illegal claimants and deter economic refugees.

During the 1980s, affluent societies became increasingly aware of the ecological and environmental impact of their own affluent lifestyles, including the waste of non-renewable resources and the dangers of pollution. These concerns related directly to population problems and led to support for zero-population growth and an anti-immigration lobby, which was particularly strong in Australia. Structural shifts in the economy, combined with postindustrialism and technological change in a global economy, generated intense competition for investment capital and led to loss of traditional livelihoods, high unemployment, inflationary pressures, and regional trade blocs in Europe, North America, and the Pacific. A growing emphasis on economic rationality and market forces created a conflict of interest between traditional rural, resource-based industries and the older manufacturing sector on the one hand and the emerging cosmopolitan populations in the service industries of metropolitan areas on the other. While urban centres continued to prosper and attract immigrants from all over the world, small towns and populations in the rural and maritime hinterlands were threatened with extinction. By 1991, the industrial heartlands were also experiencing serious economic problems. Canada and Australia were obliged to respond to the need for new investment by encouraging entrepreneurs and business-class immigrants from Japan, Hong Kong, Korea, Taiwan, Lebanon, and Arab countries. The resulting pressure on domestic real estate and housing markets created further anti-immigration backlash.

Although the numbers admitted declined, there was continued emphasis on the immigration of skilled and professionally qualified immigrants, although there was growing recognition that anachronistic licensing requirements and a failure to recognize overseas training and credentials impeded recently arrived immigrants' access to skilled trades and professions. The increasing ethnic diversification of the Australian and Canadian populations—which was a result of increased non-traditional immigration from Asia, the Middle East, the Caribbean, and Latin America—generated a racist backlash. In both countries, governments shifted the emphasis of their multicultural programs from language and cultural heritage maintenance to combatting racism and promoting better community relations. In the 1980s, both Canada and Australia faced a growing crisis of national unity that will continue in the foreseeable future. Ethnic nationalism, the collective rights of linguistic minorities, and demands for greater

Figure 10.1   Canada: Landed immigrants by last residence

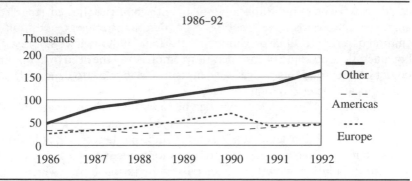

1986–92

SOURCE: Canada Employment and Immigration

regional autonomy threatened the unity of both countries, Canada in particular. This may prove to be the ultimate contradiction as Canada and
Australia adapt to a loss of sovereignty, the globalization of their respective
economies, and the consequent internationalization of their demographic
and social systems (Russell 1993:57).

Immigration policies

Canada entered the 1980s with a new Immigration Act,[3] which a leading
political scientist specializing in the comparative study of immigration
policy described as 'one of the best pieces of immigration legislation to be
found anywhere' (Hawkins 1989:xix). By the end of the decade, however, the
global refugee crisis and the flow of undocumented immigrants had forced
the Canadian government to pass three new laws (bills C-55, C-84, and C-
86), which substantially amended the earlier legislation. These laws aimed
to deter people from arriving in Canada without proper selection and
approval abroad, and to restore effective control over Canada's borders.
Meanwhile, actual immigration levels fell to a low point in the mid-1980s and
then rose steadily (see Figure 10.1). From 143,117 at the beginning of the
decade, the number of landings fell to 84,302 in 1985, rising again to more
than the planned level of 160,000 in 1989. The government reacted by
announcing still higher target levels (rising to 250,000 in 1992) despite the
prolonged recession. Furthermore, the composition of immigration
changed significantly during this period. Not only was the proportion from
non-traditional source countries increasing, but the number of those admitted as selected workers declined, the ratio of family reunion cases increased,
and, from 1988 onwards, the government was emphasizing the importance
of encouraging entrepreneurs and investors to come to Canada. Meanwhile,
a backlog of applications for refugee status or special admission after arrival

in Canada built up, reaching 85,000 claims (or approximately 125,000 persons) by the end of 1988. At this time a new set of regulations was introduced to clear the backlog and to process new refugee applications under a simplified procedure based on stricter criteria. Nevertheless, no sooner had the old backlog begun to recede when a new one emerged. In 1990, the Federal Court held that guidelines used for preliminary hearings were contrary to law, questioning the viability of the whole backlog clearance program.[4]

In the last decade, Australia accepted approximately 1 million settlers, the annual intake ranging from 80,000 in 1984–5 to 147,000 in 1988–9 and 124,000 in 1990–1. The average rate is approximately six per thousand of the Australian population. There were additional 300,000 long-term visitors in the decade, of whom a large proportion were from New Zealand, with which Australia has an agreement permitting free movement. In turn, New Zealand has a considerable in-migration from dependencies in the Pacific islands.

When emigration and remigration are taken into account, net migration accounted for 40 per cent of Australia's population growth in the decade 1981–90. Some aspects of immigration policy remain controversial, particularly in respect of the increasing proportion of immigrants from non-European sources. At the beginning of the decade, these constituted less than half the total number of settlers, but, by 1989, two-thirds of the immigrants came from Asia and the Middle East. The Australian government announced its intention of maintaining family, humanitarian, and skilled immigration streams, of which the family reunion component will be the largest. The program anticipated approximately 71,000 family migrants annually, 55,000 selected skilled workers and special eligibility cases, together with 14,000 refugees, including a contingency reserve. Meanwhile, Australian immigration law was amended to tighten control over potential asylum seekers and illegal immigrants (mainly those overstaying visitor status). A key principle of the government's policy is that 'only an Australian citizen has a right to enter Australia' (Lynch 1990; Richmond 1991a).

In some respects, Australia's immigration in the 1980s is similar to that of Canada, although there are also important differences. Although immigrants constitute nearly 20.8 per cent of the Australian population (compared with 16 per cent in Canada), those born in the UK and Ireland were a much larger proportion of the total foreign-born, as shown in tables 21 and 27. Australian immigration levels, like those in Canada, fluctuated throughout the decade. The proportion of non-Europeans increased, a points system was used to admit selected workers, family reunion cases grew proportionally, and both countries continued to emphasize multicultural policies. Australia introduced new legislation in 1989. It now exerts much stricter control over admissions and has taken measures to deter dubious refugee claims and illegal immigrants.[5] Australian immigration trends in the 1980s

Figure 10.2 Australia: Settler arrivals by birthplace

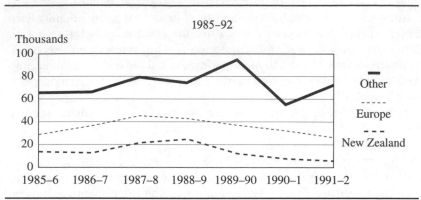

SOURCE: Bureau of Immigration Research

paralleled those of Canada. In 1981–2, 118,030 permanent settlers were admitted; the numbers fell to 77,510 in 1985, rose to 143,470 in 1987–8, and subsequently declined again (see Table 28 and Figure 10.2). Immigration from Asian countries and other non-traditional sources increased as a result of a growth in the numbers of sponsored family members and efforts to encourage investors. Due to its geographic position, Australia was less susceptible to border infringements, although some 'boat people' did arrive on its northern shores in 1977.[6] Even so, its legislation already provided more punitive and deterrent powers to discourage undocumented entry. Unlike Canada, it did not automatically grant a refugee hearing to anyone arriving at the airport seeking asylum. Generally, such people were detained temporarily and then deported without further ado.

Freda Hawkins attributes the policy similarities to the 'remarkable degree of communication and exchange of information that goes on all the time between Canada and Australia at the political and bureaucratic level' (Hawkins 1989:243). This overlooks the fact that there is similar consultation between officials in the United States, the UK, and European countries, reflecting the globalization of immigration control. From a sociological perspective, it would be more appropriate to examine the demographic, economic, and social changes occurring in both countries and at a global level, which have had similar consequences in terms of immigration policy.

World system and global crisis

It is now almost a cliché to describe the contemporary world as a 'global system', with core, semi-peripheral, and peripheral, areas (Giddens 1985; Wallerstein 1974). The consequences of economic interdependence, uneven development, and the further effects of a postindustrial technological revolution in communications are particularly evident with respect to population growth and migration (Richmond 1988c:9).

Although the pace of world population growth has slowed somewhat compared to a decade ago, the estimated 5.5 billion people in 1993 is expected to grow by another billion this decade and double before the end of the twenty-first century. Most of this growth is occurring in Asia and Africa. At the same time, the wealthier, developed countries, particularly Europe and North America, have reached the end of the demographic transition and face the possibility of an actual population decline early in the twenty-first century.

The contradiction between a global population explosion and potential demographic decline or equilibrium in advanced industrial countries has created a conflict of interest between rich and poor countries with regard to emigration and immigration. It is no coincidence that population growth rates are highest in the low-income countries. Furthermore, economic imperialism and the monetary policies imposed by banks, multinational corporations, and international bodies, such as the International Monetary Fund, have resulted in a net outflow of funds and resources from the poorer to the wealthier regions of the world (World Bank 1989).[7] Economic pressures to find employment in more developed regions is overwhelming. When superpower intervention in regional conflicts, civil and international wars (in places such as the Middle East, southeast Asia, west Asia, Africa, and Central America) are combined with economic upheavals, Malthusian natural disasters, and political revolution, it is little wonder that the world is also faced with an overwhelming refugee problem. An estimated 18 million people have been displaced in the developing world and seek to escape from violence as refugees.

Despite paying lip-service to the problem and proclaiming their dedication to humanitarian policies, countries such as Canada and Australia have been reluctant to respond to the situation in more than a token manner. In the 1980s, Canada admitted less than 200,000 refugees, a quarter of whom were from eastern Europe. Canada's target for refugee intake in the 1990s is 33,000 annually, excluding asylum applicants in Canada. Australia admitted approximately 145,000 in the decade and only committed itself to 14,000 annually after 1989. As Zolberg points out, 'the contradiction itself reflects divergent global trends: on the one hand, a more widespread adherence to a core of common humanitarian values and, on the other, the increasing economic inequality and persistence of strategic competition among national states' (Zolberg et al. 1989:30).

Environmentalism and economic growth

The environmental impact of population growth is a cause of increasing concern, particularly as developing countries endeavour to bring their level of industrialization, resource consumption, and material standards of living to those of more advanced societies. At the same time, ecological arguments are being used to oppose increased immigration to the advanced industrial societies. Although immigration to Canada or Australia at not unprecedented levels of 1 per cent per annum could maintain equilibrium and prevent population decline, it would have little effect on global demographic pressures. Even modest increases in immigration levels encounter opposition. In Canada, environmental concerns surfaced in the debate over the 'Green Paper' in 1974 when they were directly linked to restrictive immigration arguments. They surfaced again in a government report based on the demographic review (Review of Demography 1989:12–13; Richmond 1988c:95–106), which states that the upper limit of population growth 'is determined by the ability of the environment to sustain the economic activity required' and also points out that forests are expected to decline even with low rates of population growth. The ecological argument is even more evident in Australia, where an anti-immigration lobby has aligned itself with the 'Green' movement and environmental concerns to urge zero population growth, or at least a reduction in immigration levels.[8] Although the National Population Inquiry (Borrie 1975:740) said that, despite water shortages, Australia could easily grow at a rate of 1 per cent to 1.5 per cent annually (including net migration of 100,000), the advocates of constraint say that resource development does not require more people and that the problems resulting from further growth, including urban congestion and pollution, would be 'mind-boggling' (Birrell and Birrell 1987:181–200). A government-sponsored examination of immigration, population growth, and the environment (Clarke et al. 1990) rejected the more alarmist views concerning the possibility of environmental degradation due to increased immigration and tourism, but emphasized the importance of urban decongestion, environmental impact studies, and 'more efficiency-oriented pollution-control measures' (Birrell and Birrell 1987:150).

Environmentalist lobbyists are not the only critics of immigration. In both countries, radical social scientists see immigration as providing a 'reserve army of labour' and multiculturalism as an ideological device for asserting the priority of ethnicity over class while maintaining traditional bourgeois hegemony (Collins 1975; Jakubowicz 1984; Peter 1982). In fact, the 'reserve army' hypothesis fails in the light of evidence that the foreign-born in both countries were distributed widely throughout the system, and that established male immigrants, on average, had higher occupational status and were earning as much or more than native-born Canadians and Australians (Beaujot et al. 1988; Birrell and Birrell 1987; Evans and Kelly 1986, 1988; Richmond and Zubrzycki 1984).[9]

Additional criticism came from those opposed to a multicultural Australia on grounds that advocacy of increased immigration came only from those with a special interest, including federal government bureaucrats, allied with cosmopolitan intellectuals who favoured a multicultural

Australia, ethnic groups that wish to promote family reunification, and humanitarian advocates for refugees. These groups are described by their opponents as élites who manipulate public opinion in favour of policies that conflict with the interests of most Australians (Betts 1988).

The governments of Canada and Australia pursue economic growth in an increasingly competitive global economy where competition for investment capital and entrepreneurial initiatives is fierce. As a result, business immigration became a high priority in the 1980s. The number of entrepreneurs admitted to Canada increased from 1,556 in 1980 to nearly 7,000 by 1992. In 1990, they declared a total net worth of Can. $6.7 billion and funds on entry of Can. $1.24 billion (Wong 1993). Australia also had its business immigration program. In December 1988, it was announced that 'Australia would continue to encourage successful business people from all parts of the world', although it expected the numbers admitted to decline in 1988–9 from 12,000 to 10,000 annually, but there would be no cap on the numbers (Minister for Immigration and Ethnic Affairs 1988). Both countries experienced difficulty ensuring that the funds were invested in the way intended and were obliged to adopt monitoring programs to achieve this and minimize abuse (Nash 1987). The Australian program was temporarily suspended because of alleged abuses.

Business immigration is not without its critics. Some see the program as a means for wealthy families to buy their way into the country ahead of more deserving refugees and family members. Others complain that the influx of wealthy immigrants has inflated real estate prices in places such as Vancouver, BC and Brisbane, Qld, where many immigrants from Hong Kong and elsewhere settle. In Australia, Japanese investment is also controversial and the growing numbers of Japanese tourists sometimes receive a cool welcome. These factors fan the flames of anti-immigration sentiment in both countries and promote racism.

Independent immigrants, selected on the basis of their education and qualifications, were a declining element in the annual intake during the first half of the decade. However, towards the end of the 1980s, Australia and Canada recognized a continuing demand for certain skills and qualifications. According to the Fitzgerald committee, advising on Australia's immigration policies (Fitzgerald 1988:40): 'Industry protection in such industries as vehicles, clothing, textiles, and footwear has contributed to the maintenance of the kind of jobs in which many unskilled and semi-skilled immigrants have worked, instead of restructuring the economy toward high technology, and design intensive industries.' The committee went on to recommend that immigrants be selected for skill and entrepreneurship and suggested concomitant measures for retraining Australians. Subsequently, the government introduced a modified points selection system to encourage special skills and employer nominations to meet particular shortages (Minister for Immigration and Ethnic Affairs 1988).

The 1980s saw a growing trend towards 'corporatism' in Australian public policy, i.e., an emphasis upon economic rationality and management efficiency. One indicator is a growing emphasis on the material benefits of multiculturalism, in which language and ethnicity are regarded primarily as marketable resources (Foster and Stockley 1988a, 1989). Canada's experience in the 1980s was similar. Structural changes in the economy, together with the impact of shifting world markets, American protectionism, inflation and new technologies, threatened the viability of traditional resource and manufacturing industries. Not only livelihoods but whole lifestyles vanished as family farms were sold in the west and fishing communities in the Maritimes ceased to be economically viable. Even key industries such as manufacturing, transportation, and construction felt the effects of structural change. The foreign-born were less vulnerable than others in this respect, partly because immigrants of long standing in these sectors were retiring in growing numbers and not being replaced. Newer immigrants entered the expanding tertiary sectors of the economy, although not always in the highly skilled positions. Women, particularly, were more likely to be employed in low-paying service jobs (Richmond 1992; Seward and Tremblay 1989). The Economic Council of Canada (1990) reported that middle-income earners shrank in numbers in the 1980s, and that employment in Canada was tending to polarize into 'good job, bad job' sectors. Notwithstanding their educational qualifications and skills, a disproportionate number of recently arrived immigrants, especially women and visible minorities, occupied lower-paying positions (Beaujot and Rappak 1989; Richmond 1989; Verma and Basavarajappa 1989).

The effective use of immigrant skills became a public issue, particularly in Ontario.[10] Immigration policy designed to attract well educated and highly qualified immigrants clashed with overwhelming evidence that many were unable to obtain employment commensurate with those qualifications during their first years in Canada (Ornstein and Sharma 1983; Richmond 1967; Richmond and Kalbach 1980). A task force investigated the barriers to skill utilization, including trades and professional licensing requirements and related issues (Cumming et al. 1989). Its report made extensive recommendations to facilitate the recognition of credentials earned and experience gained overseas, and to remove discrimination and institutional barriers, such as the shortage of internships for medical practitioners.

Australia faced similar obstacles to the effective integration of skilled and professional immigrants into its labour force. It took a major step towards resolving the problem by establishing a National Office of Overseas Skills Recognition, an expansion of courses for bridging training, and reformed procedures for assessing overseas qualifications (Office of Multicultural Affairs 1989:35). This initiative was one component of that country's 'National Agenda for a Multicultural Australia', launched by Prime Minister Bob Hawke in July 1989.

Figure 10.3 Ethnic origin and ancestry groups

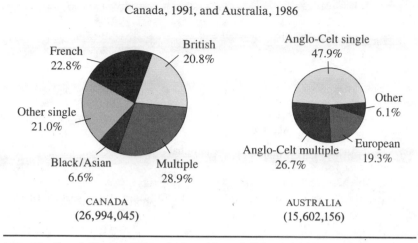

Canada, 1991, and Australia, 1986

CANADA
(26,994,045)

AUSTRALIA
(15,602,156)

SOURCES: Canada Census, 1991, and adapted from C. Price, *Ethnic Groups in Australia* (Canberra: Office of Multicultural Affairs, 1989)

Ethnic conflict and multiculturalism

During the 1980s, both countries experienced a substantial diversification of their respective populations as a consequence of migration. Although Australia remained more homogeneous than Canada, the relative difference was greater precisely because that country was, from its earliest colonial period, predominantly British (or Anglo-Celtic, to use a more fashionable term). In the mid-nineteenth century, Australia's population amounted to less than half a million, 41.5 per cent of whom were Aboriginal, 57.2 per cent Anglo-Celtic, and only 1.3 per cent of other origins. A century later, the population had risen to 7.6 million, of whom almost 90 per cent were Anglo-Celtic and less than 1 per cent Aboriginal, with less than 10 per cent from other (mainly European) ethnic backgrounds. By the mid-1980s, the proportion of European origin had doubled and the non-European, mainly Asian, population constituted 6 per cent of the 16 million people in that country (see Figure 10.3). Although restrictions on non-European immigration were removed in 1973, the full impact was only felt a decade later when 42 per cent of Australia's immigrants originated in Asia and the Pacific (Price 1987, 1989). However, people with some British (Anglo-Celtic) ancestry remain a large majority of the Australian population (75 per cent) compared with almost 50 per cent for Canada when single and multiple ancestries are combined.

In Canada, the francophone population of Quebec and other provinces prevented the British from attaining the same degree of demographic or political dominance they had in Australia. Immigration to Canada

Figure 10.4 Ethnic origin: Quebec and the rest of Canada

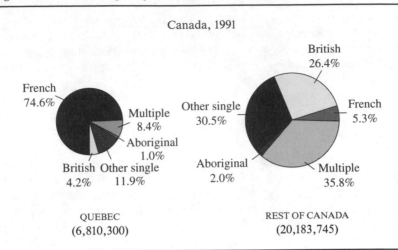

SOURCE: Canada Census, 1991

throughout the nineteenth and twentieth centuries was more ethnically mixed than immigration to Australia. Restrictions on non-European immigration were lifted in 1962. In the 1980s, immigrants from Britain and Europe comprised only 24 per cent of those admitted to Canada compared to 36 per cent admitted to Australia. Quebec, however, remains ethnically more homogeneous than Ontario or western Canada; 75 per cent of the population is of French ancestry compared with 5 per cent in the rest of Canada (see Figure 10.4). When Aboriginal origins are included, the visible minority population of Australia is approximately 7 per cent compared with less than 5 per cent in Quebec and nearly 10 per cent in the rest of Canada.

When Prime Minister Trudeau announced the federal multiculturalism policy in 1971, he was careful to give priority to official bilingualism (Burnet 1978, 1987). The need to accommodate Quebec nationalism and separatist tendencies by promoting the French language has always taken priority over policies designed to achieve ethnic pluralism or the claims of non-official language minorities. Furthermore, Quebec has expressed a growing concern about controlling its own immigration program and 'francophonizing' newcomers.[11] As a leading Quebec authority put it:

La société quebecoise ne vecut pas au même diapason que le reste du Canada le grand virage du multiculturalisme entrepris des les années soixante-dix. Trop de facteurs distinguaient le Quebec au sein de la federation canadienne pour que ce nouvel accent place sur les collectivités immigrantes émerge de la même façon au sein de la seule province a majorité linguistique française (Anctil 1986:1).

When Canada's multicultural programs began in the 1970s, they focused primarily on the needs and interests of established European immigrants and their descendants, who sought to preserve cultural traditions through government support for ethnic organizations, heritage language programs, ethnic history books, and other cultural activities, including music and dance. Eastern European groups, particularly Ukrainians, were active in multicultural affairs. In time, the emphasis shifted as new immigrant groups arrived. The political and bureaucratic separation of the federal immigration portfolio and multiculturalism, under the federal Secretary of State, impeded the coordination of short-term immigrant services and long-term ethnic programs. Moreover, by the early 1980s, growing evidence of racism in the community indicated a need for government action. Extremist organizations propagated anti-Semitic, anti-Asian and 'White' supremacist doctrines. Interracial disturbances increased. Vandals attacked synagogues and temples, and police harassed minorities, sometimes causing fatalities. 'Black' and Asian immigrants also experienced economic disadvantages. A parliamentary committee examined the problems facing visible minorities in Canada and, among other things, recommended the creation of a separate Ministry of Multiculturalism and the passing of a Multiculturalism Act (Daudlin 1984). By the end of the decade, this was achieved. Bill C-93 was passed in 1988 and at the same time a number of new programs were announced. Budgetary allocations were initially increased and then reduced again as fiscal restraint policies were adopted following an election. By 1993, the Department of Immigration was further divided. Selection and control were placed under a new Ministry of Public Security and Settlement in Human Resources. Multiculturalism diminished in importance when placed in a department concerned with 'Canadian Heritage'.

Earlier legislation (Bill C-62 in 1985) dealt with employment equity and identified visible minorities, among other groups, as possible candidates for affirmative action. This came into force in 1988. Notwithstanding these measures, evidence of racial prejudice, injustice, institutional discrimination, harassment, and violence against native peoples, 'Blacks', and Asians persisted (Dwivedi et al. 1989; Lewis 1989; Nova Scotia Royal Commission 1989).[12] In 1990, the federal government introduced Bill C-63 to establish the Canadian Race Relations Foundation with a mandate to 'facilitate throughout Canada the development, sharing and application of knowledge and expertise in order to contribute to the elimination of racism and all forms of racial discrimination in Canadian society.' Budget cuts have delayed indefinitely the implementation of this legislation.

Ethnic tensions and racism were also evident in Australia. Extreme right-wing organizations engaged in racist propaganda and occasional acts of vandalism and violence. Religious conflict broke out between the Muslim and Jewish communities (Markus and Rasmussen 1987). Rather more influential than the neo-Nazi groups were the reactionary views of historian

Geoffrey Blainey. His speech to the Rotary Club in March 1984 received extensive media coverage and comment. It led to other articles and a book (Blainey 1984) in which he argued that current levels of Asian immigration were too high, that government policy contradicted public opinion, and that social harmony was threatened along with Australia's traditional institutions and social system. Blainey's criticisms, when combined the environmentalist arguments, led to intellectual opposition to immigration and multiculturalism. It sparked a debate on the future of Australian society that set the British and Eurocentred views of 'old Australians' at odds with others who considered the country's economic and political future firmly linked to its geopolitical proximity to Asia and the Pacific (Lewins 1987). Some elements of that debate echo in British Columbia (BC Ministry of International Business and Immigration 1990; Reid 1989).

Meanwhile, Australian government policy vacillated according to the political party in power and changing perceptions of the problems. First adopted by Al Grassby, minister of immigration in 1973, the Australian version of multiculturalism was more closely linked than that of Canada to the process of integrating first-generation immigrants and winning their electoral support. This was reinforced by the Galbally report in 1978, which reviewed the postarrival programs and services for migrants (Galbally 1978). The early 1980s saw a shift to broader questions of ethnic pluralism and social justice for minorities. Multiculturalism was represented as a necessity for all Australians (ACPE 1982) and addressed issues of national unity. Attention focused on race as well as ethnicity, including the treatment of Aboriginal peoples. Some social scientists contended that the contradictions and dilemmas inherent in the concept of multiculturalism would 'force people on to a new conceptual plane and policy level of "beyond multiculturalism"' (Foster and Stockley 1984, 1988a, 1988b). Funding for multicultural programs was actually reduced in 1986 and the educational aspects absorbed into 'Australian studies'. However, multiculturalism remains a key component of political rhetoric. Support for immigrant services and government-funded multilingual broadcasting was increased again with the proclamation of a National Agenda for a Multicultural Australia (July 1989). This document specified the Hawke government's definition of the term 'multiculturalism' and identified specific goals for its multicultural policies. These included freedom from discrimination, equal life chances for all, and full economic, political, and social participation. The government also set the following limits on Australian multiculturalism:

Multicultural policies are based on the premise that all Australians should have an overriding and unifying commitment to Australia, to its interest and future first and foremost;

Multicultural policies require all Australians to accept the basic structures and principles of Australian society—the Constitution and the rule of law, tolerance and equality, Parliamentary democracy, freedom of speech and religion, English as the national language and equality of the sexes, and

Multicultural policies impose obligations as well as conferring rights: the right to express one's own culture and beliefs involves a reciprocal responsibility to accept the right of others to express their views and values (ACPE 1982:vii).

Federalism and national unity

Comparing Britain, Canada, and Australia, Anthony Birch (1989) suggested that, notwithstanding the history of 'White Australia', continuing opposition to immigration and the recent adoption of multicultural policies, Australia has absorbed its immigrant population more fully than Canada, creating more of a melting-pot than a mosaic. He described Australia as 'a rather successful example of national integration' (Birch 1989:214–15). Although not spelled out as clearly as in Australia's official pronouncements, Canada's immigration and multicultural policies also have implications for national unity. Immigration is a joint responsibility under the British North America Act (1867) and the repatriated Constitution (1982). The provinces are responsible for a major share of postarrival services and settlement programs, including education, language training, and social assistance (Hawkins 1988, 1989). Quebec entered into a special agreement with the federal government in 1977, enabling it to set up its own immigration offices abroad and became directly involved in selection within the legislative framework established by Ottawa. A clause in the now defunct Meech Lake Constitutional Agreement would have guaranteed Quebec a proportion of annual immigration equal to its share of Canada's population and greater responsibility for settlement services. Similar powers are presently being negotiated on a bilateral basis with the federal government. Other provinces may also seek greater control over immigration questions. Already, British Columbia is seeking to give priority to its own 'provincial nominees' in immigration processing.

Quebec never fully committed itself to the idea of linguistic or cultural pluralism. In fact, from the outset Trudeau's limited concept of multiculturalism within a bilingual framework generated hostility in Quebec (Hawkins 1989:221–2). While recognizing the increasing ethnic diversity of Canada and Quebec, various commentators emphasized the dominant role of the 'two founding peoples' and the distinct nature of Quebec society, in the light of its unique history and francophone majority. The debate over minority language rights in Quebec and the rest of Canada raged throughout the decade and reached its climax in the failure to ratify the Charlottetown Agreement in 1992 (Russell 1993).

Demands for Senate reform and other constitutional changes from the western provinces point to a clear trend towards a decentralization of power within the federal system. Although less dramatically expressed in Australia, which has only one official language and no state as 'distinct' as Quebec, regional interests are nevertheless asserting themselves there too. 'The Australian regions, now basically though imperfectly coterminous with the states, have become recognizably vital again . . . state governments are playing increasing roles in the political economy of the regions' (Hodgins et al. 1989:49). One Australian political scientist, comparing the immigration policies of Canada and Australia, suggested that 'Whilst both countries have worked strongly since 1978 at coordinating post-arrival services and programmes, it may be that their concern to evolve receiving country policy, weighing physical resources and social welfare capacity against growing international movements of people, is an anachronism' (Atchison 1988:23). He went on to quote James Eayrs's (1987) argument that the nation-state will be replaced by polyarchy, suggesting that increasing internationalism generates stronger localism, and that global immigration and refugee movements are contributing to the loss of sovereignty.

As the world system becomes increasingly interdependent, it becomes more difficult to maintain state sovereignty, including immigration controls. Further conflict arises when, partly as a result of immigration, the idea of a relatively homogeneous nation-state becomes untenable. The dominant position of a certain ethnic stratum or region could be challenged and trigger defensive reactions such as racism and separatism. In extreme cases, state legitimacy may be threatened by ethnic minorities seeking greater autonomy (Richmond 1988c:173–82). A variety of measures involving local democratic control, human rights issues, employment equity, and multicultural questions could be introduced to diffuse tension, restore order, and promote unity. If these fail, state authorities may resort to more coercive actions.

Anthony Birch (1989:229) argued that 'in the contemporary world the great majority of national governments are too powerful for minority nationalistic movements to have much real chance of success.' However, regional and ethnic minority separatism is resurgent precisely because central authority is weakening in the face of global trends and there is reluctance to use ultimate coercive power. In this respect, Canada and Australia have not faced the magnitude of the crises that have emerged in eastern Europe and the Soviet Union in the 1980s. Nevertheless, similar forces are at work everywhere. In Canada and Australia, Aboriginal land claims and demands for self-determination by colonized First Nations are another source of conflict that undermines state sovereignty and challenges the legitimacy of the state (Hodgins et al. 1989:412–87).

Due to its dual linguistic foundations and greater ethnic diversity, Canada is more susceptible than Australia to the destabilizing effects of these contradictions and crises. This does not mean that it has to close its doors to more immigrants. It does mean that greater efforts will have to be made to modify institutional structures to achieve what the National Agenda for a Multicultural Australia called a 'vision of the future', i.e., 'a genuinely multicultural society for future generations'. As Zubrzycki argued, there are two themes in multiculturalism. One involves cultural pluralism and the institutional forms necessary for the ongoing maintenance and adaptation of language and tradition within a rapidly changing system. The other is concerned with equality and equal opportunity (Zubrzycki 1986). To these might be added the demand for territorial self-government by those with traditional claims to founding status. Often these goals are in conflict and lead to confrontation.

In sum, the governments and people of Canada and Australia have dealt with issues relating to immigration and multiculturalism somewhat anachronistically. Policies and programs developed to achieve goals that seemed appropriate in the postwar period no longer make sense in a rapidly changing world. Policy makers are in a no-win situation. There are too many conflicting interests to reconcile and too many structural contradictions in the global economic and social system for any policy to provide a rational or optimal solution to pressing demographic, economic, political, and humanitarian concerns. High levels of immigration would not solve the population problems of developing countries and could have a further destabilizing effect on the fragile ecologies and weakening economies of the receiving countries. Further ethnic diversification could exacerbate existing racial conflicts and threaten national unity. At the same time, Canada and Australia are committed to policies of economic growth in a competitive global environment, which require capital investment and skilled labour. They are also obligated by international treaties and humanitarian values to respond to the resettlement needs of refugees and to be seen as opposing any manifestation of racism in their domestic relations. The outcome is predictable ambivalence and inconsistency. However, the contradictions are not necessarily irreconcilable in the long run. Resolving the dilemma may mean placing less emphasis on nationalism and 'statehood' and showing more concern for minority rights and freedoms, together with universal human welfare and equality in a global society occupying planet earth.

Notes

[1] This an updated version of a paper first published in the *International Journal of Canadian Studies* 3 (Spring 1991:87–110).

[2] By contradiction is meant a form of system conflict involving opposition of structural principles, or one in which the core value system of a society defines certain goals and ideals, but fails to provide the necessary institutional means for their achievement (Richmond 1988c:187).

[3] The Immigration Act of 1976 was not implemented until 1978 and the first

immigrants admitted under new regulations did not begin to arrive until the following year.

[4] The Federal Court decision in March 1990 held that the guidelines issued by the minister of immigration to determine at an initial interview who should be permitted to remain in Canada 'for humanitarian and compassionate reasons' were invalid because they limited such consideration to persons who had close family in Canada and/or those who fell into a select group of 'distinguished' individuals. The decision led to renewed calls for an amnesty for all those in the backlog, but the minister's response was to maintain the backlog clearance program using a wider range of criteria at the initial interview stage.

[5] The Australian Migration Amendment Act (1983) removed some residual discrimination between British subjects and other aliens. The Migration Legislation Amendment Act (1989) followed the Fitzgerald committee's report on immigration policy and various changes in regulations that only came into force in 1990. The act tightened control over entry to Australia, increased penalties for illegal entry and overstaying, revised the legal basis of the points system of selection, and provided for the issue of temporary entry permits with and without permission to work. It increased the penalties to carriers who brought undocumented persons to Australia and defined the conditions for detention, search, and deportation. It also established an Immigration Review tribunal with power only to undertake an internal review of certain decisions. It specifically precluded the tribunal from granting an entry permit on humanitarian grounds.

[6] Approximately 2,500 arrived in northern Australia by boat from Vietnam and 1,800 from Portuguese Timor (Price 1985).

[7] The *Annual Report* of the World Bank (1989) states 'The economic situation for the highly indebted countries as a group deteriorated in 1988. The trend in negative resource transfer (that is, net outflows) which started in 1984, continued. For the year, total disbursements amounted to $92 billion, but this was offset by total debt service of $142 billion, resulting in a net negative transfer of some $50 billion'(World Bank 1989:27). Tables 2–7 in the report show that net transfers were more than $4.6 billion in 1983, but fell steadily to less than $50.1 billion by 1988. They continue to favour the wealthier countries, creating a serious debt crisis (George 1992).

[8] Calling itself 'Australians Against Further Immigration', the group includes a number of academics. They state they 'are concerned about the deteriorating quality of life, environmental destruction and economic problems brought about by population increase due to mass immigration' (leaflet distributed from Armadale, Victoria 1989).

[9] Canada's increasing use of temporary employment visas to provide seasonal farm labour, some factory workers, and domestics, fits the concept of a reserve army of labour better than the flow of permanent or semi-permanent immigrants. A case could also be made on the basis of exploiting female immigrant labour (Boyd and Taylor 1986; Wong 1984).

[10] This was not the first time the problem of skill recognition was investigated. Barriers to interprovincial recognition of qualifications have always existed in

Canada, reducing the incentive to make any special provision for immigrants (McDade 1988).

[11] In June 1994, the Quebec government announced a cut in immigration levels to that province due in part to the difficulty in integrating immigrants into the French language and culture.

[12] For example, a Nova Scotia Commission that investigated the wrongful imprisonment of a Micmac person for a murder he did not commit revealed deeply entrenched racist attitudes in the judicial system. An Ontario Task Force on Race Relations and Policing investigated the factors responsible for the police shooting of 'Black' youths in Toronto (Lewis 1989; Nova Scotia Royal Commission 1989).

part three

New world order

chapter eleven

Migration, ethnic conflict,
and the new world order

The idea of a 'new world order' (NWO) was put forward by former President Gorbachev when he addressed the United Nations in December 1988. The phrase was repeated by George Bush in August 1990, shortly before the outbreak of the Gulf War. The concept is hardly original. Shakespeare, in 'The Tempest', speaks of a 'brave new world', a phrase echoed by Aldous Huxley. H.G. Wells, writing more than fifty years ago, at the height of the Second World War, exercised his usual prophetic zeal in a book titled *Guide to the New World: A Handbook of Constructive World Revolution*. Wells argued persuasively for the creation of a federal world state with three main responsibilities. Firstly, he saw a need to control the use of space to prevent what he called 'air terrorism', which today would be called 'Star Wars'. Secondly, he urged the establishment of an agency for world resource conservation and environmental protection. Thirdly, he recognized the need for a global rule of law, capable of maintaining security and enforcing a declaration of human rights. Wells did not expect his NWO to come about immediately or without struggle, but he was optimistic enough to believe that 'there is an accumulating splendour latent in the hearts of men' (Wells 1941:152) that would enable them to endure setbacks and ultimately succeed.

More realistically, perhaps, writing at the same time as H.G. Wells, Harvard sociologist Pitirim Sorokin published a book titled *Man and Society in Calamity*. He observed that people were then living amid one of the greatest crises in human history. 'Not only war, famine, pestilence and revolution, but a legion of other calamities are rampant over the whole world. All values are unsettled; all norms broken' (Sorokin [1942] 1968:308). He predicted that world migration would increase and that millions of people would be forcibly uprooted in the future.

Sorokin's forecast has been borne out. As well as the labour migrations that have occurred in the period since the Second World War, there are more than 23 million Convention refugees and displaced persons now recognized by the United Nations, and many more war victims and others who do not qualify for assistance but who are nevertheless internally or externally displaced. In addition, there has been an enormous increase in the number of people forced to move because of environmental disasters. Population movements have arisen from or given rise to ethnic tension in many parts of the world. The incidence of civil wars, terrorist activities, neo-Nazi movements, communal riots, racist attacks, and religious intolerance have all increased significantly in the last decade.

Ethnic conflicts

It was noted in Chapter Two that there were at least sixty-five ethnic conflicts raging around the world in 1993; more have ignited since. There are tremendous differences between them. The single common denominator is the use or threat of violence. Figure 11.1. lists the principal locations and parties to these conflicts, indicating by asterisks their severity, as measured by the estimated number of deaths up to the end of 1992 (Regehr 1993). There are several ways in which the conflict can be categorized. Neocolonial conflicts involving Aboriginal populations include disputes over territory as well as questions of human rights, access to resources, and aspirations for self-government by indigenous peoples who have been marginalized. Other intrastate conflicts assume a nationalist form as minorities seek independence, political autonomy, and self-determination. More than twenty new countries have been admitted to the United Nations in recent years, and more aspire to such recognition. Other intrastate conflicts arise from communal or ethnoreligious disputes in which one group seeks to eliminate or subordinate another. Ethnic nationalism may also take the form of irredentism and involve war between states when people sharing a common language or religion wish to join forces with others of similar origins in other countries to create new state boundaries and assert control over territory that was once part of another country. Finally, there are ethnic conflicts arising out of migration when foreign workers, refugees, and other immigrants and their descendants are exploited or subjected to racist attitudes and policies.

Ethnic conflicts can also be classified according to their duration or severity in terms of the extent of violence and the number of casualties. Some conflicts (such as those in Northern Ireland or the Americas) have

Figure 11.1 Global ethnic conflicts

Interstate
(Irredentists)

Georgia–Abkhazia*
Israel–Palestine***
Moldova–Romania
Romania–Hungary*
Serbia–Bosnia***
Serbia–Croatia**

Intrastate
(Neocolonial/Aboriginal)

Australia
Brazil
Canada
Colombia
Guatemala***
Mexico
Peru**
United States

Intrastate
(Nationalistic)

Afghanistan***
Armenia*
Azerbaijan*
Burma (Myanmar)*
Canada (Quebec)
China/Tibet*
India***
Mali
Northern Ireland*
Pakistan***
Philippines*
Russia*
Spain (Basques)
Sri Lanka**
Tajikistan**
Turkey*

Intrastate
(Communal or
ethnoreligious)

Algeria
Angola (irredentist)***
Bangladesh*
Belgium
Bhutan
Burundi*
Cambodia***
Chad*
Cyprus
Egypt
Ethiopia***
Fiji
Indonesia***
Iran**
Iraq**
Japan
Kenya
Liberia**
Malaysia
Mali
Mauritania
Mozambique***
Nigeria
Papua New Guinea*
Rwanda**
Senegal
Somalia***
South Africa***
Sudan*
Togo
Uganda**
Zaire

Intrastate
(Immigrant)

Britain
France
Germany
Greece
Italy
Portugal
Spain
United States

KEY: No. of deaths up to the end of 1993   *** more than 100,000
                                                        ** 10,000–100,000
                                                           * 1,000–10,000

roots in the earliest colonial conquests. Others were first evidenced in the nineteenth century when European powers exerted their imperial domination over territories in Africa and Asia. The seeds of other ethnic conflicts were sown in the aftermath of the two world wars as new power blocs were formed and lines drawn on maps that paid little heed to the aspirations of their inhabitants. The cold war, when surrogate battles between East and West were fought in places such as Korea, Vietnam, Afghanistan, and Mozambique, left a legacy of ethnic conflict. The breakup of the Soviet Union and the Warsaw Pact countries has created new crises in eastern Europe. Many of these conflicts spill over into immigrant- and refugee-receiving countries.

A further dimension concerns the means used by governments or dominant groups to deal with the causes of ethnic conflict or to control its overt manifestation. McGarry and O'Leary (1993:1–40) put forward a taxonomy of ethnic conflict regulation, distinguishing between methods used to eliminate and those designed to manage differences. In the former category are policies of genocide, forced mass-population transfers, partition and/or secession, and various forms of integration or assimilation of minorities. Methods of managing differences include hegemonic control, arbitration, federal-type systems of regional or local government, and consociation or power sharing. It is ironic that democratic societies appear to have been no more successful in resolving ethnic strife than those that use more authoritarian methods.

Postmodern dilemmas

The ethnic diversity of almost all postindustrial societies today raises the question of whether equality of opportunity and the coaptation of immigrants, with each other and with indigenous populations, can be reconciled with the maintenance of separate identities and cultural pluralism. Similar questions arise when polyethnic societies that have been previously subject to varying degrees of authoritarian integration by a dominant power suddenly find themselves free from totalitarian control. Will the process of globalization eventually lead to homogeneity or to the 'deterritorialization of cultures' and the persistence of heterogeneity?

This is a debate that is currently being conducted among sociologists concerned with questions of modernity and postmodernity. Roland Robertson, for example, suggests that one of the more powerful features of modernity is the homogenizing influence of the state in the face of ethnic and cultural diversity, but that, in a postmodern era, nations and states must reconstruct their collective identities in pluralistic terms (Robertson 1990a:15–30). Today we recognize the existence of an interdependent global economy in which information, goods, services, and money move relatively freely in what has been described as a 'borderless world'. The ultimate goal of the so-called interlinked economy (in which multinational enterprises based in the United States, Japan, and Germany are the major players) is the free movement of labour across borders, but this is far from having been achieved. On the contrary, despite rising numbers of international migrants in the last decade, borders are now closing against economic migrants and political refugees. Regional economic communities, such as the EEC and the proposed US–Canada–Mexico free trade area, are facilitating movement within the region while more severely restricting access to it. Nevertheless, international migration is an integral part of the world capitalist economy and the flow of refugees reflects the lack of political integration and instability of that system.

Migration may be literally a matter of life and death for those escaping violence or repressive regimes. For the least fortunate, survival may mean exile, homelessness, scraping a livelihood by begging, reliance on charity, or dependence on international humanitarian aid. Others become members of an underclass of temporary migrant workers or a middle class of transilient professionals, while the economically successful business-class immigrants transfer millions of dollars for investment from one country to another. In other words, immigrants are part of a global system of social stratification and ethclass conflict. Consequent upon the effects of postindustrialism, that system is undergoing major structural changes that have important consequences for external migration. There is a new international division of labour and a balance of economic power that no longer necessarily favour the formerly dominant Euro-American axis.

Commenting on the idea of a NWO, John K. Galbraith noted that the collapse of the communist economic system has changed the world. But he considered that it is not economics or foreign policy but anthropology that is the controlling condition. He called nationalism 'the immediate tribal response', and noted that it is the poorest countries where people are killing each other. However, it is doubtful if postmodern ethnic nationalism can be equated with premodern tribalism. Galbraith suggested that 'Reason eventually takes over which, quite possibly, is why the human species survives' (Galbraith 1991:14). The most pressing question, says Galbraith, is whether the world itself will survive: 'Nothing is impractical that ensures human survival, nothing certainly that ensures against civil disturbances degenerating into war.' The theme of survival runs through much of the discussion of a NWO and requires closer scrutiny.

Survival as a categorical imperative

Kant defined the categorical imperative as one that commands a certain conduct immediately without having as its condition the attainment of any other condition. Hence one should 'act only on that maxim whereby thou canst at the same time will that it shall become a universal law.' Notwithstanding the scepticism of some postmodern theorists concerning universal values, it can be argued that survival is such a categorical imperative.

However, what is meant by survival and what is its price? Is it the survival of particular individuals, of specific collectivities, or of the whole human species? Furthermore, do we mean 'survival' in a purely biological sense, or does it include the survival of particular languages, cultures, social institutions, and organizations? In a biological sense, individuals have a limited lifespan, which should not be arbitrarily cut short, nor prolonged beyond the natural span by artificially heroic means.

The biological survival of a collectivity or of the whole human species is of a different order. It implies procreation and genetic inheritance. Human beings have at their disposal the capacity for self-destruction, both individual and collective. Drug addiction and epidemic diseases threaten rich and poor alike. A nuclear holocaust might not immediately kill everyone in the world, but it would create such environmental and genetic damage that human civilization as we know it would likely disappear. Other unnatural disasters could also have devastating effects. Global warming, the effects of pollution, changes in the atmosphere, inadequate waste management, destruction of the rain forests (or other non-renewable resources) all place our planet under stress and constitute 'the challenge of global change' (Mungall and McLaren 1990). 'Environmental refugees' and 'Green crusaders' must be added to the categories of international migrants (Homer-Dixon 1991). Sociologists who once treated so-called 'nation-states' as closed systems must now address the reality of an interconnected global society, i.e., the world as a 'total system' (Boulding 1989; Giddens 1985). A key question is whether such a system can survive the conflicts that are endemic in its formation. Survival may be the ultimate categorical imperative. Genocidal policies or preventable actions that could lead to human extinction, such as a nuclear holocaust or severe environmental damage to the forests or to the ozone layer, are increasingly condemned, although much still needs to be done to ensure that such catastrophes do not occur.

However, the survival of languages and cultures may be less a categorical imperative than a pragmatic issue. There may be a positive value in maintaining cultural heterogeneity as a collective resource for humanity. If the speakers of a particular language, the adherents of a religion, or the bearers of a culture wish to maintain their traditional lifestyle, there should be no impediment. However, in reality, cultures change over time. When they are gradual and the result of consensual activity, they do not constitute a moral issue. But if traditional ways of life are coercively suppressed through cultural genocide or a misplaced desire on the part of powerful entities to accelerate the process of modernization, the potential value of the behaviour pattern is lost. Those who have internalized the culture and developed their social personality on that basis will suffer, sometimes to the point of suicide or loss of the collective will to survive, thereby breaching the categorical imperative.

The survival of particular forms of social organization, including corporations, nations, and states, is more problematic. Corporate structures (economic and political), all bureaucratic systems, military formations, and states, have developed as means to ends, but they are not ends in themselves. Therefore their survival cannot be defended unless they are effectively serving ends that are a matter of general agreement. Notwithstanding jingoistic claims to the contrary, there is nothing sacred about the particular boundaries of existing states. If the goal of global survival for the human race requires it, new boundaries may be required and new maps drawn. Political institutions must be created that will increase the probability of that survival. The necessary economic, social, and political changes must be achieved in a world that is experiencing a postindustrial revolution. This has radical implications for the old world order, as well as for the new.

In the contemporary, postmodern global system, there is a seeming contradiction between the universal and the particular, the worldwide and the local, the individual and the collective. Metaphorically, it is as if we were looking at the world from another planet through a giant telescope. We see the globe as a whole, rotating on its axis in a delicate atmosphere with its protective ozone layer. Then we zoom in to look more closely and the image shatters into five billion individual pieces. As in a kaleidoscope, these pieces are constantly moving and forming new groups, fresh patterns, different colour combinations. There are no clearly defined boundaries, only evidence of a constant state of flux. All seems chaotic and in a state of turmoil until we reverse the zoom and look at the total picture again. Then we realize that the pieces are not only part of a whole but are also interdependent. The individual cannot survive without the whole, the universal subsumes the particular. Out of the dialectic of thesis and antithesis emerges a new synthesis, but this does not end the process of change. Elements of the old forms linger on, and further conflicts generate new outcomes, ad infinitum (see Figure 11.2).

Neither technological nor economic changes are necessarily the determining ones. These interact with the social, cultural, and political factors, which also affect military formations, migration patterns, and subjective questions of identity and group belonging. Although ultimate consequences and long-term trends may not be predictable, some immediate outcomes are discernible at this time. Technological advances in the use of solar energy and space research are linked to biotechnology, population, and environment. Satellite communications are related to semiotics, information processing, and computerization, which, in turn, affect migration, ethnic identity, and changes in the political and military structuration of the world system. There are inherent contradictions between the political and military capacity to conduct nuclear war in space and our inability to deal effectively with 'conventional' wars on earth. The peacemaking and peacekeeping capacity of the United Nations has yet to be proved. Out of the local, the regional, and the global emerges a NWO. The survival of our planet and the species on it is contingent on the peaceful resolution of the

Figure 11.2 New world order — dialectics of change and conflict

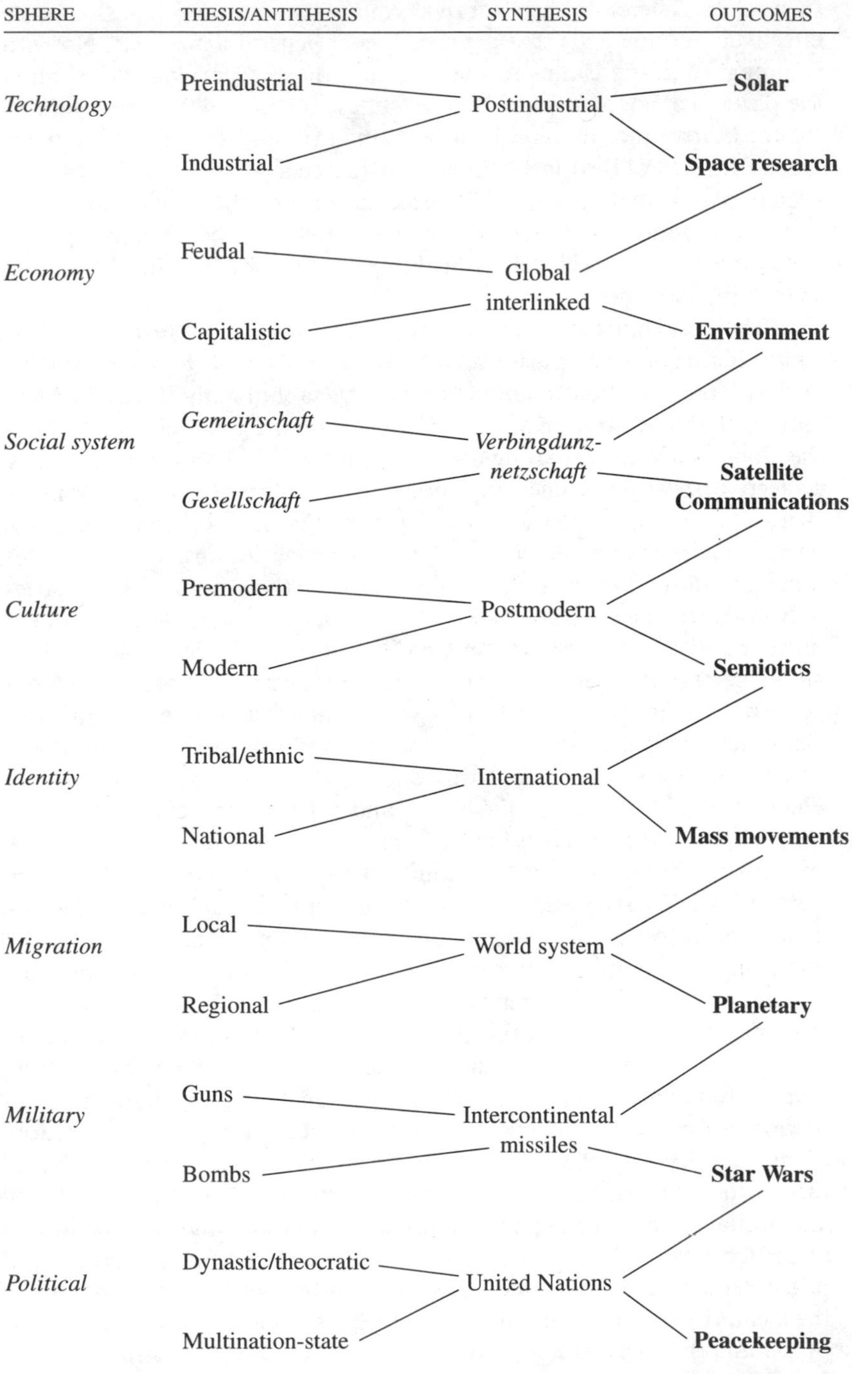

SPHERE	THESIS/ANTITHESIS	SYNTHESIS	OUTCOMES

Technology — Preindustrial / Industrial → Postindustrial → **Solar** / **Space research**

Economy — Feudal / Capitalistic → Global interlinked → **Environment**

Social system — *Gemeinschaft* / *Gesellschaft* → *Verbingdunz-netzschaft* → **Satellite Communications**

Culture — Premodern / Modern → Postmodern → **Semiotics**

Identity — Tribal/ethnic / National → International → **Mass movements**

Migration — Local / Regional → World system → **Planetary**

Military — Guns / Bombs → Intercontinental missiles → **Star Wars**

Political — Dynastic/theocratic / Multination-state → United Nations → **Peacekeeping**

resulting conflicts. Failure will mean the end of the universal and the particular.

Political aspects of postindustrialism

In all societies, information is one form of power, but in contemporary postindustrial systems, control over the generation, storage, and dissemination of information has assumed even greater significance. It is directly linked to the generation of ideology and the legitimation of political action. Through the mass media, information influences consciousness and is at the core of individual and collective identity formation (Giddens 1991; Poster 1990).

Postindustrialism and postmodernism result from the technological revolution in communications that has occurred in an accelerated fashion in the twentieth century. Premodern communities were based upon face-to-face contact and relatively low levels of hierarchical authority. They were governed by *Gemeinschaft*-type relationships. Industrialization gave way to more complex communication systems in the modern period and to the bureaucratization of formal organizations with complex authority structures in which communication tended to flow from the top down (*Gesellschaft*). In both cases, boundaries were clearly defined and communication across those boundaries were limited. When migration occurred between *Gemeinschaft* systems, assimilation was inevitable. Conformity to the norms and expectations of the majority was the only way to survive. In *Gesellschaft* systems, a limited degree of pluralistic integration was possible if the numbers involved permitted the creation of new organizations and authority structures, but these were ultimately subordinated to those of the majority. In both premodern and modern systems, power élites exercise control by the use of surveillance and by restricting the flow of information, although industrial espionage and political spying endeavoured to overcome these barriers to communication. Through socialization and education, political propaganda, etc., ideologies favourable to the preservation of power and authority were transmitted by inculcating 'national loyalty' and 'company pride'. This was most obvious in totalitarian regimes, but only partially modified in more democratic systems.

Micro-electronics, computerization, and satellite links have revolutionized information storage and retrieval and consequently the locus of power in the system. Since information is now accessible to local decision makers, instantaneous communication with others in the system (as well as mass communication with the population at large) ensures a high degree of coordination without resort to centralized systems of bureaucratic authority, although the latter persist from an earlier era. Political input at all levels is achieved by mass demonstrations (televised to the world), the constant monitoring of opinion through surveys and referenda, and by local leaders who may assume charismatic authority through media exposure. Already the 'power of the people', aided by global communication systems, has overthrown long-established political dictatorships in eastern Europe and elsewhere. In some cases, the transition has been relatively peaceful, but in others mass action has turned to violence.

As noted in Chapter Two, in postmodern systems communication flows though interpersonal and mass communication networks: *Verbindungsneztschaft* (Richmond 1969). These are capable of bypassing the power élites, facilitating direct communication (lateral and vertical, including from the ground level up), as well as between middle levels of intelligentsia, professionals, and managers. Attempts to restrict communication between countries, organizations, and individuals by censorship or other means have been defeated by the ease and speed of transportation, satellite linkages, television, telephones, fax, and all forms of radio-communication. When migration occurs under these conditions, direct communication with place and people of origin is maintained. There is no longer the same pressure to assimilate or integrate. People can maintain their distinct identities without regard to geographic distance or formal organization membership. This does not preclude changes, but these are a response to global conditions, not only to the pressures to adapt to a receiving society (Richmond 1988c).

In reality, *Gesellschaft* relationships never completely replaced *Gemeinschaft*, but were superimposed on them, creating more complex social systems. By the same token, *Verbindungsnetzschaft* relationships do not usurp the functions of communities or organizations. They add another dimension and, in the process, render human relationships and social systems more variegated and unpredictable, leading to the possibility of sudden or revolutionary change. Evolutionary and developmental theories of social change tend to assume that each new phase necessarily replaces the former, but this is not always the case. Old forms persist or adapt to new conditions, sometimes in ways that generate more conflict and further changes. Figure 11.2 illustrates the dialectical processes currently occurring in the world system. Each new synthesis generates its own contradiction without necessarily eliminating previous forms. Nuclear and solar powerplants coexist with wood- and coal-burning appliances; space research goes ahead before we have found safe ways of disposing of nuclear waste or reducing the pollution from fossil fuels; holes in the ozone layer damage the environment and threaten lifeforms, while transnational companies patent genetic innovations; satellite communications link the élites of the world, while illiteracy remains a major concern; planetary migration and space stations are promoted, while borders are closed to unwanted migrants on earth; the military continue to experiment in 'Star Wars' under the guise of surveillance and ultimate deterrence, while failing to make or keep the peace in areas under United Nations mandate.

Under postmodern conditions, nation-states, as they were understood in the industrial era, have become anachronistic. The future lies with small countries affiliated to much larger economic unions on a continental scale, although not necessarily bounded by geography. Multinational corporations and supranational governmental agencies have assumed many of the responsibilities previously exercised by smaller organizations and states. As the power of central states and federal authorities diminishes, regional and local authorities achieve greater autonomy through lateral links with their opposite numbers in other areas. Expatriate ethnic populations maintain or re-establish links with their place of origin or with the symbolic centres of their language, religion, or nationality. Ethnic nationalism is sustained and revitalized under these conditions, particularly where territorial claims are involved. At the same time, interethnic conflict is likely to be exacerbated. There is a nostalgic longing for the security of the *Gemeinschaft*, or the homogeneous 'nation-state', safely isolated by economic protectionism and military strength from the realities of the new world order.

Western Europe now functions through the EEC as a single unit for many economic purposes and plans a single currency and a more integrated banking system. Eastern Europe and parts of the former Soviet Union may become a part of this in due course. Even Israel and its Arab neighbours negotiate peace and are seriously considering closer economic union. Meanwhile, ethnic minority populations within the newly independent states are vulnerable to the domination of local majorities. 'Imperial' authorities can no longer enforce a coerced peace between old enemies, as is evident in the former Yugoslavia. A North American economic union, including the United States, Canada, and Mexico, is in the making. It is likely to lead to an assertion of states' rights, provincial rights, and steps towards local autonomy, including possible sovereignty for Quebec. Linguistic and religious minorities in Quebec and in the rest of Canada may find themselves neglected or subordinated unless they can form alliances with others who share their common culture and recognize shared interests. Thus Jews, Muslims, Buddhists, and other religious groups may benefit from economic and moral support from co-religionists elsewhere, translating religious fundamentalism into militant nationalism. Gellner (1992:15) notes that 'identification with Reformed Islam has played a role very similar to that played by nationalism elsewhere.' 'Fourth World' Aboriginal populations may establish links with other indigenous peoples in the United States, the former Soviet Union, Latin America, or Australia and (with some help from environmentalists) seek support for their respective causes through the United Nations and other supranational agencies. Lateral rather than vertical communication networks involve a significant shift in the balance of power.

There is a growing consensus among world leaders that indeed a NWO is emerging, although there is no agreement on the precise form that such a global system will take. British politician Denis Healey, commenting on George Bush's reference to a NWO on the eve of the Gulf War, rightly insisted that the major problems of the next century cannot be handled on a regional basis because ecological and population problems are now global in scale. We are moving into an age of mass migration into Europe from the east and the south, as well as into the United States and Canada from Asia and Latin America. There is an urgent need for international regulation and control, particularly since the world's population is doubling every fifty years. However, such regulation will not succeed in stemming the flow altogether. If it is too coercive, it will become counterproductive by removing the safety-valve that potential migration presently provides.

Above all, there is a need for global arms control and disarmament. This is more than a question of reducing stockpiles of nuclear weapons. The global arms bazaar in so-called 'conventional weapons' (rather than those of mass destruction) is sustaining present conflicts and creating death and destruction in Europe, Africa, Asia, and Latin America. Francis Fukuyama pointed out that 'the dominant trend in world politics over the past few decades has been for countries to grow smaller rather than larger, by fracturing along national and ethnic lines . . . [but] there are no military short-cuts to becoming a modern country . . . ' (Fukuyama 1991:30). Theo Sommer, a German expert on international relations, commenting on the consequences of the Gulf War, suggested that the NWO lost its moral underpinning when the Kurds were slaughtered by Saddam Hussein's troops. He considered that the NWO was a flawed concept because 'there cannot be such a thing as a unipolar hegemony . . . the UN is still a far cry from a world organization capable of acting under its own steam . . . we are moving from the territorial-military-political age into an economic-financial-technological age' (Sommer 1991:34). Writing before the Danes rejected the Maastricht Treaty and before the outbreak of civil war in the Balkans, he considered that Europe was moving haltingly towards unity. But he also noted the spectre of millions of international migrants, the calamity of holocausts in the Third World, the menace of an international drug mafia and organized crime, and the potential threat from Islamic fundamentalism. Such conflicts do not respond to military solutions. They require a more fundamental shift in values and institutions.

What hope is there for a NWO in which peace prevails and ethnic conflicts do not become violent? Sorokin believed that only by a reintegration of sensory and transcendental values could societies survive future calamities. More recently, some sociologists have suggested that in a postmodern age, a return to religion would provide a basis for a sense of cohesion and social solidarity (Beyer 1990; Bibby 1987). However, the historical evidence does not encourage this expectation. Organized religion has often been associated with intolerance and conflict. Ever since the Crusades, it has been closely related to statism and militarism. Globalization and religious revivalism may be closely related, but they are also the arena for ideological confrontation and fanaticism. To the present day, tensions continue between Protestants, Catholics, Jews, Muslims, Hindus, Sikhs, Buddhists, and (Chinese) Communists. These are often extremely violent. It is unlikely that any of the existing religions will serve to provide a unifying set of values at the global level.

In North America today, people tend to think of religion in terms of freedom and tolerance. Church and state are separate. Some religious leaders, such as Gandhi, Martin Luther King, Jr, Mother Teresa, and others who preach peace and understanding and champion the poor and oppressed, are revered in name but rarely followed in practice. In Europe and North America, we live in a secularized, materialistic society in which religion is rarely a matter of fanatical belief. It does not require us to condemn those neighbours who do not share the faith in which we happen to have been raised. Even the more evangelical sects do not condone violent action against non-believers, although there are cases where violence is self-inflicted or used in self-defence.

Religious tolerance was not always so evident. In Canada, the conflicts now attributed mainly to language and ethnicity were once perceived as essentially religious in origin. English Protestants were opposed to French Catholics, and both were determined to suppress native religions. Louis Riel paid the ultimate price for these powerfully held beliefs. Anti-Semitism was another strongly held prejudice that was widespread among Protestants and Catholics alike. Although Canada provided sanctuary for Mennonites, Hutterites, Mormons, and Doukhobors escaping persecution in Europe, these religious minorities were not well liked. Sometimes the opposition to them was outspoken and violent, as it was to any manifestations of Aboriginal beliefs and ceremonies.

In Europe, religious prejudice and the conflicts it generated remained salient throughout the nineteenth and twentieth centuries. In Germany, anti-Semitism reached its obscene depths in the Holocaust and is showing signs of revival in neo-Nazi movements that appeal to the young and disillusioned, faced with prolonged unemployment. Protestant-Catholic conflict persists in Northern Ireland, inflamed by the bigotry of Ulster loyalists and the nationalism of the IRA. In eastern Europe, ancient rivalry between Catholics and Eastern Orthodox Christians has been revived. Christian communities, together with the Jewish and Muslim minorities in the former Yugoslavia and the former Soviet Union, felt oppressed by communist ideology and are now seeking new converts. It was not without reason that Marx and Lenin saw religion as 'the opium of the masses', dividing the proletariat against each other, rendering them open to capitalist exploitation. Stalin's ruthless suppression of all religions in the name of socialist revolution was an attempt to unite a disparate empire that was always in danger of disintegrating into warring factions based on religious, linguistic, and national differences. The end of the cold war and the collapse of the Soviet empire provided the opportunity for these ethnoreligious conflicts to surface again. At the same time, these historical antagonisms only provided the underlying conditions that predispose conflict. Economic competition and fanatical power struggles between leaders are the intervening determinants. Precipitating factors include real or alleged atrocities and the effects of economic collapse. The means are readily available in stockpiles of arms and unemployed young men and women eager to fight for a cause.

Meanwhile, outside of Europe and North America, religion never ceased to be a matter of open conflict, often violent in nature. Hindus, Muslims, and Sikhs fought openly on the Indian subcontinent, causing enormous bloodshed and creating massive refugee movements. The rise of Islamic fundamentalism drew attention to the fact that there were divisions within the world's Muslim populations, as well as between them and other religious groups in the same regions. Arabs fought Arabs in Iran and Iraq, while Arabs and Jews fought in Palestine, Muslims opposed Christians in Lebanon, Muslims oppressed Buddhists in Malaysia and Indonesia, while other Muslims warred with non-Muslims in Nigeria and the Horn of Africa. Religious conflict and nationalism combined everywhere to ferment civil war, oppression of minorities, and terrorist revolts. When the opposing sides were supported militarily by one or all of the superpowers, the conflicts were prolonged and exacerbated. Secular humanism, or 'enlightenment rationalist fundamentalism' as Gellner (1992:80–96) calls it, does not evoke the commitment to grand endeavours and sacrificial efforts that religion has done in the past.

Environmental concerns, as expressed in the Earth Summit in 1992, might focus attention on survival as a global issue, but there appears to be little political will to translate the good intentions expressed on that occasion into practical reforms on any significant scale. A substantial proportion of the world's population is still excluded from the more affluent regions, and some are in danger of being exiled in perpetuity. Vietnamese boat people, Kurds who fled to the mountains, Somalis dying of war-induced starvation, Romanian gypsies, and Bosnian refugees are among the unwanted minorities. But there is no emigration from this planet, not even to satellite stations in outer space. As H.G. Wells recognized, we cannot wait for the fear of 'air terrorism', imminent space invaders, or 'Star Wars' with a mythical global enemy to galvanize us into the peaceful settlement of our disputes!

The world capitalist system has transformed internal class conflicts into a global contradiction between the interests of the wealthy and the technological élites, wherever they may come from, and the illiterate or innumerate poor, whatever their nationality. Contrary to Marxian predictions, the workers of the world have not united against their global capitalist oppressors. Racial and national consciousness have proven to be far more powerful bases of social formation than economic class. Instead, class consciousness is transformed into ethnic conflict and demands for regional autonomy. Local élites exploit the discontents of marginalized populations in a struggle for power, aided and abetted by nationalist intelligentsia who take advantage of the waning influence of former imperial regimes to promote an ethnic revival (Smith 1981, 1990). Civil wars replace the class struggle as previously subordinate populations and indigenous minorities endeavour to liberate themselves from control by once-dominant ethnic strata, or in irredentist fervour pursue genocidal policies of 'ethnic cleansing'.

Notwithstanding the end of the cold war between the NATO alliance and the Warsaw Pact countries, the global system is an unstable one in which war, with or without the use of nuclear and chemical weapons, remains a realistic option for power-hungry leaders. There is still a global military-industrial complex, an international arms bazaar, and massive weapons transfers. The transnational corporations that make up the global economic system (and the populations whose lifestyles they facilitate) are united in their dependence on energy from fossil fuels and will stop at nothing to ensure a continued supply of cheap oil and cheap labour. The result of internal conflicts and external wars will be a massive increase in the number of refugees seeking asylum. Our global society has yet to adapt itself to such a prospect. Having failed to respond to the needs of the millions of displaced persons, who were already victims of past crises, it has created still more political, economic, and environmental refugees as a consequence of recent military actions and their aftermath. Social conflict has been globalized and is a product of both internal and external forces linked to form distinctive transnational patterns. There is a relentless inevitability about change, which brings with it structural contradictions and social conflict. Like city dwellers on a geological fault line, we prefer to pretend disaster could never happen. When it does, we are generally unprepared.

What does this mean in practical terms for politicians, bureaucrats, and academics charged with the responsibility of formulating policies concerning peacekeeping, international migration, and refugee movements? Firstly, it means that all previous plans and programs are anachronistic; we have to rethink the whole system in global terms, and that means international cooperation. Secondly, it means that short-term self-interest must give way to policies that are aimed at the long-term interest of all concerned, including the so-called developing countries whose people must actively participate in the decisions concerning them. Thirdly, state sovereignty can no longer be maintained in an absolute way; all boundaries are permeable and borders can no longer be defended with walls, iron curtains, armed guards, or computer surveillance systems. Power-sharing and cooperation are essential. Fourthly, territories and their resources, material and human, must be held in trust for posterity and not consumed wantonly for present profit. Finally, there is no exit from a global society. We must learn to live together, respecting our differences and embracing our common humanity, whether in our immediate neighbourhood or a hemisphere away. As we approach the twenty-first century, we have a choice between the optimism of H.G. Wells or the pessimism of Pitirim Sorokin.

chapter twelve

Global apartheid: Migration, racism, and the world system[1]

It may seem strange to juxtapose terms such as 'apartheid', 'asylum', and 'refuge' and to link them to concepts such as 'ethnic cleansing', 'reservation', 'prison', and 'hospital' (see Figure 12.1). However, from a sociological perspective, these are all actions, structures, and institutions associated with forcible isolation of people who are different. Because of the differences, they are perceived as having actually (or potentially) conflicting relationships. Distancing is used to deal with the conflict. When separation is imposed by a dominant group upon a less powerful one, the conflict is only temporarily resolved. In the long run, the opposition is generally exacerbated. Restitution and retribution may be delayed for generations, but the power struggle continues. As processes of structuration, apartheid and asylum have much in common.

The word apartheid literally means 'apart*hood*' (c.f. neighbourhood*)*, that is, the separation of people into different areas. The term 'asylum' (literally meaning non-seizure) originated with the Church's refusal to allow wanted criminals and others sought by the authorities to be forcibly removed from the altar. Later the term was applied to mental hospitals, sanatoria, and other institutions where anyone who might contaminate others, disturb the peace, or in some way come into conflict with the general public could be kept apart. As Michel Foucault (1973) showed in his study of *Madness and Civilization*, the nineteenth-century insane asylum brought to bear on the mentally ill all the means of social control in the

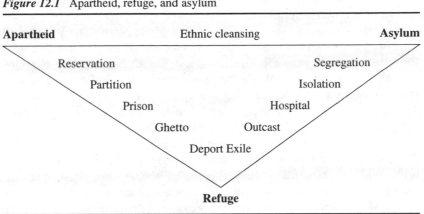

Figure 12.1 Apartheid, refuge, and asylum

power of 'keepers'.[2] They used segregation, surveillance, subordination, and silencing as instruments. These replaced physical coercion with self-restraint, judgement, and the patriarchal authority of the medical profession.

Totalitarian states have long used the device of exile or forcible confinement in prisons or hospitals as a means of dealing with dissidents and political enemies. Thus 'asylum' acquired a dual meaning. On the one hand, it is a way in which a more powerful (or majority) group segregates 'others' who do not conform or who are seen as threatening. On the other hand, the asylum offers sanctuary and some protection for the minority or outcast who might otherwise face death. The term 'refugee' (from the Latin *refugium*, meaning to flee back) was first applied to the Protestant Huguenots escaping the threat of death and persecution in France, following the revocation of the Edict of Nantes in 1685.

The principle of separation as a means of social control is widely used and has a long history in Canada and elsewhere. The expulsion of the Acadians from the Maritimes in 1756, the separation of Upper and Lower Canada, the creation of Indian reserves and, in some provinces, the formation of separate school systems for Catholics and Protestants are all examples of the principle of separation being used as a device to reduce tension and maintain control. When South Africa introduced its system of African reserves (later called Bantustans or homelands), it was following a well-established precedent in colonial history. The English 'Pale' in France and Ireland, the partition of Ireland and later India (establishing Pakistan and later Bangladesh), the division of Cyprus, are all examples of the political application of the principle. The so-called 'ethnic cleansing' of areas in former Yugoslavia is the latest example and one that comes close to genocide. Serbian, Croatian, and Muslim peoples who have lived together for centuries are being separated by military force in an attempt to create homogeneous ethnoreligious areas, expanding the power and territorial control of fanatical nationalist leaders. Numerous civilian casualties and vast refugee movements are the result.

Residential segregation by ethnicity and religion created the ghettoes of European cities and eventually led to the Holocaust. In the United States, the emergence of separate residential areas ('Black' ghettoes) and separate schools for 'Blacks' and 'Whites' is another example. In 1954, the American Supreme Court found separate schools and colleges for Afro-Americans 'inherently unequal' and therefore unconstitutional, but, despite busing, *de facto* residential and educational segregation have persisted. In some cases, electoral boundaries have been redrawn in order to emphasize ethnic homogeneity, thereby giving a spurious legitimacy to residential segregation. In determining the legitimacy of any case of ethnic segregation, it is necessary to consider the extent to which it is voluntary on both sides, or how far it is a result of coercion and domination by one group over another. The latter is nearly always the case.

As far as immigration is concerned, the question becomes are we creating a system of global apartheid based on discrimination against migrants and refugees from poorer developing countries? Or are we simply acting rationally to protect the integrity of our social systems and harmonize our immigration policies? Will the emerging new world order ensure justice and equality of treatment for immigrants and refugees, or will it create a system that privileges some and deprives others of their rights? In order to determine whether it is accurate to describe present trends as contributing to global apartheid, it is necessary to summarize the key elements in the South African experience concerning external and internal migration, in the context of state-legislated apartheid in that country.

Apartheid in South Africa

When the Nationalist party came to power in South Africa in 1948, building on existing forms of discrimination and segregation, it proceeded to create the system that came to be known as 'apartheid'. In defending the South African Group Areas Act in 1951, then President Dr Malan argued that it was essential to keep the groups apart in order to maintain 'racial peace' (Richmond 1961:81–137). An integral element of the system was the control of internal migration, combined with the selective immigration to South Africa of people who were racially defined as 'European'. Forty-four years later, the system is gradually being dismantled, although South Africa is a long way from institutionalizing equality, democracy, and racial integration. Apartheid failed for a number of reasons, among which were the internal contradictions and conflicts within the system itself. Revolutionary change could only be contained by the use of excessive force, with consequent loss of legitimacy in the eyes of the world and its own people. Internal resistance to oppression was reinforced by pressure from outside the country. Externally imposed economic sanctions were used to symbolize disapproval of the regime and provide leverage for reform.

'White' South Africans are outnumbered by a ratio of six to one within the republic. They are an affluent and politically dominant minority enjoying a material standard of living comparable to that of middle-class Canadians, while the majority of the African population have average incomes that are only one-tenth of those of 'Whites'. This inequality has been maintained by systemic discrimination beginning with the Labour Regulation Act (1911) regulating the recruitment of labour and the Native Lands Act of 1913, which created the 'reserves', later to be described as 'homelands', confining the African population to 13 per cent of the total area of the country. Subsequent legislation, up to and including the Abolition of Influx Control Act (1986), regulated the movement of people into urban areas. Other measures included the Blacks (Urban Areas) Consolidation Act (1945), the Population Registration Act (1950), which required everyone to carry racially classified identification, the Group Areas Acts (1950 and 1966), and the Prevention of Illegal Squatting Act (1951). Added to these were a series of measures entrenching the dominant economic and political power of the 'White' population by denying full citizenship and the franchise, suppressing political opposition, and restricting access to education and social rights (Adam 1979).

The selective immigration of 'White' settlers to South Africa was encouraged in part to compensate for the demographic imbalance between 'White' and non-'White' and to provide a source of skilled manpower. An immigrant to South Africa had to be 'readily assimilable by the White inhabitants' and not a threat to 'the language, culture or religion of any white ethnic group', according to the minister of immigration (Couper 1990). In fact, more than 1 million immigrants of European ethnic origin were admitted to South Africa between 1945 and 1985. At the same time, South Africa forced into exile many opponents of apartheid and hunted down Mozambican refugees who crossed the border, deporting those they caught (US Committee for Refugees 1991:53).

Notwithstanding these measures, the South African economy is dependent on a supply of temporary workers from within and outside the country. Agriculture, mining, manufacturing, and domestic services all rely heavily on migrant workers. These are drawn from neighbouring countries such as Malawi, Mozambique, and Zambia, as well as from the homelands, such as Transkei, Ciskei, etc. Such migrant workers were confined to separate townships or to hostels away from the 'White' areas. A third of the 'Black' population is now urban, but have no security of tenure. In 1981, it was estimated that 74,000 'Blacks' commuted daily from homelands into 'White' areas to work, and a further 1.5 million worked for longer periods as contract labourers (Glavovic 1987:47).

The South African situation gives rise to numerous external refugees and internally displaced persons. Opponents of apartheid were often obliged to flee to Swaziland or other neighbouring countries to avoid persecution. Compulsory removal to homelands, factional disputes within Bantustans and between tribal groups, together with squatter camps made up of those seeking employment have created internal refugees, whose numbers may range from hundreds of thousands to millions (Mabin 1987:80–5). Despite some changes to the system, it seems that current trends represent 'relatively insignificant changes from past apartheid policies' (Robertson 1987:116), but there is no guarantee that these will bring peace. Regional divisions remain and the possibility of secession cannot be ruled out (Adam and Moodley 1993). The African National Congress is pressing the all-'White' government to introduce more radical reforms that will enable the non-'White' majority to participate democratically in the political process. For the first time, democratic elections with universal franchise were held in 1994. Meanwhile, factional fighting between Zulus and other African groups vying for power, and armed reaction by 'White' extremists demanding their own separate state do not augur well for the future. Southern Africa will continue to generate its own refugees, 'Black' and 'White'.

Racism outside South Africa

However, as apartheid in South Africa is gradually giving way to political reform and social change, the rest of the world appears to be moving in a different direction. In eastern and central Europe, following the collapse of the Soviet empire, nationalism and irredentism have revived, causing widespread violence. Ethnic cleansing provides the ideological rationale for civil war in the former Yugoslavia. The idea that only one dominant racial or ethnoreligious group should be allowed to occupy a particular territory is precisely the meaning of apartheid. When military force is used to bring about such territorial separation, killing or displacing hundreds of thousands (possibly millions) of people in the process, it is no exaggeration to speak of 'apartheid'.

Faced with the prospect of mass migration from poorer to richer countries, from those where governmental systems have collapsed to those with more stable political environments (and with huge refugee flows from Bosnia-Herzegovina), coordinated efforts are being made to stem the potential flow into western Europe. The legislation used and the regulative institutions created have a remarkable similarity to those that South Africa adopted to control the movement of people from outside and within its borders. Furthermore, the ideological justifications used to defend these measures echo those adopted by the dominant 'White' minority in South Africa to defend their actions in imposing the system of apartheid on the non-'White' majority. As well as explicit racism and claims to 'superiority', they include an obligation to limit intertribal conflict, the need to preserve ethnic identity, expressions of religious fanaticism, the defence of existing cultural and social institutions, state security, the maintenance of law and order, preservation of economic privilege and the need to regulate and manage population movements. These themes, which were constantly repeated by defenders of the South African system, are now recurring in the rhetoric of those who wish to restrict immigration into western Europe, North America, and Australia.

People in most countries have an ambivalent attitude towards questions of race, ethnicity, and migration. On the one hand, the United Nations Subcommission on Prevention of Discrimination and Protection of Minorities and the Commission on Human Rights condemn apartheid and, on the other, they note an upsurge in racism, discrimination, intolerance, and xenophobia in many parts of the world (*Human Rights Newsletter*, October 1990, April 1991). In Europe and North America, neo-Nazi and other right-wing extremist groups are gaining support. Recent riots in Los Angeles and lesser outbreaks of violence in Toronto serve to remind us how volatile interracial situations are. Public opinion surveys in many countries reveal a backlash against immigration and growing support for reactionary political parties. In France, the Front National, led by Jean-Marie Le Pen, mobilized 15 per cent of the popular vote in recent elections, and demonstrations against non-'White' immigrant workers are frequent events, as are antiracist marches (Husbands 1991; Singer 1991). In Germany, a tenfold increase in racist attacks (from 200 to 2,386) was reported in 1991 (*Migration News Sheet*, February 1992). There was a further escalation of ethnic violence in Germany in 1992, much of it instigated by neo-Nazi skinheads, targeted towards asylum applicants, gypsies, and other foreigners, including long-resident Turkish workers and their families. The government reacted by proposing stricter controls over immigration and an amendment to the constitutional right to asylum. The Republican party in Germany proposed mass repatriation of foreigners and the confinement of accepted refugees in camps away from cities.

Immigration controls

There is a worldwide trend towards stricter immigration controls and attempts to limit the flow of refugees and asylum applicants. It is part of a growing nostalgia for a simpler world in which people felt secure in homogeneous communities where neighbours shared 'traditional' values. It is also a reaction to the insecurity felt by many faced with a rapidly changing global society. This is evident in the growth of racism, xenophobia, and religious and ethnic conflict in various countries, including those that have traditionally been receptive to both political and economic migrants. Politically, it is expressed in the coordinated efforts of countries in western Europe, North America, and Australia to deter asylum applications and limit mass migration to these regions. There is a growing fear in Europe concerning the possibility of mass migration from east to west and an equal concern about the potential flow from south to north, including from the

Maghreb territories of the southern Mediterranean and Africa to France and Germany.

The reunification of East and West Germany reduced the FRG's dependency on immigrant workers, while at the same time leaving the country vulnerable to mass migration from east and central Europe as well as from the former Soviet Union. Under the German constitution, 'ethnic Germans', from wherever they may come, have privileged rights of entry and citizenship, although long-time residents of the country who are not of German descent (including their children born in Germany) are denied similar privileges. Recently, new immigration legislation was introduced in Germany that will severely restrict the number of asylum applicants accepted and allows the government to segregate them in camps. Britain introduced an asylum bill that will require refugees to be fingerprinted, restrict access by asylum applicants to public housing, permit deportation where an asylum claim has been refused, and require airlines or other carriers to ensure that travellers hold a visa to enter or even pass through the United Kingdom en route to another country.

Notwithstanding the European Economic Community's abolition of internal border checks, Britain, Ireland, and Denmark have expressed reservations and indicated exceptions. The UK intends to retain frontier controls for all non-EEC nationals, including those entering Britain via other EEC countries. A limit of three months' stay will be placed on non-UK nationals entering the country. Britain is one of the twelve European countries that signed the Dublin Convention in June 1990. Neither this nor the related Schengen Agreement have yet been ratified by all the countries involved, although their provisions are expected to come into force in 1994, having been delayed by preparation of a computerized data bank concerning immigrants. Meanwhile, France, Germany, Belgium, and other countries tightened their control over asylum applicants and refugee movements.

Schengen Agreement and Dublin Convention

The Schengen Agreement was signed in 1985 by Belgium, Denmark, France, Germany, and Luxembourg. When the subsequent Dublin Convention and Maastricht Treaty are ratified, it will apply to all twelve EEC members. The agreement provides that persons with valid documents who can show that they have sufficient means to support themselves during their stay and to return to their country of origin will be allowed entry, but only if they are not considered a 'threat to public policy, national security or international relations of the Contracting Parties'. Once admitted, they may travel freely within the EEC, subject to any limitations that Britain or other dissenting countries may impose. In order to enforce the regulations, the countries in question may take any necessary steps to verify documents and may use mobile units to exercise surveillance at external borders. Every contracting party is obliged to supply the others with information concerning individuals requesting admission (including asylum applicants), and this information may be computerized.

As well as extending the provisions of the Schengen Agreement to all countries in the EEC, the Dublin Convention also deals specifically with the question of asylum applicants and determines who is responsible for processing them. It reiterates the 1951 Geneva Convention's definition of a refugee, as amended by the 1967 New York Protocol. In order of precedence, the state responsible for hearing an asylum application is either the one that issued a residence permit or an entry visa; when no visa is required, the state that first admitted the person into the EEC territory is responsible. The other EEC states are bound by the decision of the one that processes the application.

Critics of the Schengen Agreement and Dublin Convention note that there is no recognition of the growing numbers of cases of *de facto* humanitarian refugees who may not meet the 1951 Convention definition. It is felt that the effect of visa requirements, entry regulations, and carrier sanctions will be to deter or exclude many legitimate claimants and those trying to escape wartorn countries. It will also increase the traffic in forged documents. Third-country nationals (i.e., non-EEC citizens) resident in the EEC will find their right to travel and work in other countries restricted. These agreements must also be considered in the context of increasing cooperation within and between European countries and others in matters of international policing and security. The Trevi Group is an intergovernmental body that coordinates efforts to combat terrorism and organized crime. Among the measures it has recommended (and that are being widely adopted) are uniform documentation of travellers; the fingerprinting of migrants and asylum applicants; the creation of a computerized database and information exchange on criminals, deported persons, and unwanted persons; training of police officers and border guards for surveillance; and the harmonization of legislation governing immigration and security measures at borders. The Maastricht Treaty, when ratified, will create a European Union with even greater coordination of immigration controls. A provisional list of countries whose nationals will require visas to enter any European Union country covers most Third World states, including many commonwealth countries whose citizens do not at present require a visa to visit Britain, although they will do so in the future.

It is probably not a coincidence that many of these measures have been incorporated into the new Canadian legislation on immigration (Bill C-86). Canada is one of the sixteen states participating in the Inter-governmental Consultations on Asylum, Refugee, and Migration Policies in Europe, North America, and Australia. Described as 'informal', these consultations enable governments to be kept informed of developments in other countries and facilitate the harmonization process. The participating states acknowledge the value of cooperation, endorse the principles established in the Dublin Convention, and seek to intensify cooperation in combatting illegal immigration. The aim is to adopt a concerted approach that will also include the countries of eastern Europe, so that they will adopt policies that correspond with those in western Europe.

Canada's new Immigration Act enables this country to harmonize its immigration law and practice with that of other countries. As in the McCarthy era in the United States, guilt by association with allegedly subversive organizations or a criminal record, however minor, will be sufficient to exclude potential immigrants and asylum applicants. Asylum applicants will be fingerprinted and the use of forged documents will be grounds for exclusion. Immigrants may be required to work in particular places and to remain in such employment for two years after arrival, as if they were indentured. Business immigrants and investors will be given top priority for admission. Officials will have greater control over numbers admitted annually in various categories. As at present, the extensive use of temporary employment visas will enable the government to limit the number of people allowed to settle permanently. None of these measures, in themselves, appears particularly draconian. However, the combined effect will be to give considerable advantage to the wealthy and well educated over 'your tired, your poor, your huddled masses yearning to breathe free'. The delayed reaction of Canada and many other countries to the prolonged plight of refugees in Somalia and other regions of Africa, compared with the response to those in former Yugoslavia, suggests that the 'huddled masses' should preferably be 'White' if they are to receive much help at all. The United States (in the Bush and Clinton administrations) has applied a double standard in its treatment of Cuban as compared with Haitian asylum applicants. 'Fortress Europe' is matched by 'Fortress North America'.

Africa and the Middle East

The African continent has experienced large population movements induced by economic conditions and political instability. South Africa has always relied on a flow of workers from neighbouring countries who are employed on a contract basis in mining and other industries. Reliable statistics are difficult to obtain, but the number of people living and working outside their country of birth runs into millions. The situation is summarized by Aderanti Adepoju (1988) as follows:

> International migration in West Africa is dominated by clandestine or undocumented migration of unskilled persons. In southern Africa migration is temporary and oscillatory, conditioned largely by South African immigration laws. Refugee migration is a major feature in Central and especially East Africa. Clandestine migrations are most frequent among nomads—especially between Somalia, Kenya and Tanzania (Adepoju 1988:78).

The growing number of refugees and others displaced by war and ecological disasters is a disturbing feature of the African scene, particularly in the region of the Horn and Sudan, where more than 5 million people live under the most primitive conditions in and outside organized camps (Harrell-Bond 1986; Mazur 1988).

The Middle East and the Gulf region are experiencing the combined effects of economic and political instability. Israel has always been a country of immigration and has welcomed Jewish settlers from any country. In recent years the numbers of Soviet Jews emigrating to that country has grown more rapidly than the regular immigration and settler assistance system can handle. Israel is reported to have budgeted for 400,000 Soviet Jewish immigrants in 1991 and still more in 1992. Meanwhile, the Palestinian problem and the *Intifadah* continued to exacerbate an already prolonged refugee crisis in the region throughout the 1980s and early 1990s (Abu-Lughod 1988). It remains to be seen whether the PLO/Israel peace accord of 1993 will reduce the bloodshed and relieve the refugee problem in Jordan and elsewhere.

The oil-rich Gulf region always attracted professional, skilled, and managerial personnel from Britain, Europe, and the United States, but after 1970, the number of Asian workers in the region has risen to over 3 million. They provided much-needed remittances to their countries of origin as well as a significant cultural impact as the two-way flow of contract labour has a profound influence on families in the sending countries. The average length of a contract is two to three years. The reintegration of return migrants has caused problems for the countries of origin. The war between Iraq and Iran led to some diminution in the flow of migrants, but when it ended, the numbers began to increase again until the crisis over Kuwait and the war in the Persian Gulf (Amjad 1990; Seccombe 1988). This resulted in more than half a million workers who were forced to leave (Curmi 1993). Some were trapped in Jordan where they spent months in makeshift camps. In the aftermath of the war, a major refugee crisis occurred as thousand of Kurds tried to escape to Turkey or Iran.

Asia

Asia has long been a source of permanent and temporary migration to the rest of the world. This is particularly true of east and south Asia (especially China, India, and Pakistan) whose emigrants now form permanently established minorities in Britain, North America, Australia, and elsewhere. Asia has a large refugee problem involving people from Tibet, Afghanistan, Bangladesh, Sri Lanka, Vietnam, and Kampuchea. Many have sought asylum in neighbouring countries, as well as farther away (Centlivres and Centlivres-Dumont 1988; Zolberg et al. 1989).

In recent years, the NIE countries, together with those that have become part of the ILE, have experienced net inward migration as well as outward flows. There is a growing interdependence of the economies of Asia, as well as cross-national labour migration, particularly within and between

Thailand, Malaysia, Singapore, Brunei, Indonesia, and the Philippines and the leading ILE countries such as Japan and Hong Kong (Gunasekaran 1990). It is impossible to document the detailed flows, but the multiway nature of the movements must be emphasized. Hong Kong is losing some of its wealthiest and best-qualified people who are emigrating in anticipation of mainland China's repossession in 1997 but, at the same time, it has over two million foreign-born residents, mainly from China, but also from ILE countries such as Britain, the United States, and Japan (Abella 1990). Hong Kong, Thailand, and other Asian countries also have a serious refugee problem.

Some Asian countries, such as Singapore, rely heavily on temporary workers from Thailand and elsewhere. There are strict controls to deal with illegal migrants. Malaysia supplies labour to Singapore, but is also a receiver of labour migration from other countries. Brunei is an oil-rich country that makes use of migrant workers (including women working as domestics) from the Philippines and elsewhere. Indonesia is a net exporter of labour. Appleyard (1988:159) noted that many of the issues relating to international migration in Asia also apply to the Pacific islands, where there is a proportionally greater outward flow reflecting the poverty and deteriorating economic conditions in the islands compared with the relative prosperity of some Asian countries. Nevertheless, as in other regions, remittances from nationals working abroad are important. Throughout Asia, as elsewhere, these multiway flows of population create severe strains on sending and receiving areas alike, sometimes exacerbating existing ethnic tensions and cultural clashes (Appleyard 1989; Claval 1990; Stahl 1988).

The World System

We are living in a global society, although we still lack effective world governmental institutions. Nevertheless, the most economically developed and affluent countries are banding together to protect their privileged position in much the same way that Afrikaners and others of European descent sought to maintain their dominance in South Africa. Europeans and those of European descent in the Americas and Oceania are outnumbered in the world in a ratio of four to one. This leads to fear that they will lose their power and territorial control as the peoples of Africa and Asia restructure their economies and participate in a global postindustrial society where mass migration is the norm. As the senior legal adviser to the UNHCR has stated, even if the developed countries 'were prepared to betray the very values on which their societies are based, by building new iron curtains and Berlin Walls around their common territory, the human flood would still find its ways' (von Blumenthal 1991). In other words, a system of global apartheid is bound to fail.

What then is the alternative? The director of the agency for intergovernmental consultations echoes the view of many experts that uncontrolled, large-scale international migration threatens social cohesion, international solidarity, and peace (Widgren 1991). Coordinated efforts to deter irregular movements, encourage voluntary repatriation, harmonize immigration and asylum policies, and promote economic development in the Third World are seen as essential. But the economic, political, and social costs of effective measures to deal with root causes are enormous. They would involve long-term developmental assistance, large-scale planned migration, and concerted efforts to promote human rights and equality in sending and receiving countries alike. Contrary to the view that economic growth will itself remove the need for migration, it must be recognized that the emerging global economic and social system is one in which population movements will continue to increase rather than decline. A comprehensive, non-exodus approach, such as that advocated by the intergovernmental committee and its advisers, will be self-defeating. Global apartheid will collapse as surely as the South African version has done. In the postmodern world, we must all learn to live with ethnocultural diversity, rapid social change, *and* mass migration. There is no peaceful alternative.

Notes

[1] This is a revised version of an article published in *Refuge* 13, no. 1 (April 1993). Pages 214–16 are from my article, 'International Migration and Global Change' in *Asian Transmigration*, edited by O.J. Hui, C.K. Bun, and C.S. Beng (Singapore: Prentice-Hall, 1994).

[2] Foucault (1973:241–78) compared the humanitarian efforts of the Religious Society of Friends and Samuel Tuke at the Retreat in York, England, with those of Scipion Pinel at Bicêtre near Paris, France. Although the former was based on religious ideals and the latter on secular, rational principles, they had in common the imposition of self-discipline, order, and justice to modify behaviour in conformity with majority expectations.

chapter thirteen

Alternative visions

The practice of violence, like all action, changes the world, but the most probable change is to a more violent world.

—Hannah Arendt (1970:80)

Every generation believes itself to be at the end of an era and the beginning of a new age. It is fashionable for contemporary writers to look forward to the twenty-first century, as if this were a particularly important turning point. The artificiality of the Gregorian calendar is ignored and its universality taken for granted. It is one example of the globalization process that this western European/Christian concept of time has been so widely adopted. There remain some doubts whether the new century actually begins with the year 2000 or 2001. Journalists, eager for a scoop, will undoubtedly prefer the earlier date. However, there is no reason to suppose that the next decade will be markedly different from the last. We shall be constrained and enabled by the same structuration processes already occurring, the competing goals and values now embedded in local, national, and global cultures, and by the institutions that have been created. Change is ubiquitous but that is not a new discovery. The new world order is likely to be more like the old than many would hope, but it may still contain some surprises.

Paul Kennedy (1993), in *Preparing for the Twenty-first Century*, identified a number of key issues that are likely to be critical. They include the demographic explosion in Asia and Africa; the neo-Malthusian problem of population and limited resources, which could generate mass migration; the dangers to the natural environment; the communications revolution; and the questionable future of the nation-state. Beyond emphasizing the importance of education and enlightened political leadership, he offers few solutions. He notes that 'we face not a "new world order" but a troubled and fractured planet' (Kennedy 1993:149)

Max Dublin (1990) argues persuasively that attempts to prophesy the future are dangerous. When undertaken by those in power, such prophecies tend to be self-fulfilling. If a certain outcome is inevitable, it is better to 'go with the flow' and make the best of it. Most forecasting in the social sciences is simple extrapolation of existing trends. This is particularly true in demography. Population experts cover themselves by denying that they are actually forecasting the future. Their 'projections' are based on sets of alternative assumptions concerning fertility, mortality, and migration. In turn, these are generally based on past trends with low, medium, and high alternatives combined in various patterns. The possibility of sudden reversal is rarely considered, even in the most sophisticated computer simulations. Catastrophic increases in mortality, substantial rises or falls in fertility, and sudden changes in the scale and direction of population movements across national boundaries or between continents are regarded as improbable. Therefore such contingencies rarely enter the equations, yet such unpredictable events cannot be ruled out.

It is not an exercise in what Dublin (1990) calls 'futurehype' to consider some hypothetical scenarios based on existing social patterns and movements. When the distribution of power behind these movements is known, it may even be possible to apply a probability coefficient to calculate the likelihood of a particular outcome. However, such attempts at prediction are about as reliable as a long-term weather forecast, and have odds similar to those available at the racetrack or the lottery.

It is a characteristic of the human condition that, individually and collectively, we monitor our own actions and their consequences. Organizations and individuals are guided by the feedback of information. We are capable of learning from our mistakes. The tragedy is that we so often fail to do so. Blinded by political ideology, economic dogmatism, and/or religious fervour, we persist in courses of action that lead to unintended disasters.

Without engaging in wild speculation, it is possible to identify three broad visions of the future that are likely to influence the direction of events in the next several decades. All are present and discernible already as social trends and movements. However, each represents a very different perception of the world as it is and as it might be. As scenarios, they are ultimately contradictory and incompatible. However, it is possible that some combination of all three may influence policies and programs, at various levels of governmental and non-governmental action. The result, clearly, would be to generate further conflict.

Figure 13.1 New world order: Alternative scenarios

	Nostalgic	Pragmatic	Utopian
Orientation	Past	Present	Future
Focus	Cultural	Political-economic	Bioenvironmental
Goal	Ethnic survival	State survival	Species survival
Fear	Loss of identity	Loss of sovereignty	Extinction
Means	Separation/ exclusion	Border control surveillance	Emancipation/ empowerment
Structural form	*Gemeinschaft* (Community)	*Gesellschaft* (Organization)	*Verbindungs-neztschaft* (Network)
Migration	Restricted (Reactive) Selective criteria Cultural	Restricted (Reactive) Selective criteria Economic	Planned (Proactive) Selective criteria Ecological
Possible outcome	Global apartheid (monologic)	Global domination/ subordination	Global equality participation (dialogic)
Risks	Racism Fundamentalism Genocide	Conventional/ nuclear wars Armageddon	Fragmentation/ anarchy Chaos

I call these three visions of the future the pragmatic, the nostalgic, and the utopian, respectively (see Figure 13.1). All are 'realistic' in the sense that they are grounded in present, practical concerns, have influential leaders pressing their merits, and are backed by human and material resources. The pragmatic vision is presently the most powerful and influential of the three. It is oriented to the present and immediate future, and is concerned mainly with political and economic questions. It contrasts with the nostalgic vision, which looks to the past for inspiration and focuses mainly on questions of language, culture, and religion. The utopian outlook, which has gained considerable support in recent years, is oriented to a longer-term future and focuses primarily on environmental and developmental issues. All three scenarios, when translated into practical policies and programs, have significant implications for international migration and ethnic relations within a rapidly changing world system. They each have positive and negative implications, expressing both hopes and fears for the future, promising the achievement of desirable goals, but at the same time are accompanied by serious risks if carried to extremes.

Pragmatic view

The pragmatic view reflects the existing distribution of political and economic power within the world system. It is represented in the deliberations of the G7 group of countries, the EEC and various UN agencies. The Informal Consultations body (representing western European countries, together with Australia, Canada, and the United States on issues relating to migration) is influential in developing common policies with regard to refugees and related issues (Widgren 1991). The Conference on Security and Cooperation in Europe, which also included representation from the United States and Canada, debated issues that concern migration, refugees, and displaced persons (Brett and Eddison 1993). Unfortunately, no agreement was reached on appropriate measures. The main thrust of the policies so far endorsed is to create the conditions for non-exodus, i.e., reducing proactive and reactive migration to the minimum compatible with economic needs and the fulfilment of legal obligations. It is expected that this can be achieved through the development of early warning systems that will permit prompt intervention to prevent ethnic conflicts or other refugee-generating situations from exploding into unmanageable proportions. Those adopting the pragmatic approach believe that economic migration from developing to developed countries can be reduced by appropriate investment and economic growth in the former. Development aid is deliberately seen as a migration-hampering strategy. There are few grounds for believing that it will work. In the short run, the reverse could happen as aspiration levels rise and the means to travel become available.

The single common denominator of the pragmatic approach adopted by these countries and by international organizations (such as the UN and its agencies) is state security and the preservation of sovereignty. This translates into a preoccupation with border control, as evident in the EEC.

Europe is not alone in this respect. Other countries and regions have introduced similar measures, including Canada and the United States within the North American free trade region. Enforcement of immigration laws is seen as closely related to other aspects of public security and measures to combat organized crime and drug dealing. It has even been alleged that smuggling people may prove to be more lucrative than smuggling drugs. Already there is a flourishing business in stolen and forged passports, visas, and other documents. Concern with state sovereignty and border control has led to a criminalization of potential refugees and economic migrants (proactive and reactive). Until proven otherwise, all are regarded as potentially illegal and therefore subject to deportation if caught without proper documents. 'States' powers to refuse entry and expel aliens and their discretion to confer nationality has been treated as an integral part of this territorial power since the late nineteenth century . . . Such powers are by no means treated as absolute under current international law' (Bosniak 1991:7430). There have been challenges to the Maastricht Treaty in Europe on the ground that it interferes with the fundamental sovereignty of states. Some countries are reluctant to sign conventions relating to the rights of migrant workers if these are held to apply to undocumented migrants and asylum seekers.

The fortress mentality reflects a concern with personal and collective security. It begins with the individual's fear of assault and consequent carrying of defensive weapons, the use of personal alarms, and training in self-defence. It extends to the carrying of knuckle-dusters, knives, and guns by young people in school. It includes the installation of security systems in homes and offices, and the employment of armed security guards by government agencies and corporations. It is fuelled by fears of violent crime and increasing evidence of the global reach of political terrorism. It is used to justify increased budgets for police forces, as well as the enforcement branch of immigration departments. There is a pervasive fear of 'strangers', which makes physically or culturally 'visible minorities' targets for hostility. The latter are also more likely to be singled out for more stringent inspection at airports and border crossings.

From a psychological point of view, there is a direct connection between concern with personal, family, and corporate security and the question of state security. The state is held responsible for public well-being. Loss of sovereignty by the state threatens ontological security and the foundations of individual identity. It is also related with the concept of citizenship in both its legal and political form, and those aspects related to entitlement in connection with health, welfare, education, and income maintenance. The right to vote in a democratic system and the right to benefits in an affluent society are closely guarded privileges. State control of immigration is seen as an essential means to the end of maintaining economic advantage in an increasingly competitive global system. This is particularly true at a time of recession and fiscal restraint when the welfare state itself is threatened and the principle of universality in entitlement to benefits is being questioned. In any case, such 'universality' does not extend to those who are not citizens or denizens of the country in question (Hammar 1990a).

Key concepts in the pragmatic vision of the world are management and control. In this respect, it is an understandable dimension of late modernity. Bureaucratic solutions are seen as necessary and appropriate. It is a manifestation of *Gesellschaft*. Complex organizational solutions are sought for the practical problems facing the political and economic power élites. In a rapidly changing world, managed competition within a global economy is regarded as the only rational response. A new international division of labour is emerging as a result of the globalization of production. Developed countries must now compete with 'awakening giants' in Third World countries. Within this global system, labour migration and free movement for investors and entrepreneurs is regarded as necessary as long as it is controlled. The management of international migration flows in the interests of economic efficiency is the key consideration. Since tourism is a major industry, this too must be facilitated even when it conflicts with the need to control borders. The needs of large corporations for trained personnel (and access to a supply of less skilled workers to undertake routine assembly work, construction, and service jobs) is a priority consideration. Selection of temporary migrants according to these economic criteria and the encouragement of entrepreneurs is combined with the assumption that they will leave on their own accord or can be required to depart when their economic services are no longer needed.

The pragmatic approach extends to questions of ethnic conflict, nationalist movements, the aftermath of Soviet disintegration, and the longer-term consequences of colonialism, cold war politics, and wars in Asia, Africa, and Latin America. Border clashes and territorial disputes in former colonial countries and in those that have achieved independence from communist regimes are disputes over sovereignty. The sovereignty aspect is highlighted in internal as well as external conflicts. It arises in connection with Aboriginal land claims, property rights, resource management (fishing, forestry, and mining), and the right to live and work in particular places. Key questions are 'Who owns this land?', 'What is the basis of their title to it?', and 'Who may benefit from its resources?'.

For majority groups and advanced industrial countries, the principal goal is the maintenance of the status quo in terms of political and economic power. For minorities it is how to change the balance of power in their favour. Some countries and peoples will be winners, and others will lose in a struggle for world domination and market share. The global arms trade, on which many countries have come to depend, together with the proliferation of nuclear weapons and the capacity to manufacture them, introduces an inherent instability in the world's interstate system. The proliferation of automatic weapons, and the ready availability of explosives has also made civil disturbances more dangerous and terrorists' activities more lethal. The absence of any form of effective world government (and legitimate fear that if one existed it would be tyrannical in form) has left the United Nations peacekeeping functions in disarray. To date, it has failed dismally to prevent civil wars from occurring on all continents. The potential for large-scale reactive migration remains enormous. The refugee problem is not about to go away.

The pragmatic approach requires a managed solution. This means keeping numbers of migrants as low as possible (by declaring many of the victims of war and disaster ineligible for refugee status) and preventing those that are eligible from fleeing to distant countries. Thus, the preferred responses to reactive migration are refugee camps as close as possible to countries of origin, provision for temporary asylum and eventual repatriation, and interdiction measures to ensure that asylum applicants and others designated 'illegal immigrants' do not even reach the more affluent and industrialized countries. Those that do will not be allowed to seek the most favourable place to apply for asylum but must be dealt with in the first one they arrive in.

The pragmatic response to ethnic conflicts, civil disturbances, local wars, and the ambitions of petty dictators is generally a military one. Law and order must be restored and insubordination punished. Following well-established tradition, major powers (with or without the support of the UN Security Council) consider a 'preemptive strike' the most appropriate response, irrespective of the civilian casualties (described as collateral damage) that may ensue. Military intervention may be preceded or followed by economic sanctions that also cause much civilian suffering. The provision of humanitarian aid, with or without the support of peacekeeping forces, is also tied to political objectives. Any other approach would be regarded as incompatible with the national interest of those who presently hold the balance of political and economic power. Foreign aid, including the forgiveness of international indebtedness, becomes a tool for inducing compliance (George 1993). Although early warning of disaster may facilitate a humanitarian response, it may also make it easier for other countries to take measures for self-protection.

Nostalgic view

The nostalgic vision of a new world order is one that looks back romantically to a real or imagined situation in which traditional cultural values could be maintained, free from the threat of globalization. Whereas the pragmatic vision is concerned with the survival and security of the state, the nostalgic perspective regards the survival of the ethnie as the dominant value. The community may be defined by language, religion, 'race', and nationality, or simply as an extended family that wants to be reunited. Its structural form is that of *Gemeinschaft*, i.e., a territorially defined space within which a relatively homogeneous population can maintain its integrity as a 'people' and pass on its traditions to the next generation. The means to this goal is separation from and the exclusion of the 'Others'.

The term 'nostalgia' literally means 'homesickness'. It is particularly evident among emigrés and diasporic populations. It is also a powerful emotive component of most nationalist movements seeking independence, and irredentist groups endeavouring to unite previously divided people of similar ethnocultural origin. The cultural traditions in question may be genuine, but often they are mythologized, or invented traditions that are deliberately designed by ethnic community leaders to stir emotions and mobilize support. Past achievements are glorified and former defeats and humiliations exaggerated as nationalistic fervour is promoted. Ideas of 'family reunion', 'return to the motherland', 'manifest destiny', 'chosen peoples', 'ancestral rights', and 'Aboriginal claims' all reflect the nostalgia for community, a sense of belonging, and an attempt to retain or regain a coherent identity.

Nostalgia is an identifiable component of much late modern literature, music, painting, architecture, and cultural artefacts. It is also evident in the antiurban sentiments of many writers who yearn for a simpler agrarian lifestyle. Sociologists themselves have expressed nostalgic sentiments, beginning with Herbert Spencer and continuing through the writings of Durkheim and others when they lamented the loss of integration induced by industrialization and the large-scale movements of population that it entailed. Robertson (1990b:49) observes, 'One of the major features of modernity which has had a particularly powerful impact with respect to nostalgia is undoubtedly the homogenizing requirements of the modern nation state in the face of ethnic and cultural diversity.' He points out that nineteenth-century nationalism endeavoured to overcome ethnocultural diversity by producing loyal citizens in a standard mould. Universal public education was one of the means used, and war was often the occasion for testing that loyalty. The efforts were only partially successful, and many rebelled against the imposed uniformity.

It is ironic that the international conflicts of the last century and the aftermath of imperialism created the norm of self-determination. In turn, this has generated the nostalgic aspirations of so many minorities and formerly colonized or defeated peoples for their own homogeneous nation-state. The ideal of the self-determination of peoples was entrenched in international law and the United Nations Charter, yet the concept of a 'people' is not defined, and the idea of 'self-determination' is open to various interpretations. The UN began with fifty members; it now has almost 200. Where will it end? One possibility is a world made up of city-states!

Quoting H.R. Isaacs, Daniel Moynihan (1993:25) observes that we have entered the postindustrial age before much of the world has emerged from the preindustrial era. It is little wonder that so many yearn for the security of their own community. As Anthony Smith (1991:74) demonstrates, nationalism is a cultural doctrine, an ideology that seeks to maintain the autonomy, unity, and identity of a nation. Fear of losing this identity, or the desire to restore it, drives the movements aimed at ethnic survival. The means most often chosen towards this goal is separation (even isolation) from those who are different. Anyone who does not share the same language, religion, culture, and history are seen as threatening the unity and solidarity of the community in question. They must be excluded, by force if necessary.

The concept of unity also has a plain and a more esoteric nationalist meaning. At the simple level it refers to unification of the national territory or homeland, if it is divided, and the gathering together within the homeland of all nationals (Smith 1991:75).

Unity also means redeeming lost lands, reclaiming those who have been separated from the homeland, and promoting the cohesion or 'fraternity' of all those who truly belong to the ethnic community. The criterion for 'belonging' is invariably 'blood', i.e., descent from putative ancestors. In its most extreme form, nationalist ideology and the cult of ethnoreligious survival is used to justify ethnic cleansing, the policies of apartheid, the expulsion of minorities, and racist pogroms. It is also at the root of much religious fundamentalism. Protestant sects shun, Catholics excommunicate, and Muslims declare 'holy wars' against those who threaten the orthodox view through their beliefs and writings, or who endanger the solidarity of the community by their behaviour.

When applied to questions of international migration, the nostalgic vision leads to restrictive policies and selective criteria, which are primarily cultural. They favour family reunification, ethnic and national preferences, privileged entry for 'patrials' (i.e., second- or subsequent generation descendants of former emigrants), and exclusionary rules directed against particular ethnocultural groups or nationalities. Once admitted to a particular country, immigrants are expected to assimilate to the majority language and culture. However, in its less totalitarian forms, nostalgic emphasis on ethnic survival within more heterogenous populations leads to residential segregation, social separation, institutional completeness, Aboriginal self-government, and various programs of a multicultural nature designed to preserve identity.

A new world order based on the nostalgic principle of community and ethnically homogeneous territories would endeavour to reverse the consequences of mass communications, satellite links, and international travel. Censorship would prevail, satellite signals would be scrambled, and information controlled for indoctrination purposes. In concert with the pragmatic policies already in place, borders would be carefully guarded. Only those deemed ethnically acceptable and culturally compatible would be admitted for permanent residence. Others would be excluded altogether or subject to strict temporary licensing. It would be the fulfilment of global apartheid.

Utopian view

Giddens (1990:154–62) defines utopian realism as avenues for desired social change that are 'connected to institutionally imminent possibilities'. He recognizes four political dimensions of utopian realism in the late modern world. They are the local, the global, the politics of inequality, and those concerned with self-actualization. In turn, these are linked to particular types of social movement and to the institutional dimensions of modernity. Capitalism gives rise to labour movements, primarily concerned with questions of inequality and what Giddens calls 'emancipatory politics'. Industrialism generates movements concerned with ecology and the local environment. While militarization spurs peace movements, the all-pervasive surveillance and supervisory activities characteristic of the modern state are countered by democratic movements emphasizing free speech, freedom of information, and participation. The latter includes 'life politics' or the politics of self-actualization (Giddens 1990:157).

In considering the implications of utopian realism in relation to questions of migration and ethnic conflict, there are obvious contrasts with the nostalgic and pragmatic perspectives. Rather than a past or present orientation, utopian realism is future-oriented, adopting a longer time perspective than those concerned with current crises. It is the survival of species (human and animal) and of planet earth itself, which is the main focus (Mungall and McLaren 1990). Although it is universal in its scope, it is also very much concerned with local effects. It is summed up in the slogan 'think globally, act locally'. From a sociological perspective, it introduces the concept of 'glocalization' that Robertson (1992:173–4) borrows from Japanese marketing jargon. It is an attempt to reconcile the macroscopic concerns of a planet under stress with a world more closely linked by economic and communication networks, and with a recognition of persisting and desirable microscopic differences. It is related to the distinction between cosmopolitans and locals, which has long been recognized (Hannerz 1990). In a sense, everyone in contemporary society is compelled to be both, responding willingly or unwillingly to global influences while coming to terms with the immediate environment. This is most evident when a major disaster occurs, such as an earthquake, a flood, or a volcanic eruption. By the same token, human interventions in local situations have worldwide repercussions. The Earth Summit in Brazil, the activities of UN agencies, such as UNICEF and the UNHCR, are examples of the glocalization process at work.

Migration policies influenced by a realistically utopian view would begin by fully implementing existing international conventions concerning human rights, recognition of refugees, and the rights of migrant workers. The Universal Declaration of Human Rights, first signed in 1948, entrenches the right to leave a country, but, as mentioned earlier, there is no reciprocal right of admission elsewhere. This lack of symmetry could be remedied by broadening the definition of a refugee along the lines of one used by the Organization of African Unity. It could be further strengthened by ensuring that in a time of crisis, refugees would be recognized collectively rather than requiring individuals to prove that they were personally victims of persecution. The international community, through the UNHCR or a new organization combining humanitarian aid, peace promotion, and refugee assistance, would be responsible for ensuring that safe havens and temporary asylum were available for the victims of war, political persecution, and environmental disasters.

There are a number of other international conventions on human rights and related issues. If ratified and fully implemented, they would substantially improve the situation of refugees, migrant workers, ethnic minorities, and the victims of environmental disasters, torture, slavery, child abuse, and racial discrimination. Many countries have yet to ratify these agreements. Among those that have done so, there remain differences in interpretation and ineffective measures to implement the conventions in question. Governmental and non-governmental agencies have an important role to play. The UN Centre for Human Rights in Geneva provides a valuable documentation centre and forum for discussion and action in these matters.

A good example of what is being achieved in the area of minority rights is provided by a report by the United Nations. In pointing the way ahead, it noted:

> The body of international law that can be applied to minorities has shown a welcome development in the past two decades. The field of non-discrimination is well covered in international conventions and declarations and some special rights for minorities are already found in international human rights instruments.
>
> New human rights standards for minorities are under discussion and the volume of national legislation on the subject is growing. Further evidence that minority rights are a live issue is provided in reports by governments to international organizations, in the studies by special human rights rapporteurs, by the work of NGO's, and by academic research.
>
> There is also evidence that much remains to be done. Many minorities are subject to grave and persistent violations of their basic rights. Long experience has shown that neither oppression—applied in defiance of international law— nor neglect of minority problems provide a basis for relations between groups with different characteristics in the same country (United Nations 1992).

The report states that special measures are needed to safeguard the identity, heritage, and dignity of minorities, including recognition of the right to exist, the enjoyment of culture and language, the establishment of schools, guarantees of political representation, and autonomy in cultural and social affairs. The empowerment of minorities by giving them a previously unheard 'voice' in decision making is the intended direction. At the same time, it must be recognized that some cultural traditions are at variance with a 'universal' view of human rights, particularly in relation to the rights of women and children. Reconciling such differences constitutes a challenge.

One of the instruments available to improve the welfare of proactive and reactive migrants is the International Convention on the Protection of the Rights of All Migrant Workers and Members of their Families. This was approved by the UN General Assembly in December 1990, following ten years of arduous negotiation. However, it must be ratified by at least twenty states before it enters into force as international law. This may never happen. Already some Western countries have indicated that they do not intend to pursue ratification. The Convention defines a 'migrant worker' as 'a person who is to be engaged, or has been engaged, in a remunerated activity in a State of which he or she is not a national.' It includes the self-employed and members of families of migrant workers, protecting them from collective expulsion and endeavouring to ensure that their legal, economic, and social (including health and safety) rights are not less than those of nationals of the country concerned (Bohning 1991).

As the World Conference on Human Rights (held in Vienna in 1993) showed, 'the achievement of basic human rights has become one of the central challenges of civilization. There is new hope for the cause of human rights. But there are new and dangerous challenges as well' (Boutros-Ghali 1993). One of those challenges arises from a postmodern rejection of the idea of universality. Arguments were put forward at the conference that suggested the definition and interpretation of human rights could be culturally specific. This challenges the very foundation of the UN Convention, which emphasizes the 'universality and indivisibility' of human rights. It is particularly threatening to women and to minorities subject to racial or religious persecution on ideological grounds.

A realistically utopian approach to migration questions, refugees, and ethnic minority issues would be guided, among other considerations, by an overwhelming concern for species survival and for sustainable development. Its structural form would build on the advanced communication technologies and networks (*Verbindungsnetzschaft*) typical of the postindustrial, postmodern world. Already these processes are at work in realm of emancipatory and life politics. Questions relating to the status of women, women as refugees and victims of abuse, the rights and welfare of children, actions to protect forests and wildlife, and efforts to promote world peace, have benefited from the global networks of communication and support that have come about. Such networks link governmental and non-governmental agencies and individuals, mobilizing informational resources as tools of empowerment.

Giddens (1990:164) defines the 'contours of a post-modern order' as consisting of multilayered democratic participation, demilitarization, humanization of technology, and an economic postscarcity system. The latter may be moving beyond utopian realism into an area of wishful thinking. Nevertheless, decisions relating to migration would be governed by humanitarian, developmental, and ecological considerations. This must include the reduction of pollution and the promotion of viable technologies at the local level, or what Schumacher (1973) called 'small is beautiful' types of development. Although migration in these circumstances would be, to a large extent, proactive as it would not be compelled by overwhelming political or economic pressures, it would need to be facilitated in ways that benefited all concerned. Receiving societies would have to support settlement services and training programs more effectively than in the past. Clearly, this will not happen unless there is participation in the planning process at all levels.

Dialogical models

To achieve such goals, a 'dialogical' model of applied sociology would be needed (Giddens 1987:44–8). Rather than imposing plans from above or seeking bureaucratic solutions to problems, policy makers would work more closely with those most directly affected by the proposals in question. Indeed, the proposals themselves would more often come from the grass roots. Structuration theory recognizes the link between knowledge and agency, suggesting that the findings of the social sciences spiral in and out of actual life. 'A dialogical model introduces the notion that the most effective forms of connection between social research and policy making are forged through an extended process of communication between researchers, policy makers and those affected by whatever issues are under consideration' (Giddens 1987:47).

An example of how this works in practice is provided by the experiences of educators, mediators, and peacemakers who have worked closely with people in a variety of contexts, successfully defusing situations of extreme tension and conflict and contributing to the building of new forms of cooperation. In *Tools for Transformation*, Adam Curle (1990) gives a number of illustrations drawn from his own experiences in Africa and Asia, where he applied principles based on a mixture of Buddhist philosophy, applied psychology, and Quaker traditions of reconciliation. He rejects the view that the Western model of an ideal society, with its emphasis upon material affluence, can be imposed on other countries. Development should mean improvement in the quality of life without generating waste and pollution. Peacemaking can only be achieved when the protagonists are helped to find their own way out of the trap of violence. From the perspective of utopian realism, it is also essential that the concept of security be given a positive connotation, removing fears and threats, rather than the negative one associated with military preparations. In helping others towards liberation, Curle concluded, 'here I find a wonderful paradox. The more we understand that human beings are not self-sufficient, self-existent, and separate creatures, the more we appreciate and value their individuality' (Curle 1990:176). However, as in the case of the pragmatic and nostalgic visions, utopian realism involves risk.

High-consequence risks

Giddens (1990:171) identifies the 'high-consequence risks' of modernity as the growth of totalitarian power, the collapse of economic growth mechanisms, ecological disasters, and large-scale warfare, including nuclear conflict. To these might be added the extreme fragmentation, loss of binding consensus, relativism, and nihilism, which could be the consequence of contemporary postmodern trends when taken to extremes (Gellner 1992:22–39).

The three alternative visions of a new world order that I have described do not eliminate these risks (see Figure 13.1). They are present in varying degrees, regardless of which view is most influential in governing the actions of individuals and collectivities (governmental and non-governmental). The outstanding risks associated with the nostalgic outlook are a rise in totalitarianism, authoritarianism, neofascist movements, and the eventual creation of a world in which apartheid is the dominant form. Racism and religious fundamentalism would flourish in these circumstances. In turn, this would lead to opposing camps determined to exclude and eventually exterminate those who did not conform to type.

In a system of global apartheid, 'seditious' or 'blasphemous' publications would be banned and their authors subject to severe penalties. Radio and television programs would be censored and the education system used for strict indoctrination. The surveillance technology is readily available, so that the kind of 'thought control' envisaged by George Orwell in his book *1984* could be imposed. Genocide would be a state-supported program, as it was in Nazi Germany, Cambodia, and Bosnia.

The risks associated with a pragmatic vision are only too evident in the present day. They include short-term crisis management, technological 'fixes', together with the protection of existing economic privilege and political power through 'practical' policies and those designed to ensure patriotic fervour and electoral success. Emphasis upon global economic competition, productivity, and growth can only have a deleterious effect on the environment. Reliance on arms sales, and the use of conventional weaponry in local wars (even by those assigned the task of peacekeeping) exacerbates existing conflicts. The sixty or more ethnic conflicts and the other political crises presently generating massive flows of reactive migrants will continue in the foreseeable future. There are very real possibilities that countries who have not signed the nuclear non-proliferation treaties (and even some that have) may be provoked into using atomic weapons in some future conflagration. Retaliation by other powers could lead to a third world war that could appropriately be described as 'Armageddon'.

At first sight, policies and programs (many already in place) that fall into the category of utopian realism appear to hold out greater hope for the human species and the future of planet earth. However, it also carries with it high-consequence risks that could lead to social fragmentation, anarchy, and chaos. The greatest risk is that, because of this, such policies will not be taken seriously. To the corporate executives and politicians (whose mandate it is to do what is most profitable and in the interests of their own organizations and communities), the so-called 'Green parties' are a laughing-stock. They rarely attract more than 5 per cent of the popular vote in elections. Since the onset of the latest global recession, these parties appear to have lost whatever influence they had, at least in Western countries, during more affluent times.

Even if the future-oriented realistically utopian policies were to be adopted on a large scale, it is not possible to say what the eventual outcome would be. If it meant that the inhabitants of advanced industrial countries were obliged to accept substantial reductions in their own material standards of living in order to benefit those in less developed countries, a backlash could be expected. Already there are signs that a coalition between the nostalgic and the utopian visions may be responsible for more restrictive immigration policies in some countries. Immigrants and tourists are sometimes blamed for urban congestion, pollution, and potential ecological damage, as well as competition for employment (Clarke et al. 1990; Richmond 1980). Furthermore, there is evidence that improved education and material improvements in rural areas or in the urban areas of less developed countries may actually increase the potential for proactive migration. This occurs as a result of raised expectations and new aspirations that cannot be realized in the immediate locality, leading to proactive migration.

The cultural and psychological consequences of postmodern trends are potentially divisive. The rapidity of change undermines ontological security and generates anxiety. A new version of anomie is apparent. It is one that reflects the normlessness of a postmodern society. A society that celebrates difference, denies universal metanarratives, and insists that collective rights take priority over individual rights could quickly degenerate into anarchy or even a Hobbesian 'war of all against all'. The problem of order and its compatibility with individual liberty is still as central to sociological theory and political practice as it was when Talcott Parsons (1961) wrote the *Structure of Social Action*. It has not yet been solved. As issues relating to postmodernism and multiculturalism enter political discourse, they raise contested questions concerning 'trajectories of change' (Robertson 1992:186).

We live in an age of crisis management. Half a century ago, Harvard sociologist Pitirim Sorokin examined 'man and society in calamity' and observed that 'We live amidst one of the greatest crises in human history. Not only war, famine, pestilence and revolution, but a legion of other calamities are rampant over the whole world. All values are unsettled; all norms broken' (Sorokin [1942] 1968:308). He argued that only by a reintegration of sensory and transcendental values could societies survive future calamities. Following Durkheim, some sociologists have suggested that in a postmodern age, a return to religion would provide a basis for a sense of cohesion and social solidarity (Bell 1976; Beyer 1990; O'Neill 1988a). Unfortunately, religion often leads to fanaticism. In a global society, it may be divisive. A global religion, if it were to emerge, could be seen as threatening by established secular and spiritual powers. As Robertson and Chirico (1985:238) noted, globalization and religious revivalism may be closely related, but 'societal civil-religion concerns (may be seen) as sites of potential religious, ideological and religious-ideological conflict'. To the present day, religious tensions continue. These are often extremely violent. It is unlikely that any of the existing religions will serve to provide a unifying set of values at the global level.

Perhaps the Gaia hypothesis, which some naturalist scientists endorse, provides a thread of hope (Lovelock 1987, 1988; Mungall and McLaren 1990).[1] A pantheistic return to the worship of 'Mother Earth' seems absurd to our rational, technocratic minds, but environmentalists have recognized the imperative of stewardship if the planet is to survive and the human species with it. At a more immediate and practical level, the effective implementation of all United Nations' conventions and other international instruments on human rights, including those relating to migrant workers, refugees, and racism, would be a step towards a less exploitative global system. Failure to create the conditions under which migrants and those who remain sedentary can live together in our global cities or hinterlands will be far more disastrous than the crises that led millions to leave the Old World for the New, or the Third World for the First World. Notwithstanding the economic trend towards a 'borderless world', globalization is far from complete. A substantial proportion of the world's population is still excluded from the more affluent regions and some are in danger of being perpetually exiled. Vietnamese and Haitian boat people, those who fled to the Kurdish mountains, and the victims of ethnic cleansing in Bosnia symbolize the unwanted minorities. But there is no emigration from this planet, not even to satellite stations in perpetual orbit.

Note

[1] The Gaia hypothesis put forward by British medical doctor and biochemist James Lovelock (1987, 1988) suggests that the earth is a self-regulating biosystem, and that life and the environment must be considered a unity.

Appendix 1

Extract from the 1951 UN Convention relating to the Status of Refugees

Article 1
Definition of the term 'refugee'

A. For the purpose of the present Convention, the term 'refugee' shall apply to any person who:

(1) Has been considered a refugee under the Arrangements of 12 May 1926 and 30 June 1928 or under the Conventions of 28 October 1933 and 10 February 1938, the Protocol of 14 September 1939 or the Constitution of the International Refugee Organization;

(2) As a result of events occurring before 1 January 1951 and *owing to well-founded fear of being persecuted for reasons of race, religion, nationality, membership of a particular social group or political opinion, is outside the country of his nationality and is unable or, owing to such fear, is unwilling to avail himself of the protection of that country; or who, not having a nationality and being outside the country of his formal habitual residence as a result of such events, is unable or, owing to such fear, is unwilling to return to it* [emphasis added].

In the case of a person who has more than one nationality, the term 'the country of his nationality' shall mean each of the countries of which he is a national, and a person shall not be deemed to be lacking the protection of the country of his nationality if, without any valid reason based on well-founded fear, he has not availed himself of the protection of one of the countries of which he is a national.

B. (1) For the purpose of this Convention, the words, 'events occurring before 1 January 1951' in Article 1, Section A, shall be understood to mean either

(a) 'events occurring in Europe before 1 January 1951'; or

(b) 'events occurring in Europe or elsewhere before 1 January 1951', and each Contracting State shall make a declaration at the time of signature, ratification or accession, specifying which of these meanings it applies for the purpose of its obligations under this Convention.

(2) Any Contracting State which has adopted alternative (a) may at any time extend its obligations by adopting alternative (b) by means of a notification addressed to the Secretary-General of the United Nations.

C. This Convention shall cease to apply to any person falling under the terms of Section A if:

(1) He has voluntarily re-availed himself of the protection of the country of his nationality; or

(2) Having lost his nationality, he has voluntarily re-acquired it; or

(3) He has acquired a new nationality, and enjoys the protection of the country of his new nationality; or

(4) He has voluntarily re-established himself in the country which he left or outside which he remained owing to fear of persecution; or

(5) He can no longer, because the circumstances in connection with which he has been recognized as a refugee have ceased to exist, continue to refuse to avail himself of the protection of the country of his nationality;

Provide that this paragraph shall not apply to a refugee falling under Section A (1) of this Article who is able to invoke compelling reasons arising out of previous persecution for refusing to avail himself of the protection of the country of his nationality;

(6) Being a person who has no nationality he is, because the circumstances in connection with which he has been recognized as a refugee have ceased to exist, able to return to the country of his former habitual residence;

Provided that this paragraph shall not apply to a refugee falling under Section A (1) of this Article who is able to invoke compelling reasons arising out of previous persecution for refusing to return to the country of his former habitual residence.

D. This Convention shall not apply to persons who at present receiving from organs or agencies of the United Nations other than the United Nations High Commissioner for Refugees protection or assistance.

When such protection or assistance has ceased for any reason, without the position of such persons being definitely settled in accordance with the relevant resolutions adopted by the General Assembly of the United Nations, these persons shall *ipso facto* be entitled to the benefits of this Convention.

E. This Convention shall not apply to a person who is recognized by the competent authorities of the country in which he has taken residence as having the rights and obligations which are attached to the possession of the nationality of that country.

F. The provisions of this Convention shall not apply to any person with respect to whom there are serious reasons for considering that:

(a) he has committed a crime against peace, a war crime, or a crime against humanity, as defined in the international instruments drawn up to make provision in respect of such crimes;
(b) he has committed a serious non-political crime outside the country of refuge prior to his admission to that country as a refugee;
(c) he has been guilty of acts contrary to the purposes and principles of the United Nations.

Article 2
General obligations

Every refugee has duties to the country in which he finds himself, which require in particular that he conform to its laws and regulations as well as to measures taken for the maintenance of public order.

Article 3
Non-discrimination

The Contracting State shall apply the provisions of this Convention to refugees without discrimination as to race, religion or country of origin . . .

Article 31
Refugees unlawfully in the country of refuge

1. The Contracting States shall not impose penalties, on account of their illegal entry or presence, on refugees who, coming directly from a territory where their life or freedom was threatened in the sense of Article 1, enter or are present in their territory without authorization, provided they present themselves without delay to the authorities and show good cause for their illegal entry or presence.

2. The Contracting States shall not apply to the movements of such refugees restrictions other than those which are necessary and such restrictions shall only be applied until their status in the country is regularized or they obtain admission into another country. The Contracting States shall allow such refugees a reasonable period and all the necessary facilities to obtain admission into another country.

Article 32
Expulsion

1. The Contracting States shall not expel a refugee lawfully in their territory save on grounds of national security or public order.

2. The expulsion of such a refugee shall be only in pursuance of a decision reached in accordance with due process of law. Except where compelling reasons of national security otherwise require, the refugee shall be allowed to submit evidence to clear himself, and to appeal to and be represented for the purpose before competent authority or a person or persons especially designated by the competent authority.

3. The Contracting States shall allow such a refugee a reasonable period within which to seek legal admission to another country. The Contracting States reserve the right to apply during that period such internal measures as they may deem necessary.

Article 33
Prohibition of expulsion or return ('refoulement')

1. *No Contracting States shall expel or return ('refouler') a refugee in any manner whatsoever to the frontiers of territories where his life or freedom would be threatened on account of his race, religion, nationality, membership of a particular social group or political opinion* [emphasis added].

2. The benefit of the present provision may not, however, be claimed by a refugee whom there are reasonable grounds for regarding as a danger to the security of the country in which he is, or who, having been convicted by a final judgement of a particularly serious crime, constitutes a danger to the community of that country.

Article 34
Naturalization

The Contracting States shall as far as possible facilitate the assimilation and naturalization of refugees. They shall in particular make every effort to expedite naturalization proceedings and to reduce as far as possible the charges and costs of such proceedings.

Extract from the Protocol of 1967
relating to the Status of Refugees

Article 1
General provision

1. The States party to the present Protocol undertake to apply articles 2 to 34 inclusive of the Convention to refugees as hereinafter defined.

2. *For the purpose of the present Protocol, the term 'refugee' shall, except as regards the application of paragraph 3 of this article, mean any person within the definition of article 1 of the Convention as if the words 'As a result of events occurring before 1 January 1951 and . . . ' and the words '. . . as a result of such events', in article 1 A (2) were omitted* [emphasis added].

3. The Present Protocol shall be applied by the States Parties hereto without any geographic limitation, save that existing declarations made by States already Parties to the Convention in accordance with article 1 B(1)(a) of the Convention, shall, unless extended under article 1 B(2) thereof, apply also under the present Protocol.

Appendix 2
Statistical tables

World

Table 1 Estimated and projected world population by region, 1970–2025

	1970	%	1990	%	2000	%	2025	%
				(MILLIONS)				
Africa	362	9.79	642	12.13	867	13.85	1,597	18.78
North America	226	6.11	276	5.22	295	4.71	332	3.90
Latin America	286	7.73	448	8.47	538	8.59	757	8.90
Asia and Pacific	2,121	57.36	3,139	59.32	3,743	59.78	4,950	58.21
Europe*	703	19.01	787	14.87	818	13.07	867	10.20
TOTAL	3,698	100.00	5,292	100.00	6,261	100.00	8,503	100.00
Industrialized	1,049	28.37	1,207	22.81	1,264	20.19	1,354	15.92
Developing	2,649	71.63	4,086	77.21	4,997	79.81	7,150	84.09

*Includes former USSR

SOURCE: Adapted from UN Population Division, *World Population Prospects* (New York: UN Population Division, 1990)

Table 2 Principal sources of the world's refugees and asylum seekers (as of 31 December 1993)

Afghanistan	3,429,800*	Iraq	134,700
Palestinians	2,801,300	China (Tibet)	133,000
Mozambique	1,332,000*	Sri Lanka	106,650*
Former Yugoslavia	1,319,650*	Bhutan	105,100*
Burundi	780,000	Mali	87,000
Liberia	701,000*	Western Sahara	80,000*
Somalia	491,200*	Zaire	79,000
Eritrea	421,500*	Mauritania	79,000
Sudan	373,000	Bangladesh	53,500
Angola	335,000	Uzbekistan	51,000
Vietnam	303,500	Guatemala	49,200
Azerbaijan	290,000*	Iran	39,000
Burma	289,500*	Cambodia	35,500
Rwanda	275,000*	Chad	33,400
Sierra Leone	260,000*	Laos	26,500
Togo	240,000	Nicaragua	23,050
Ethiopia	232,200	El Salvador	21,900
Armenia	200,000*	Uganda	20,000
Tajikistan	153,000*	Senegal	18,000
Georgia	143,000*	South Africa	10,600

*Indicates that sources vary widely in number reported

SOURCE: US Committee for Refugees, *World Refugee Survey, 1994* (Washington: US Committee for Refugees, 1994)

Table 3 Principal regions and countries of asylum, December 1993

REGION	COUNTRY	NUMBERS	MAIN SOURCES
Africa		5,825,000	
	Malawi	700,000	Mozambique
	Sudan	633,000	Ethiopia/Eritrea
Middle East		4,924,000	
	Iran	1,995,000	Afghanistan
	Jordan	1,073,600	Palestine
South & Central Asia		2,151,000	
	Pakistan	1,482,300	Afghanistan
East Asia & Pacific		468,000	
	China	296,900	Vietnam
	Thailand	108,300	Burma
	Hong Kong	3,550	Vietnam
Europe		2,614,100	
	Yugoslavia	357,000	Serbia
	Germany	529,100	Yugoslavia and others
Americas & Caribbean		272,900	
	United States	150,400	Various
	Mexico	52,000	Guatemala
	Canada	20,500	Various
TOTAL		16,255,000	

SOURCE: US Committee for Refugees, *World Refugee Survey, 1994* (Washington: US Committee for Refugees, 1994)

Table 4a   Estimates of asylum applications in Europe, North America, and Australia, 1987–91 (rounded)

	1987	1988	1989	1990	1991
Europe	203,150	243,950	321,900	461,100	599,400
North America	61,100	102,000	122,000	109,600	100,500
Australia			500	3,600	16,000
TOTAL	264,250	345,950	444,400	574,300	715,900

SOURCE: UNFPA, *The State of the World Population 1993* (New York: UN Fund for Population Activities, 1993)

Table 4b   Spontaneous arrivals of asylum seekers in Europe, 1992 and 1993

REGION OF NATIONALITY	1992	1993
Africa	113,840	74,650
Americas	8,510	4,310
Asia	71,780	54,040
Australasia	n.a.	5
Europe	463,140	343,705
Middle East	40,490	28,300
Stateless	640	950
Various	2,435	845
TOTAL	700,840	506,800

SOURCE: Based on statistics supplied by UN High Commissioner for Refugees (numbers are rounded)

Table 5 Selected populations in refugee-like situations (as of 31 December 1993)

Information on these groups is fragmentary, and estimates of their numbers widely, especially those marked with an asterisk (*).

HOST COUNTRY	ORIGIN	NUMBER
Jordan	Palestinians	750,000*
Iran	Iraq	500,000*
Russia	Former USSR	460,000*
Pakistan	Afghanistan	400,000*
Thailand	Burma	350,000*
Bangladesh	Pakistan (Biharis)	238,000
Burundi	Rwanda	170,000
Saudi Arabia	Somalia	150,000*
Iraq	Kuwait (Bidoon)	130,000*
Lebanon	Palestinians	125,000*
Kuwait	Bidoon	120,000*
Uganda	Rwanda	120,000*
Egypt	Palestinians	100,000
Mexico	Guatemala	100,000*
Iraq	Palestinians	70,000*
Turkey	Iran	50,000*
Cameroon	Chad	40,000
Syria	Palestinians	40,000*
Ecuador	Colombia	30,000*
Honduras	Central Americans	30,000*
Jordan	Iraq	30,000*
Uzbekistan	Tajikistan	30,000*
Venezuela	Colombia	30,000*
Hong Kong	Vietnam	27,560
Kuwait	Palestinians	25,000
Dominican Republic	Haiti	25,000*
Mauritania	Senegal	22,000
Hungary	Former Yugoslavia	20,000*
Namibia	Angola	20,000
Southeast Asia	Vietnam	19,600

SOURCE: US Committee for Refugees, *World Refugee Survey, 1994* (Washington: US Committee for Refugees, 1994)

Table 6   Selected list of significant populations of internally displaced civilians
(as of 31 December 1993)

Table 6 identifies selected countries in which substantial numbers of people have been displaced within their homelands as a result of human conflict or forced relocations. Although they share many characteristics with refugees who cross international borders, they are generally not eligible for international refugee law. Because information on internal displacement is fragmentary, this table presents only reported estimates, and no total is provided. In some countries, such as Turkey and the Russian Federation, significant displacement exists, but reliable estimates of the number of persons displaced are unavailable. It is important to note that even this selected list includes 25 million people, and that the total number of internally displaced civilians is undoubtedly much higher.

Sudan	4,000,000	Sierra Leone	400,000
South Africa	4,000,000	Croatia	350,000
Mozambique	2,000,000	Colombia	300,000–600,000
Angola	2,000,000	Kenya	300,000
Bosnia	1,300,000	Rwanda	300,000
Liberia	1,000,000	Haiti	300,000
Iraq	1,000,000	Cyprus	265,000
Lebanon	700,000	Iran	260,000
Somalia	700,000	Georgia	250,000
Zaire	700,000	India	250,000
Azerbaijan	600,000	Philippines	200,000–1,000,000
Sri Lanka	600,000	Eritrea	200,000
Peru	600,000	Guatemala	200,000
Burma	500,000–1,000,000	Togo	150,000
Burundi	500,000	Djibouti	140,000
Ethiopia	500,000	Cambodia	95,000

SOURCE: US Committee for Refugees, *World Refugee Survey, 1994* (Washington: US Committee for Refugees, 1994)

Table 7 Defence expenditures of NATO countries, 1970–92

COUNTRY CURRENCY UNIT (MILLION)		CURRENT PRICES AND EXCHANGE RATES									1985 PRICES AND EXCHANGE RATES								
(0)		1970 (1)	1975 (2)	1980 (3)	1985 (4)	1988 (5)	1989 (6)	1990 (7)	1991 (8)	1992e (9)	1970 (1)	1975 (2)	1980 (3)	1985 (4)	1988 (5)	1989 (6)	1990 (7)	1991 (8)	1992e (9)
Belgium*	B.fr.	37,388	70,899	115,754	144,183	150,647	152,917	155,205	157,919	130,943	92,077	121,248	145,395	144,183	147,490	143,906	142,113	139,922	113,210
Denmark	D.Kr.	2,967	5,355	9,117	13,344	15,620	15,963	16,399	17,091	16,844	12,201	11,934	13,227	13,344	13,991	13,849	13,885	14,110	13,616
France	F.fr.	32,672	55,872	111,672	186,715	215,073	224,985	232,376	239,411	241,417	130,500	141,963	173,364	186,715	192,421	194,671	195,020	195,072	191,163
Germany	DM	22,573	37,589	48,518	58,650	61,638	63,178	68,376	65,579	66,143	44,169	53,867	56,938	58,650	57,633	57,582	60,277	55,804	54,108
Greece	Dr.	14,208	45,936	96,975	321,981	471,820	503,032	612,344	693,846	809,387	129,660	238,472	244,924	321,981	304,126	287,711	293,606	280,912	287,132
Italy	1,000 lt. l.	1,562	3,104	7,643	17,767	25,539	27,342	28,007	30,191	30,250	13,192	14,722	15,551	17,767	19,935	19,747	18,701	18,348	–
Luxembourg	Lux.fr.	416	836	1,534	2,265	3,163	2,995	3,233	3,681	3,882	1,056	1,498	2,033	2,265	3,065	2,816	2,944	3,215	3,287
Netherlands	DG	3,909	7,119	10,476	12,901	13,300	13,571	13,513	13,548	13,822	10,479	10,882	11,647	12,901	13,559	13,725	13,372	13,055	12,893
Norway	N.Kr.	2,774	4,771	8,242	15,446	18,865	20,248	21,252	21,316	23,763	10,961	11,091	12,643	15,446	16,035	16,517	16,653	16,100	17,613
Portugal	Esc.	12,538	19,898	43,440	111,375	194,036	229,344	267,299	305,643	325,663	149,631	138,698	116,610	111,375	129,753	135,768	138,421	139,329	133,383
Spain	Ptas.	–	–	350,423	674,883	835,353	923,375	922,808	947,173	984,276	–	–	600,198	674,883	672,558	695,051	647,366	621,978	609,757
Turkey	TL	6,399	32,833	203,172	1,234,547	3,788,920	7,158,471	13,865,971	23,656,518	38,738,512	412,650	899,319	1,132,939	1,234,547	1,423,630	1,594,439	1,833,609	1,884,924	1,932,940
United Kingdom	£	2,607	5,571	11,593	18,301	19,290	20,868	22,466	24,495	23,758	16,490	16,256	16,429	18,301	16,476	16,850	16,886	16,917	15,739
NATO Europe	US $	–	–	112,255	92,218	155,778	154,147	186,592	188,144	190,092	–	–	84,729	92,218	92,026	93,044	93,617	91,681	–
Canada	Ca $	1,999	3,360	5,788	10,332	12,336	12,854	13,473	13,192	13,722	7,129	6,983	7,732	10,332	10,984	10,931	11,124	10,657	10,890
United States	US $	79,846	88,400	138,191	258,165	293,093	304,085	306,170	280,292	314,319	240,211	179,715	192,288	258,165	269,654	268,622	262,024	227,803	249,821
North America	US $	81,754	91,704	143,141	265,731	303,117	314,942	317,717	291,806	326,124	245,431	184,828	197,950	265,731	277,698	276,627	270,170	235,608	257,796
NATO total	US $	–	–	255,396	357,949	458,894	469,088	504,309	479,951	516,216	–	–	282,679	357,949	369,723	369,671	363,787	327,288	–

NOTES: *Decrease in 1992 Belgian defence expenditure reflects the decision by the Belgian government to demilitarize the Gendarmerie.   e Estimate

SOURCE: *NATO Review* (Brussels: NATO Information Services, February 1993)

Canada

Table 8 Canadian military exports to major regions of the Third World, 1991 and 1992 (millions)

REGION	PER CENT	
	1991	1992
Middle East	51.6	91.3
Asia	41.5	5.2
Sub-Saharan Africa	3.5	1.9
Western hemisphere	3.4	1.6
TOTAL	100.0	100.0
Estimated value	$57.7	$253,416

NOTE: US military exports to Third World $14,300
　　　　　Other countries $10,242

SOURCE: Compiled from E. Regehr, 'Canada's Military Exports to the Third World in 1992: Arming the Repression', *Ploughshares Monitor* 14, no. 3 (1993):8–10; and B. Robinson, '1992–93 Military Budget: Stills Swords, Not Ploughshares' *Ploughshares Monitor* 13, no. 2 (1992):1–3

Table 9 Ethnic origin[a] by birthplace and period of immigration

	TOTAL	NON-IMMIG[b]	IMMIG	PERIOD OF IMMIGRATION				
				1946	1946–66	1967–77	1978–82	1983–6
British	6,332,720	5,527,930	804,790	178,535	338,580	205,520	62,885	18,230
%	25.3	26.2	20.6	43.9	21.7	16.9	13.0	7.5
French	6,093,165	6,002,785	90,380	15,575	32,195	29,160	9,005	4,450
%	24.4	28.4	2.3	3.8	2.1	2.4	1.9	1.8
German	895,715	645,540	251,175	32,550	169,790	30,775	10,830	7,235
%	3.6	3.1	6.4	8.0	10.9	2.5	2.2	3.0
Italian	709,590	339,535	370,055	10,195	281,880	58,400	7,140	2,445
%	3.6	1.6	9.5	2.5	18.1	4.8	1.5	3.0
Portuguese	199,595	55,205	144,390	355	40,830	84,340	11,295	5,435
%	0.8	.3	3.7	.1	2.6	6.9	2.3	2.2
Chinese	369,320	93,330	266,990	2,215	34,375	105,710	81,330	40,360
%	1.5	.4	6.8	.5	2.2	8.7	16.9	16.6
South Asian	265,890	68,545	144,390	315	11,640	120,315	42,470	23,515
%	1.1	.3	3.7	.1	.7	9.9	8.8	9.6
Other single origins	3,176,760	1,877,580	1,299,080	115,375	479,980	397,525	192,040	113,150
%	12.7	8.9	33.2	28.4	30.8	32.6	39.9	46.4
Multiple origins	6,785,345	6,503,310	483,035	50,130	187,230	173,880	62,810	26,880
%	27.1	30.8	12.4	12.3	12.0	14.3	13.0	11.0
TOTAL	25,010,995	21,113,855	3,908,145	406,300	1,557,555	1,218,710	481,885	243,705
%	100.1	100.0	98.6	99.7	101.2	98.9	99.6	101.1

NOTES: [a] Ethnic origin is based on question 17 in the 1986 Census of Canada, which read 'To which ethnic or cultural group(s) do you or did your ancestors belong? Mark or specify as many as applicable.' There were fifteen preselected categories and room for three other write-in descriptions. A note in the Census *Guide* indicated that ethnic or cultural group referred to 'roots' and should not be confused with citizenship or nationality; [b] Non-immig is defined as persons born in Canada, excluding those whose parents were diplomatic or military personnel temporarily resident in Canada; [c] Immig is defined as persons born outside Canada, excluding those who acquired Canadian citizenship by birth. Not all columns sum to total due to rounding and omission of 'not known'.

SOURCE: Statistics Canada, Census of Canada, 1986. Profile of Immigrants, Cat. 93–155, Table 1

Table 10 Population 15 years and over: Highest level of schooling by sex, birthplace, and period of immigration

LEVEL OF EDUCATION	TOTAL	NON-IMMIG	IMMIG	PERIOD OF IMMIGRATION				
				1946	1946-66	1967-77	1978-82	1983-6
		MALES						
Less than grade 9	1,625,950	1,259,275	366,875	75,885	184,760	66,630	25,700	13,825
%	16.9	16.2	20.2	43.1	23.5	11.7	13.3	15.4
Grades 9–13, without cert.	2,530,405	2,180,255	350,150	41,485	128,485	115,770	43,870	20,540
%	26.3	28.0	19.3	23.6	16.4	20.3	22.8	22.9
Grades 9–13, with cert.	1,075,075	923,075	152,000	9,465	56,865	54,870	20,155	10,555
%	11.2	11.8	8.4	5.4	7.2	9.6	10.5	11.7
Trades cert. or diploma	397,070	320,680	75,390	8,485	42,800	18,595	4,555	1,840
%	4.1	4.1	4.2	4.8	5.5	3.3	2.4	2.0
Other non-university, without cert.	631,850	527,430	104,420	7,370	45,530	34,685	11,685	5,150
%	6.6	6.8	5.3	4.2	5.8	6.1	6.1	5.7
Other non-university, with cert.	1,395,975	1,094,225	299,750	14,055	149,550	97,585	28,700	9,850
%	14.5	14.0	16.5	8.0	19.1	17.1	14.9	11.0
University, without degree	856,880	676,370	190,510	8,550	71,870	73,785	24,500	11,825
%	8.9	8.7	10.5	4.9	9.2	12.9	12.7	13.2
University, with degree	1,085,050	810,170	274,770	11,000	104,705	109,665	33,315	16,185
%	11.3	10.4	15.1	6.2	13.3	19.2	17.3	18.0
TOTAL	9,606,255	7,791,480	1,814,770	176,080	784,565	571,580	192,580	89,880
%	99.9	100.0	100.0	100.1	100.0	100.0	99.9	99.9

Table 10 (continued)

LEVEL OF EDUCATION	TOTAL	NON-IMMIG	IMMIG	PERIOD OF IMMIGRATION				
				1946	1946-66	1967-77	1978-82	1983-6
		FEMALES						
Less than grade 9	1,757,775	1,274,880	493,090	101,845	222,320	104,190	41,815	23,120
%	17.5	15.7	25.9	44.2	28.8	17.9	20.1	22.6
Grades 9–13, without cert.	2,790,825	2,353,190	437,635	64,280	172,315	130,105	48,235	22,695
%	27.8	29.0	23.0	27.9	22.3	22.4	23.2	22.2
Grades 9–13, with cert.	1,435,145	1,217,420	218,725	16,770	89,875	72,425	26,520	13,135
%	14.3	15.0	11.5	7.3	11.6	12.5	12.8	12.8
Trades cert. or diploma	204,430	170,720	33,705	2,535	15,150	10,780	3,590	1,640
%	2.0	2.1	1.8	1.1	2.0	1.9	1.7	1.6
Other non-university, without cert.	705,870	584,940	118,935	12,830	46,930	38,735	13,330	6,110
%	7.0	7.2	6.2	5.6	6.1	6.7	6.4	6.0
Other non-university, with cert.	1,459,695	1,202,550	250,940	15,655	108,470	92,320	27,975	11,520
%	14.6	14.8	13.2	6.8	14.0	15.9	13.5	11.3
University, without degree	871,780	705,315	160,470	9,535	57,730	65,450	21,780	10,880
%	8.7	8.7	8.4	4.1	7.5	11.3	10.5	10.6
University, with degree	793,430	614,655	178,780	5,870	60,194	74,810	24,610	13,290
%	7.9	7.6	9.4	2.5	7.8	12.9	11.8	13.0
TOTAL	10,027,845	8,123,565	1,904,285	230,220	772,890	580,815	207,855	102,395
%	99.9	100.0	99.4	99.6	100.0	101.4	100.0	100.0

SOURCE: Statistics Canada, Census of Canada, 1986, Profile of Immigrants, Cat. 93–155, Table 1

Table 11   Structural change in employment by industry, 1971–86

INDUSTRIES[a]	EMPLOYMENT 1971	EMPLOYMENT 1986	CHANGE 1971–86	% CHANGE 1971–86
TOTAL	7,584,396	11,569,900	3,985,504	52.55
All primary	703,295	748,240	44,945	6.39
All secondary	2,195,296	2,571,320	376,024	17.13
All tertiary	4,685,805	7,908,745	3,222,940	68.78
SECONDARY				
Food & beverages	220,694	264,625	43,931	19.91
Tobacco products	9,582	6,950	-2,632	-27.47
Rubber & plastics	44,928	70,135	25,207	56.11
Leather industries	28,017	22,185	-5,832	-20.82
Primary textiles	69,487	21,290	-48,197	-69.36
Textile products	23,948	34,685	10,737	44.83
Clothing industries	99,516	122,170	22,654	22.76
Wood industries	93,040	121,960	28,920	31.08
Furniture & fixtures	44,580	65,955	21,375	47.95
Paper & allied	119,102	123,265	4,163	3.50
Printing & publishing	85,862	141,260	55,398	64.52
Primary metal	112,889	113,055	166	.15
Metal fabricating	138,992	152,265	13,273	9.55
Machinery	71,441	75,695	4,254	5.95
Transportation equipment	150,597	211,705	61,108	40.58
Electrical products	123,450	148,600	25,150	20.37
Non-metallic mineral	51,925	54,690	2,765	5.32
Petroleum & coal	14,056	22,980	8,924	63.49
Chemical	77,445	94,795	17,350	22.40
Miscellaneous manufacturing	57,971	85,955	27,984	48.27
Construction	557,774	617,085	59,311	10.63
TERTIARY				
Transportation & storage	376,319	537,145	160,826	42.74
Communications	144,003	229,705	85,702	59.51
Electric & other utilities	63,523	126,585	63,062	99.27
Wholesale trade	343,942	524,330	180,388	52.45
Retail trade	929,854	1,385,270	455,416	48.98
Finance, insurance & real estate	336,183	632,920	296,737	88.27
Business services	267,943	545,285	277,342	103.51
Government services	639,585	874,815	235,230	36.78
Education	569,485	773,915	204,430	35.90
Health & welfare	513,095	940,555	427,460	83.31
Amusement & recreation	45,351	132,380	87,029	191.90
Accommodation & food	297,922	662,410	364,488	122.34
Other personal & miscellaneous	158,600	543,430	384,830	242.64

NOTE: [a] Excluding 'Other' and not specified

SOURCE: Statistics Canada, Census of Canada, 1971 and 1986

Table 12 Percentage distribution and index of relative concentration of immigrants by industrial sector

	TOTAL L.F.[a]	NON-IMMIG[b]	ALL IMMIG[c]	TRAD[d]	LONG <1971	INTER 1971-80	RECENT 1981-6	NON-TRAD[e]	LONG[f] <1971	INTER 1971-80	RECENT[g] 1981-6
MALES											
Primary %	9.2	10.2	4.8	5.8	5.7	5.5	6.8	2.6	2.6	2.4	3.0
Index	100.0	110.9	52.2	63.0	62.0	59.8	73.9	28.3	28.3	26.1	32.6
Secondary %	30.6	29.2	37.0	39.1	39.0	39.6	38.5	32.4	26.3	34.7	35.7
Index	100.0	95.4	120.9	127.8	127.5	129.4	125.8	105.9	85.9	113.4	116.7
Tertiary %	60.2	60.7	58.2	55.1	55.2	54.9	54.6	65.1	71.0	62.9	61.3
Index	100.0	100.8	96.7	91.5	91.7	91.2	90.7	108.1	117.9	104.5	101.8
FEMALES											
Primary %	3.6	3.8	3.0	3.4	3.5	3.2	4.2	2.2	1.6	2.2	3.3
Index	100.0	105.6	83.3	94.4	97.2	88.9	116.7	61.1	44.4	61.1	91.7
Secondary %	13.2	11.7	20.2	19.4	19.4	19.8	17.8	21.9	13.4	23.7	30.2
Index	100.0	88.6	153.0	147.0	147.0	150.0	134.8	165.9	101.5	179.5	228.8
Tertiary %	83.1	84.6	76.7	77.2	77.2	77.0	78.0	75.9	85.0	74.1	66.5
Index	100.0	101.8	92.3	92.9	92.9	92.7	93.9	91.3	102.3	89.2	80.0

NOTES: [a] L.F. is labour force; [b] Non-immig is defined as persons born in Canada, excluding those whose parents were diplomatic or military personnel temporarily resident in Canada; [c] Immig is defined as persons born outside Canada, excluding those who acquired Canadian citizenship by birth; [d] Trad is defined as immigrants from traditional source countries i.e, Britain, Europe, and the United States.; [e] Non-trad is defined as all other source countries; [f] Long are immigrants arriving before 1971; [g] Recent are immigrants arriving 1981-6.

SOURCE: Statistics Canada/IRPP, Special Tabulations, Census of Canada, 1986, adapted from S. Seward and M. Tremblay, *Immigrants in the Canadian Labour Force: Their Role in Structural Change* (Ottawa: Institute for Research in Public Policy, 1989)

Table 13 Percentage distribution and index of relative concentration of immigrants by industry, 1986, total (male and female) by specific industries

	TOTAL L.F.[a]	NON-IMMIG[b]	ALL IMMIG[c]	TRAD[d]	LONG <1971	INTER 1971-80	RECENT 1981-6	NON-TRAD[e]	LONG[f] <1971	INTER 1971-80	RECENT[g] 1981-6
Declining labour force											
Tobacco products %	.1	.1	.1	.1	.1	.0	.0	.1	.1	.0	.0
Index	100.0	100.0	100.0	100.0	100.0	.0	.0	100.0	100.0	.0	.0
Leather prod. %	.2	.2	.4	.4	.4	.6	.5	.4	.1	.5	.8
Index	100.0	100.0	200.0	200.0	200.0	300.0	250.0	200.0	50.	250.0	400.0
Primary textiles %	.2	.2	.2	.2	.2	.2	.2	.2	.2	.2	.3
Index	100.0	100.0	100.0	100.0	100.0	100.0	100.0	100.0	50.	100.0	150.0
SUBTOTAL %	.5	.5	.7	.7	.7	.8	.7	.7	.3	.7	1.1
Fast growing labour force											
Utilities	1.1	1.1	.9	1.0	1.1	.7	.4	.6	1.1	.6	.2
Index	100.0	100.0	81.8	90.9	100.0	63.6	36.4	54.5	100.0	54.5	18.2
Business serv. %	4.6	4.5	5.2	5.1	4.8	5.5	7.0	5.5	6.1	5.3	4.8
Index	100.0	97.8	113.0	110.9	104.3	119.6	152.2	119.6	132.6	115.2	104.3
Fin. ins. & real est.	5.4	5.4	5.7	5.3	5.5	5.0	4.3	6.4	6.7	7.1	4.1
Index	100.0	100.0	105.6	98.1	101.9	92.6	79.6	118.5	124.1	131.5	75.9
Accom. & food ser. %	6.3	6.0	7.7	6.1	5.4	8.6	8.4	10.9	8.2	10.8	15.4
Index	100.0	95.2	122.2	96.8	85.7	136.5	133.3	173.0	130.2	171.4	244.4
Health & welfare	8.2	8.2	8.1	7.2	7.1	7.5	8.1	9.9	13.5	9.5	5.5
Index	100.0	100.0	98.8	87.8	86.6	91.5	98.8	120.7	164.6	115.9	67.1
Amuse & rec.	4.6	4.7	4.3	4.2	4.3	4.0	4.2	4.3	4.2	4.3	4.5
Index	100.0	102.2	93.5	91.3	93.5	87.0	91.3	93.5	91.3	93.5	97.8
Other pers. & misc.	12.6	12.9	11.1	11.0	11.0	11.1	10.2	11.0	10.5	12.0	11.6
Index	100.0	102.4	88.1	87.3	87.3	88.1	81.0	91.3	83.3	95.2	92.1
SUBTOTAL %	42.8	42.8	43.0	39.9	39.2	42.4	42.6	49.1	50.3	49.6	46.1

NOTES: [a] L.F. is labour force.; [b] Non-immig is defined as persons born in Canada, excluding those whose parents were diplomatic or military personnel temporarily resident in Canada; [c] Immig is defined as persons born outside Canada, excluding those who acquired Canadian citizenship by birth; [d] Trad is defined as immigrants from traditional source countries, i.e., Britain, Europe, and the United States; [e] Non-trad is defined as all other source countries; [f] Long are immigrants arriving before 1971; [g] Recent are immigrants arriving 1981-6.

SOURCE: Statistics Canada/IRPP, Special Tabulations, Census of Canada, 1986, adapted from S. Seward and M. Tremblay, *Immigrants in the Canadian Labour Force: Their Role in Structural Change* (Ottawa: Institute for Research in Public Policy, 1989)

Table 14 Population 15 years and over, in labour force, by birthplace, period of immigration, and occupation

OCCUPATIONAL GROUP	TOTAL	NON-IMMIG[a]	IMMIG[b]	1956	1946-66	1967-77	1978-82	1983-6
		MALES						
Managerial, administrative, etc.	919,690	735,375	184,310	8,400	98,015	58,905	13,890	5,105
%	12.6	12.4	13.5	17.8	15.9	12.1	9.1	8.3
Professional & related	957,140	737,395	219,745	5,925	93,540	87,610	24,135	8,540
%	13.1	12.4	16.1	12.5	15.1	18.1	15.8	13.9
Clerical & related	494,410	413,945	80,465	2,735	30,865	33,135	9,795	3,930
%	6.8	7.0	5.9	5.8	5.0	6.8	6.4	6.4
Sales	641,511	541,250	100,490	4,855	45,480	35,745	9,485	3,930
%	8.8	9.1	7.4	10.3	7.4	7.4	6.2	6.4
Service	742,515	584,355	158,250	3,760	59,575	57,370	26,125	11,325
%	10.2	9.9	11.6	8.0	9.6	11.8	17.1	18.4
Primary	575,020	522,015	53,005	8,415	24,745	12,125	5,335	2,380
%	7.9	8.8	3.9	17.8	4.0	2.5	3.5	3.9
Processing	597,985	461,730	136,255	2,385	58,545	49,850	18,505	6,980
%	8.2	7.8	10.0	5.0	9.5	10.3	12.1	11.4
Product fabricating, assembling, etc.	725,155	555,855	159,265	3,535	71,700	61,915	22,705	9,505
%	9.9	9.4	11.7	7.5	11.6	12.8	14.9	15.5
Construction trades	735,385	599,115	135,275	2,855	76,335	44,015	9,135	3,955
%	10.1	10.1	9.9	6.0	12.4	9.1	6.0	6.4
Other occupations	905,065	779,525	125,530	4,400	58,105	44,470	13,880	5,785
%	12.4	13.1	9.2	9.3	9.4	9.2	9.1	9.4
All occupations	7,294,215	5,929,610	1,364,605	47,235	617,825	485,145	152,880	61,425
%	100.0	100.0	99.1	100.1	99.8	100.0	100.1	100.0

Table 14 (continued)

OCCUPATIONAL GROUP	TOTAL	NON-IMMIG[a]	IMMIG[b]	1956	1946-66	1967-77	1978-82	1983-6
FEMALES								
Managerial, administrative, etc.	422,280	347,530	74,755	2,435	36,980	27,755	5,825	1,755
%	7.8	7.8	7.5	8.9	9.1	7.1	4.7	3.7
Professional & related	1,136,740	948,435	188,305	4,560	77,995	79,280	20,030	6,475
%	20.9	21.3	18.9	16.7	19.2	20.4	16.2	13.5
Clerical & related	1,824,210	1,544,185	280,020	8,520	118,045	114,680	28,755	9,025
%	33.5	34.7	28.2	31.2	29.0	29.5	23.3	18.9
Sales	511,410	426,520	84,795	3,490	37,830	31,920	8,255	3,295
%	9.4	9.6	8.5	12.8	9.3	8.2	6.7	6.9
Service	874,905	701,310	173,500	4,280	63,600	64,890	27,705	13,120
%	16.1	15.8	17.4	15.7	15.6	16.7	22.5	27.4
Primary	136,130	114,150	21,985	1,815	9,510	5,730	3,455	1,475
%	2.5	2.6	2.2	6.7	2.3	1.5	2.8	3.1
Processing	129,550	99,055	30,485	530	10,935	12,190	4,940	1,895
%	2.4	2.2	3.1	1.9	2.7	3.1	4.0	4.0
Product fabricating, assembling, etc.	229,990	129,560	100,435	925	35,660	37,445	18,325	8,080
%	4.2	2.9	10.1	3.4	8.8	9.6	14.9	16.9
Construction trades	18,095	15,005	3,090	35	1,345	1,185	380	145
%	.3	.3	.3	.1	.3	.3	.3	.3
Other occupations	152,700	125,675	30,025	590	13,945	14,190	5,610	2,575
%	2.8	2.8	3.0	2.2	3.4	3.6	4.6	5.4
All occupations	5,446,010	4,451,535	994,480	27,280	406,815	389,250	123,280	47,845

NOTES: [a] Non-immig is defined as persons born in Canada, excluding those whose parents were diplomatic or military personnel temporarily resident in Canada; [b] Immig is defined as persons born outside Canada, excluding those who acquired Canadian citizenship by birth.

SOURCE: Statistics Canada, Census of Canada, 1986, Profile of Immigrants, Cat. 93-155, Table 1

Table 15 Total and employment income, 1985, by sex, birthplace, and period of immigration

	TOTAL	NON-IMMIG[a]	IMMIG[b]	<1946	1946-66	1967-77	1978-82	1983-6
Median total income, $								
Males	19,797	19,326	21,345	12,922	25,587	22,378	15,884	9,323
Females	9,540	9,420	9,983	8,753	10,839	11,175	8,954	8,219
Average employment income worked full year, full time, $								
Males	30,504	30,153	31,843	33,708	33,577	31,460	25,559	21,815
Females	19,995	20,052	19,721	20,211	20,882	19,905	15,817	13,222
Average employment income worked part year, or part time								
Males	13,474	12,977	16,070	15,972	18,931	14,949	11,576	8,219
Females	8,012	7,810	8,897	9,017	10,055	8,898	7,479	5,885

NOTES: [a] Non-immig is defined as persons born in Canada, excluding those whose parents were diplomatic or military personnel temporarily resident in Canada; [b] Immig is defined as persons born outside Canada, excluding those who acquired Canadian citizenship by birth.

SOURCE: Statistics Canada, Census of Canada, 1986, Profile of Immigrants, Cat. 93–155, Table 1

Table 16 Canada, landed immigrants by world area (country of last permanent residence), 1984–93

WORLD AREA	1984	1985	1986	1987	1988	1989	1990	1991	1992	1993*
Africa & Middle East	8,633	9,056	12,360	19,948	22,132	30,931	13,497	15,523	19,611	16,727
Asia & Pacific	38,144	34,354	35,490	58,149	69,286	76,326	114,409	119,301	142,776	148,160
Americas (Excl. US)	13,813	15,532	21,701	29,009	22,274	25,430	28,375	35,856	37,839	33,576
United States	6,923	6,670	7,283	7,983	6,520	6,918	6,088	6,279	7,524	7,933
Europe (excl. UK)	15,808	14,423	17,654	29,108	31,392	43,638	47,003	39,164	37,708	38,782
United Kingdom	5,105	4,458	5,091	8,554	9,164	8,413	13,241	7,372	7,116	6,959
TOTAL	88,426	84,493	99,579	152,751	160,768	191,656	222,613	223,495	252,574	252,137

*Provisional

				PERCENTAGE DISTRIBUTION (ROUNDED)						
	1984	1985	1986	1987	1988	1989	1990	1991	1992	1993
Africa & Middle East	10	11	12	13	14	16	6	7	8	7
Asia & Pacific	43	41	36	38	43	40	51	53	57	59
Americas (Excl. US)	16	18	22	19	14	13	13	16	15	13
United States	8	8	7	5	4	4	3	3	3	3
Europe (Excl. UK)	18	17	18	19	20	23	21	18	15	15
United Kingdom	6	5	5	6	6	4	6	3	3	3
TOTAL	100	100	100	100	100	100	100	100	100	100

SOURCE: Compiled from Canada Employment and Immigration, immigration levels, annual reports, and special tabulations

Table 17   Refugee and humanitarian movements, Canada, 1947–91

YEAR	MOVEMENT	NUMBER
1947–57	Postwar European	186,150
1956–7	Hungarian	37,149
1968–9	Czechoslovakian	11,943
1970	Tibetan	228
1972–3	Ugandan Asian	7,069
1973–9	South American	7,016
1975	Cypriot	700
1975–8	Vietnamese/Cambodian	9,060
1976	Iraqi Kurdish	98
1976–7	Angolan/Mozambican	2,100
1976–9	Lebanese	11,321
1978	Argentine	9
1979–80	Indochinese	60,049
1981–91	All countries	283,887
	(including asylum applicants accepted)	

SOURCE: Compiled from Canada Employment and Immigration, immigration levels, annual reports, and special tabulations.

Table 18 Canada, landings by class of immigrant, 1984–93

CLASS #	1984	1985	1986	1987	1988	1989	1990	1991	1992	1993**
Convention refugee†	5,681	6,126	6,557	7,566	8,637	10,170	11,401	17,012	28,682	22,152
Designated classes	9,783	10,738	12,764	14,185	17,938	26,735	28,302	34,194	23,161	8,038
Administrative review	0	0	6,596	17,139	855	0	0	0	0	0
Other humanitarian*	9,043	8,725	6,251	5,709	4,222	0	0	0	0	
Total humanitarian	24,507	25,589	32,168	44,599	31,652	36,905	39,703	51,206	51,843	30,190
Family class	43,849	38,556	42,165	53,436	51,003	60,685	73,481	83,585	99,830	111,178
Assisted relatives	8,188	7,417	5,903	12,316	15,493	21,473	25,395	21,998	19,863	22,191
Independent	3,303	4,341	9,982	28,631	44,583	51,496	53,718	45,761	47,452	48,372
Total selected	11,491	11,758	15,885	40,947	60,076	72,969	79,113	67,759	67,315	70,563
Entrepreneurs	3,557	4,968	5,876	8,466	11,215	12,962	12,265	9,787	15,684	16,571
Investors	0	0	23	316	1,016	2,266	4,211	5,069	9,617	12,585
Self-employed	2,705	1,522	1,629	2,321	2,682	2,309	1,975	1,936	2,816	3,345
Total business	6,262	6,490	7,528	11,103	14,913	17,537	18,451	16,792	28,117	32,501
Retirees	2,317	2,100	1,833	2,666	3,124	3,560	3,534	4,153	5,469	7,705
TOTAL	88,426	84,493	99,579	152,751	160,768	191,656	214,282	223,495	252,574	252,137

**Provisional
† After 1989, includes approved asylum applicants
* Includes 'special measures' program and others admitted on relaxed criteria
# All classes include dependants admitted with applicant

Table 18 (continued)

CLASS #	PERCENTAGE DISTRIBUTION (ROUNDED)									
	1984	1985	1986	1987	1988	1989	1990	1991	1992	1993
Convention refugee†	6	7	7	5	5	5	5	8	11	9
Designated classes	11	13	13	9	11	14	13	15	9	3
Administrative review	0	0	7	11	1	0	0	0	0	0
Other humanitarian*	10	10	6	4	3	0	0	0	0	0
Family class	50	46	42	35	32	32	34	37	40	44
Assisted relatives	9	9	6	8	10	11	12	10	8	9
Independent	4	5	10	19	28	27	25	20	19	19
Entrepreneurs	4	6	6	6	7	7	6	4	6	7
Investors	0	0	0	0	1	1	2	2	4	5
Self-employed	3	2	2	2	2	1	1	1	1	1
Retirees	3	2	2	2	2	2	2	2	2	3
TOTAL	100	100	100	100	100	100	100	100	100	100

**Provisional

† After 1989, includes approved asylum applicants

* Includes 'special measures' program and others admitted on relaxed criteria

All classes include dependants admitted with applicant

SOURCE: Canada Employment and Immigration, immigration levels, annual reports, and special tabulations

Table 19 Convention refugees and designated classes by world area (country of last permanent residence) Canada, 1990–3

REGION	1990	1991	1992	1993*
Europe				
Convention	499	950	2,289	3,514
Designated	15,783	11,526	6,121	1,116
Africa				
Convention	3,635	4,968	7,369	4,944
Designated	420	1,835	2,238	1,240
Asia				
Convention	4,622	8,311	15,014	11,419
Designated	8,244	11,731	8,337	2,250
Australasia				
Convention	5	0	0	0
Designated	0	1	0	4
North and Central America				
Convention	2,070	2,247	2,703	1,067
Designated	3,481	7,567	4,744	2,456
South America				
Convention	504	348	780	605
Designated	312	1,161	1,043	697
Caribbean				
Convention	32	122	260	379
Designated	25	122	227	51
Oceania				
Convention	34	66	267	107
Designated	37	251	451	124
Total				
Convention	11,401	17,012	28,682	22,035
Designated	28,302	34,194	23,161	8,045

*Provisional (includes CR8 dependants)

SOURCE: Compiled from Canada Employment and Immigration, immigration levels, annual reports, and special tabulations.

Table 20 Refugee determination hearings, regional summary,
1 January–31 December 1993

	OTTAWA/ ATLANTIC	QUEBEC	ONTARIO	PRAIRIES	BC	NATIONAL
Claims heard to completion (includes cases before 1993)	1,513	7,899	15,049	562	1,141	26,164
Decisions rendered	1,507	7,955	14,453	561	1,073	25,549
Claims rejected	472	3,503	6,534	199	740	11,448
Claims upheld	1,035	4,452	7,919	362	333	14,101
Withdrawn/abandoned	173	1,186	3,238	51	356	5,004
Decisions pending*	153	553	2,143	37	263	3,149
Claims pending**	1,565	5,603	10,385	288	2,111	19,952

 * Decisions pending include all claims heard to completion for which no decision had been
   rendered by the end of the reporting period
** Claims pending include all claims referred to the Convention Refugee Determination
   Division that have not been finalized (i.e., by a positive or negative decision or by
   withdrawal or abandonment) as of the end of the reporting period

SOURCE: Immigration and Refugee Board, *News Release, 28 February 1994* (Ottawa:
Immigration and Refugee Board, 1994)

Table 21 Canada, immigrants and non-permanent residents by selected places of birth and period of immigration (rounded)

PLACE OF BIRTH	%	IMMIGRANT POPULATION	BEFORE 1961	1961–70	1971–80	1981–7	1988–91	NON-PERMANENT
United States	5.74	249,080	61,790	55,450	76,430	37,070	18,345	18,160
C&S America	5.05	219,390	6,995	19,320	72,085	66,955	54,035	25,285
Caribbean & Bermuda	5.35	232,525	8,175	46,300	100,150	46,010	31,885	14,940
United Kingdom	16.53	717,745	328,180	178,630	139,570	48,630	22,735	9,300
N&W Europe	11.86	514,930	311,910	91,035	60,430	32,715	18,840	9,585
E&S Europe	26.07	1,132,025	474,995	302,190	170,815	91,350	92,675	24,410
Africa	3.83	166,170	5,605	27,135	59,805	32,930	40,700	19,805
W. Asia & Middle East	3.38	146,795	5,400	13,755	30,225	37,825	59,585	19,725
E. Asia	8.69	377,210	22,225	39,220	108,825	88,015	118,930	33,305
SE Asia	7.18	311,970	2,920	14,710	116,455	99,380	78,515	23,305
S. Asia	5.27	228,795	5,065	30,040	85,300	56,115	52,275	21,870
Oceania & Other	1.07	46,255	5,770	10,190	17,360	7,980	4,965	3,725
TOTAL		4,342,890	1,239,035	827,960	1,037,440	644,975	593,480	223,410
Per cent	100.00	100.00	28.53	19.06	23.89	14.85	13.67	

SOURCE: Adapted from Census of Canada, 1991

United States

Table 22 Inflows of permanent settlers by birthplace, 1980–90, United States (thousands) fiscal years (rounded)

	1980	1981	1982	1983	1984	1985	1986[1]	1987	1988	1989[2]	1990[2]
Europe	72.1	66.7	69.2	58.9	64.1	63.0	62.6	61.2	64.8	82.9	112.4
Asia	236.1	264.3	313.3	277.7	256.3	264.7	268.4	257.7	264.5	312.1	338.6
Africa	14.0	15.0	14.3	15.1	15.5	17.1	17.5	17.7	18.9	25.2	35.9
Oceania	4.0	4.2	3.8	3.5	3.8	4.1	3.6	4.0	3.8	4.4	6.2
Canada	13.6	11.2	10.8	11.4	10.8	11.4	11.1	11.9	11.8	12.2	16.8
Mexico	56.7	101.3	56.1	59.1	57.6	61.1	66.5	72.4	95.0	405.2	679.1
Caribbean	73.3	73.3	67.4	73.3	74.3	83.3	101.1	102.9	112.4	88.9	115.4
Central America	21.0	24.5	23.6	24.6	24.1	26.3	28.3	29.3	30.7	101.0	146.2
South America	39.7	35.9	35.4	36.1	37.5	39.1	42.1	44.4	41.0	58.9	85.8
Other and not stated	0.2	0.2	0.2	0.1	—	—	—	0.1	0.1	0.1	0.2
TOTAL	530.6	596.6	594.1	559.8	543.9	570.0	601.7	601.5	643.0	1,090.9	1,536.5

[1] The distribution by region of birth has been estimated.
[2] Data for 1989 and 1990 include respectively around 479,000 and 880,000 immigrants who obtained a permanent residence permit following the 1986 Immigration Reform and Control Act.

SOURCE: OECD-SOPEMI, *Trends in International Migration* (Paris: OECD, 1992)

Table 23 Inflows of permanent settlers by entry class, 1980–90, United States[1] (thousands) fiscal years (rounded)

	1980	1981	1982	1983	1984	1985	1986	1987	1988	1989	1990
Immediate relatives of US citizens[2]	157.7	152.4	168.4	177.8	183.2	204.4	223.5	218.6	219.3	217.5	231.7
Relative preferences[3]	216.9	226.6	206.1	213.5	212.3	213.3	212.9	211.8	200.8	217.1	214.6
Worker preferences[4]	44.4	44.3	51.2	55.5	49.5	50.9	53.6	53.9	53.6	52.8	53.7
Western hemisphere[5]	15.9	58.4	2.3	—	—	—	—	—	—	—	—
IRCA legalization[6]	—	—	—	—	—	—	—	—	—	478.8	880.4
Non-preference[7]	—	—	—	—	—	—	—	3.0	6.0	7.1	20.4
Refugees[8]	88.1	107.6	156.6	102.7	92.1	95.0	104.4	96.5	110.7	84.3	97.4
Others[8]	7.7	7.4	9.6	10.3	6.7	6.4	7.3	17.7	52.6	33.4	38.4
TOTAL	530.6	596.6	594.1	559.8	543.9	570.0	601.7	601.5	643.0	1,090.9	1,536.5

[1] With the exception of immediate relatives of US citizens, immigrants in a class of admission include principal beneficiaries, i.e., those aliens who directly qualify for the class of admission under US immigration laws, and derivative beneficiaries, i.e., the spouses and unmarried children of principal immigrants.

[2] Numerically unrestricted immigrants comprising spouses, unmarried minor children, and orphans adopted by US citizens as well as parents of adult US citizens.

[3] Numerically restricted relatives comprise the following four preference classes: First: Unmarried adult sons and daughters of US citizens; Second: Spouses and unmarried sons and daughters of US permanent resident aliens; Fourth: Married sons and daughters of US citizens; Fifth: Brothers and sisters of adult US citizens

[4] Numerically restricted workers comprise the following two preference classes:
Third: Members of the professions or persons of exceptional ability in the sciences and arts
Sixth: Skilled and unskilled workers in short supply

[5] For the period 1968–77, immigrants from independent Western hemisphere countries were not included under the preference system; however, they were subject to a 120,000 cap. Although the Western hemisphere category of admission was eliminated in 1977 through the extension of the preference system to that hemisphere, a number of Western hemisphere immigrants were admitted after 1977 as a result of lawsuits.

[6] Under the 1986 Immigration Reform and Control Act, foreigners who had been accorded temporary legal status could apply, between December 1988 and December 1990, for a permanent residence permit.

[7] If preference classes are undersubscribed, the unused numbers become available to non-preference immigrants (who have established that their admission will not have an adverse effect on the US labour force). Although non-preference slots have been unavailable since 1978, recent lawsuits have resulted in the admission of a small number of non-preference immigrants. Under the 1986 Immigration Reform and Control Act, immigrants from certain countries determined to have been adversely affected by the 1965 immigration reform were admitted under a special 'non-preference' category.

[8] Refugees were admitted under various laws. The Refugee Act of 1980 now governs all refugee admissions.

SOURCE: OECD-SOPEMI, *Trends in International Migration* (Paris: OECD, 1992)

Great Britain

Table 24 United Kingdom 1982–91, acceptances for settlement by nationality (on arrival and removal of time limit) (rounded)

NATIONALITY	1982	1983	1984	1985	1986	1987	1988	1989	1990	1991
Europe	7,100	6,520	6,370	6,270	5,240	5,070	5,620	4,880	5,120	5,530
United States	3,350	3,940	3,750	4,170	3,790	3,710	3,570	3,070	3,750	3,910
Other America	2,470	2,590	2,690	2,960	2,590	2,690	2,910	2,440	3,050	3,310
Africa	4,120	4,670	4,380	4,710	4,130	5,130	5,840	6,480	8,310	9,580
Indian subcon	20,180	16,690	14,840	17,510	14,550	11,620	12,180	12,520	13,170	14,290
Middle East	2,580	3,280	2,870	3,580	3,030	2,680	2,810	3,670	3,030	2,900
Other Asia	5,020	5,070	4,860	5,000	5,030	5,620	6,020	5,950	7,430	7,720
Australasia	4,220	4,660	6,040	6,660	5,380	5,720	6,190	6,840	5,350	2,440
Other n.e.s.	4,820	6,030	5,150	4,500	3,980	3,790	4,140	3,800	4,000	4,220
All nationalities	53,870	53,460	50,950	55,360	47,820	45,980	49,280	49,650	53,200	53,900
Old Commonwealth	5,160	5,800	7,440	8,160	6,610	6,900	7,380	7,890	6,230	3,120
%	9.58	10.85	14.60	14.74	13.82	15.01	14.98	15.89	11.71	5.79
New Commonwealth & Pakistan	30,380	27,550	24,800	27,050	22,660	20,830	22,800	23,160	25,980	27,930
%	56.40	51.53	48.68	48.86	47.39	45.30	46.27	46.65	48.83	51.82
Foreign (excl. Pakistan)	18,330	20,120	18,720	20,150	18,530	18,240	19,100	18,600	20,990	22,850
%	34.03	37.64	36.74	36.40	38.75	39.67	38.76	37.46	39.45	42.39

SOURCE: Adapted from Home Office, *Control of Immigration Statistics* (annual) (London: HMSO)

Table 25 Work permit holders and dependants given leave to enter, excluding EC nationals,[1] 1981–91

UNITED KINGDOM YEAR OF ADMISSION	TOTAL	EMPLOYMENT FOR 12 MONTHS OR MORE	EMPLOYMENT FOR LESS THAN 12 MONTHS	TRAINEES	DEPENDANTS OF WORK PERMIT HOLDERS
1981	16,700	3,750	7,050	1,120	4,790
1982	17,980	3,920	8,050	490	5,020
1983	18,490	4,720	7,980	910	4,870
1984	18,910	5,040	8,060	800	5,030
1985	19,560	5,400	8,340	560	5,270
1986	21,300	5,960	9,490	580	5,280
1987	26,020	6,710	12,550	520	6,250
1988	30,620	7,680	15,020	490	7,420
1989	40,450	10,860	18,460	650	10,570
1990	48,750	14,740	19,880	700	13,430
1991	46,920	11,060	21,100	640	14,120

[1] Spain and Portugal are included prior to 1986, when they entered the EC. Figures also include admissions recorded as German Democratic Republic prior to the unification of Germany on 3 October 1990.

SOURCE: Adapted from Home Office, *Control of Immigration Statistics* (annual) (London: HMSO)

Table 26 Great Britain, applications received for refugee status or asylum; from selected countries, 1988–91

COUNTRY	1988	1989	1990	1991
Afghanistan	25	85	200	—
Angola	45	220	1,030	3,300
Bangladesh	10	10	55	—
Bulgaria	5	30	130	240
Ivory Coast	0	15	50	625
Ethiopia	225	560	1,840	1,035
Ghana	170	325	790	1,595
India	290	630	1,415	1,085
Iran	390	345	335	290
Iraq	165	210	915	465
Lebanon	150	175	1,035	590
Nigeria	10	20	90	—
Uganda	410	1,240	1,895	1,110
Pakistan	330	245	1,295	1,830
Poland	70	45	20	20
Romania	10	15	295	280
Somalia	305	1,845	1,850	1,225
Sudan	20	110	220	260
Ceylon	405	1,785	3,325	2,410
Turkey	335	2,360	1,100	1,260
USSR	5	30	93	115
Zaire	145	490	1,490	3,650
Others	465	720	> 2,250	2,410
TOTAL	3,985	11,465	>22,000	23,775
Dependants	1,715	5,070	> 8,000	—
Overall total	5,700	16,535	>30,000	—

SOURCE: Compiled from Home Office, *Control of Immigration Statistics, United Kingdom 1988* (London: HMSO, 1989); and J. Salt, *International Migration and the United Kingdom* (London: Migration Research Unit, University College):Table 12

Australia

Table 27 Australia, immigrants by year of arrival

PLACE OF BIRTH	%	IMMIGRANT POPULATION	PRIOR TO 1976	1976–80	1981–5	1986–7	1988–9	1990–1	NOT STATED
North America	1.80	66,375	27,815	6,971	9,210	4,718	6,640	9,826	1,195
UK & Ireland	31.41	1,158,979	849,547	71,332	88,563	37,478	47,750	38,486	25,823
N&W Europe*	5.60	206,606	173,035	6,909	13,296	3,189	3,368	3,051	3,758
E&S Europe**	19.41	716,426	610,495	22,876	29,228	11,617	13,777	9,918	18,515
South Africa	1.33	49,001	12,447	9,181	10,328	7,310	5,670	3,295	770
Lebanon	1.87	68,831	30,805	13,502	6,367	6,174	5,420	3,962	2,601
E. Asia †	3.67	135,302	24,108	11,864	20,235	16,204	36,623	24,023	2,245
SE Asia ‡	7.22	266,280	23,315	47,586	71,067	35,966	45,907	37,312	5,127
S. Asia °	1.65	61,015	30,493	4,052	7,687	4,746	5,960	6,960	1,117
New Zealand	7.16	264,147	67,128	49,875	47,315	31,633	42,956	19,155	6,085
Other	18.89	697,248	291,425	69,789	101,048	66,993	83,079	68,806	16,108
TOTAL		3,690,210	2,140,613	313,937	404,344	226,028	297,150	224,794	83,344
%			58.01	8.51	10.96	6.13	8.05	6.09	2.26

* Germany & Netherlands
** Greece, Italy, Malta, Yugoslavia, Poland, and USSR
† Hong Kong & China exc. Taiwan
‡ Malaysia, Philippines, and Vietnam
° India

SOURCE: Information supplied from Census of Australia, 1991

Table 28 Australia, region of birth of settler arrivals, 1982–3 to 1991–2

REGION	1982–3	1983–4	1984–5	1985–6	1986–7	1987–8	1988–9	1989–90	1990–1	1991–2
Oceania	8,626	7,315	10,746	15,610	16,564	25,654	27,999	15,270	10,970	10,362
UK & Ireland	27,424	13,731	12,376	16,119	22,523	27,250	27,978	25,591	21,861	15,187
S. Europe	4,972	3,524	4,524	5,798	6,549	7,271	5,820	4,175	3,793	3,834
N&W Europe	8,676	3,615	2,746	3,142	3,777	4,457	4,210	3,453	3,114	2,367
E. Europe	6,177	3,342	2,683	2,961	3,585	4,588	4,430	5,167	3,565	5,482
Middle East	2,102	3,576	4,771	5,692	6,405	8,508	6,549	4,956	6,200	5,909
North Africa	2,485	4,043	5,280	6,499	7,484	10,021	8,044	5,754	7,154	7,021
SE Asia	19,827	18,655	18,414	17,907	23,004	29,491	31,702	28,201	29,417	22,325
NE Asia	3,540	4,668	7,682	8,190	8,926	12,679	15,874	16,395	22,100	21,473
S. Asia	2,579	3,367	4,794	4,486	6,253	6,719	7,025	6,011	9,389	10,594
N. America	2,769	2,301	2,392	2,651	2,854	3,069	3,068	3,015	2,811	2,570
Other Americas*	1,714	2,127	3,660	4,068	4,268	4,630	4,322	4,125	3,745	3,308
TOTAL	90,891	70,264	80,068	93,123	112,192	144,337	147,021	122,113	124,119	110,432

SOURCE: Bureau of Immigration and Population Research, *Australian Immigration Consolidated Statistics, No. 17* (Canberra: Australian Government Publishing Service, June 1993)

*Includes Caribbean

Europe

Table 29 Inflows of foreign population into selected OECD countries, 1980–90[1] (thousands)

	1980	1981	1982	1983	1984	1985	1986	1987	1988	1989	1990
Belgium	46.8	41.3	36.2	34.3	37.2	37.5	39.3	40.1	38.2	43.5	52.3
France[2]	59.4	75.0	144.4	64.2	51.4	43.4	38.3	39.0	44.0	53.2	63.1
Germany	523.6	451.7	275.5	253.5	295.8	324.4	378.6	414.9	545.4	649.5	—
Luxembourg	7.4	6.9	6.4	6.2	6.0	6.6	7.4	8.3	9.0	9.1	—
Netherlands	78.5	49.6	39.7	34.4	34.7	40.6	46.9	47.4	50.8	51.5	60.1
Norway[3]	11.8	13.1	14.0	13.1	12.8	14.9	16.5	15.2	16.4	14.0	11.7
Sweden[4]	—	—	—	18.3	14.1	13.4	19.4	19.0	24.9	28.9	23.9
Switzerland[5]	70.5	80.3	74.7	58.3	58.6	59.4	66.8	71.5	76.1	80.4	101.4
United Kingdom[6]	69.8	59.1	53.9	53.5	51.0	55.4	47.8	46.0	49.3	49.7	52.4

[1] Data, except for France and United Kingdom, are taken from population registers. Asylum seekers are excluded.
[2] Entries of new foreign workers, including holders of provisional work permits (APT) and foreigners admitted on family reunification grounds. Does not include residents of EEC countries (workers and family members) who have not been brought in by the International Migration Office (IMO).
[3] Entries of foreigners intending to stay longer than six months in Norway.
[4] Some short duration entries are not counted (mainly citizens of other Nordic countries).
[5] Entries of foreigners with annual residence permits, and those with settlement permits (permanent permits) who return to Switzerland after a temporary stay abroad. Includes, up to 31 December 1982, holders of permits of duration under twelve months. Seasonal and frontier workers (including seasonal workers who obtain permanent permits) are excluded.
[6] Entries correspond to permanent settlers within the meaning of the 1971 Immigration Act and subsequent amendments.

SOURCE: OECD-SOPEMI, *Trends in International Migration* (Paris: OECD, 1992)

Table 30 Inflows of asylum seekers into selected OECD countries, 1980–91 (thousands)

	1980	1981	1982	1983	1984	1985	1986	1987	1988	1989	1990	1991*
Austria	9.3	34.6	6.3	5.9	7.2	6.7	8.6	11.4	15.8	21.9	22.8	27.3
Belgium	2.7	2.4	3.1	2.9	3.7	5.3	7.6	6.0	4.5	8.1	13.0	15.2
Denmark	0.2	0.3	0.3	0.3	4.3	8.7	9.3	2.7	4.7	4.6	5.3	4.6
Finland	—	—	—	—	—	—	0.1	0.1	0.1	0.2	2.5	2.1
France	18.8	19.8	22.5	22.3	21.6	28.8	26.2	27.6	34.3	61.4	54.7	50.0
Germany	107.8	49.4	37.2	19.7	35.3	73.8	99.7	57.4	103.1	121.3	193.1	256.1
Greece	—	—	—	0.5	0.8	1.4	4.3	6.3	9.3	6.5	4.1	—
Italy	—	—	—	3.1	4.6	5.4	6.5	11.0	1.4	2.2	4.7	27.0
Netherlands	1.3	0.8	1.2	2.0	2.6	5.6	5.9	13.5	7.5	13.9	21.2	21.6
Norway	0.1	0.1	0.1	0.2	0.3	0.8	2.7	8.6	6.6	4.4	4.0	3.0
Portugal	1.6	0.6	0.4	0.6	0.2	0.1	0.1	0.2	0.3	0.1	0.1	—
Spain	—	—	—	1.4	1.1	2.3	2.8	3.7	4.5	4.0	8.6	8.0
Sweden	—	—	—	4.0	12.0	14.5	14.6	18.1	19.6	30.0	29.4	26.5
Switzerland	6.1	5.2	7.1	7.9	7.4	9.7	8.5	10.9	16.7	24.4	35.8	41.6
United Kingdom	9.9	2.9	4.2	4.3	3.9	5.4	4.8	5.2	5.7	16.5	30.0	57.7

*Provisional data

SOURCE: OECD-SOPEMI, *Trends in International Migration* (Paris: OECD, 1992)

Bibliography

Abella, M. 1990. *Structural Change and Labour Migration within the Asian Region*. Nagoya: UN Centre for Regional Development, Expert Group Meeting on Cross-National Labour Migration in the Asian Region.

Abella, R. 1984. *Equality in Employment: A Royal Commission Report*. Ottawa: Ministry of Supply and Services Canada.

Abu-Lughod, J.L. 1988. 'Palestinians: Exiles at Home and Abroad', *Current Sociology* 36, no. 2:61–70.

ACPE (Australian Council on Population and Ethnic Affairs). 1982. *Multiculturalism for All Australians: Our Developing Nationhood*. Canberra: Australian Government Publishing Service.

Adam, H. 1979. *Ethnic Power Mobilized: Can South Africa Change?* New Haven: Yale University Press.

———, and K. Moodley. 1993. *The Opening of the Apartheid Mind: Options for the New South Africa*. Berkeley: University of California Press.

Adelman, H., ed. 1991. *Refugee Policy: Canada and the United States*. Toronto and New York: York Lanes Press and Center for Migration Studies.

———, and C.M. Lanphier, eds. 1990. *Refuge or Asylum? A Choice for Canada*. Toronto: York Lanes Press.

Adepojo, A. 1988. 'International Migration in Africa South of the Sahara'. In

International Migration Today, Vol. 1: Trends and Prospects, edited by R. Appleyard. Paris: UNESCO.

Adorno, T.W. 1950. *The Authoritarian Personality*. New York: Harper.

Aguiar, M. 1986. *Political Comments on Emigration*. Porto: Centro de Estudos.

Aircraft Movement Statistics. 1990. *Annual Reports*. Ottawa: Statistics Canada, Aviation Statistics Centre.

Akyeampong, E.B., and J. Winters. 1993. 'International Employment Trends by Industry—a Note'. *Perspectives* (Summer):33–45.

Alomes, S., and D. de Hartog, eds. 1991. *Postpop: Popular Culture, Nationalism and Postmodernism*. Victoria: Footprint.

Altemeyer, R.A. 1988. *Enemies of Freedom: Understanding Right-Wing Authoritarianism*. San Francisco: Jossey-Bass.

———. *Right-Wing Authoritarianism*. Winnipeg: University of Manitoba Press.

Amin, S. 1974. 'Modern Migrations in Western Africa'. In *Modern Migration in Western Africa*, edited by S. Amin. London: Oxford University Press, 65–124.

Amjad, R. 1990. *Asian Labour in the Middle East: Lessons and Implications*. Nagoya: UN Centre for Regional Development, Expert Group Meeting on Cross-National Labour Migration in the Asian Region.

Amnesty International. 1992. *A Comprehensive Report on Human Rights Violations Around the World*. New York: Amnesty International Publications.

Anctil, P. 1986. 'Le Pluralisme au Quebec', *Etude Ethniques au Canada* XVIII, no. 2:1–6.

Anwar, M. 1979. *The Myth of Return: Pakistanis in Britain*. London: Heinemann Educational Books.

Appadurai, A. 1990. 'Disjuncture and Difference in the Global Cultural Economy', in *Global Culture: Nationalism, Globalization and Modernity*, edited by M. Featherstone. London: Sage Publications.

Appleyard, R., ed. 1988. *International Migration Today, Vol. 1: Trends and Prospects*. Paris: UNESCO.

———, ed. 1989. *The Impact of International Migration on Developing Countries*. Paris: Organization for Economic Co-operation and Development.

———. 1991. *International Migration: The Challenge of the Nineties*. Geneva: International Organization for Migration.

Arac, J., ed. 1991. *After Foucault: Humanistic Knowledge, Postmodern Challenges*. New Brunswick: Rutgers University Press.

Arendt, H. 1970. *On Violence*. London: Allen Lane/The Penguin Press.

Atchison, J. 1988. 'Immigration in Two Federations: Canada and Australia', *International Migration* 26, no. 1:5–32.

Bakan, A. 1987. 'International Market for Female Labour and Individual Deskilling: West Indian Women Workers in Toronto'. *Canadian Journal of Latin American and Caribbean Studies* 12, no. 24:69–85.

Balakrishnan, T.R., and K. Selvanathan. 1990. 'Ethnic Residential Segregation in Metropolitan Canada'. In *Ethnic Demography: Canadian Immigrant, Racial and Cultural Variations*, edited by S.S. Halli, F. Trovato, and L. Driedger. Ottawa: Carleton University Press.

Banton, M. 1977. *The Idea of Race*. London: Tavistock Publications.

———. 1983. *Racial and Ethnic Competition*. Cambridge: Cambridge University Press.

———. 1985. *Promoting Racial Harmony*. Cambridge: Cambridge University Press.

———. 1990. 'The International Defence of Racial Equality', *Ethnic and Racial Studies* 13, no. 4:568–83.

Barrett, M. 1991. *Politics of Truth: From Marx to Foucault*. Cambridge: Polity Press.

Barth, F. 1969. *Ethnic Groups and Boundaries*. Boston: Little, Brown.

Baubock, R. 1992. *Legitimate Immigration Control*. Vienna: Institute for Advanced Studies. Paper presented at the International Conference on Mass Migration in Europe: Implications in East and West.

Bauman, Z. 1992. *Intimations of Postmodernity*. London: Routledge.

BC Ministry of International Business and Immigration. 1990. *British Columbia's Pacific Visions*. Victoria: BC Ministry of International Business and Immigration.

Beach, C., and A.G. Green, eds. 1988. *Policy Forum on the Role of Immigration in Canada's Future*. Kingston: Queen's University Press.

Bean, F.D., B. Edmonston, and J.S. Passel, eds. 1990. *Undocumented Migration to the United States: The IRCA and the Experience of the 1980s*. Washington: Rand Corporation and the Urban Institute.

———, G. Vernez, and C.B. Keeley, eds. 1989. *Opening and Closing the Doors: Evaluating Immigration Reform and Control*. Washington: Rand Corporation and the Urban Institute.

Beaujot, R., K.G. Basavarajappa, and R.B.P. Verma. 1988. *Income of Immigrants in Canada, 1980*. Ottawa: Statistics Canada.

———, and P. Rappak. 1989. 'The Role of Immigration in the Changing Socio-Economic Structures'. *The Review of Demography and Its Implications for Economic and Social Policy* 5:57–62.

———. 1991. *Population Change in Canada: The Challenge of Policy Adaptation*. Toronto: McClelland and Stewart.

Beiser, M. 1988. *After the Door Has Been Opened: Mental Health Issues Affecting Immigrants and Refugees in Canada*. Ottawa: Health and Welfare Canada.

Bell, D. 1973. *The Coming of Post-industrial Society: A Venture in Social Forecasting*. London: Heinemann.

———. 1976. *The Cultural Contradictions of Capitalism*. New York: Basic Books.

Benyon, J., ed. 1984. *Scarman and After: Essays Reflecting on Lord Scarman's Report, the Riots and Their Aftermath*. Oxford: Pergamon.

Bercuson, D.J., and B. Cooper. 1991. *Deconfederation: Canada Without Quebec*. Toronto: Key Porter Books.

Bernard, W.S. 1976. 'Immigrants and Refugees: Their Similarities, Differences and Needs'. *International Migration* 14, no. 4:267–81.

Berry, J.W. 1991. *Sociopsychological Costs and Benefits of Multiculturalism*. Ottawa: Economic Council of Canada.

———, R.K. Kalin, and D.M. Taylor. 1977. *Multiculturalism and Ethnic Attitudes in Canada*. Ottawa: Supply and Services.

Berting, N.J., et al. 1983. *Beyond Progress and Development: Proceedings of the Symposium on Macro Political and Societal Change*. Rotterdam: Faculty of Social Sciences, Erasmus University.

Betts, K. 1988. *Ideology and Immigration: Australia 1976–1987*. Melbourne: Melbourne University Press.

Beyer, P.F. 1990. 'Privatization and the Public Influence of Religion in Global Society'. In *Global Culture*, edited by M. Featherstone. London: Sage Publications.

Bibby, R.W. 1987. *Fragmented Gods: The Poverty and Potential of Religion in Canada*. Toronto: Irwin.

———. 1990. *Mosaic Madness: The Poverty and Potential of Life in Canada*. Toronto: Stoddart.

Birch, A.H. 1989. *Nationalism and National Integration*. London: Unwin Hyman.

Birrell, R., and T. Birrell. 1987. *An Issue of People: Population and Australian Society* (2nd ed.). Melbourne: Longman Cheshire.

Blainey, G. 1984. *All for Australia*. North Ryde: Methuen Haynes.

Blalock, H.M. 1989. *Power and Conflict: Towards a General Theory*. Newbury Park: Sage Publications.

Bohning, R. 1991. 'The ILO and the New UN Convention on Migrant Workers: The Past and the Future'. *International Migration Review* 24, no. 4:698–709.

Borjas, G.J. 1988. *International Differences in the Labor Market Performance of Immigrants*. Kalamazoo: W.E. Upjohn.

———, and R.B. Freeman, eds. 1992. *Immigration and the Workforce: Economic Consequences for the United States and Source Areas*. Chicago: University of Chicago Press.

Borrie, W.D. 1975. *Population and Australia: Report of the National Population Inquiry*. Canberra: Australian Government Publishing Service.

Bosniak, L.S. 1991. 'Human Rights, State Sovereignty and the Protection of Undocumented Workers under the International Migrant Workers Convention'. *International Migration Review* 24, no. 4:737–70.

Boulding, K. 1962. *Conflict and Defense: A General Theory*. New York: Harper.

———. 1985. *The World as a Total System*. Beverly Hills: Sage Publications.

———. 1989. *Three Faces of Power*. Newbury Park: Sage Publications.

Boutros-Ghali, Boutros. 1993. *World Conference on Human Rights, Newletter No. 2*. Geneva: UN Centre for Human Rights.

Boxhill, W. 1984. *Limitations to the Use of Ethnic Origin Data to Identify Visible Minorities in Canada*. Ottawa: Statistics Canada, cat. no. 99–957.

———. 1990, 'Making Tough Choices in Using Census Data to Count Visible Minorities in Canada'. Unpublished paper, Statistics Canada.

Boyd, M. 1989. 'Family and Personal Networks in International Migration: Recent Developments and New Agendas'. *International Migration Review* 23, no. 3:638–70.

———, and C. Taylor. 1986. 'The Feminization of Temporary Workers: The Canadian Case'. *International Migration Review* 24, no. 4:717–34.

———, et al. 1986. 'Temporary Workers in Canada: A Multi-faceted Program'. *International Migration Review* 20, no. 4:929–50.

Boyne, R., and A. Rattansi, eds. 1990. *Postmodernism and Society*. London: Macmillan.

Braham, P., A. Rattansi, and R. Skellington, eds. 1992. *Racism and Antiracism: Inequalities, Opportunities and Policies*. London: Sage Publications.

Breton, R., et al. 1990. *Ethnic Identity and Equality: Varieties of Experience in Canada*. Toronto: University of Toronto Press.

Brett, R. 1992. *The Challenge of Change: Report of the Helsinki Follow-Up Meetings of the Conference on Security and Co-operation in Europe*. Colchester: University of Essex, Human Rights Centre.

———, and E. Eddison. 1993. 'Migration, Refugees and Displaced Persons: Report on the CSCE Human Dimensions Seminar on Migration, Including Refugees and Displaced Persons'. *Papers in the Theory and Practice of Human Rights*, no. 4.

Brown, C. 1984. *Black and White Britain: The Third PSI Survey*. London: Heinemann.

Brubaker, W.R., ed. 1989. *Immigration and the Politics of Citizenship in Europe and North America*. Lanham: University Press of America.

Bryan, G.A., and D. Jary. 1991. *Giddens' Theory of Structuration: A Critical Appreciation*. London: Routledge.

Bullivant, B. 1981. *The Pluralist Dilemma in Education: Six Case Studies*. Sydney: Allen & Unwin.

Burnet, J. 1978. 'The Policy of Multiculturalism within a Bilingual Framework: A Stocktaking'. *Canadian Ethnic Studies* 10:107–11.

———. 1987. 'Multiculturalism in Canada'. In *Ethnic Canada: Identities and Inequalities*, edited by L. Driedger. Toronto: Copp Clark Pitman.

Burnley, I.H., and W.E. Kalbach. 1985. *Immigrants in Canada and Australia, Vol. 3: Urban and Ecological Aspects*. Toronto: Institute for Behavioural Research, York University.

Buttrick, J. 1992. 'Migration between Canada and the United States, 1970–1985: Some New Estimates'. *International Migration Review* 26, no. 4:1448–56.

Canada Employment and Immigration. 1992. *Annual Report*. Ottawa: Canada Employment and Immigration.

Cashmore, E., and B. Troyna. 1982. *Black Youth in Crisis*. London: George Allen & Unwin.

Castles, C., et al. 1984. *Here for Good: Western Europe's New Ethnic Minorities*. London: Pluto Press.

CEIAC (Canada Employment and Immigration Advisory Council). 1991a. *Immigrants and Language Training*. Ottawa: CEIAC.

———. 1991b. *Immigrants in the 1990's*. Ottawa: CEIAC.

———. 1991c. *National Symposium on Settlement and Integration*. Ottawa: CEIAC.

Centlivres, P., and M. Centrelivres-Dumont. 1988. 'The Afghan Refugees in Pakistan: A Nation in Exile'. *Current Sociology* 36, no. 2:71–92.

Centre for Contemporary Cultural Studies. 1982. *The Empire Strikes Back: Race and Racism in 70's Britain*. London: Hutchison.

Centre for Refugee Studies. 1993. *Report of the Early Warning Workshop*. Toronto: Centre for Refugee Studies.

Chiswick, B.R., ed. 1992. *Immigration, Language and Ethnicity: Canada and the United States*. Washington: The AEI Press.

Clark, S.D. 'Sociology in Canada: An Historical Overview'. *Canadian Journal of Sociology* 1, no. 2:225–34.

Clarke, H.R., et al. 1990. *Immigration, Population and the Growth of the Environment*. Canberra: Bureau of Immigration Research.

Clarke, S.E., and J.R. Obler. 1976. *Urban Ethnic Conflict: A Comparative Perspective*. Chapel Hill: University of North Carolina, Institute for Research in Social Science.

Claval, P. 1990. *Cultural Dimension of Cross-Labour Migration*. Nagoya: UN Centre for Regional Development, Expert Group Meeting on Cross-National Migration in the Asian Region.

Cohen, I.J. 1989. *Structuration Theory: Anthony Giddens and the Constitution of Social Life*. London: Macmillan.

Cohon, J.D. 'Psychological Adaptation and Dysfunction among Refugees'. *International Migration Review* 15, no. 1:255-75.

Collins, J. 1975. 'The Political Economy of Post-war Immigration'. In *Essays in the Political Economy of Australian Capitalism*, edited by E.L. Wainwright and K. Buckley. Sydney: Australia and New Zealand Book Company.

Commonwealth of Australia, Office of Multicultural Affairs. 1989. *National Agenda for a Multicultural Australia*. Canberra: Australian Government Publishing Service.

Coombe, R.J. 1991. 'Encountering the Postmodern: New Directions in Cultural Anthropology'. *Canadian Review of Anthropology and Sociology* 28, no. 2:188-205.

Cooper, P. 1985. 'Competing Explanations of the Merseyside Riots of 1981'. *British Journal of Criminology* 25, no. 1:60-9.

Couper, M.P. 1990. 'Immigrant Adaptation in South Africa'. Unpublished doctoral dissertation, Rhodes University, South Africa.

Cox, O.C. 1948. *Caste, Class and Race*. New York: Monthly Review Press.

Craib, I. 1992. *Anthony Giddens*. London: Routledge.

CRE (Commission for Racial Equality). 1985. *Ethnic Minorities in Britain*. London: Commission for Racial Equality.

Cruz, A., ed. 1992. *Migration News Sheet*. Brussels: European Information Network.

Cumming, P.A., et al. 1989. *Access! Task Force on Access to Trades and Professions in Ontario* Toronto: Ministry of Citizenship.

Cuny, F.C. 'The UNHCR and Relief Operations: A Changing Role'. *International Migration Review* 15, no. 1-2:16-19.

Curle, A. 1990. *Tools for Transformation: A Personal Study*. Stroud: Hawthorn Press.

Curmi, B. 1993. 'Gestation de la crise des refugies au detour de la crise du gulfe: le role des organizations internationales'. In *International Union for the Scientific Study of Population*, vol. 2, 59-67. International Population Conference, Montreal, August.

Dahrendorf, R. 1959. *Class and Class Conflict in Industrial Society*. London: Routledge & Kegan Paul.

Daudlin, B. 1984. *Equality Now: Report of the Special Committee in Visible Minorities in Canadian Society*. Ottawa: Queen's Printer.

Davis, A. 1983. *Women, Race and Class*. New York: Women's Press.

Davis, K. 1974. 'The Migrations of Human Populations'. *Scientific American*, 231.

De Jong, G., and R.W. Gardner. 1981. *Migration Decision Making: Multi-disciplinary Approaches to Micro-level Studies in Developed and Developing Countries*. New York: Pergamon Press.

De Vos, G.A., and M. Saurez-Orozco. 1990. *Status Inequality and the Self in Culture*. Newbury Park: Sage Publications.

Deschenes, J. 1986. *Commission of Inquiry into War Criminals: Report*. Ottawa: The Commission of Inquiry into War Criminals.

Dex, S. 1985. 'The Use of Economists' Models in Sociology'. *Ethnic and Racial Studies* 8, no. 4:516–33.

Dezalay, Y. 1990. 'The Big Bang and the Law: The Internationalization and Restructuration of the Legal Field'. In *Global Culture: Nationalism, Globalization and Modernity*, edited by M. Featherstone. London: Sage Publications.

Dirks, G.E. 1977. *Canadian Refugee Policy: Opportunism or Indifference?* Montreal: McGill-Queen's University Press.

———. 1984. 'A Policy within a Policy: The Identification and Admission of Refugees to Canada'. *Canadian Journal of Political Science* 17, no. 2:279–307.

Dowty, A. 1987. *Closed Borders: The Contemporary Assault on Freedom of Movement*. New Haven: Yale University Press.

Drew, D., and J. Gray. 1991. 'The Black-White Gap in Examination Results: A Statistical Critique of a Decade's Research'. *New Community* 17, no. 2:159–72.

Driedger, L. 1987. *Ethnic Canada: Identities and Inequalities*. Toronto: Copp Clark Pitman.

Drucker, P.F. 1993. *Post-Capitalist Society*. New York: Harper Business.

Dublin, M. 1990. *Futurehype: The Tyranny of Prophecy*. Markham: Penguin Books.

Duleep, H.O., and M.C. Regrets. 1992. 'Some Evidence of the Effects of Admissions Criteria on Immigrant Assimilation'. In *Immigration, Language and Ethnicity: Canada and the United States*, edited by B.R. Chiswick. Washington: The AEI Press, 410–32.

Dwivedi, O.P., et al. 1989. *Canada 200: Race Relations and Public Policy*. University of Guelph: Department of Political Studies.

Eayrs, J. 1987. 'The Outlook for Statehood'. *International Perspectives* (March/April):3–7.

Economic Council of Canada. 1990. *Good Jobs, Bad Jobs*. Ottawa: Economic Council of Canada.

Egan, J. 1992. 'Access of Migrant and Seasonal Farmworkers to Medicaid-Covered Health Care Services'. In *In Defense of the Alien*, Vol. XIV, edited by L. Tomasi. New York: Center for Migration Studies.

Eichenbaum, J. 'A Matrix of Human Movement'. *International Migration* 13, no. 1–2:21–41.

Eisenstadt, S.N. 1954. *The Absorption of Immigrants*. London: Routledge and Kegan Paul.

El-Hinnawi, E. 1985. *Environmental Refugees*. New York: UN Development Program.

Employment Equity Commission. 1991. *Working Towards Equality: Discussion Paper on Employment Equity Legislation*. Toronto: Ministry of Citizenship.

Employment Gazette. 1990. 'Ethnic Origins and the Labour Market', *Employment Gazette* (March):125-37.

Etzioni, A. 1968. *The Active Society: A Theory of Societal and Political Processes*. New York: Free Press.

Evans, M.D.R., F.L. Jones, and J. Kelley. 1988. 'Job Discrimination Against Immigrants'. In *Australian Attitudes*, edited by J. Kelley and C. Bean. Sydney: Allen & Unwin.

———, and J. Kelley. 1986. 'Immigrants' Work: Equality and Discrimination in the Australian Labour Market'. *Australian & New Zealand Journal of Sociology* 2:187-207.

Fairchild, H.P. 1913. *Immigration: A World Movement and Its American Significance*. New York: McMillan.

Fanon, F. 1967. *The Wretched of the Earth*. Harmondsworth: Penguin Books.

Featherstone, M., ed. 1990. *Global Culture: Nationalism, Globalization and Modernity*. London: Sage Publications.

Feliciano, F. 1983. *International Humanitarian Law and Coerced Movements of Peoples across State Boundaries*. San Remo: International Institute of Humanitarian Law.

Ferris, E.G., ed. 1985. *Refugees and World Politics*. New York: Praeger.

Fishman, J.A. 1989. *Language and Ethnicity in Minority Socio-Linguistic Perspective*. Philadelphia: Multilingual Matters Ltd.

Fitzgerald, S. 1988. *Immigration: A Commitment to Australia*. Canberra: Australian Government Publishing Service.

Fleras, A., and J.L. Elliott. 1992. *The Challenge of Diversity: Multiculturalism in Canada*. Scarborough: Nelson.

Foster, L., and D. Stockley. 1984. *Multiculturalism: The Changing Australian Paradigm*. Clevedon: Multilingual Matters Ltd.

———. 1988a. *Australian Multiculturalism: A Documentary History and Critique*. Clevedon: Multilingual Matters Ltd.

———. 1988b. 'The Rise and Decline of Australian Multiculturalism'. *Politics* 23, no. 2:1-10.

———. 1989. 'The Politics of Ethnicity: Multicultural Policy in Australia'. *Journal of Intercultural Studies* 10, no. 2:16-33.

Foucault, M. 1973. *Madness and Civilization: A History of Insanity in the Age of Reason*. New York: Vintage Books.

———. 1978. *The History of Sexuality*. Translated by R. Hurley. New York: Pantheon Books.

———. 1979. *Discipline and Punishment: The Birth of the Prison*. New York: Vintage Books.

Fragomen, A.T. 1979. 'New Asylum Regulations'. *International Migration Review* 13, no. 2:347–51.

Frankel, B. 1987. *The Postindustrial Utopians*. Cambridge: Polity Press.

Freeman, G. 1992. 'Migration Policies and Politics in Receiving States'. *International Migration Review* 26, no. 4:1144–67.

Freire, P. 1973. *Pedogogy of the Oppressed*. New York: Seabury Press.

Fried, C., ed. 1983. *Minorities: Community and Identity*. Berlin: Springer.

Fromm, E. 1941. Escape from Freedom. New York: Farrer and Rinehart.

———. 1977. *The Anatomy of Human Destructiveness*. Harmondsworth: Penguin Books.

Fukuyama, F. 1991. 'New World Order'. *Guardian Studies* April:29–32.

Galbally, F. 1978. *Migrants Services and Programs*. Canberra: Australian Government Publishing Service.

Galbraith, J.K. 1985. *Anatomy of Power*. London: Corgi.

———. 1991. 'The New World Order'. *Guardian Studies* April:13–18.

Gellner, E. 1992. *Postmodernism, Reason and Religion*. London: Routledge.

George, S. 1992. *The Debt Boomerang: How Third World Debt Harms Us All*. London: Pluto Press.

———. 1993. 'Debt as Warfare'. *The Ploughshares Monitor* 14, no. 2:1–4.

Giddens, A. 1968. 'Power in the Recent Writings of Talcott Parsons'. *Sociology* 2, no. 3:257–72.

———. 1979. *Central Problems in Social Theory: Action, Structure and Contradiction in Social Analysis*. London: Macmillan.

———. 1981. *The Class Structure of the Advanced Societies* (2nd ed.). London: Hutchison.

———. 1984. *The Constitution of Society*. Cambridge: Polity Press.

———. 1985. *The Nation–State and Violence*, Vol. 2 of *A Contemporary Historical Materialism*. Cambridge: Polity Press.

———. 1987. *Social Theory and Modern Sociology*. Cambridge: Polity Press.

———. 1990. *The Consequences of Modernity*. Cambridge: Polity Press.

———. 1991. *Modernity and Self-Identity: Self and Society in the Late Modern Age*. Stanford: Stanford University Press.

Gillborn, D., and D. Drew. 1992. '"Race", Class and School Effects'. *New Community* 18, no. 4:551–65.

Gilroy, P. 1982. 'Police and Thieves'. In *The Empire Strikes Back: Race and Racism in 70's Britain*, edited by the Centre for Contemporary Studies. London: Hutchinson.

Glavovic, P.D. 1987. 'State Policy, Agriculture and Environmental Values'. In *Race and the Law in South Africa*, edited by A.J. Rycroft et al. Cape Town: Juta.

Glazer, N. 1975. *Affirmative Discrimination: Ethnic Inequality and Public Policy*. New York: Basic Books.

———, and D.P. Moynihan. 1963. *Beyond the Melting Pot*. Cambridge: MIT Press.

———, and D.P. Moynihan, eds. 1975. *Ethnicity: Theory and Experience*. Cambridge: Harvard University Press.

———, and K. Young. 1983. *Ethnic Pluralism and Public Policy: Achieving Equality in the United States and Britain*. Lexington: D.C. Heath & Co.

Gleditsch, N.P., and O. Njolstadt, eds. 1990. *Arms Races: Technological and Political Dynamics*. Newbury Park: Sage Publications.

Gleick, J. 1987. *Chaos: Making a New Science*. New York: Viking.

Gleick, P.H., and M.R. Lowi. 1992. *Water and Conflict: Occasional Paper, No. 1*. Toronto: University of Toronto, Peace and Conflict Studies Program.

Glenn, H.P. 1992. *Strangers at the Gate: Refugees, Illegal Entrants and Procedural Justice*. Montreal: Les editions Yvon Blais Inc.

Gobineau, A. 1915. *The Inequality of Human Races*. London: Heinemann.

Goldlust, J., and A.H. Richmond. 1974. 'A Multivariate Model of Immigrant Adaptation'. *International Migration Review* 8, no. 2:193–225.

Goodwin-Gill, G.S. 1986. 'International Law and the Detention of Refugees and Asylum Seekers'. *International Migration Review* 20, no. 2:193–219.

———. 1989. 'International Law and Human Rights: Trends Concerning International Migrants and Refugees'. *International Migration Review* 23, no. 3:526–46.

Gordenker, L. 1986. 'Early Warning of Disastrous Population Movement'. *International Migration Review* 20, no. 2:170–92.

Gordon, M.M. 1978. *Human Nature, Class and Ethnicity*. New York: Oxford University Press.

Gordon, P. 1989. *Fortress Europe? The Meaning of 1992*. London: Runnymede Trust.

Gorman, R. 1986. 'Beyond ICARA II: Implementing Refugee-Related Development Assistance'. *International Migration Review* 20, no. 2:283–98.

Gramsci, A. 1988. *An Antonio Gramsci Reader: Selected Writings 1916–1935*. Edited by D. Forgues. New York: Schocken Books.

Grey, J. 1989. 'Refugee Legislation in Canada'. In *The Refugee Crisis: British and Canadian Responses*. Oxford: Refugee Studies Programme, Queen Elizabeth College.

Gunasekaran, S. 1990. *Cross-National Labour Migration within Asia: Patterns and Problems*. Nagoya: UN Centre for Regional Development, Expert Group Meeting on Cross-National Labour Migration in the Asian Region.

Gurr, T.R. 1970. *Why Men Rebel*. Princeton: Princeton University Press.

———, and H.D. Graham, eds. 1989. *Violence in America*. Beverly Hills: Sage Publications.

Habermas, J. 1976. *Legitimation Crisis*. London: Heinemann.

———. 1990. *Moral Consciousness and Communicative Action*. Cambridge: Polity Press.

Hall, S. 1980. 'Race, Articulation and Societies Structured in Dominance'. In *Sociological Theories: Race and Colonialism*, edited by UNESCO. Paris: UNESCO.

Halli, S.S., F. Trovato, and L. Driedger, eds. 1990. *Ethnic Demography: Canadian Immigrant, Racial and Cultural Variations*. Ottawa: Carleton University Press.

Hammar, T. 1990a. *Democracy and the Nation State*. Aldershot: Avebury Gower.

———. 1990b. *Managing International Migration: Experiences, Emerging Trends, and Issues*. Nagoya: UN Centre for Regional Development, Expert Group Meeting on Cross-National Labour Migration in the Asian Region.

Hampson, F.O. 1990. 'Peace, Security and New Forms of International Governance'. In *Planet under Stress: The Challenge of Global Change*, edited by C. Mungall and D.J. McLaren. Toronto: Oxford University Press.

Hannerz, U. 1990. 'Cosmopolitans and Locals in World Culture'. In *Global Culture: Nationalism, Globalization and Modernity*, edited by M. Featherstone. London: Sage Publications.

Hannum, H. 1985. *The Right to Leave and Return in International Law and Practice*. Washington: International Law Unit.

Hansard. 1965. Parliamentary Debates (House of Commons), 23. London: Her Majesty's Stationery Office.

Hansen, A., and A. Oliver-Smith. 1981. *Forced Migration and Resettlement: The Problems and Responses of Dislocated Peoples*. Boulder: Westview Press.

Harrell-Bond, B. 1986. *Imposing Aid: Emergency Assistance to Refugees*. Oxford and New York: Oxford University Press.

Hathaway, J. 1992. 'The Conundrum of Refugee Protection in Canada: From Control to Compliance to Collective Deterrence'. *Journal of Policy History* 4, no. 1:71–91.

———, and L. MacMillan. 1993. *Rebuilding Trust: Report on Fundamental Justice in Information Gathering and Dissemination at the Immigration and Refugee Board of Canada*. Toronto: Osgoode Hall, York University.

Hawkins, F. 1988. *Canada and Immigration: Public Policy and Public Concern* (2nd ed.). Montreal: McGill-Queen's University Press.

————. 1989. *Critical Years in Immigration: Canada and Australia Compared*. Kingston and Montreal: McGill-Queen's University Press.

Hazarika, S. 1993. 'Bangladesh and Assam: Land Pressures, Migration and Ethnic Conflict'. Occasional Paper Series, project on environmental change and acute conflict. Cambridge and Toronto: American Academy of Sciences and University of Toronto.

Healey, D. 1991. 'The New World Order?' *Guardian Studies* 1, April:5–7.

Hechter, M. 1975. *Internal Colonialism: The Celtic Fringe in British National Development, 1536–1966*. Berkeley: University of California Press.

————. 1978. 'Group Formation and the Cultural Division of Labour'. *American Journal of Sociology* 84, no. 2:293–318.

————. 1986. 'Rational Choice Theory and the Study of Race'. In *Theories of Race and Ethnic Relations*, edited by J. Rex and D. Mason. Cambridge: Cambridge University Press.

Hein, J. 1993. 'Refugees, Immigrants and the State'. *Annual Review of Sociology* 19:43–59.

Helmes-Hayes, R. 1990. '"Hobhouse Twice Removed": John Porter and the LSE Years'. *Canadian Review of Sociology and Anthropology* 27, no. 3:357–89.

Henry, F. 1978. 'The Dynamics of Racism in Toronto: Research Report'. Toronto: York University.

Herberg, W. 1960. *Protestant, Catholic, Jew: An Essay on American Religious Sociology*. New York: Anchor.

Hewson, H.H. 1989. *Hedge of Wild Almonds: South Africa, the Pro-Boers and the Quaker Conscience*. London: James Currey Ltd.

Herman, E.S., and N. Chomsky. 1988. *Manufacturing Consent: The Political Economy of the Mass Media*. New York: Pantheon Books.

Hiebert, J. 1993. 'Rights and Public Debate: The Limitations of the "Rights Must Be Paramount" Perspective'. *International Journal of Canadian Studies* 7–8: 117–36.

Hobsbawm, E.J., and T. Ranger, eds. 1983. *The Invention of Tradition*. Cambridge: Cambridge University Press.

Hodgins, B.W., et al. 1989. *Federalism in Canada and Australia: Historical Perspectives 1920–1988*. Peterborough: Frost Centre, Trent University.

Hoffman-Nowotny, H. 1981. 'A Sociological Approach Towards a General Theory of Migration'. In *Global Trends in Migration*, edited by M.M. Kritz et al. New York: Center for Migration Studies.

Home Office. 1989. *Control of Immigration Statistics, United Kingdom 1988.* London: Her Majesty's Stationery Office.

Homer-Dixon, T.F. 1991. 'Environmental Change and Human Security'. *Behind the Headlines* 48, 3:7–16.

———, J.H. Boutwell, and G.W. Rathjens. 1993. 'Environmental Change and Violent Conflict'. *Scientific American* February:38–45.

Hubbel, D., and N. Rajesh. 1992. 'Thailand's Program of Reforestation by Forced Eviction: Not Seeing People for the Forest'. *Refuge* 12, no. 1:20–1.

Hulse, F.S. 1969. 'Ethnic, Caste and Genetic Miscegenation'. *Journal of Bio-Social Science*, Supplement no. 1.

Human Rights Newsletter. October 1990. Geneva: UN World Campaign for Human Rights.

———. April 1991. 'Commission on Human Rights Concludes Annual Session'. Geneva: UN World Campaign for Human Rights.

Husbands, C.T. 1991. 'The Support for the Front National: Analyses and Findings'. *Ethnic and Racial Studies* 14, no. 3:382–416.

Immigration Canada. 1989. *Immigration to Canada: A Statistical Review.* Ottawa: Canada Employment and Immigration.

Indian and Northern Affairs Canada. 1989. *Highlights of Aboriginal Conditions, vols 1–3.* Ottawa: Indian and Northern Affairs Canada.

International Migration Review. 1992. 'Migration and the Environment'. *International Migration Review* 30, no. 2:225–8.

Intriligator, M.D., and D.L. Briot. 1990. 'A Possible Future for the Arms Race'. In *Arms Races: Technological and Political Dynamics*, edited by N.P. Gleditsch and O. Njolstadt. London: Sage Publications.

IOM (International Organization for Migration). 1992. *Migration and the Environment.* Geneva: IOM and Refugee Policy Group.

Isajiw, W.W. 1990. 'Ethnic Identity Retention'. In *Ethnic Identity and Equality*, edited by R. Breton et al. Toronto: University of Toronto Press.

Jackson, J., ed. 1969. *Sociological Studies 2: Migration.* Cambridge: Cambridge University Press.

Jacobson, J. 1988. *Environmental Refugees: A Yardstick of Habitability.* Washington: Worldwatch Institute.

Jakubowicz, A. 1984. 'State and Ethnicity: Multiculturalism as Ideology". In *Ethnic Politics in Australia*, edited by J. Jupp. Sydney: Allen & Unwin.

Jameson, F. 1991. *Postmodernism, or the Cultural Logic of Late Capitalism.* Durham: Duke University Press.

JanMohamed, A.R., and D. Lloyd, eds. 1990. *The Nature and Context of Minority Discourse.* New York: Oxford University Press.

Jansen, C.J. 1970. 'Migration: A Sociological Problem'. In *Readings in the Sociology of Migration*, edited by C.J. Jansen. London: Pergamon Press.

Jencks, C. 1992. *The Postmodern Reader*. London: Academy Editions.

Joly, D. 1989. *Harmonising Asylum Policy in Europe*. Coventry: Centre for Research on Ethnic Relations, University of Warwick.

————, and R. Cohen. 1989. *Reluctant Hosts: Europe and Its Refugees*. Aldershot: Avebury Gower.

Jones, F.L. 1988. *The Recent Employment and Unemployment Experiences of First, Second and Later Generations of Immigrants in Australia*. Canberra: Office of Multicultural Affairs.

————. 1989. *Ancestry Groups in Australia: A Descriptive Overview*. Canberra: Office of Multicultural Affairs.

Jones, T. 1993. *Britain's Ethnic Minorities: An Analysis of the Labour Force Survey*. London: Policy Studies Institute.

Kalbach, W.E. 1990. 'Ethnic Residential Segregation and Its Significance for the Individual in an Urban Setting'. In *Ethnic Identity and Equality*, edited by R. Breton et al. Toronto: University of Toronto Press.

Kalin, W. 1986. 'Troubled Communications: Cross-Cultural Misunderstandings in the Asylum Hearing'. *International Migration Review* 20, no. 2:230–44.

Kasinsky, R.G. 1976. *Refugees from Militarism: Draft-Age Americans in Canada*. New Brunswick: Transaction Books.

Keely, C. 1981. *Global Refugee Policy: The Case for a Development-Oriented Strategy*. New York: The Population Council.

Keller, S.W. 1975. *Uprooting and Social Change: The Role of Refugees in Development*. Delhi: Manohar Book Service.

Kelley, J., and C. Bean, eds. 1988. *Australian Attitudes*. Sydney: Allen & Unwin.

Kennedy, P. 1993. *Preparing for the Twenty-First Century*. Toronto: Harper-Collins.

King, A.D. 1990. *Global Cities: Post-Imperialism and the Internationalization of London*. London and New York: Routledge.

King, M. 1993. 'The Impact of Western European Border Policies on the Control of Refugees in Eastern and Central Europe'. *New Community* 19, no. 2:183–200.

Kondrashov, S. 1991. 'Domestic Issues Place Shackles on Soviet Foreign Policy'. *Los Angeles Times*, 15 January, H2.

Kosinski, L., and P. Mansill. 1975. *People on the Move*. London: Methuen.

Kraly, E.P., and R. Warren. 1991. 'Long-Term Immigration to the United States: A New Approach to Measurement'. *International Migration Review* 25, no. 1:60–92.

Krause, K. 1992. *Arms and the State: Patterns of Military Production and Trade*. Cambridge: Cambridge University Press.

Kritz, M.M., et al. *Global Trends in Migration: Theory and Research on International Population Movements*. New York: Center for Migration Studies.

————, ed. 1983. *U.S. Immigration and Refugee Policy: Global and Domestic Issues*. Lexington: D.C. Heath.

Krotki, K., and D. Odynak. 1990. 'The Emergence of Multiethnicities in the 1980's'. In *Ethnic Demography*, edited by S.S. Halli et al. Ottawa: Carleton University Press.

Kubat, D., and H. Hoffman-Nowotny. 1981. 'Migration: Towards a New Paradigm'. *International Social Science Journal* 33, no. 2:307–29.

Kumar, K. 1978. *Prophecy & Progress: The Sociology of Industrial and Post-Industrial Society*. Harmondsworth: Penguin Books.

Kunz, E. 1973. 'The Refugee in Flight: Kinetic Models and Forms of Displacement'. *International Migration Review* 7, no. 2:125–46.

————. 1981. 'Exile and Resettlement: Refugee Theory'. *International Migration Review* 15, no. 1:42–51.

Laferriere, M. 1978. 'The Education of Black Students in Montreal Schools: An Emerging Anglophone Problem'. In *Ethnic Canadians: Culture and Education*, edited by M.L. Kovacs. Regina: Canadian Plains Research Centre.

Laing, R.D. 1960. *The Self and Others: Further Studies in Sanity and Madness*. New York: Pantheon.

Lal, B.B. 1986. 'The "Chicago School" of American Sociology, Symbolic Interactionism and Race Relations Theory'. In *Theories of Race and Ethnic Relations*, edited by J. Rex and D. Mason. Cambridge: Cambridge University Press.

Lam, L. 1983. 'Vietnamese Chinese Refugees in Montreal'. Unpublished doctoral dissertation, York University.

Lassailly-Jacob, V., and M. Zmolek, eds. 1992. 'Environmental Refugees'. *Refuge* 12, no. 1:1–4.

Lee, E. 1969. 'A Theory of Migration'. In *Sociological Studies 2: Migration*, edited by J. Jackson. Cambridge: Cambridge University Press.

Leiken, R.D., ed. 1984. *Central America: Anatomy of a Conflict*. New York: Pergamon.

Lewins, F. 1987. 'The "Blainey Debate" in Hindsight'. *Australian and New Zealand Journal of Sociology* 23, no. 2:261–73.

Lewis, C. 1989. *The Report of the Race Relations and Policing Task Force*. Toronto: Office of the Ontario Solicitor General.

Lewis, S. 1992. *Report on Race Relations in Ontario*. Toronto: Office of the Premier, Queen's Park.

Li, P., ed. 1990. *Race and Ethnic Relations in Ontario*. Toronto: Oxford University Press.

Lieberson, S., and A.R. Silverman. 1965. 'The Precipitating and Underlying Conditions of Race Riots'. *American Sociological Review* 30, 6:887–98.

——, and M.C. Waters. 1988. *From Many Strands: Ethnic & Racial Groups in Contemporary America*. New York: Russell Sage.

Loescher, G. 1992. *Refugee Movements and International Security*. London: Brassey.

Long, R.E., ed. 1992. *Immigration to the United States (The Reference Shelf)*. New York: H.W. Wilson Co.

Lovelock, J.E. 1987. *A New Look at Life on Earth*. London: Oxford University Press.

——. 1988. *The Ages of Gaia: A Biography of Our Living Earth*. London: Oxford University Press.

Luciuk, L.Y. 1986. 'Unintended Consequences in Refugee Settlement: Postwar Ukrainian Refugee Immigrants in Canada'. *International Migration Review* 20, no. 2:467–82.

Lundahl, M. 1979. *Peasants and Poverty: A Study of Haiti*. London: Croom Helm.

Lutz, W., C. Prinz, and J. Langgassner. 1993. 'World Population Projections and Possible Ecological Feedbacks'. *Population Network Newsletter* 23:1–11.

Lynch, M.A. 1990. 'Australian Immigration: Policy Development'. *Immigration History and Policy: Australia and Canada*, edited by P. Hanks. Victoria: Monash University.

Mabin, A. 1987. 'Unemployment, Resettlement and Refugees in South Africa'. In *Refugees: A Third World Dilemma*, edited by J.R. Rogge. Totowa: Rowman & Littlefield.

Mabogunje, A.L. 1970. 'Systems Approach to a Theory of Rural-Urban Migration'. *Geographical Analysis* 2, no. 1:1–18.

McAll, C. 1991. 'Beyond Culture: Immigration in Contemporary Quebec' (Working Paper No. 25). Ottawa: Economic Council of Canada.

McDade, K. 1988. *Barriers to the Recognition of the Credentials of Immigrants in Canada*. Ottawa: Institute for Research on Public Policy.

McGarry, J., and B. O'Leary. 1993. *Politics of Ethnic Conflict Regulation: Case Studies of Protracted Ethnic Conflict*. London: Routledge.

McLellan, J. 1987. 'Religion and Ethnicity: The Role of Buddhism in Maintaining Ethnic Identity'. *Canadian Ethnic Studies* 19, 1:64–76.

——, and A.H. Richmond. 1994. 'Multiculturalism in Crisis: A Postmodern Perspective on Canada'. *Ethnic and Racial Studies*. Forthcoming.

McLuhan, M. 1964. *Understanding Media: The Extension of Man*. New York: McGraw Hill.

MacMillan, L. 1993. 'The Review of Rejected Refugee Claims'. *Refuge* 12, no. 6:1–3.

McNeill, W.H. 1983. *The Great Frontier: Freedom and Hierarchy*. Princeton: Princeton University Press.

Majthay, A. 1985. *Foundations of Catastrophe Theory*. Boston: Pitman.

Mangalam, J.J. 1968. *Human Migration: A Guide to Migration Literature in English*. Lexington: University of Kentucky Press.

Manpower and Immigration. 1974. *Three Years in Canada*. Ottawa: Supply and Services.

Markus, A., and R. Rasmussen. 1987. *Prejudice in the Public Arena: Racism*. Melbourne: Centre for Migrant and Intercultural Studies, Monash University.

Marr, W.L. 1986. 'Are the Canadian Foreign-Born Under-represented in Canada's Occupational Structure?' *International Migration Review* 24, no. 4:769–75.

Marrus, M.R. 1985. *The Unwanted: European Refugees in the Twentieth Century*. Oxford: Oxford University Press.

Marshall, T.H. 1965. *Class, Citizenship and Social Development*. Garden City: Doubleday.

Martin, P.L. 1990. *Foreign Workers in the United States: Past, Present and Future*. Nagoya: UN Centre for Regional Development, Expert Group Meeting on Cross-National Labour Migration in the Asian Region.

Mason, D. 1986. 'Controversies and Continuities in Race and Ethnic Relations Theory'. In *Theories of Race and Ethnic Relations*. Cambridge: Cambridge University Press.

Matas, D. 1989. *Closing the Doors: The Failure of Refugee Protection*. Toronto: Summerhill Press.

Mazur, R.E. 1988. 'Refugees in Africa: The Role of Sociological Analysis and Praxis'. *Current Sociology* 36, no. 2:43–60.

Meissner, D., et al. 1986. *Legalization of Undocumented Aliens: Lessons from Other Countries*. Washington: Carnegie Endowment Fund.

Michalowski, M. 1991. 'Foreign Temporary Residents to Canada: Short-Term Movers or Long-Term Immigrants?' Paper presented to American Population Association meetings, Washington: American Population Association.

———. 1993. 'Redefining the Concept of Immigration to Canada'. *Canadian Studies in Population* 20, no. 1:59–84.

Migration News Sheet. February 1992. Brussels: European Information Network.

Miles, R. 1987. *Capitalism and Unfree Labour: Anomoly or Necessity?* London and New York: Tavistock Publications.

———, and A. Phizakalea. 1980. *White Man's Country: Racism in British Politics*. London: Pluto Press.

Miller, R.M. 1992. 'An Overview of the Immigration Act 1990'. In *In Defence of the Alien, Vol. 14*, edited by L. Tomasi. New York: Center for Migration Studies.

Mills, C.W. 1956. *The Power Elite*. New York: Oxford University Press.

Minister for Immigration and Ethnic Affairs. 1988. *News Release*, 8 December. Canberra: Minister for Immigration and Ethnic Affairs.

Moynihan, D.P. 1993. *Pandaemonium: Ethnicity in International Politics*. New York: Oxford University Press.

Mumford, L. 1938. *The Culture of Cities*. New York: Harcourt Brace.

Mungall, C., and D.J. McLaren, eds. 1990. *Planet under Stress*. Toronto: Oxford University Press.

Myrdal, A. 1976. *The Game of Disarmament: How the United States and Russia Run the Arms Race*. New York: Pantheon Books.

Myrdal, G. 1944. *An American Dilemma: The Negro Problem and Modern Democracy*. New York: Harper.

Nagata, J. 1985. 'Religion, Ethnicity and Language: Indonesian Chinese Immigrants in Toronto'. Paper presented at symposium, Australian National University, Melbourne.

Nash, A. 1987. *The Economic Impact of the Entrepreneur Program*. Ottawa: Institute for Research on Public Policy.

———. 1989. *International Refugee Pressures and the Canadian Public Policy Response*. Ottawa: Institute for Research on Public Policy.

Newcomb, T.M., and B.M. Hartley, eds. 1947. *Readings in Social Psychology*. New York: Holt.

Nova Scotia Royal Commission. 1989. 'On the Donald Marshall, Jr. Prosecution'. *Digest of Findings and Recommendations*. Halifax: The Royal Commission.

O'Neill, J. 1972. *Sociology as a Skin Trade: Towards a Reflexive Sociology*. New York: Harper Torchbooks.

———, ed. 1973. *Modes of Individualism and Collectivism*. London: Heinemann.

———. 1985. 'Decolonization and the Ideal Speech Community: Some Issues in the Theory and Practice of Communicative Competence'. In *Critical Theory and Public Life*, edited by J. Forrester. Cambridge: MIT Press.

———. 1988a. 'Religion and Postmodernism: The Durkheimian Bond'. *Theory, Culture and Society* 5, 2–3:403–508.

———. 1988b. 'Techno-culture and the Specular Functions of Ethnicity: With a Methodological Note'. In *Ethnicity in a Technological Age*, edited by I.H. Angus. Edmonton: University of Alberta Press.

———. 1990. 'AIDS as a Globalizing Panic'. In *Global Culture: Nationalism, Globalization and Modernity*, edited by M. Featherstone. London: Sage Publications.

Office of Multicultural Affairs (Australia). 1989. *Issues in Multicultural Australia 1988*. Canberra: Department of Prime Minister and Cabinet.

Ohmae, K. 1990. *The Borderless World: Power and Strategy in the Interlinked Economy*. New York: Harper.

Ornstein, M., and R.D. Sharma. 1983. *Adjustment and Economic Experience of Immigrants in Canada: An Analysis of the 1976 Longitudinal Survey of Immigrants*. Toronto: Institute for Behavioural Research, York University.

Ostow, R. 1984. 'Everett Hughes: The McGill Years'. *Society/Société* 8, no. 3:12–16.

———. 1991. *Ethnicity, Structured Inequality and the State in Canada and the Federal Republic of Germany*. New York: Lang.

Otunnu, O. 1992. 'Environmental Refugees in Sub-Saharan Africa: Causes and Effects'. *Refuge* 12, no. 1:11–14.

Palantzas, T. 1991. 'A Search for "Autonomy" at Canada's First Sociology Department'. *Society/Société* 15, no. 2:10–18.

Papademetriou, D.G. 1991. *The Immigration Act of 1990*. Washington: US Department of Labor.

Parsons, T. 1951. *The Social System*. Glencoe: The Free Press.

———. 1960. 'The Distribution of Power in American Society'. In *Structure and Process in Industrial Societies*, edited by T. Parsons. Glencoe: The Free Press.

———. 1961. *The Structure of Social Action*. Glencoe: The Free Press.

———. 1963. 'On the Concept of Influence'. *Public Opinion Quarterly* 27:37–62.

———. 1971. *The Systems of Modern Societies*. Englewood Cliffs: Prentice-Hall.

Patel, D. 1980. *Dealing with Interracial Conflict: Policy Alternatives*. Montreal: The Institute for Research on Public Policy.

Peach, C., et al. 1986. *Ethnic Segregation in Cities*. London: Croom Helm.

Pedraza-Bailey, S. 1985. *Political and Economic Migrants in America*. Austin: University of Texas Press.

Peter, K. 1982. 'The Myth of Multiculturalism and Other Political Fables'. In *Ethnicity, Power and Politics in Canada*, edited by J. Dahlie and T. Fernando. Toronto: Methuen.

Petersen, W. 1958. 'A General Typology of Migration'. *American Sociological Review* 23, no. 3:256–65.

Petras, E. 1981. 'The Global Labour Market in the Modern World Economy'. In *Global Trends in Migration: Theory and Research on International Population Movements*, edited by M.M. Kritz, C.B. Keely, and S.M. Tomasi. New York: Center for Migration Studies.

Plaut, W.G. 1985. *Refugee Determination in Canada*. Ottawa: Supply and Services Canada.

Porter, J. 1965. *The Vertical Mosaic*. Toronto: University of Toronto Press.

Portes, A. 1983. 'International Labor Migration and National Development'. In

U.S. Immigration and Refugee Policy: Global and Domestic Issues, edited by M.M. Kritz. Lexington: D.C. Heath and Co.

——, and J. Borocz. 1989. 'Contemporary Immigration: Theoretical Perspectives on Its Determinants and Modes of Incorporation'. *International Migration Review* 23, no. 3:606–30.

——, and R. Mozo. 1985. 'The Political and Adaptation Process of Cubans and Other Ethnic Minorities in the United States'. *International Migration Review* 51, no. 6:35–63.

——, and A. Stepick. 1985. 'Unwelcome Immigrants: The Labour Market Experience of Cuban and Haitian Refugees in South Florida'. *American Sociological Review* 50, no. 4:493–514.

Poster, M. 1990. *The Mode of Information: Poststructuralism and Social Context.* Chicago: University of Chicago Press.

Poulantzas, N.A. 1975. *Classes in Contemporary Capitalism.* London: NLB.

Price, C. 1969. 'Assimilation'. In *Sociological Studies 11: Migration*, edited by J. Jackson. Cambridge: Cambridge University Press.

Price, E. 1985. 'Refugee and Mass Migration'. Paper presented at a meeting of the International Sociological Association Research Committee on Migration, Dubrovnick.

——. 1987. 'Australia: Multicultural and Non-racist'. *New Community* 14, no. 1–2:241–4.

——. 1989. *Ethnic Groups in Australia.* Canberra: Office of Multicultural Affairs.

Pryor, E.T., et al. 1990. *Migration between the United States and Canada.* Ottawa: Statistics Canada.

Rabinow, P., ed. 1984. *The Foucault Reader.* New York: Pantheon.

Radhakrishnan, R. 1990. 'Ethnic Identity and Post-Structuralist Difference'. In *The Nature and Context of Minority Discourse*, edited by A.R. JanMohamed and D. Lloyd. New York: Oxford University Press.

Ramcharan, S. 1982. *Racism: Non-Whites in Canada.* Toronto: Butterworths.

Rampton, A. 1981. *Committee of Inquiry: West Indian Children in Our Schools.* London: Her Majesty's Stationery Office.

Rao, G.L., et al. 1984. *Immigrants in Canada and Australia, Vol. 1: Demographic Aspects and Education.* Toronto: Institute for Behavioural Research, York University.

Rattansi, A. 1992. 'Changing the Subject: Racism, Culture and Education'. In *'Race', Culture and Difference.* London: Sage Publications.

Ravenstein, E.G. 1885. 'The Laws of Migration'. *Journal of the Royal Statistical Society* 48:242–305.

Regher, E. 1992. 'A World Made Safe for War? Armed Conflicts in the World, 1992'. *Ploughshares Monitor* 13, no. 4:13–17.

———. 1993. 'Canada's Military Exports to the Third World in 1992: Arming the Repression'. *Ploughshares Monitor* 14, no. 3:8–11.

Reid, A. 1989. *Attitudes and Perceptions of Selected Dimensions of Refugee and Immigration Policy in Canada*. Ottawa: Canada Employment and Immigration.

Reitz, J.G. 1988. 'The Institutional Structure of Immigration as a Determinant of Inter-Racial Competition: A Comparison of Britain and Canada'. *International Migration Review* 22, no. 1:117–46.

Review of Demography. 1989. *Charting Canada's Future*. Ottawa: Health and Welfare Canada.

Rex, J. 1981. *Social Conflict: A Conceptual and Theoretical Analysis*. London: Longman.

———. 1985. 'Kantianism: Methodological Individualism and Michael Banton'. *Ethnic and Racial Studies* 8, no. 4:548–62.

———. 1986. *Race and Ethnicity*. Milton Keynes: Open University Press.

———, and D. Mason, eds. 1986. *Theories of Race and Ethnic Relations*. Cambridge: Cambridge University Press.

———, and R. Moore. 1967. *Race, Community and Conflict: A Study of Sparkbrooke*. London: Oxford University Press.

Rex, J., and S. Tomlinson. 1979. *Colonial Immigrants in a British City: A Class Analysis*. London: Routledge.

Richmond, A.H. 1950. 'Economic Insecurity and Stereotypes as Factors in Colour Prejudice'. *Sociological Review* 17:147–70.

———. 1954. *West Indian Workers in Liverpool, 1941–1951*. London: Routledge & Kegan Paul.

———. 1955. *The Colour Problem: A Study of Racial Relations*. Harmondsworth: Penguin Books.

———. 1961. *The Colour Problem* (rev. ed.). Harmondsworth: Penguin Books.

———. 1967. *Postwar Immigrants in Canada*. Toronto: University of Toronto Press.

———. 1969. 'Sociology of Migration in Industrial and Postindustrial Societies'. In *Sociological Studies 2: Migration*, edited by J. Jackson. Cambridge: Cambridge University Press.

———. 1974. *Aspects of the Absorption and Adaptation of Immigrants*. Ottawa: Manpower and Immigration.

———. 1976. 'Urban Ethnic Conflict in Britain and Canada: A Comparative Perspective'. In *Urban Ethnic Conflict: A Comparative Perspective*, edited by S.E. Clarke and J.L. Obler. Chapel Hill: Institute for Research in Social Science, University of North Carolina.

———. 1980. 'Environmental Conservation: A New Racist Ideology?' In *Sourcebook on the New Immigration*, edited by R.S. Bryce Laporte. New Jersey: Transaction Books.

———. 1984. 'Ethnic Nationalism and Postindustrialism'. *Ethnic and Racial Studies* 7, no. 1:4–18.

———. 1986. 'Ethnogenerational Variation in Educational Achievement'. *Canadian Ethnic Studies* 18, no. 3:75–89.

———. 1988a. 'Sociological Theories of International Migration: The Case of Refugees'. *Current Sociology* 36, no. 2:7–25.

———. 1988b. *Race and Violence in Britain: A Systems Analysis*. Toronto: The LaMarsh Research Program, York University.

———. 1988c. *Immigration and Ethnic Conflict*. London: Macmillan.

———. 1989. *Caribbean Immigrants in Canada: A Demo-Economic Analysis*. Ottawa: Statistics Canada.

———. 1990. 'Race Relations and Immigration: A Comparative Perspective'. *International Journal of Comparative Sociology* 21, 3–4:156–76.

———. 1991a. 'Immigration and Multiculturalism in Canada and Australia: The Contradictions and Crises of the 1980s'. *International Journal of Canadian Studies* (Spring):87–110.

———. 1991b. 'Foreign-Born Labour in Canada: Past Patterns, Emerging Trends and Implications'. *Regional Development Dialogue* 12, no. 3:145–61.

———. 1992. 'Immigration and Structural Change: The Canadian Experience 1971–1986'. *International Migration Review* 26, no. 4:1200–21.

———. 1993a. 'Reactive Migration: Sociological Aspects of Refugee Movements'. *Journal of Refugee Studies* 6, no. 1:7–24.

———. 1993b. 'Education and Qualifications of Caribbean Migrants in Metropolitan Toronto'. *New Community* 19, no. 2:263–80.

———. 1994. 'International Migration and Global Change'. In *Asian Transmigration*, edited by J.H. Ong, K.B. Chan, and S.B. Chew. Singapore: Prentice-Hall.

———, et al. 1989. 'Some Consequences of Third World Immigration to Canada'. In *The Impact of International Migration on Developing Countries*, edited by R. Appleyard. Paris: Organization for Economic Co-operation and Development, Development Centre.

———, and W.E. Kalbach. 1980. *Factors in the Adjustment of Immigrants and Their Descendants*. Ottawa: Statistics Canada.

———, and A. Mendoza. 1990. 'Education and Qualifications of Caribbean Immigrants and Their Children in Britain and Canada'. In *In Search of a Better Life: Perspective on Migration from the Caribbean*, edited by R.W. Palmer. New York: Praeger.

——, and R.B.P. Verma. 1978. 'The Economic Adaptation of Immigrants: A New Theoretical Perspective'. *International Migration Review* 17, no. 1:3–28.

——, and J. Zubrzycki. 1974. *Immigrants in Canada and Australia, Vol. 2*. Toronto: Institute for Behavioural Research, York University.

Riesman, D. 1958. *The Lonely Crowd: A Study of the Changing American Character*. New York: Doubleday.

Robertson, M.K. 1987. 'Orderly Urbanization: The New Influx Control'. In *Race and the Law in South Africa*, edited by A.J. Rycroft et al. Cape Town: Juta.

Robertson, R. 1990a. 'Mapping the Global Condition: Globalization as the Central Concept'. In *Global Culture: Nationalism, Globalization and Modernity*, edited by M. Featherstone. London: Sage Publications.

——. 1990b. 'After Nostalgia? Wilful Nostalgia and the Phases of Globalization'. In *Theories of Modernity and Postmodernity*, edited by B.S. Turner. London: Sage Publications.

——. 1992. *Globalization: Social Theory and Global Culture*. Newbury Park: Sage Publications.

——, and J. Chirico. 1985. 'Humanity, Globalization and Worldwide Religious Resurgence'. *Sociological Analysis* 46:219–42.

Robinson, B. 1992. '1992–93 Military Budget: Stills Swords, Not Ploughshares'. *Ploughshares Monitor* 13, no. 2:1–3.

Rockefeller, S.C. 1992. 'Comment'. In *Multiculturalism and the 'Politics of Recognition'*, edited by C. Taylor. Princeton: Princeton University Press.

Rodal, A. 1987. *Nazi War Criminals in Canada: The Historical and Policy Setting from the 1940s to the Present*. Ottawa: Supply and Services Canada.

Roderick, R. 1986. *Habermas and the Foundations of Critical Theory*. London: Macmillan.

Rogers, R. 1992. 'The Future of Refugee Flows and Policies'. *International Migration Review* 26, no. 4:1112–43.

Rogg, E.M. 1974. *The Assimilation of Cuban Exiles: The Role of Community and Class*. New York: Aberdeen Press.

Rogge, J.R. 'Some Comments on Definitions and Typologies of Refugees'. *Zambian Geographical Journal* no. 33–34, cited in *Refuge* 2, no. 5:12.

Rose, E.J.B., et al. 1969. *Colour and Citizenship: A Report on British Race Relations*. London: Oxford University Press.

Rose, M. 1991. *The Post-modern and the Post-industrial: A Critical Analysis*. Cambridge: Cambridge University Press.

Rose, P.I. 1981. 'Some Thoughts about Refugees and the Descendants of Theseus'. *International Migration Review* 15, no. 1–2:8–15.

Ross, R.J.S., and K.C. Trachte. 1990. *Global Capitalism: The Leviathan*. Albany: State University of New York Press.

Rossi, P.H. 1985. *Why Families Move*. Glencoe: The Free Press.

Runnymede Trust. 1989. 'Immigration Statistics'. *Race and Immigration* (September) 228:5–6.

Russell, P.H. 1993. 'Attempting Macro Constitutional Change in Australia and Canada'. *International Journal of Canadian Studies* 7, no. 8:41–62.

Salt, J. 1992. 'The Future of International Labour Migration'. *International Migration Review* 26, no. 4:1077–1111.

———, and R.T. Kitching. 1990. 'Labour Migration and the Work Permit System in the United Kingdom'. *International Migration Review* 28, no. 3:267–94.

Samson, A. 1977. *The Arms Bazaar.* London: Hodder & Stoughton.

Samuel, J.T. 1987. *Immigration and Visible Minorities in the Year 2001: A Projection*. Ottawa: Carleton University Press.

Sassen, S. 1988. *The Mobility of Labour and Capital*. Cambridge: Cambridge University Press.

———. 1991. *The Global City*. Princeton: Princeton University Press.

———. 1993. 'Economic Internationalism: The New Migration in Japan and the United States'. *International Migration Review* 31, no. 1:73–102.

———. 1994. *Cities in a World Economy*. Thousand Oaks: Pine Forge Press.

Sassen-Koob, S. 1986. 'New York City: Economic Restructuring and Immigration'. *Development and Change* 17, no. 1:85–119.

Satzewich, V. 1988. 'The Canadian State and the Racialization of Caribbean Migrant Farm Labour, 1947–1966'. *Ethnic and Racial Studies* 11, no. 3:282–304.

———. 1991. *Racism and the Incorporation of Foreign Labour: Farm Labour Migration to Canada Since 1945*. London: Routledge.

Saul, J.R. 1992. *Voltaire's Bastards: The Dictatorship of Reason in the West*. Toronto: Penguin Books.

Scarman, Lord. 1981. *The Brixton Disorders, 10–12 April 1981*. London: Her Majesty's Stationery Office.

Schlesinger, Jr, A.M. 1992. *The Disuniting of America: Reflections on a Multicultural Society*. New York: W.W. Norton Co.

Schumacher, E.F. 1973. *Small Is Beautiful: A Study of Economics As If People Mattered*. London: Blond and Briggs.

Sciulli, D. 1986. 'Voluntaristic Action as a Distinct Concept: Theoretical Foundations of Societal Constitutionalism'. *American Sociological Review* 51, no. 6:743–66.

Seccombe, I.J. 1988. 'International Migration in the Middle East: Historical Trends, Contemporary Patterns and Consequences'. In *International Migration Today, Vol. 1: Trends and Prospects*, edited by R. Appleyard. Paris: UNESCO.

Seidman, S., and D.J. Wagner, eds. 1992. *Postmodernism and Social Theory: The Debate over General Theory*. Cambridge: Blackwell.

Serow, W.J., et al., eds. 1990. *Handbook of International Migration*. New York: Greenwood Press.

Seward, S. 1990. *Challenges of Labour Adjustment: The Case of Immigrant Women in the Clothing Industry*. Ottawa: Institute for Research on Public Policy.

———, and M. Tremblay. 1989. *Immigrants in the Canadian Labour Force: Their Role in Structural Change*. Ottawa: Institute for Research in Public Policy.

———. 1990. 'Immigration and the Changing Labour Market'. Paper presented at the Canadian Population Society, Victoria, BC.

———. 1991. *Immigrants in Canada: Their Response to Structural Change (1981–1986)*. Ottawa: Institute for Research on Public Policy.

Sharma, R.D. 1981a. *Perceived Difficulties of Foreign-Born Population and Services of Agencies*. Toronto: Institute for Behaviour Research, York University.

———. 1981b. *Immigrant Needs in Metropolitan Toronto*. Toronto: Ontario Council of Agencies Serving Immigrants.

Shaw, C. 1988. 'Latest Estimates of Ethnic Minority Populations'. *Population Trends* 51.

Simey, M. 1985. *Government by Consent: The Principle and Practice of Accountability in Local Government*. London: Bedford Square Press.

Simmons, A. 1985–6. 'Recent Studies in Place-Utility and Intentions to Migrate in International Comparison'. *Population and Environment* 8, no. 1–2:120–41.

———. 1990. '"New Wave" Immigrants: Origins and Characteristics'. In *Ethnic Demography: Canadian Immigrants, Racial and Cultural Variations*, edited by S.S. Halli et al. Ottawa: Carleton University Press.

———, et al. 1977. *Social Change and Internal Migration: A Review of Findings from Africa, Asia and Latin America*. Ottawa: International Development Research Centre.

Singer, D. 1991. 'The Resistable Rise of Jean-Marie Le Pen'. *Ethnic and Racial Studies* 14, no. 3:368–81.

Sivard, R.L. 1985. *World Military and Social Expenditures, 1985*. Washington: World Priorities, Inc.

Skerry, P. 1982. 'Commentary'. In *Immigration, Language and Ethnicity: Canada and the United States*, edited by B.R. Chiswick. Washington: AEI Press.

———. 1993. *Mexican Americans: The Ambivalent Minority*. New York: Free Press.

Smil, V., and J.A. Gladstone. 1992. 'Environmental Change and Acute Conflict', Occasional Paper No. 2. Toronto: Peace and Conflict Studies Program.

Smith, A.D. 1981. *The Ethnic Revival in the Modern World*. Cambridge: Cambridge University Press.

———. 1989. 'The Origins of Nations'. *Ethnic and Racial Studies* 12, no. 3:340–67.

———. 1991. *National Identity*. Harmondsworth: Penguin Books.

———. 1992. 'Chosen Peoples: Why Ethnic Groups Survive'. *Ethnic and Racial Studies* 15, no. 2:435–56.

Smith, D.J., and S. Tomlinson. 1989. *The School Effect: A Study of Multi-Racial Comprehensives*. London: Policy Studies Institute.

Smith, M.G. 1985. 'Race and Ethnic Relations as Matters of Rational Choice'. *Ethnic and Racial Studies* 8, no. 4:484–99.

Smolowe, J. 1991. 'The Arsenal: Who Armed Baghdad?' *Time*, 11 February:34–5.

Sniderman, P.M. 1993. *Working Papers on Anti-Semitism in Quebec*. Toronto: Institute for Social Research, York University.

Sommer, T. 1991. 'The New World Order'. *Guardian Studies* April:33–7.

Sorokin, P.A. [1942] 1968. *Man and Society in Calamity: The Effects of War, Revolution, Famine, Pestilence Upon the Human Mind, Behavior, Social Organization and Cultural Life*. New York: Dutton.

Sparks, A. 1990. *The Mind of South Africa*. New York: Alfred A. Knopf.

Spicer, K. 1991. *Citizens' Forum on Canada's Future*. Ottawa: Supply and Services.

Stahl, C., ed. 1988. *International Migration Today, Vol 2: Emerging Issues*. Paris: UNESCO.

Stasiulis, D.K. 1990. 'Theorizing Connection: Gender, Race, Ethnicity and Class'. In *Race and Ethnic Relations in Canada*, edited by P. Li. Toronto: Oxford University Press.

Statistics Canada. 1984. *Canada's Immigrants*. Ottawa: Supply and Services.

———. 1989a. *User's Guide to the Quality of 1986 Census Data: Sampling and Weighting*. Ottawa: Statistics Canada.

———. 1989b. *1986 Census of Canada: Profile of Immigrants*, Cat. 93–155. Ottawa: Supply and Services.

———. 1990. *International Travel, National and Provincial Counts, Education, Culture and Tourism*. Ottawa: Supply and Services.

Stein, B.N. 1981. 'The Refugee Experience: Defining the Parameters of a Field of Study'. *International Migration Review* 15, no. 1–2:320–93.

Stepick, A., and A. Portes. 1986. 'Flight into Despair: A Profile of Recent Haitian Refugees in South Florida'. *International Migration Review* 20, no. 2:329–50.

Stewart, I. 1989. *Does God Play Dice? The Mathematics of Chaos*. Oxford: Basil Blackwell.

Stouffer, S.A. 1940. 'Intervening Opportunities: A Theory Relating to Mobility and Distance'. *American Sociological Review* 5:845–67.

———. 1960. 'Intervening Opportunities and Competing Migrants'. *Journal of Regional Science* 2:1–26.

Straubhaar, T. 1993. 'Migration Pressure'. *International Migration* 31, no. 1:5–45.

Suhrke, A. 1992. *Pressure Points: Environmental Degradation, Migration and Conflict*. Fantoft-Bergen: Chr. Michelson Institute.

———, and A. Visentin. 1991. 'The Environmental Refugee: A New Approach'. *Ecodecision* (September):73–4.

Swan, N. 1991. *Economic and Social Impacts of Immigration*. Ottawa: Economic Council of Canada.

Swann, Lord. 1985. *'Education for All': Report of the Committee of Inquiry into the Education of Children from Ethnic Minority Groups*. London: Her Majesty's Stationery Office.

Taran, P.A. 1992. 'Migration and the Environment'. *Migration Today* 43:6–7.

Taylor, C. 1992. *Multiculturalism and 'the Politics of Recognition'.* Princeton: Princeton University Press.

Thomas, B. 1968. 'Migration: Economic Aspects'. *International Encyclopedia of the Social Sciences* 10:293.

Thomas, J.F. 'Documentary Note: Refugees—a New Approach'. *International Migration Review* 15, no. 1–2: 20–5.

Tinker, J. 1992. 'Immigration Reform: Yesterday and Today'. In *In Defense of the Alien, Vol. 14*, edited by L. Tomasi. New York: Center for Migration Studies.

Tiryakian, E.A. 1984. 'The Global Crisis as an Interregnum of Modernity'. *International Journal of Comparative Sociology* 25, 1–2:123–30.

Toffler, A. 1970. *Future Shock*. New York: Random House.

Tomasi, L., ed. 1992. *In Defense of the Alien, Vol. 14*. New York: Center for Migration Studies.

Tonnies, F. [1887] 1957. *Community and Society*. Translated and edited by L.P. Loomis. East Lansing: Michigan State University Press.

Tos, N., and P. Klinar. 1976. 'A System Model for Migration Research: Yugoslav Workers in the Federal Republic of Germany'. In *International Migration and Adaptation in the Modern World*, edited by A.H. Richmond. Toronto: International Sociological Association, Research Committee on Migration.

Touraine, A. [1969] 1971. *The Post-Industrial Society*. New York: Random House.

Trolldalen, J.M. 1992. *Environmental Refugees: A Discussion Paper.* Oslo: Norwegian Refugee Council.

Troyna, B., and J. Williams. 1986. *Racism, Education and the State: The Racialization of Education Policy*. London: Croom Helm.

Tuck, M., and P. Southgate. 1981. *Ethnic Minorities, Crime and Policing*. London: Her Majesty's Stationery Office.

Turner, B.S., ed. 1990. *Theories of Modernity and Postmodernity*. London: Sage Publications.

Turner, J.H. 1987. 'Toward a Sociological Theory of Motivation'. *American Sociological Review* 52, no. 1:15–27.

———. 1988. *A Theory of Social Interaction*. Stanford: Stanford University Press.

———. 1992. The Promise of Positivism'. In *Postmodernism and Social Theory*, edited by S. Seidman and D.G. Wagner. Oxford: Basil Blackwell.

Turpel, M.E. 1990. 'Aboriginal Peoples and the Canadian Charter: Interpretive Monopolies, Cultural Differences'. In *Canadian Human Rights Year Book 1989–90*, edited by M. Boivin et al. Ottawa: Human Rights Research and Education Centre, University of Ottawa.

Tyhurst, L. 1977. 'Psychosocial First Aid for Refugees'. *Mental Health and Society* 4:319–43.

UN Association of Canada. 1991. 'National Round Table on the Environment and the Economy': The Earth Summit. Ottawa: UNAC.

UNFPA (UN Fund for Population Activities). 1993. *The State of World Population 1993*. New York: UN Fund for Population Activities.

UNHCR (UN High Commissioner for Refugees). 1994. *Populations of Concern to UNHCR: A Statistical Overview, 1993*. Geneva: Food and Statistical Unit, UNHCR.

United Nations. 1989. *Human Rights: UN Training Course on International Norms and Standards in the Field of Human Rights*. New York: UN Centre for Human Rights.

———. 1991. *Report of the Working Group on Solutions and Protection*. Geneva: Executive Committee, UN High Commissioner for Refugees.

———. 1992. *Minority Rights: Fact Sheet No. 18*. New York: UN Centre for Human Rights.

Urry, J. 1991. 'Time and Space in Giddens's Social Theory'. In *Giddens's Structuration Theory: A Critical Appreciation*, edited by C.G.A. Bryant and D. Jury. London: Routledge.

US Committee for Refugees. 1991. *World Refugee Report, 1991*. Washington: American Council for Nationalities Service and US Committee for Refugees.

———. 1993. *World Refugee Survey, 1993*. Washington: American Council for Nationalities Service and US Committee for Refugees.

US Department of Justice. 1991. *Statistical Year Book, 1990*. Washington: US Department of Justice, Immigration and Naturalization Service.

US Department of Labor. 1989. *Effects of Immigration on the U.S. Economy and Labor Market*. Washington: Bureau of International Labor Affairs.

———. 1991. *Employer Sanctions and the U.S. Labor Markets*. Washington: Immigration Policy and Research, Bureau of International Labor Affairs.

US Refugee Resettlement Program. 1992. *Report to Congress*. Washington: US Refugee Resettlement Program.

Verma, R.B.P., and K.G. Basavarajappa. 1989. 'Employment Income of Immigrants in Metropolitan Areas of Canada, 1980'. *International Migration Review* 27, no. 3:441–66.

Volek, Z. 1978. 'Changing Characteristics of Refugees as Immigrants to Australia'. *International Migration* 16, no. 2:43–51.

von Blumenthal, U. 1991. 'Dublin, Schengen and the Harmonization of Asylum in Europe'. Paper presented at the First European Lawyers Conference.

Waddington, D. 1992. *Contemporary Issues in Public Disorder*. London: Routledge.

———, et al. 1989. *Flashpoints: Studies in Public Disorder*. London: Routledge.

Wallerstein, I. 1974. *The Modern World System: Capitalist Agriculture and the Emergence of the European World Economy in the Sixteenth Century*. New York: Academic Press.

Weber, M. 1947. *Theory of Social and Economic Organization*. Translated by A.R. Henderson and T. Parsons. London: William Hodge & Co.

———. 1968. *Economy and Society: An Outline of Interpretive Sociology*. New York: Bedminster.

Weiner, M. 'On International Migration and International Relations'. *Population and Development* 11, no. 30:441–56.

Wells, H.G. 1941. *Guide to the New World: A Handbook of Constructive World Revolution*. London: Gollancz.

Westing, A.H., ed. 1990. *Environmental Hazards of War: Releasing Dangerous Forces in an Industrializing World*. Newbury Park: Sage Publications.

Wexler, P. 1990. 'Citizenship in the Semiotic Society'. In *Theories of Modernity and Postmodernity*, edited by B.S. Turner. London: Sage Publications.

Widgren, J. 1991. 'The Management of Mass Migration in a European Context'. Statement at the Royal Institute of International Affairs, London.

Wolpert, J. 1965. 'Behavioral Aspects of the Decision to Migrate'. *Papers of the Regional Science Association* 19:159–69.

Wong, D. 1989. 'The Semantics of Migration'. *Sojourn* 4:2–7.

———. 1991. 'Asylum as a Relationship of Otherness: A Study of Asylum Holders in Nuremberg, Germany'. *Journal of Refugee Studies* 4, no. 2:150–63.

Wong, L. 1984. 'Canada's Guestworkers: Some Comparisons of Temporary Workers in Europe and North America'. *International Migration Review* 18, no. 1:85–98.

———. 1993. 'Immigration and Capital Accumulation: The Impact of Business Immigration to Canada'. *International Migration* 31, no. 1:171–90.

World Bank. 1984. *World Development Report, 1984*. New York: Oxford University Press.

———. 1989. *Annual Report, 1989*. Washington: International Bank for Reconstruction and Development (World Bank).

Wright, P. 1987. *Spycatcher*. Toronto: Stoddart.

Yarnold, B.M. 1990. *Refugees Without Refuge: Formation and Failed Implementation of U.S. Political Asylum Policy in the 1980s*. Lanham: University Press of America.

Yon, D. 1991. 'Migration, Schooling and the Politics of Identity'. MA thesis, graduate program in social anthropology, York University.

Zeeman, E.C. 1977. *Catastrophe Theory: Selected Papers, 1972–77*. Reading: Addison-Wesley.

Zmolek, M. 1992. 'Damming the Narmada and the Three Gorges'. *Refuge* 12, 1:33–8.

Zolberg, A. 1989. 'The Next Waves: Migration Theory for a Changing World'. *International Migration Review* 23, no. 3:403–30.

———, et al. 1981. 'International Migration in Political Perspective'. In *Global Trends in Migration: Theory and Research on International Population Movements*, edited by M. Kritz et al. New York: Center for Migration Studies.

———, et al. 1986. 'International Factors in the Formation of Refugee Movements'. *International Migration Review* 20, no. 2:151–69.

———, et al. 1989. *Escape from Violence: Conflict and the Refugee Crisis in the Developing World*. New York: Oxford University Press.

Zubrzycki, J. 1986. 'Multiculturalism and Beyond: The Australian Experience in Retrospect and Prospect'. *New Community* 13, no. 2:167–76.

———. 1987. 'Public Policy in Multicultural Australia'. *International Migration Review* 25, no. 1:63–72.

Zucker, N.L., and N.F. Zucker. 1991. 'The 1980 Refugee Act: A 1990 Perspective'. In *Refugee Policy: Canada and the United States*, edited by H. Adelman. Toronto and New York: York Lanes Press and the Center for Migration Studies.

Zwingmann, C., and M. Pfister-Ammende, eds. 1973. *Uprooting and After*. New York: Springer-Verlag.

Index